Elections in Hard Times: Southern Europe 2010-11

Southern Europe has been at the heart of the European sovereign debt crisis and in the vanguard of the programmes of radical economic austerity implemented to confront it. During the first two crisis years, the consequences for domestic political stability were dramatic. Across the region, 2010-11 saw the overthrow of incumbent governments, the breaking down of established political affiliations and the emergence of new political actors. The culmination was the simultaneous downfall of three South European governments in the space of eighteen days in November 2011.

This volume offers a collection of case studies of the twelve popular votes during this period in Italy, Greece, Portugal, Spain, Turkey, Cyprus and the Turkish Cypriot community. The contests include legislative, presidential and sub-national elections and a national-level referendum. In our control case, Turkey, there was no economic crisis and no government change. Elsewhere in Southern Europe, the studies indicate the progression of the crisis, from the limited disapproval of the Berlusconi government registered in the Spring 2010 Italian regional election to the electoral collapse of the Spanish socialists in late 2011. The volume indicates a build-up of popular frustration with the democratic process which can only be dangerous for the future of South European democracy.

This book was previously published as a special issue of *South European Society and Politics*.

Anna Bosco is Associate Professor of Comparative Politics and European Government at the University of Trieste and co-editor of the journal *South European Society and Politics*.

Susannah Verney is Assistant Professor of European Integration at the University of Athens and co-editor of the journal *South European Society and Politics*.

South European Society and Politics series
Series editors:
Susannah Verney, University of Athens, Greece
Anna Bosco, University of Trieste, Italy

The parallel regime transitions of the 1970s, when Southern Europe was the vanguard of the 'third wave' of democratisation, the impact of EU membership and Europeanisation and more recently, the region's central role in the eurozone crisis have all made Southern Europe a distinctive area of interest for social science scholars. The *South European Society and Politics* book series promotes new empirical research into the domestic politics and society of South European states. The series, open to a broad range of social science approaches, offers comparative thematic volumes covering the region as a whole and on occasion, innovative single-country studies. Its geographical scope includes both 'old' and 'new' Southern Europe, defined as Italy, Greece, Portugal, Spain, Cyprus, Malta and Turkey.

Voters and Parties in the Spanish Political Space
Edited by Ignacio Sánchez-Cuenca and Elias Dinas

Elections in Hard Times: Southern Europe 2010-11
Edited by Anna Bosco and Susannah Verney

Transformations of the Radical Left in Southern Europe
Bringing Society Back In?
Edited by Myrto Tsakatika and Marco Lisi

Previously published in the journal *South European Society and Politics*

Europeanization and the Southern Periphery
Edited by Kevin Featherstone and George Kazamias

Who Governs Southern Europe?
Edited by Pedro Tavares de Almeida, Nancy Bermeo and António Costa Pinto

Spain and Portugal in the European Union
The First Fifteen Years
Edited by Paul Christopher Manuel and Sebastián Royo

Mobilising Politics and Society?
The EU Convention's Impact on
   Southern Europe
*Edited by Sonia Lucarelli and
   Claudio Radaelli*

Reinventing Democracy
Grassroots Movements in Portugal
*Edited by João Arriscado Nunes and
   Boaventura de Sousa Santos*

When Greeks think about Turks
The View from Anthropology
Edited by Dimitrios Theodossopoulos

Party Change in Southern Europe
*Edited by Anna Bosco and
   Leonardo Morlino*

**The South European Right in the 21st
   Century**
Italy, France and Spain
Edited by Jocelyn A. J. Evans

Spain's 'Second Transition'?
The Socialist government of José Luis
   Rodríguez Zapatero
Edited by Bonnie N. Field

**Dealing with the Legacy of
   Authoritarianism**
The "Politics of the Past" in Southern
   European Democracies
*Edited by António Costa Pinto and
   Leonardo Morlino*

**Perspectives of National Elites on
   European Citizenship**
A South European View
*Edited by Nicolò Conti, Maurizio Cotta
   and Pedro Tavares de Almeida*

Euroscepticism in Southern Europe
A Diachronic Perspective
Edited by Susannah Verney

**Turkey and the EU: Accession and
   Reform**
Edited by Gamze Avci and Ali Çarkoğlu

Elections in Hard Times: Southern Europe 2010-11

Edited by
Anna Bosco and Susannah Verney

LONDON AND NEW YORK

First published 2014
by Routledge

2 Park Square, Milton Park, Abingdon, Oxfordshire OX14 4RN
711 Third Avenue, New York, NY 10017

Routledge is an imprint of the Taylor & Francis Group, an informa business

First issued in paperback 2018

Copyright © 2014 Taylor & Francis

All rights reserved. No part of this book may be reprinted or reproduced or utilised in any form or by any electronic, mechanical, or other means, now known or hereafter invented, including photocopying and recording, or in any information storage or retrieval system, without permission in writing from the publishers.

Notice:
Product or corporate names may be trademarks or registered trademarks, and are used only for identification and explanation without intent to infringe.

British Library Cataloguing in Publication Data
A catalogue record for this book is available from the British Library

ISBN 13: 978-0-415-70489-2 (hbk)
ISBN 13: 978-1-138-37734-9 (pbk)

Typeset in Times New Roman
by Taylor & Francis Books

Publisher's Note
The publisher accepts responsibility for any inconsistencies that may have arisen during the conversion of this book from journal articles to book chapters, namely the possible inclusion of journal terminology.

Disclaimer
Every effort has been made to contact copyright holders for their permission to reprint material in this book. The publishers would be grateful to hear from any copyright holder who is not here acknowledged and will undertake to rectify any errors or omissions in future editions of this book.

Contents

Citation Information	ix
1. Electoral Epidemic: The Political Cost of Economic Crisis in Southern Europe, 2010–11 *Anna Bosco and Susannah Verney*	1
2. The 2010 Regional Elections in Italy: Another Referendum on Berlusconi *Piergiorgio Corbetta*	27
3. The Turkish Cypriot Presidential Election of April 2010: Normalisation of Politics *Sait Akşit*	47
4. The Eurozone's First Post-bailout Election: The 2010 Local Government Contest in Greece *Susannah Verney*	67
5. The 2010 Regional Election in Catalonia: A Multilevel Account in an Age of Economic Crisis *Guillem Rico*	89
6. The 2011 Portuguese Presidential Elections: Incumbency Advantage in Semi-presidentialism? *Carlos Jalali*	111
7. The Twilight of the Berlusconi Era: Local Elections and National Referendums in Italy, May and June 2011 *Alessandro Chiaramonte and Roberto D'Alimonte*	133
8. In the Whirlwind of the Economic Crisis: Local and Regional Elections in Spain, May 2011 *Belén Barreiro and Ignacio Sánchez-Cuenca*	153
9. Disengaging Citizens: Parliamentary Elections in the Republic of Cyprus, 22 May 2011 *Christophoros Christophorou*	167
10. After the Bailout: Responsibility, Policy, and Valence in the Portuguese Legislative Election of June 2011 *Pedro C. Magalhães*	181

CONTENTS

11. No Crisis, No Change: The Third AKP Victory in the June 2011 Parliamentary Elections in Turkey
    Senem Aydın-Düzgit   201

12. The 2011 General Election in Spain: The Collapse of the Socialist Party
    Irene Martín and Ignacio Urquizu-Sancho   219

    Index   237

Citation Information

The chapters in this book were originally published in *South European Society and Politics*, volume 17, issue 2 (June 2012). When citing this material, please use the original page numbering for each article, as follows:

Chapter 1
Electoral Epidemic: The Political Cost of Economic Crisis in Southern Europe, 2010–11
Anna Bosco and Susannah Verney
South European Society and Politics, volume 17, issue 2 (June 2012) pp. 129-154

Chapter 2
The 2010 Regional Elections in Italy: Another Referendum on Berlusconi
Piergiorgio Corbetta
South European Society and Politics, volume 17, issue 2 (June 2012) pp. 155-174

Chapter 3
The Turkish Cypriot Presidential Election of April 2010: Normalisation of Politics
Sait Akşit
South European Society and Politics, volume 17, issue 2 (June 2012) pp. 175-194

Chapter 4
The Eurozone's First Post-bailout Election: The 2010 Local Government Contest in Greece
Susannah Verney
South European Society and Politics, volume 17, issue 2 (June 2012) pp. 195-216

Chapter 5
The 2010 Regional Election in Catalonia: A Multilevel Account in an Age of Economic Crisis
Guillem Rico
South European Society and Politics, volume 17, issue 2 (June 2012) pp. 217-238

Chapter 6
The 2011 Portuguese Presidential Elections: Incumbency Advantage in Semi-presidentialism?
Carlos Jalali
South European Society and Politics, volume 17, issue 2 (June 2012) pp. 239-260

CITATION INFORMATION

Chapter 7
The Twilight of the Berlusconi Era: Local Elections and National Referendums in Italy, May and June 2011
Alessandro Chiaramonte and Roberto D'Alimonte
South European Society and Politics, volume 17, issue 2 (June 2012) pp. 261-280

Chapter 8
In the Whirlwind of the Economic Crisis: Local and Regional Elections in Spain, May 2011
Belén Barreiro and Ignacio Sánchez-Cuenca
South European Society and Politics, volume 17, issue 2 (June 2012) pp. 281-294

Chapter 9
Disengaging Citizens: Parliamentary Elections in the Republic of Cyprus, 22 May 2011
Christophoros Christophorou
South European Society and Politics, volume 17, issue 2 (June 2012) pp. 295-308

Chapter 10
After the Bailout: Responsibility, Policy, and Valence in the Portuguese Legislative Election of June 2011
Pedro C. Magalhães
South European Society and Politics, volume 17, issue 2 (June 2012) pp. 309-328

Chapter 11
No Crisis, No Change: The Third AKP Victory in the June 2011 Parliamentary Elections in Turkey
Senem Aydın-Düzgit
South European Society and Politics, volume 17, issue 2 (June 2012) pp. 329-346

Chapter 12
The 2011 General Election in Spain: The Collapse of the Socialist Party
Irene Martín and Ignacio Urquizu-Sancho
South European Society and Politics, volume 17, issue 2 (June 2012) pp. 347-363

Please direct any queries you may have about the citations to
clsuk.permissions@cengage.com

Electoral Epidemic: The Political Cost of Economic Crisis in Southern Europe, 2010–11

Anna Bosco and Susannah Verney

This article introduces a collection of essays on the elections of 2010–11 in Italy, Greece, Portugal, Spain, Turkey, Cyprus and the Turkish Cypriot community. It examines the impact of the European sovereign debt crisis on electoral trends in the era of the Greek and Portuguese bailouts. After briefly examining the crisis economies, it investigates patterns of abstention, incumbent punishment and opposition success, including the rise of regional, anti-party, far-right and racist parties. The article concludes, following Krastev (Journal of Democracy, vol. 13, no. 3, 2002, pp. 39–53), that the crisis is creating 'democracy without choices' in Southern Europe with potentially destabilising consequences throughout the region.

To govern has become electorally very costly in Southern Europe. The international economic crisis has hit this region particularly hard, with deeply destabilising consequences for national political systems. The aim of this special issue is to investigate the political cost of economic crisis through a case-by-case examination of the unusually large number of elections that took place in 2010–11. The two-year period covered starts from the point when the European sovereign debt crisis first became critical at the beginning of 2010 and ends with the dramatic developments of November 2011. Each article in this volume stands alone as a study of a particular popular vote, providing us with detailed insight into the country-specific characteristics of each contest. When read together, this collection allows us to see the big picture of the electoral trends developing across the region as a whole—a picture that can only be disquieting for those concerned with the health of South European democracy.

In the following sections, this article first aims to establish just how exceptional the developments of this period were. It then sets the case of the South European region in a broader perspective, by discussing the malaise affecting political parties more generally even before the onset of the international economic crisis. Subsequently, it briefly delineates how that crisis affected South European economies, before turning to the pattern of electoral trends in the region as these emerge from our country case studies. The article concludes by attempting to assess the impact of these two years of economic crisis on the political health of Southern Europe. The overall goal of this introduction is to give a sense of the political consequences that governing in crisis conditions are having throughout the region.

Hard Times in Europe's South

November 2011 marked an exceptional moment in European politics. An unprecedented series of events saw the simultaneous downfall of the Greek, Italian and Spanish governments. On Thursday 3 November, Greek Prime Minister Georgios Papandreou asked parliament for a vote of confidence in order to negotiate the formation of a new coalition government that he would not lead. His successor was sworn in eight days later. The day after that, on Saturday 12 November, Italian Prime Minister Silvio Berlusconi tendered his resignation to the President of the Republic, with the new government taking office four days later. Just four more days went past before the Spanish Prime Minister, José Luis Rodríguez Zapatero, was defeated in the parliamentary elections. This triple dethronement took just 18 days. The November events were preceded five months earlier by another electoral defeat, that of the Portuguese government headed by José Sócrates. Thus, the year 2011 witnessed the ousting of the incumbents in all four countries of 'core' Southern Europe.

The joint downfall of the four governments was even more striking, given that only one was near the end of its term in office. In the case of Spain, elections would normally have been held four months later, in March 2012. But the Portuguese government was three months short of its mid-term point, which the Greek and Italian governments had just passed by one and two months, respectively.[1]

Of the four prime ministers, Sócrates was on his second term and had already suffered a significant 8.4 per cent loss in vote share in the 2009 election. However, Zapatero, also a second-term incumbent, had, unusually, been re-elected with an increased majority in 2008. Berlusconi, who had previously been elected twice (in 1994 and 2001), was now on his first term following the premature collapse of the preceding centre-left government. His centre-right coalition had won the 2008 election with a crushing 9.3 per cent lead over the centre-left. Papandreou, on his first prime-ministerial term, had been elected with an even more overwhelming lead, in this case of 10.4 per cent. Thus, such a rapid downfall of their governments would hardly have been expected under non-crisis conditions.

While the Spanish and Portuguese incumbents left after elections, both the Greek and Italian premiers quit when their parliamentary majorities were about to collapse, in both cases reflecting a prior loss of confidence among public opinion. After the Spanish and Portuguese elections, new governments were formed by the official opposition. In Greece and Italy, however, elections were viewed as a luxury that these two countries could not afford.

In both cases, new governments were formed based on new majorities shaped from the existing parliaments. Both the Italian and Greek successor governments were rather unusual. The Italian government consisted entirely of technocrats. This was not a complete novelty on the Italian political scene, as there had been the precedent of the technocratic cabinet headed by Lamberto Dini (January 1995 to May 1996). Dini was a former general director of the Bank of Italy, who had previously served as Treasury minister in the first Berlusconi government. In contrast, Mario Monti, appointed prime minister in November 2011, did not have any previous national political experience although he had served twice as a European Commissioner.[2] The Monti government, including civil servants and university professors, but no party or elected representatives, was sworn in with the support of all parliamentary groups, with the exception of the northern regionalist Lega Nord. The wide parliamentary majority and its internal differences have led Monti to term his government 'a large non-coalition' (Bosco & McDonnell forthcoming).

Meanwhile Greece, ever since the fall of the military dictatorship in 1974, had been ruled by one-party majority governments, except for nine brief months of coalition rule in 1989–90. Apart from short-term service governments formed to conduct elections, there had only been one case (the Zolotas government of November 1989 to March 1990) when the prime minister had not been an elected parliamentarian. Overturning national tradition, the new Greek government of November 2011 was a three-party coalition headed by a non-elected technocrat (Lucas Papademos, a former governor of the Bank of Greece and former vice-president of the European Central Bank). The coalition set a further national precedent by legitimating government participation by the far right.[3]

While the fate of the four national governments was spectacular, the rot was not limited to their abrupt demise. Even an election that saw the triumphant return of the incumbent—the Portuguese presidential contest of January 2011—resulted in a significant vote for independent candidates, indicating dissatisfaction with the main parties. At the sub-national level, the previous year saw the fall of the Catalan regional government while the defeat of incumbents emerged as a significant trend in the Greek municipal election (including the country's three major cities). In Italy, the regional elections of March 2010 were characterised by the emergence of an anti-politics tendency led by Beppe Grillo, a former comedian turned political blogger, whose 5-Stars Movement (Movimento 5 stelle, M5S) was consolidated in the local elections the following year.

Elsewhere in Southern Europe, in the presidential system of the Republic of Cyprus, the 2011 legislative elections could not bring about a change in the executive, but left the latter clearly weakened. In the northern part of the island, the Turkish Cypriots replaced their president, although this election did not appear to cause particular concern for the health of the party system. Only in Turkey did the incumbent government emerge triumphant from the 2011 parliamentary elections. But then in 2011 Turkey—unlike our five eurozone economies—was enjoying rapid economic growth.

While the picture drawn above is certainly striking, just how unusual were these South European elections and the rejection of governing parties which they entailed?

Putting Southern Europe into Perspective

As noted by Peter Mair, political parties in contemporary democracies have shown a diminishing capacity to exercise simultaneously the basic functions that allowed the development of modern democracies: to govern and to represent. According to Mair, 'in contemporary democracies, these two functions have begun to grow apart, with many of today's parties downplaying, or being forced to downplay, their representative role, and enhancing, or being forced to enhance their governing role' (Mair 2011, p. 8). More specifically, parties seem to have become less and less able to reconcile the demands for responsiveness (and therefore representation) with the demands of responsibility which are at the basis of party government.

Responsiveness—'whereby political leaders or governments listen to and then respond to the demands of citizens and groups' (Mair 2011, p. 10)—has become a difficult goal to attain, for reasons rooted in the development of contemporary democracies. Organisational changes that moved parties away from civil society and reduced the size of their memberships, the decline of large and homogeneous electorates which resulted in more fragmented and volatile groups of voters, and diminishing levels of party identification have made parties less able, on the one hand, to listen to their electoral base and to express the latter's demands and, on the other, to mobilise and persuade their voters.

At the same time, responsiveness has come into conflict with responsibility. Responsibility, 'whereby leaders and governments are expected to act prudently and consistently and to follow accepted procedural norms and practices', means that parties must live up to commitments and agreements 'with other governments and institutions' and this, in turn, involves 'an acceptance that in certain areas and in certain procedures, the leaders' hands will be tied' (Mair 2011, p. 11). Central banks, courts, international agencies and organisations, and European Union (EU) institutions are among the actors that have contributed to tie the leaders' hands.

As a consequence, parties are not only less capable than in the past of listening to and representing their voters, but also when in office they are unable to craft and implement the policies their voters asked for, since governments' freedom is severely constrained. This is particularly clear in the case of the EU, where 'much of the policy discretion and room for manoeuvre open to governments has been severely curtailed by the transfer of decision-making authority to the supranational level' (Mair 2011, p. 12). In short, tensions between the representative and governing roles played by parties are nothing new: they were already developing before the start of the financial and economic crisis and are not specific to Southern Europe. It is the international economic crisis, however, that has dramatically deepened these tensions in the European periphery.

The economic downturn has left government parties stuck between the devil and the deep blue sea, squeezed between the demands of their voters and those of a whole bunch of external actors such as the prime ministers of their EU partners, EU institutions, the International Monetary Fund (IMF), bond markets and rating agencies, and the European Central Bank. As the latter have come to control the supply of financial resources necessary to a state's survival, their sway over national governments has grown accordingly. Pulled between the pressures from their electoral constituencies for fiscal expansion and the demands of the resource suppliers for financial retrenchment, parties in office have had no easy choice.

The economic storm that has broken out in Southern Europe has shown that when incumbents are 'responsible'—abiding by the agreements with the external actors—they end up neglecting their voters' demands. This has imposed a heavy electoral toll on South European government parties, as the literature on economic voting has recently shown (Bellucci, Costa-Lobo & Lewis-Beck 2012). On the other hand, when incumbents avoid being 'responsible' and/or try to be primarily responsive to their voters, they lose international credibility, with dangerous consequences for the management of national sovereign debt and hence for the economic health of the country.

These two extremes are well represented by the trajectories followed on the one side by Zapatero in Spain and on the other by Berlusconi in Italy. Zapatero lost the 2011 elections because his voters felt betrayed by the U-turn in economic policy precipitated by EU pressures. In contrast, the Berlusconi government fell because it had not been 'responsible' enough, having put off the reforms necessary to promote the country's economic growth and financial stability. As a consequence of the above, political parties—and government parties in particular—have become among the least trusted institutions in Southern Europe.

While dissatisfaction with parties is a worldwide trend, it also has specific local causes. These need to be taken into account when it comes to understanding the factors that are changing South European democracies. For example, in Greece, government corruption scandals were a major cause of discontent, while in Italy the prime minister's involvement in sex scandals contributed to undermining his credibility. On the divided island of Cyprus, the lack of progress on the national question following the failure of the UN reunification plan in 2004 has obviously been a significant factor in explaining voter dissatisfaction among both Greek and Turkish Cypriots.

However, once the bomb of the economic crisis exploded in domestic politics, it tended to overshadow other issues. It is striking that even in the rather unusual case of Cyprus, where the island's division has always dominated the political scene, Christophorou (2012) cites opinion polls suggesting that in 2011 the state of the economy weighed more heavily than the national question among Greek Cypriot voters, while, as noted by Akşit (2012), the urgent need for economic restructuring was encouraging a shift in the issue focus of Turkish Cypriot politics.

However, the economic crisis has done much more than add yet another issue to such nationally specific causes of discontent as those cited above. Instead, it has brought all the failings of the national political systems into sharp relief. Voters distrust their political class not only because of the economic pain they are going through, but also because the crisis has brought a realisation of the role played in the economic problems afflicting their own country by the mismanagement—or, at best, lack of management—of their own governments. The advent of the crisis, in other words, has taught South Europeans an 'intensive class' in economic policy, highlighting the poor governance that characterised each national administration. This, in turn, has contributed to creating strong dissatisfaction with the parties and disillusion with politics in general. The next section will take a closer look at this powerful economic trigger of political discontent.

Crisis Economies

Milestones of the South European Crisis

The economic crisis in Southern Europe essentially dates back to the end of 2008, the year the Spanish housing bubble burst. The most significant event for the region as a whole was the collapse of Lehman Brothers in the US, triggering an intense new phase of crisis in the international financial system. Once money markets began reassessing comparative sovereign credit risk, Southern Europe became especially vulnerable. In particular, the countries of the southern eurozone, recipients of cheap credit over the previous decade, faced rapidly growing borrowing costs, soon to have dramatic consequences for both state finances and the real economy.

However, the moment that brought Southern Europe to the centre of the world map occurred in October 2009. This was the shock announcement by the recently elected socialist government that the country's real budget deficit for the year was likely to reach 12.7 per cent (four times the eurozone's specified limit) rather than the 3.7 per cent reported by its predecessor. At the same time, the national debt was recalculated at over 112 per cent of GDP, nearly twice the eurozone reference rate. With Greek public finances clearly unsustainable, the prospect of a Southern sovereign debt default had entered the agenda.

In April 2010, Greece became the first eurozone member to have its sovereign credit rating downgraded to junk status, effectively pricing it out of the markets. In May 2010, a bailout for Greece, entailing a €110 billion loan, was agreed by the EU, the IMF and the European Central Bank (rapidly known as the 'Troika'), on condition the country implement a radically front-loaded austerity policy and structural reform. As soon became apparent, the EU/IMF programme was drawn up on the basis of wildly unrealistic economic forecasts by the international lenders.[4] The austerity policy aggravated the recession already affecting the country, driving the debt-to-GDP ratio up to dizzying heights.

But the lack of credibility of the rescue programme was not the only cause of contagion to other states on the eurozone periphery. The original message of the Greek rescue was that markets could be confident the eurozone would intervene to prevent the bankruptcy of a member-state, hence making it safe to invest in the area. In autumn 2010, this was undermined by the agreement between the German Chancellor and French President that future bailouts should include debt restructuring, with the private sector asked to pay part of the cost. Following this development, confidence that South European debt would be repaid was further shaken and the sovereign debt crisis rapidly spread.

After a similar bailout was devised for Ireland (November 2010), it was the turn of Portugal, which in May 2011 agreed on a €78 billion loan package. In Spain, the eurozone crisis made its main entrance on the political scene in May 2010, at the time of the Greek bailout. Pressure from Ecofin (the EU Economic and Financial Affairs Council) forced the socialist incumbent to adopt a policy U-turn, abandoning the social expenditures that had become the government trademark and moving abruptly onto an austerity path. In July 2011, faced with the failure of the Greek rescue programme, a eurozone summit agreed there would be a second bailout for the country, to include private investors taking a 21 per cent loss on their Greek government bonds. This also proved a crunch point for other South European economies.

In Italy, the key moment occurred the following month, when the European Central Bank President, Jean-Claude Trichet, and the Governor of the Bank of Italy, Mario Draghi, sent a letter to Prime Minister Berlusconi, calling on his government to implement a rich menu of reforms aimed at promoting growth and ensuring financial stability. Summer 2011 also saw international attention turn to the Republic of Cyprus, given the exposure of its banks to Greek sovereign debt and their resulting threatened losses from the planned Greek bond 'haircut'. Speculation followed in the international financial press about a future Troika package for the Republic of Cyprus, although this prospect seemed to have been averted, at least temporarily, when the government signed an agreement for a €2.5 billion loan from Russia in December.

The last act in the South European financial drama before the startling political denouement in November was the emergency eurozone summit of October 2011. With the 21 per cent bond 'haircut' agreed three months earlier clearly inadequate to contain Greece's spiralling debt, the summit decided to increase private sector losses to 50 per cent. It seemed highly doubtful that this step would be sufficient to resolve the Greek debt problem, while the changing parameters of the crisis resolution policy further undermined confidence in the financial markets, indicating a likely perpetuation of the crisis.

National Variations within the Broader Picture

Data show that each South European economy has been struggling with a crisis that presented a different mix of features. The starting point of the recession, as shown in Tables 1 to 7, was not the same in all countries. For Cyprus, Portugal, Spain and Turkey, the first year of negative GDP growth was 2009, while in Greece, Italy and also in the non-internationally recognised 'TRNC' ('Turkish Republic of Northern Cyprus') recession had started a year earlier. In addition, by the end of 2011, the various South European economies had been struggling with recession for different time spans: ranging from the 12 months of Cyprus and Turkey to the dramatic four years of Greece (2008–11), while Portugal seemed to be the only case of double-dip recession (recession, then short-term recovery followed by recession again). Turkey and its dependency, the 'TRNC', on the other hand, both showed sustained growth after the severe decline of 2009. Accordingly, at the end of the period covered in this special issue, South European countries can be divided into three groups: those still in recession (Portugal and Greece), those stuck in a borderland characterised by low growth rates (Cyprus, Italy and Spain), and those that seem to have overcome the crisis and exhibited high growth rates (Turkey and the 'TRNC'). Each group, however, presents internal differences.

Table 1 Economic Indicators of Crisis: The Case of Greece

Indicator	2007	2008	2009	2010	2011
Real GDP growth (% of GDP)	3.9*	−0.2	−3.1	−4.9	−7.1
Unemployment (%)	8.3	7.7	9.5	12.6	17.7
Public debt (% of GDP)	107.4	112.9	129.7	148.3	170.6
Government deficit (−) or surplus (+) (% of GDP)	−6.5	−9.8	−15.6	−10.7	−9.4

Source: Eurostat.
* Annual average for 1998–2007.

The hardest hit: the two bailout countries. The two countries in recession at the end of 2011—Greece and Portugal—had different economic backgrounds. The Greek economy had been booming in the years immediately before the 2008 financial crisis, when it had enjoyed the fastest growth rates in the eurozone, accompanied by a sharp reduction in unemployment (Pagoulatos & Triantopoulos 2009, p. 36). However, the country suffered from chronic high public indebtedness and fiscal deficit due, among other causes, to the low reform capacity of its political class, the clientelistic use of public-sector jobs, and extensive tax evasion (Kaplanoglou & Rapanos forthcoming). This had already led to Greek entry into the EU's excessive deficit procedure in 2004, which Greece had exited in 2007. Following the revelations about the true state of public finances in October 2009, the country's low credibility played against it: its sovereign debt rating was repeatedly downgraded and speculative attacks in the financial markets made the bailout inevitable. The extent of Greece's subsequent downward spiral really became apparent in 2011, when the unprecedented drop in GDP suggested the economy had entered a death spiral, the unemployment rate was almost double its 2007 level and the debt-to-GDP ratio had risen by more than 60 per cent of GDP in just five years (see Table 1).

Table 2 Economic Indicators of Crisis: The Case of Portugal

Indicator	2007	2008	2009	2010	2011
Real GDP growth (% of GDP)	2.1*	0.0	−2.9	1.4	−1.7
Unemployment (%)	8.9	8.5	10.6	12.0	12.9
Public debt (% of GDP)	68.4	71.7	83.2	93.5	108.1
Government deficit (−) or surplus (+) (% of GDP)	−3.1	−3.6	−10.2	−9.8	−4.4

Source: Eurostat.
* Annual average for 1998–2007.

Unlike Greece, Portugal had been characterised at least since 2002 by weak growth (which had turned negative in 2003) and by rising unemployment and fiscal imbalances that had cost the country two spells under the EU's excessive deficit procedure, in 2001 and 2005. Just before the eruption of the 2008 financial turmoil, the incumbent socialist government began to implement austerity policies and reforms aimed at fiscal consolidation. The new financial downturn, therefore, 'caught Portugal in the middle of an adjustment process' that had been 'slow and partial' (Torres 2009, p. 67), adding new austerity to old and inaugurating a painful new phase of stagnation and recession, characterised by rising unemployment and public debt (see Table 2).

Despite their different starting points, a point that the two countries had in common was that the financial rescue and harsh restrictive measures that Greece and Portugal were required to implement did not seem to have ameliorated the debt burden, which reached new heights in 2011, instead driving the two countries further into recession and driving up unemployment to historical records.

No bailout, no growth. While the micro-state of the Republic of Cyprus and the big EU members, Italy and Spain, may not immediately spring to mind as a likely grouping, in 2010–11 these three countries shared two important features. Unlike Greece and Portugal, they did not need a financial rescue but nor were they on a sustained growth path.

Within this group, the Republic of Cyprus showed remarkable stability: in the crunch year of 2009 it experienced the smallest contraction in GDP growth of all our South European cases, unemployment rose less than elsewhere and the burden of public debt was slightly lower than in 2007, while the government even managed to maintain a budget surplus in 2007 and 2008 (see Table 3). Behind these relatively positive data were local factors such as strong population growth, the low-tax corporate regime and the recent transition to a service economy (Besim & Mullen 2009, p. 89), but also the fact that the Republic of Cyprus had joined the EU in 2004 and had adopted the euro in 2008. With euro membership in sight, in other words, Cyprus's economic policy had been devoted to 'putting the house in order' in the years preceding the 2008 financial crisis and this initially allowed it to resist the economic turmoil better than elsewhere. It was only during 2011, when the viability of the main

Table 3 Economic Indicators of Crisis: The Case of the Republic of Cyprus

Indicator	2007	2008	2009	2010	2011
Real GDP growth (% of GDP)	4.0*	3.6	−1.9	1.3	0.5
Unemployment (%)	4.1	3.8	5.5	6.4	7.9
Public debt (% of GDP)	58.8	48.9	58.5	61.3	71.1
Government deficit (−) or surplus (+) (% of GDP)	3.5	0.9	−6.1	−5.3	−6.3

Source: Eurostat.
*Annual average for 1998–2007.

Cypriot banks was threatened by the planned write-off of Greek public debt, that the problems became more serious and a possible future bailout entered the agenda.

When the financial crisis landed in the eurozone in 2008, Italy and Spain, the two largest economies of the South European periphery, had different weaknesses. In the decade preceding the crisis, Italy's growth performance had been the worst among the South European member states (and indeed in the EU as a whole). Convergence with the criteria for Economic and Monetary Union (EMU) had involved tightening both the budget deficit and the public debt. However, even after the reforms undertaken to join the eurozone in 1999, many of Italy's main problems remained unsolved (including a large unofficial economy, limited R&D investment, low productivity, high unit labour costs, lack of competition in the service sector and serious territorial imbalances, to name but a few) while fiscal policy reverted to a loose pattern. As a result, the Italian government faced the consequences of the 2008 crisis constrained by a rising budget deficit and a public debt considerably in excess of 100 per cent of GDP (see Table 4). The high level of Italian indebtedness was nothing new and the capacity of the Italian Treasury to issue, manage and honour the debt was recognised worldwide (Jones forthcoming). However, when the prospect of a Greek default turned the credit crunch into a sovereign debt crisis, confidence in the Italian bond market rapidly declined, bringing it under speculative attack and raising the external pressure on the government to work for financial stability—as the August 2011 letter from Trichet and Draghi made clear. At the same time, the scale of the debt and deficit ruled out expansive fiscal policies to counteract the negative effects of the crisis on the real economy.

Table 4 Economic Indicators of Crisis: The Case of Italy

Indicator	2007	2008	2009	2010	2011
Real GDP growth (% of GDP)	1.5*	−1.2	−5.5	1.8	0.4
Unemployment (%)	6.1	6.7	7.8	8.4	8.4
Public debt (% of GDP)	103.0	106.1	116.4	119.2	120.7
Government deficit (−) or surplus (+) (% of GDP)	−1.6	−2.7	−5.4	−4.5	−3.9

Source: Eurostat.
* Annual average for 1998–2007.

Table 5 Economic Indicators of Crisis: The Case of Spain

Indicator	2007	2008	2009	2010	2011
Real GDP growth (% of GDP)	3.8*	0.9	−3.7	−0.3	0.4
Unemployment (%)	8.3	11.3	18.0	20.1	21.7
Public debt (% of GDP)	36.3	40.2	53.9	61.5	69.3
Government deficit (−) or surplus (+) (% of GDP)	1.9	−4.5	−11.2	−9.7	−9.4

Source: Eurostat.
* Annual average for 1998–2007.

The opposite happened in Spain, where expansive policies were introduced and later reversed. Before 2008, Spain had been the protagonist of one of the most commented-on success stories in Europe. In contrast to the situation in Italy, the 1998–2007 decade was characterised by vigorous economic growth, the reduction of unemployment, a relatively small public debt (36.3 per cent in 2007) and a comfortable government surplus for three years in a row (2005–07) (see Table 5). The Spanish economic miracle, however, rested on feet of clay. Once the financial crisis and the related credit crunch touched the country, the flourishing household consumption and the boom in the real-estate market, which had sustained the long period of growth, turned into high private indebtedness, threatening the stability of the banking system. In just three years (2007–09), Spain's growth, from its earlier annual average of 3.8 per cent, declined to an equivalent level of negative growth (−3.7 per cent), while the country's public debt increased by almost 18 points and its former budget surplus turned into a two-digit deficit. The most dramatic consequence of the crisis, however, concerned the unemployment rate, which more than doubled in 2007–09. The data become really impressive in the case of those aged under 25. The *generación perdida* (lost generation) included almost half the Spanish youth in 2011, a truly poisonous aspect of the Spanish crisis.

The Italian and Spanish governments, both elected in 2008, when the financial turmoil was already on the horizon, initially tried to buy time, denying the gravity of the economic problems. In Italy, where growth had been sluggish for over a decade but unemployment rose very little between 2008 and 2011, the strategy of denial seemed to work until 2011. In Spain, on the other hand, the economic stop could not be ignored, as the country had just emerged from a boom decade that contrasted sharply with the current state of crisis. Zapatero was therefore forced to abandon the strategy of denial much earlier than Berlusconi and to promote expansionary policies to assuage the consequences of the crisis (Royo 2009). These policies, however, could not be implemented for an extended period and, as already noted, the Spanish government was obliged to discard them in May 2010 in favour of harsh austerity measures.

Short crisis, rapid recovery. Turkey and its Turkish Cypriot satellite shared a short V-shaped recession, with an impressive GDP contraction in 2009 (−4.8 and −5.5 per cent, respectively) followed by a recovery in the next two years. The striking passage from recession to growth brought employment creation following the job losses that had taken

Table 6 Economic Indicators of Crisis: The Case of Turkey

Indicator	2007	2008	2009	2010	2011
Real GDP growth (% of GDP)	4.3*	0.7	−4.8	9.0	8.5
Unemployment (%)	8.8	9.7	12.5	10.7	8.8
Public debt (% of GDP)	39.9	40.0	46.1	42.4	40.1
Government deficit (−) or surplus (+) (% of GDP)	−1.5	−2.8	−7.0	−2.6	−

Source: Eurostat; for public debt 2011, Economist Intelligence Unit Report, September 2012.
* Annual average for 1998–2007.

place in 2009. These are the only cases in Southern Europe where the number of unemployed in 2011 was lower or only slightly higher than in 2007, before the beginning of the crisis (see Tables 6 and 7). During the two-year period 2010–11, Turkey recorded particularly strong growth rates, analogous to those it had enjoyed in 2004–05. Meanwhile, the short recession and strong recovery helped Turkey to reduce the weight of its budget deficit and public debt. After rising in 2008 and 2009, in 2011 the latter was back at approximately the same level as in 2008. By 2011, the former poor cousin to the Southern eurozone had thus gained the status of the most dynamic South European economy.

Table 7 Economic Indicators of Crisis: The Case of the Turkish Cypriot Economy

Indicator	2007	2008	2009	2010	2011
Real GDP growth (% of GDP)	2.8	−2.9	−5.5	3.7	3.3
Unemployment (%)	9.4	9.8	12.4	11.9	9.7
Public debt (% of GDP)	100.0	116.0	130.0	139.0	141.0
Government deficit (−) or surplus (+) (% of GDP)	−6.2	−9.3	−13.5	−10.1	−

Source: State Planning Organisation (SPO), *Dünya ve KKTC Ekonomisine Bakış: 2012 Yılı I. Çeyrek*, 3 August 2012, Lefkoşa, KKTC.

It should be noted that the economy of northern Cyprus is highly dependent on Turkey and this explains the similarity in economic trends. While the 'TRNC' has strikingly high levels of budget deficit (13.5 per cent in 2009), these are financed with transfers from Turkey which are never paid back. As a consequence, deficit financing does not create any risk to the financial market and the economy. In the same vein, the astonishing level of 2011 public debt—141 per cent of GDP—was in reality much lower. Domestic debt in 2011 amounted to 53 per cent of GDP while the rest consisted of foreign debt (i.e. loans from Turkey) which is not expected to be repaid.[5]

Having established the crisis climate, now let us turn to its impact on elections.

Crisis Elections: The Case Studies

The case studies examined in this volume concern 12 votes that took place across Southern Europe during 2010–11 (shown in Table 8). Four of these took place in 2010 and the remaining eight, including the early parliamentary elections in Portugal and

Table 8 Electoral Contests in Southern Europe, 2010–11

Date	Country	Level
28–29 March 2010	Italy	Regional
18 April 2010	'TRNC'	Presidential
7 & 14 November 2010	Greece	Regional and municipal
28 November 2010	Spain (Catalonia)	Regional
23 January 2011	Portugal	Presidential
15–16 May 2011	Italy	Municipal and provincial
22 May 2011	Spain	Municipal and regional
22 May 2011	Cyprus	Parliamentary
5 June 2011	Portugal	Parliamentary
12 June 2011	Turkey	Parliamentary
12–13 June 2011	Italy	National referendums
20 November 2011	Spain	Parliamentary

Spain, in 2011. Of the seven South European states, Malta was the only one that did not hold either general or local elections during this period.[6] There were three votes in Italy (a national-level referendum and two sub-national elections) and in Spain (one national and two sub-national), two in Portugal (both national) and one in Greece (sub-national) and in Turkey (national). On the divided island of Cyprus, there was a national election in the Republic of Cyprus and a community-wide vote within the Turkish Cypriot community in the northern part of the island. Our case studies thus include four cases of legislative and two presidential elections, five sub-national contests and one national-level referendum (with four questions). This provides a varied range of case studies across different national contexts, with which to measure the level of political discontent across the region.

In examining the case studies, the coincidence of the election dates with the unfolding of the crisis at the European and national levels outlined in the previous section may have a bearing on the punishment meted out by the electorate. In some cases, there seemed little scope for voter clemency towards the party in power. All three Spanish elections followed both the Greek bailout and the national switch to an unpopular austerity policy and took place against a background of rapidly rising unemployment. In Portugal, both contests occurred after a protracted period of socialist austerity, the parliamentary election coming just a few weeks after the agreement on the EU/IMF bailout.

In contrast, in the Republic of Cyprus, the parliamentary elections took place with black clouds already gathering on the horizon but before the crucial decision for Greek debt restructuring with private sector involvement had been taken. Curiously, in Greece itself, the only popular vote of this period may also be seen as an interim election. Although the local government elections came six months after the EU/IMF bailout, they preceded the really dramatic deterioriation of the economy which, as we saw, took place in 2011. Meanwhile, the three Italian votes, taking place at different points in the evolution of the crisis, provided a clear illustration of how the latter was mirrored in rising political discontent. The limited disapproval of the Berlusconi government recorded in the regional elections held two months before the first Greek bailout had risen to a crescendo by the time of the national referendum held 15 months later.

For the Turkish Cypriots, the vote for their president came after two years of recession and rising unemployment, for which the incumbent could be expected to pay. However, as we have seen, the election was followed by a return to growth and job creation, suggesting that this defeat was unlikely to be followed by a deeper political crisis. Finally, the Turkish parliamentary poll occurred when the country had already fully recovered from the brief recession of 2009 and was enjoying real growth rates unthinkable elsewhere in Southern Europe. Turkey thus becomes a 'control case' for the political impact of the economic crisis, against which its crisis-struck South European neighbours can be measured.

The aim of the following sections is to provide an overall view of these elections, indicating the electoral trends that were emerging across the South European region in the new climate of crisis.

Incumbent Punishment

As we have already seen, incumbent punishment seems to have become the hallmark of crisis elections in Southern Europe. Given our substantial number of sub-national elections, the question arises of whether the incumbent being punished is the local or the national one. One of the characteristics of the period under consideration is that not only national elections but also sub-national ones became rather exciting. In some cases, they even attracted considerable international interest, notably the Greek local government elections of 2010, the crucial first electoral test after an EU/IMF bailout. All our authors seem to agree that in 2010–11, national political considerations were at centre stage in the sub-national contests. Against the backdrop of the economic crisis with its deeply destabilising effects, regional and local polls thus acted as important indicators of central government viability—and, in the cases of both Italy and Spain, as portents of their approaching downfall.

A Rule with Few Exceptions

Of our 12 votes, only two could be regarded as unequivocal victories for the incumbent. Both these cases can be regarded as exceptions that proved the rule. The first was our 'control case' of the parliamentary election in Turkey, where, as Aydın-Düzgit (2012) so neatly puts it, there was 'no crisis, no change' of government. In considering the Turkish case, it should be borne in mind that this country had already undergone its own political earthquake a decade earlier. In the wake of an economic crisis and IMF intervention, the 2002 Parliament had included none of the five parties elected in 1999, regardless of whether they had been in government or opposition. This rout of the old political class had resulted in the rise of the Islamist AKP (Justice and Development Party), which in 2011 was re-elected for its third term. Turkey's governmental stability, which in 2011 stood in marked contrast to the instability in the southern eurozone, was thus built on a previous period of turmoil which had resulted in the reshaping of the party system.

However, this did not mean that the Turkish governing party was immune to economic pressures. As we have seen above, in 2009 the Turkish economy suffered a sudden drop in growth, accompanied by a rise in unemployment. This was reflected in the results of the 2009 municipal elections, in which support for the governing party decreased, whether compared with the 2004 local elections (three per cent) or the 2007 parliamentary election (seven per cent) (see Çarkoglu 2009). Analysts' predictions that this marked the beginning of the end of AKP hegemony were confounded by the rapid growth and falling unemployment of the following years, the context in which the 2011 parliamentary election took place.

The second exception concerned the presidential election in Portugal. As Carlos Jalali (2012) explains in some detail, this election was a special case due to the way in which semi-presidentialism creates an incumbency advantage. This is attributable both to the direct benefits of holding office and to the way in which the system serves to deter high-quality challengers. It could also be noted that, although under the Portuguese Constitution the president potentially has quite wide-ranging powers, in practice Portuguese presidents have tended not to use them. Because the president does not play a direct day-to-day role in the running of the country, he or she is less likely to be held accountable for present ills by the electorate.

In two other cases, the national incumbent claimed victory in a sub-national election. Six months after the collapse of Lehman Brothers, the Italian regional elections confirmed that, despite some expression of discontent, the ruling centre-right coalition remained the first political force (Corbetta 2012). Even more striking, the governing socialists in Greece remained first party six months after the country's 2010 bailout by the EU and IMF. In the Greek case, though, another incumbent Greek government had already been ousted as a result of the crisis. In fact, the Greek legislative election of October 2009 had been the first manifestation of a pattern that was to become all too familiar two years later. In this early 'crisis election', the centre-right New Democracy had called an early vote halfway through the parliamentary term. The result was the party's ejection from office with its lowest-ever electoral support since its foundation 35 years earlier, entailing the loss of 20 per cent of its 2007 vote share.[7] Just one year later, perhaps it was a little early for a second governing party to suffer a similar fate. Moreover, in both the Italian and Greek sub-national contests, although the governing parties came first, the elections also indicated a significant loss of electoral support, so that both could also be interpreted as defeats.

It is also worth noting that both of these elections were held in 2010. Our case studies indicate a progression of the political impact of economic crisis in Southern Europe. The first of our elections, the Italian regional contest of March 2010, was the closest to suggesting business as usual. In contrast 2011 became a year of nemesis. Apart from these four contests, in all the other elections, the incumbent was the clear loser.

ELECTIONS IN HARD TIMES: SOUTHERN EUROPE 2010-11

The Punished Incumbents

In Spain, the key feature of all three electoral contests of 2010–11 was the dramatic decline in the socialist vote. The previously popular Zapatero was held widely responsible by the electorate for not responding earlier to the national economic crisis following the bursting of the Spanish property bubble and subsequently for the abrupt switch from an expansionary economic policy to fiscal retrenchment in May 2010, with the latter leaving socialist voters feeling betrayed. This was clearly reflected in the election for the Catalan parliament in November 2010. The socialists, the leading party in the Catalan regional government, lost 8.4 per cent of the total vote, falling to their lowest ever level in Catalonia. Six months later, in the local and regional elections of May 2011, held against the background of the 'Indignados' protest movement against the austerity policy, the Spanish socialist party obtained 'its worst results since 1977' (Barreiro & Sánchez-Cuenca 2012). The PSOE ceased to govern several regions while in the municipal election the party's vote was reduced to 27.8 per cent, falling by 7.1 per cent of the total vote compared with the previous elections of 2007. Six months after that, in the national parliamentary election of November 2011 the socialist vote plunged by a staggering 15.1 per cent, down to 28.8 per cent from the 43.9 per cent the party had won three-and-a-half years earlier.

In Italy, the common outcome of both votes in 2011 was the major blow to the personal prestige of Prime Minister Berlusconi and his government. In the May local elections, the centre-right governing coalition won only 40 of the 133 municipalities with at least 15,000 inhabitants, compared with the 55 that it had held previously. The key defeat, because of its impact on the Prime Minister's prestige, occurred in Berlusconi's home town of Milan. The Prime Minister personally campaigned on behalf of the centre-right candidate, who was defeated by a startling margin of over ten per cent in the second round. One month later, the referendum, whose four questions all concerned legislation passed by the centre-right government, resulted in a resounding rejection of the latter's policy, with over 94 per cent of voters supporting the repeal of every one of the laws. In Portugal, where the legislative elections followed shortly after the EU/IMF bailout, the incumbent socialists lost 8.5 per cent of the total vote, reduced to 28.1 per cent from the 36.6 per cent they had polled just 21 months earlier. As in Spain, this election left the socialists' support limited to significantly less than one-third of the electorate (Magalhães 2012).

In the Republic of Cyprus, the communist AKEL (Progressive Party of the Working People), the party of the President of the Republic, actually increased its vote share in the parliamentary elections by 1.6 per cent and gained an additional parliamentary seat. However, as Christophorou (2012) points out, this percentage rise was due to a significant jump in abstention whereas in absolute numbers the party lost voters. At the same time, AKEL was relegated to second place, losing the position as first political force which it had occupied since 2001. Although under the presidential system the government did not fall, it emerged from the election with its legitimacy clearly reduced. Meanwhile, in the non-internationally recognised northern part of the island, the incumbent president of the Turkish Cypriots, Mehmet Ali Talat, was ousted after one term in office, losing a substantial 12.7 per cent of the total electorate and falling to 42.9 per cent compared with the 55.6 per cent he had won in his 2005 victory.

Thus, leaving aside the exceptional cases mentioned above, the overall picture from our South European elections is one of incumbent punishment seeming to become a rule across the region. Moreover, governing party losses often occurred on a scale exceeding the expected swings between governing parties alternating in power. In the Spanish case, for example, the extent of the socialists' decline and its repetition across electoral contests at different levels within the polity suggested something more than a run-of-the-mill political defeat. It indicated rather a development with potential long-term consequences for the party system.

Opposition Success?

Reinforcing this picture was the fact that in several of our South European elections, the incumbent parties' loss was not, as would normally have been expected, the official opposition's gain. Perhaps the most notable instance concerned Spain. As Barreiro and Sánchez-Cuenca (2012) note, by the end of 2011 the centre-right PP (Partido Popular) appeared to have become a hegemonic force in Spanish politics, not only holding power at the national level, but also heading or participating in 12 of the 17 regional governments and running many of the major cities. Yet in the parliamentary elections, despite the 15.1 per cent of the total vote lost by the socialists, the PP increased its own vote by only 4.7 per cent. Similarly, in the local and regional elections six months earlier, the PP vote rose by only 2.1 per cent, less than one-third of the socialists' 7.1 per cent drop. Thus, the party's new dominance in Spanish politics was not founded on a significant expansion of its electoral base.

Italy provides another example. In the municipal elections of May 2011, Berlusconi's humiliation brought only limited benefits for the centre-left opposition. The latter, while gaining an additional nine of the municipalities with over 15,000 residents, actually suffered a 1.2 per cent decline in vote share compared with the previous year's regional elections in the same municipalities (Chiaramonte & D'Alimonte 2012). However, this picture of limited gain for the official opposition did not apply, for example, in the case of Portugal, where the vote increase for the centre-right PSD, the parliamentary election winner, exceeded the socialists' loss.

The Far Left

Another interesting development was that the capitalist crisis brought only limited gains for the traditional far left. In the Republic of Cyprus, the communist party had always been a major political force and from 2003 had participated in government. In contrast, in Turkey, the far left did not participate in Parliament at all. Elsewhere in Southern Europe, the traditional far left was a minor player—and remained so in 2010–11.

Thus, in the Spanish parliamentary election, the traditional third party, IU (Izquierda Unida – United Left), almost doubled its electoral strength, from 3.8 per cent in 2008 to 6.9 per cent in 2011. But the increase of 3.1 per cent of the total vote, while significant for IU, represented only a small proportion of the socialists' 15.1 per cent loss. Similarly, in the earlier local elections, IU gained less than an additional one per cent of the total vote despite the socialists' 7.1 per cent loss. In the Portuguese parliamentary contest, in which the socialists lost 8.5 per cent of the vote, the far left vote actually fell. While communist party support at 7.9 per cent remained unchanged, the Left Bloc lost 4.6 per cent of the total vote, almost half its 2009 vote share. Thus, in the Portuguese case, the crisis seemed to have led the electorate to make a distinct shift to the right.

In post-bailout Greece, the communist party did capture some of the protest vote, registering a nationwide total of 9.9 per cent in the country's first regional elections[8] while its vote reached double figures in two of the three main municipalities that serve as the main measure of success in Greek local elections. But, despite a limited increase in its electoral strength, the Greek communist party essentially consolidated its traditional position as the third force playing a marginal role in a two-party system. Meanwhile, the Radical Left Coalition (SYRIZA), the other parliamentary party in this area of the Greek political spectrum, did not succeed in increasing its vote.[9] However, a big surprise of the 2010 local government elections in Greece was the performance of an extra-parliamentary party, ANDARSYA (Anticapitalist Left Collaboration for the Overthrow), which won a single seat on seven regional and 12 municipal councils. While this hardly turned ANDARSYA into a significant player in local government, it did suggest that in the Greek case there might be potential for a radicalisation of the electorate towards the left (Verney 2012).

If, with the Greek exception, the protest vote was not mainly moving in a traditional anti-capitalist direction, where were disaffected voters turning?

Spain: The Regionalist Alternative

In Spain, the period 2010–11 saw a significant rise in support for regional nationalist parties, although this was not always because of the crisis. The most striking result in the 2011 local elections occurred in the Basque Country, where Batasuna, regarded as the political wing of the terrorist ETA (Basque Homeland and Liberty), had been banned since 2003. In 2011, a new situation developed following ETA's decision to announce a truce. Bildu, a left-wing separatist party officially launched six weeks before the election and initially also banned for alleged links with Batasuna, emerged as second party in the election with 25.4 per cent of the vote. This outcome, indicating new prospects for Basque separatism if it pursued a peaceful path, contributed to ETA's official decision to renounce violence a few months later.

Meanwhile in the Catalan parliamentary election, the main beneficiary of the socialist decline was the moderate nationalist CiU (Convergència I Unió), up from 31.5 per cent of the vote in 2006 to 38.4 per cent in 2010. The centre-right CiU had been the traditional party of power in Catalonia from 1980 to 2003, so after two terms of a left-wing coalition the CiU's return to power could be seen as a normal alternation in government. However, in 2010 the question of Catalonia's relations with the Spanish state had been at centre stage for several years, following the reform of the Catalan Statute of Autonomy in 2006 to grant more powers to the region and the subsequent limitation of this reform by a Constitutional Court decision. This election, occurring against a background of multiple municipal 'referendums' on Catalan independence during the previous year, also saw the entry to parliament of a pro-secessionist party, Catalan Solidarity for Independence, which gained 3.3 per cent of the vote in its first electoral contest (see Rico 2012).

Then in the national parliamentary election of 2011, CiU increased its vote from 3.0 to 4.2 per cent while three regional parties entered the Spanish national parliament for the first time. They included a new Basque coalition, Amaiur, founded by former members of Bildu and other Basque nationalist groups, which gained 1.4 per cent of the national vote and seven seats.

This outcome may have significant consequences for Spain's future political stability. In the previous national parliamentary election of 2008, the two main parties had reached the highest concentration of votes in the democratic period, together receiving 83.8 per cent of the votes and holding 92.3 per cent of the seats in the Congreso de los Diputados, the parliament's powerful lower chamber. In the 2011 election, however, the proportion of votes (73.4 per cent) and Congreso seats (84.6 per cent) showed a reversal in the concentration trend that had been a feature of Spanish elections since 1996, when the PP won office for the first time. The main consequence of this U-turn was the increase in party fragmentation at the parliamentary level, as the number of parties represented in the Congreso jumped from 10 to 13, one of the highest figures since 1977. With the three new entrants, the number of regional parties rose from six to nine, together accounting for over ten per cent of MPs.[10]

At a time of economic crisis, regional and regional-nationalist parties, such as those from Catalonia and the Basque Country, may be tempted to raise demands for fiscal and political autonomy in order to mobilise their voters. Such demands are not easily manageable, especially in an era of fiscal retrenchment and by a right-wing governing party that has in the past been hostile to every form of decentralisation. This suggests that the decline of the socialists as a result of the economic crisis and the concomitant rise in support for regionally based parties may encourage centrifugal tendencies dangerous for the integrity of the Spanish state.

New Challengers

In the Spanish case, the crisis gave birth in May 2011 to the Indignados social movement, a non-party protest against fiscal retrenchment, operating in a non-traditional manner and mobilised by social media. However, the movement did not develop into a new political party. Elsewhere in Southern Europe, other electorates appeared willing to turn in new directions. In the period 2010–11, several new challenger parties emerged, whose common characteristic was the rejection of the existing system.

In Italy, the M5S, which took shape in the late 2000s, was founded by comedian and popular blogger Beppe Grillo. The party, largely built through social networking, campaigned primarily on an anti-corruption and anti-party platform with an added environmental politics dimension. The M5S made its first electoral appearance in the spring 2010 regional elections, in which it won its first four council seats. The party's vote share averaged 3.7 per cent across the five regions it contested, with a high point of 7.0 per cent in Emilia-Romagna. In the 2011 municipal elections, the M5S won 3.1 per cent of the total vote and appointed four mayors. This included a striking victory in the city of Parma, where the party's candidate won 60 per cent of the vote in the second-round run-off.

Meanwhile, the economic crisis, by aggravating the problem of unemployment, made the issue of undocumented immigration in the EU's southern frontline even more explosive than before. In some countries, this opened new opportunities for the far right. In Greece, a radical right party had been represented in Parliament since 2007. LAOS (Popular Orthodox Rally), which had supported the Greek bailout and was the only opposition party in May 2010 to vote in favour of the Memorandum of Understanding with the country's international creditors, emerged clearly weakened from the local government elections six months later. Its relative defeat included the failure to elect a single municipal councillor in the country's capital. Instead a seat on the Athens city council was won by a neo-nazi group, Golden Dawn, known for its violent attacks on immigrants. Golden Dawn had existed on the far fringes of the Greek political system for decades. In the context of the economic crisis, the party was able to win its first elected post.

Meanwhile, Golden Dawn's sister party in the Republic of Cyprus, ELAM (National Popular Front), founded in 2008, won 1.1 per cent of the vote in its first parliamentary election in 2011. Although this was not enough to win a seat, this dynamic first appearance suggested potential for the future. In Catalonia, the PxC (Platform for Catalonia), an issue party that focuses on immigration from Islamic countries, failed to enter the Catalan parliament in 2010. However, with 2.4 per cent, it had the highest vote share of all the extra-parliamentary parties. In the 2011 municipal election, PxC won 2.3 per cent of the vote and 67 out of 9,137 local council seats, up from 17 in 2007.

Two South European states constitute exceptions to this rise of new challengers. Once again, one of these is our 'control' case, Turkey, where the 2011 election saw the same constellation of political forces[11] returned to Parliament as in 2007. The other was Portugal, where the parliamentary elections produced no new entrants to Parliament and only a small rise in support for extra-parliamentary parties (from 4.1 to 5.3 per cent). However, it is worth noting that in the Portuguese presidential elections—as we have seen, one of the exceptions to our pattern of incumbent punishment—a substantial 14.0 per cent of the vote went to a non-affiliated candidate, who ran a campaign stressing that he was not a political system insider.[12]

Abstention

The level of electoral participation is always regarded as an important gauge of support for a democratic political system. Thus, in a period of economic crisis, voter demobilisation could be an important indicator of political alienation. The case that most clearly suggested that this was taking place was Greece. In the local and regional elections of 2010, abstention reached an unprecedented level for any post-dictatorship election in the country (and not just for local government contests). Particularly disturbing was the fact that, in the second round, abstention at both the regional and municipal levels exceeded the crucial 50 per cent deemed to indicate political system delegitimation. Moreover, this rejection of political participation occurred in a country where voting had traditionally been compulsory, although sanctions were no longer applied. Another case where the rise in abstention caused shock was the Republic of Cyprus. On a comparative basis, the 21.3 per cent abstention rate in the 2011 parliamentary election may not seem particularly high. However, for Cyprus, which also had a tradition of compulsory voting, this was almost double the 11.0 per cent of 2006.

Elsewhere, the picture was less clearcut. In Spain, abstention rose by 4.9 per cent in the national parliamentary election to reach 31.1 per cent. As noted by Martín and Urquizu-Sancho (2012), this was the third-highest level since 1977. Perhaps more striking was that this made abstention the second-largest force behind the PP and over two percentage points ahead of the defeated socialists. However, in both the 2010 Catalan parliamentary election and the Spanish local and regional elections of 2011, abstention dropped (by 2.8 and 2.2 per cent, respectively). In the latter case, the Indignados protest movement, then at its height, advocated that citizens use the ballot to express their views (without suggesting how they should vote). Interestingly enough, in this contest, blank and invalid votes, a traditional way of expressing dissatisfaction with the whole party system, reached a historical high of 4.2 per cent, making spoiled ballots the fourth political force after the two main parties and the United Left (Barreiro & Sánchez-Cuenca 2012).

In Italy, abstention rose to a record level of 36.5 per cent in 2010, marking a jump of 7.9 per cent of the total electorate compared with the previous regional elections in 2005. In the local elections of 2011, however, abstention fell compared with the rate registered in the same municipalities in the regional elections of the previous year. Thus, in both Spain and Italy, abstention rose in some elections and declined in others. This suggests that rather than a general alienation from the political system, citizens' assessment of the value of voting changed according to the contest. Elsewhere, abstention does not seem to have been an issue. It actually fell in the Turkish Cypriot presidential election compared with the previous contest in 2005, while it rose marginally in Turkey, from 15.8 in 2007 to 16.8 per cent in 2011. In Portugal, rising abstention levels do not seem to have been politically significant.[13]

There was, however, one case where a fall in abstention operated as a form of political protest. This was the Italian referendums of June 2011. Referendums in Italy require a 50 per cent turnout in order for the vote to be regarded as valid, so that parties opposed to the referendum question campaign for their supporters to abstain rather than to vote against. In the six referendums held since 1997, less than one-third of the electorate had turned out on each occasion, with the result that all had been declared invalid. In contrast, in June 2011, over 54 per cent of the voters turned out to express their opposition to Berlusconi's legislation, resulting in its repeal. A further interesting aspect was that the unexpectedly high turnout built up outside party channels (Carrozza, forthcoming), another indication of declining political party influence.

Assessing the Fallout from the Economic Bomb

The preceding analysis has confirmed the impact of the economic crisis on political developments in Southern Europe. In our control case, Turkey, where the recession was already over by 2010, the incumbent party was consolidated in power, no new challenger parties appeared and the rise in electoral abstention was marginal. In a second case, with the economy returning to growth after a short-lived recession, the Turkish Cypriots voted out their president, but without the disquieting symptoms of political malaise manifested elsewhere in Southern Europe. In contrast, in the five countries affected by the eurozone sovereign debt crisis, there was a clear spillover of crisis from the economy to politics.

As we have seen, in four cases this entailed the summary departure of the incumbent, three of them at a relatively early point in their government term. However, the political cost of economic crisis in Southern Europe went well beyond the ousting of the parties in power at the time. In Spain, part of the price paid was the weakening of one of the traditional parties of power to a point potentially presaging the undermining of the two-party system. Another consequence was the rise of regionalist parties with all the potential implications for the Spanish state. More generally, the electoral epidemic spreading in Southern Europe included the growth of abstention, increasing parliamentary fragmentation and the emergence of new political forces, notably those expressing anti-party, extreme right-wing or even racist positions. Not discussed in this article but also a clear consequence of the crisis was a tendency towards the bypassing of political parties as a means of political participation. Alternative channels that emerged during this period included local referendums (in Spain) and the occupation of town squares (the Spanish Indignados and their Greek equivalent, the Aganaktismenoi).

Growing distrust of political parties provided fertile soil for the electoral epidemic. Scandals taking place at the national level, past economic mismanagement, the economic costs generated by parties' failure to be responsible, the economic pain of the austerity measures—in hard times there seem to be many good reasons to distrust political parties and none to like them. Eurobarometer data (see Table 9) on this point are very revealing. In the Turkish and Turkish Cypriot cases, trust in parties actually grew in 2008–11. In contrast, in all five eurozone cases, trust in parties declined significantly, while in three countries (Spain, the Republic of Cyprus, and Greece) the

Table 9 Trust in Political Parties: Southern Europe, 2008-11

	2008 (%)	2011 (%)	Difference (%)
Spain	40	12	−28
Cyprus	33	8	−25
Greece	17	5	−12
Portugal	19	14	−5
Italy	13	9	−4
Average EU 27	18	14	−4
Turkey	18	27	+9
Cyprus (Turkish Cypriot community)	22	27	+5

Source: Eurobarometer no. 69 (2008), fieldwork carried out in April–May 2008; and no. 76 (2011), fieldwork carried out in November 2011.

level of change ranged from three to seven times the average for the EU-27, indicating a startling delegitimation of parties. Data mined at the national level would undoubtedly offer a more detailed panorama, but it is clear that an increase of anti-party sentiment on such a scale can lead to destabilising consequences for national political systems and party government in Southern Europe.

Moreover, this picture seems unlikely to be ameliorated in the near future. At the end of 2011, there was no indication that the South European economic crisis would be resolved in the near future. Its likely perpetuation and deepening would make it even more difficult for parties to reconcile the tension between 'responsiveness' and 'responsibility', between the demands of voters and the constraints of government management, as discussed above. In particular, growing dependence on external lenders results in a situation where, as Krastev noted for the Balkans, 'governments get elected by making love to the electorate, but they are married to the international donors'. The result is the development of 'democracy without choices' in which citizens can change governments far more easily than they can change policies (Krastev 2002, p. 51). The likely outcome is a build-up of popular frustration with the democratic process which can only be dangerous for the future of South European democracy.

Notes

[1] The last elections had been held on 27 September 2009 in Portugal, 4 October 2009 in Greece and 13–14 April 2008 in Italy. It should be noted that the parliamentary term is five years in Italy and four years in Portugal, Greece and Spain.

[2] For Internal Market (1995–99) and Competition (1999–2004).

[3] The party concerned was the radical right LAOS (Popular Orthodox Rally), which campaigned on a nationalist, anti-immigrant and soft Eurosceptic platform.

[4] The European Commission's spring 2010 forecast, published in the month in which the Greek bailout was signed, predicted a 0.5 per cent drop in GDP for 2011. The autumn forecast, when there had been ample time to take into account the effects of the austerity programme, revised

this to three per cent. Even the latter was startlingly wrong. The real GDP decline in 2011, at 7.1 per cent, was 130 per cent higher than the Commission's autumn 2010 prediction.

[5] We warmly thank Mustafa Besim for providing data on the Turkish Cypriot economy and helping us to interpret them. See also Besim and Mullen (2009, p. 94).

[6] There was one popular vote in Malta: a referendum on 28 May 2011, which resulted in the passage of a bill later in the year, permitting divorce in this country for the first time. The Maltese referendum has not been included in this volume, as the theme concerned a significant social issue, views on which were strongly influenced by religious beliefs, and hence was not regarded as relevant to our study of the potential decline in the legitimacy of party systems in the region.

[7] Specifically, New Democracy (ND) lost an 8.4 per cent of the total vote, falling from 41.9 per cent in 2007 to 33.5 per cent in 2009.

[8] That is, 592,977 out of 5,988,678 total votes cast. Figures from the Greek Ministry of the Interior elections site, www.ypes.gr/el/Elections/

[9] As explained by Verney (2012) in this volume, the peculiarities of the Greek system for local government elections, in which parties are forbidden to run under their own names, result in electoral lists running under a kaleidoscope of different banners across the country. This makes it impossible to gather nationwide figures for party support. In 2010 the only exception to this was the communist party, which ran under the same title everywhere. In addition, due to the 2010 reform that redrew the territorial map, party scores are not generally comparable with the previous local government elections in 2006.

[10] The Spanish proportional electoral system—based on small districts and the D'Hondt electoral formula—has a strong majoritarian representational bias that overrepresents the two largest parties, underrepresents smaller nationwide ones and offers proportional representation to regional parties with geographically concentrated bases of support. For this reason, the emergence of regional parties is easier than that of state-wide parties. In the Congreso de los Diputados the number of parties has always been lower than 13, with two exceptions: the 1979 and 1989 elections, which resulted, respectively, in 14 and 13 parties.

[11] Officially, three political parties and a group of Kurdish candidates, running as independents because of the ten per cent national electoral threshold for political party representation.

[12] This was a rather different case from the 'independent' candidacy of a well-known socialist party member running against the wish of his party in 2006.

[13] The historical high of 42.0 per cent in the parliamentary election did not mark a particularly significant rise over the 40.3 per cent of 2009 and can be partly attributed to administrative problems in the management of electoral registers. In the presidential election, a 53.5 per cent abstention rate seemed significant when compared with the 38.5 percent of the previous presidential contest in 2006. However, it was comparable to the 51.3 per cent of the 2001 presidential election and can be attributed to the lack of excitement about an election that the incumbent was widely expected to win.

References

Akşit, S. (2012) 'The Turkish Cypriot presidential election of April 2010: normalisation of Turkish Cypriot politics', *South European Society and Politics*, vol. 17, no. 2, pp. 175–194.

Aydın-Düzgit, S. (2012) 'No crisis, no change: the third AKP victory in the June 2011 parliamentary elections in Turkey', *South European Society and Politics*, vol. 17, no. 2, pp. 329–346.

Barreiro, B. & Sánchez-Cuenca, I. (2012) 'In the whirlwind of the economic crisis: local and regional elections in Spain, May 2011', *South European Society and Politics*, vol. 17, no. 2, pp. 281–294.

Bellucci, P., Costa Lobo, M. & Lewis-Beck, M. S. (2012) 'Economic crisis and elections: the European periphery', *Electoral Studies*, vol. 31, pp. 469–471.

Besim, M. & Mullen, F. (2009) 'Cyprus in the global financial crisis: how lack of banking sophistication proved an advantage', *South European Society and Politics*, vol. 14, no. 1, pp. 87–101.

Bosco, A. & McDonnell, D. (forthcoming) 'Introduction: the Monti government and the downgrade of Italian parties', in *Italian Politics: From Berlusconi to Monti*, eds A. Bosco & D. McDonnell, Berghahn, New York.

Çarkoglu, A. (2009) 'The March 2009 local elections in Turkey: a signal for takers or the inevitable beginning of the end for AKP?', *South European Society and Politics*, vol. 14, no. 3, pp. 295–316.

Carrozza, C. (forthcoming) 'The June referendums. A partial victory', in *Italian Politics: From Berlusconi to Monti*, eds A. Bosco & D. McDonnell, Berghahn, New York.

Chiaramonte, A. & D'Alimonte, R. (2012) 'The twilight of the Berlusconi era: local elections and national referendums in Italy, May and June 2011', *South European Society and Politics*, vol. 17, no. 2, pp. 261–279.

Christophorou, C. (2012) 'Disengaging citizens: parliamentary elections in the Republic of Cyprus, 22 May 2011', *South European Society and Politics*, vol. 17, no. 2, pp. 295–307.

Corbetta, P. (2012) 'The 2010 regional elections in Italy: another referendum on Berlusconi', *South European Society and Politics*, vol. 17, no. 2, pp. 155–173.

Jalali, C. (2012) 'The 2011 Portuguese presidential elections: incumbency advantage in semi-presidentialism?', *South European Society and Politics*, vol. 17, no. 2, pp. 239–260.

Jones, E. (forthcoming) 'The Berlusconi government and the sovereign debt crisis', in *Italian Politics: From Berlusconi to Monti*, eds A. Bosco & D. McDonnell, Berghahn, New York.

Kaplanoglou, G. & Rapanos, V. T. (forthcoming) 'Tax and trust: the fiscal crisis in Greece', *South European Society and Politics*, DOI:10.1080/13608746.2012.7233.

Krastev, I. (2002) 'The Balkans: democracy without choices', *Journal of Democracy*, vol. 13, no. 3, pp. 39–53.

Magalhães, P. C. (2012) 'After the bailout: responsibility, policy, and valence in the Portuguese legislative election of June 2011', *South European Society and Politics*, vol. 17, no. 2, pp. 309–327.

Mair, P. (2011) 'Bini Smaghi vs. the parties: representative government and institutional constraints', Robert Schuman Centre for Advanced Studies and EU Democracy Observatory, EUI working paper no. 2011/22, European University Institute, Florence.

Martín, I. & Urquizu-Sancho I. (2012) 'The 2011 general election in Spain: the collapse of the socialist party', *South European Society and Politics*, vol. 17, no. 2, pp. 347–363.

Pagoulatos, G. & Triantopoulos, C. (2009) 'The return of the Greek patient: Greece and the 2008 global financial crisis', *South European Society and Politics*, vol. 14, no. 1, pp. 35–54.

Rico, G. (2012) 'The 2010 regional election in Catalonia: a multilevel account in an age of economic crisis', *South European Society and Politics*, vol. 17, no. 2, pp. 217–238.

Royo, S. (2009) 'After the fiesta: the Spanish economy meets the global financial crisis', *South European Society and Politics*, vol. 14, no. 1, pp. 19–34.

Torres, F. (2009) 'Back to external pressure: policy responses to the financial crisis in Portugal', *South European Society and Politics*, vol. 14, no. 1, pp. 55–70.

Verney, S. (2012) 'The eurozone's first post-bailout election: the 2010 local government contest in Greece', *South European Society and Politics*, vol. 17, no. 2, pp. 195–216.

Anna Bosco is Associate Professor of Comparative Politics and European Government at the University of Trieste and, with Susannah Verney, one of the two Editors of *South European Society and Politics*. She has carried out research on party politics in Italy, Spain, Portugal, Greece and East-Central Europe. Among her publications are *Party Change in Southern Europe* (2007, edited with L. Morlino), *La España de Zapatero. Años de cambios, 2004–2008* (2009, edited with I. Sánchez-Cuenca) and *Italian Politics: From Berlusconi to Monti* (forthcoming, edited with D. McDonnell).

Susannah Verney is Assistant Professor of European Integration at the University of Athens and, with Anna Bosco, one of the two Editors of *South European Society and Politics*. Recent publications include *Turkey's Road to European Union Membership: National Identity and Political Change* (2009, edited with K. Ifantis) and *Euroscepticism in Southern Europe: A Diachronic Perspective* (edited, 2011).

The 2010 Regional Elections in Italy: Another Referendum on Berlusconi

Piergiorgio Corbetta

This article analyses the 2010 regional elections in Italy, in which the centre-right, led by Silvio Berlusconi, was successful. This followed on from its victory in the 2008 general election and the 2009 European elections. The article analyses the extremely conflictual political climate in which the elections took place. The analysis of the election results concentrates on four points: the large increase in abstentionism, the contest in the northern regions between the Lega Nord and the Popolo della libertà, the failure of the centre political formations to realise their ambitions, and the success of far-left 'anti-political' groups.

The March 2010 regional elections in Italy took place in 13 out of 20 regions. There were no elections in the five regions with a 'special status' (characterised by greater autonomy) and in two other regions (Abruzzo and Molise), which for various reasons voted on a different date.[1] Forty-one million voters were eligible to vote, representing 83 per cent of the total national electorate. So, from a quantitative point of view, it was effectively a consultation of national significance. But the electoral test was also qualitatively of national importance. In Italy, 'second-order elections'—whether to a supranational parliament like the European one or to subnational parliaments like those in the regions—have always had a bearing on the national political debate. (Indeed, in the 2009 European elections the question of Europe never came up in the campaign, which was dominated by national issues.) It should be added that today in Italy the regions—set up in 1970—are very important because they have a lot of power and are likely to have even more in the future as a process is underway to extend their authority.

The electoral system for regional elections is rather complex, with a double vote: (a) one vote for a regional president, which under a majoritarian system translates into 20 per cent of the seats; (b) one vote for a party, which assigns the remaining 80 per cent of the seats with a proportional mechanism. It is therefore a mixed system (majoritarian–proportional) but mainly proportional (Di Virgilio 2005).[2] Every candidate for regional president is linked to supporting parties or lists. In every region, two main coalitions were formed: the centre-right coalesced into the Popolo della Libertà (People of Freedom, PDL) and the centre-left into the Partito Democratico (Democratic Party, PD).[3] In summary, the principal alliances were:

- the centre-right coalition formed by the PDL and the Lega Nord (Northern League, LN);
- the centre-left alliance, formed by the PD and Italia dei Valori (Italy of Values, IDV), which ran in every region with the exception of Calabria;
- the centrist party Unione di Centro (Union of the Centre, UDC), allied with the PD in Piemonte, Liguria, Marche and Basilicata, with the PDL in Lazio, Campania and Calabria, and ran alone in the other regions;
- the Radicali Italiani (Italian Radicals) formed the Lista Bonino-Pannella (Bonino-Pannella List), which allied with the centre-left in four regions, ran with the IDV in Calabria and stood alone in Tuscany;
- the Partito Socialista Italiano (Italian Socialist Party, PSI) allied with the centre-left;
- the Federazione della Sinistra (Left Federation, FS, one of the two radical-left formations that came from the 2008 Sinistra Arcobaleno, Rainbow Left) stood mainly as part of the centre-left, but ran alone in Lombardy and in Campania, and with the SEL (see below) in Marche;
- Sinistra, Ecologia, Libertà (Left, Ecology, Freedom SEL, the other list that came from the Sinistra Arcobaleno) stood with the centre-left throughout Italy, but allied with FS in Marche;
- the new Movimento Cinque Stelle (Five Star Movement) stood in Campania, Emilia-Romagna, Piedmont, Veneto and Lombardy and did not form part of any coalition.

As the reader can see, the picture might seem confusing. But it is only apparently so. The regional differences outlined above are small and negligible and in reality the political contest in every region was between the centre-left and centre-right coalitions formed around the PDL and PD. But, above all, it was a national referendum regarding Berlusconi himself.

A Referendum for or against Berlusconi

The so-called 'second republic' was born in Italy in 1993, when the new electoral law—moving from a proportional to a mainly majoritarian system—swept away the old parties and initiated a bipolar system. The transition from a multi-party system to the present one was complex and not without contradictions (Newell 2000). It should be noted that at present the Italian political system is not a two-party one, but a multi-party system with two main parties, the PD on the left and the PDL on the right, and other smaller parties gravitating around one or the other of these.

For half a century Italian politics had been dominated by a classical centre party (Christian Democrats) in various coalitions, excluding from government a numerically small right wing (the inheritors of the Monarchist Party and the Fascists) and a left that was much larger and more rooted in the country but dominated by the Communist Party, which was still tied to Moscow and greatly feared by the economic powers in Italy, Europe and above all the US.

The transformation of the Italian political system in a bipolar direction has had two main consequences: (a) it has allowed the left to govern after being excluded for 50 years; (b) it has given rise to a centre-right political pole (not right-wing but centre-right, it should be noted), something completely new in post-war Italian politics. It should be added that in the 1994 general election the centre-right did not just come into being but also found a leader: Silvio Berlusconi. He has shown extraordinary resilience in his position as leader. Between 1994 and 2010 the centre-left has had seven leaders in succession (Occhetto, Prodi, D'Alema, Rutelli, Veltroni, Franceschini, Bersani), while Berlusconi has never left his command post on the centre-right.

He is above all a leader with the charisma typical of populist leaders,[4] that is the ability to arouse opposing emotions: love and hate, with nothing in between. There are those, including the author of this article, who believe that if the Italian system is bipolar today it is due to Berlusconi's ability to create only friends or enemies. As far as his attractiveness is concerned, his popularity ratings have been consistently high and his leadership abilities have enabled him to fuse together politically diverse centre-right souls (Catholic, Liberal and post-Fascist). With regards to his ability to repel, he has given rise to a widespread anti-Berlusconi feeling which is often the only glue binding together the confused and contradictory centre-left, which is united only when it can attack the bogeyman of Italian politics or when it is attacked by him.

In the period 1994–2010, 13 elections took place in Italy at a national level: almost one a year, which means that there has been a permanent election campaign for 16 years and daily politics has been a continual aggressive and argumentative polemic. Each election became a referendum for or against Berlusconi. Excluding the elections that are about to be analysed here, Berlusconi won seven of these hard battles and lost five (see Table 1). So, this poses the question: did Berlusconi also win the referendum of the 2010 regional election?

The Electoral Campaign

According to two of Italy's most renowned political journalists—the presenter of a state television talk show and an opinion writer in the daily newspaper *La Stampa*—this electoral campaign was 'the ugliest, the most unseemly and even the most violent ever' (Vespa 2010) and 'the worst in the history of the Republic' (Sorgi 2010). It is

Table 1 Elections of national importance which took place from 1994 to 2010, and their winners

	1994	1995	1996	1999	2000	2001	2004	2005	2006	2008	2009	2010
General	CR		CL			CR			CL	CR		
Regional		CL			CR			CL				CR
European		CR		CR			CL				CR	

CR = centre-right. CL = centre-left.

difficult to disagree with this opinion. And this assessment is not limited to the brief period of the electoral campaign.

In fact, the nine months between the European elections of 6–7 June 2009 and the regional elections of 27–28 March 2010 were a continuous election campaign, concentrated on the figure of Berlusconi. Already at the end of 2009, a few weeks before the European election, Berlusconi's wife, Veronica Lario, sent a letter to the main Italian press agency in which—faced with the possibility that Berlusconi was running various soubrettes as candidates on his party list for the European election—spoke about 'shameless rubbish … for the amusement of the emperor'. A few days later she asked for a divorce, following news in the papers about an ambiguous relationship that her husband was having with an underage girl (Noemi Letizia), news that had already appeared in the press some time previously. In the middle of June the newspapers, still focusing on the Prime Minister's family morals, published audiotapes of a meeting between Silvio Berlusconi and the escort Patrizia D'Addario. From this a turbid scenario emerged of parties organised in Berlusconi's villa in Sardinia with prostitutes offered by businessmen who, in exchange, were interested in obtaining public contracts for their companies. This affair, together with a constant repetition of further news and spicy details, dragged on for months. On 10 September, at a press conference at the Italian–Spanish summit, Berlusconi felt the need to publically declare in front of a European audience that he had 'never paid for sex', and on 1 October Patrizia D'Addario was a guest on the popular television programme *Annozero*, where she stated that 'Berlusconi knew I was an escort' (Gundle 2010).

In addition to this Boccaccio-like affair, Berlusconi continually had to face legal problems. On 4 October 2009, the Civil Court in Milan established that Fininvest, Berlusconi's company, had to pay €750 million to the Cir company (an important holding, also involved in the media) as compensation for an event dating back to the early 1990s (regarding a controversial judgement about control of the country's main publishing house, which also owns influential daily and weekly newspapers), when a judge was bribed to rule in favour of Berlusconi. The Prime Minister himself was not tried because of the statute of limitations, but his lawyer was found guilty, and the sentence passed in October 2009 implicitly confirmed that the company owned by Berlusconi was involved in corrupt practices with the aim of possessing important media assets. On 7 October the Consitutional Court rejected the so-called *Lodo Alfano* (named after Berlusconi's minister who had proposed this law in Parliament), which had been approved in June 2008 following a ferocious parliamentary battle, with the aim of shielding those holding the three highest political positions (and therefore also Berlusconi) from being brought to court for as long as they held office. Berlusconi really wanted this law because it was explicitly aimed at protecting him personally from legal investigations, and obviously its rejection by the Constitutional Court represented a big defeat for him, as he faces trials on several fronts, with the possibility of being found guilty in some of them. This could seriously jeopardise his institutional role (no democratic country would tolerate a prime minister convicted by the courts). So Berlusconi's lawyers and the ministers closest to him—beginning with the Justice

Minister (Angelino Alfano)—embarked on frenetic activity to put in place a law (*legge ad personam*) aimed at protecting Berlusconi from the trials already underway. Of particular concern was an impending trial which Berlusconi faced. This was connected to the British lawyer, David Mills who had already been sentenced to four years and six months for giving false testimony in court. It was alleged that Berlusconi had paid him to do so in order that Berlusconi and his company could be immune from prosecution for charges brought against them in a previous trial.

Berlusconi's lawyers drew up three draft laws to protect their beneficiary. These were the law of *legittimo impedimento* (the prime minister can refuse to face trial if he or she is engaged in government activity), the *processo breve* (the limit for the statute of limitations is cut considerably and comes into effect two years after the original request to send the case to court, meaning that all Berlusconi's trials would be timed out, together with 50 per cent of proceedings pending in the country, according to the National Association of Magistrates), and another version of the *Lodo Alfano*. This gave rise to ferocious controversy. Berlusconi repeatedly attacked the magistrates with statements of a kind that are not easily acceptable in a democracy ('There is a climate of civil war, the public prosecutors want to bring me down', 26 November; 'Parliament's sovereignty has been passed to the judges', 10 December; 'The judges are the Taliban', 26 February; 'The Public Prosecutor' Party has come on to the field, distorting the election campaign', 23 March).[5]

But Berlusconi was under attack on other fronts. The Prime Minister managed the aftermath of the Aquila earthquake—which happened on 6 April 2009—by heavily involving himself personally and using the media, in order to show Italians how his government (and he himself) was different from all the other governments and prime ministers who had gone before (and who had often been accused of inefficiency in similar emergency situations). Guido Bertolaso was the man who became the symbol of this mass media campaign (and also had the job of restoring the popularity of Berlusconi, under attack for the mentioned affairs concerning his family and female escorts). Bertolaso was the head of Civil Protection, omnipresent on TV—the archetypal 'actions not words', 'we act while you talk' person. But on 10 February, Bertolaso was investigated for corruption related to contracts that he had assigned for 'big events'. A vast network of corruption with many ramifications emerged, and public opinion became aware that doing away with the bureaucracy linked to contracts, something that Berlusconi wanted as part of his much extolled 'can-do government', had consequently led to a lack of controls and therefore to corruption.

Other factors soured Berlusconi's relationship with centre-left public opinion. Two weeks before the elections, Berlusconi was investigated by magistrates for having put pressure on the Communications Agency (a body independent from the government) to gag the political talk show *Annozero*, which Berlusconi opposed because it strongly criticised him. On this subject it should be mentioned that at the beginning of March the executive committee of the body responsible for state radio and television (which in Italy has three of the most important television channels, while the other three are owned by Berlusconi) decided to suspend political talk shows. These are very popular in Italy, and many are critical of Berlusconi. The left accused the government of 'gagging' freedom of political expression, and the controversy in this case also continued until election day.

Finally, in the last two weeks before the vote, the electoral campaign was further embittered by events closely linked to the elections themselves. First of all, magistrates in the province of Rome and then in Milan ruled that the electoral lists of Berlusconi's PDL were not eligible because of irregularities in the way that they were presented. In Milan this decision was overturned, but not in Rome. There the affair, involving judgements, appeals and counter-judgements, dragged on almost until election day; in the end the PDL's list was not accepted in the province of Rome, and even here Berlusconi did not miss an opportunity to blame the magistrates (declaring that his party was a victim of bureaucracy).

In this climate it is not surprising that these elections were once again presented as a referendum for or against Berlusconi. But it was Berlusconi himself who was pushing in this direction, appealing—in typical populist style—to public opinion in opposition to 'bureaucratic institutional fetters', and presenting himself as the 'only one directly elected by the people'.

Abstentionism

For the reasons just mentioned, the elections took place in a climate that was greatly scrutinised by the mass media; and they seemed to be alarmed when, with voting still underway, the Minister for Home Affairs released the usual initial figures on the elections, which revealed a low turnout. On Monday 29 March, when the polling stations were already open, the three most important daily newspapers had the headlines, 'Turnout down 9 per cent. Big fall in the whole of Italy' (*Corriere della Sera*), 'Turnout collapses in the regional elections' (*La Repubblica* and *La Stampa* had the same headline).

This alarm was justified. In fact, the turnout in these elections, at 63.5 per cent, was the lowest in the history of the Italian Republic. In the previous regional elections in 2000 and 2005, the turnout was 73.0 per cent and 71.4 per cent, respectively, and in 2010 the figure was six percentage points below that of the European elections just nine months before. More than a third of Italians did not go out to vote in 2010. These figures mean little to the non-Italian observer, considering that in the four most important European nations (Germany, France, Britain and Spain) average turnout in recent general elections has been 69 per cent and has been even lower in local elections. Regional elections took place in France just 15 days before those in Italy, with half of the French people not turning out to vote. But this is a misleading comparison because in France the turnout is always much lower than in Italy, and goes up and down dramatically. In Italy, on the other hand, turnout has always been very high[6] (going to vote was part of both the Socialist/Communist and Christian Democrat political culture) and has been declining for many years. As we can see from Figure 1, in the 1970s a very high percentage of Italians voted, well above 90 per cent. Since then, this percentage has constantly fallen, speeding up particularly in the middle of the 1990s when the old parties disappeared and the proportional electoral system was replaced with a mainly majoritarian one. But this is not only a problem of turnout. All of the indicators concerning the relationship between citizens and politics point to a growing disaffection amongst the electorate with political parties and politicians, which has spread to political institutions, to parliament and to local councils, and affects all forms of political participation.

This is a tendency that is general throughout the Western world but appears particularly accentuated in Italy. In Italian society, something is happening to the relationship between citizens and democracy and these elections could represent the beginning of a collapse rather than an anomalous wave that will recede. There are many reasons for concern: the confusion of an election campaign with its toing and froing regarding the presentation of lists (to such a point that in Rome people still did not know which lists would be on the ballot paper five days before the elections); the squabbling between political opponents trying to discredit each other rather than put forward a programme for government; the scandals involving the highest ranks of the political class, including the opposition; the left's lack of leadership and clear political line; and above all the presence of a leader (Berlusconi) who in the purest populist style undermines political institutions and appeals directly to the 'people'. All this reveals

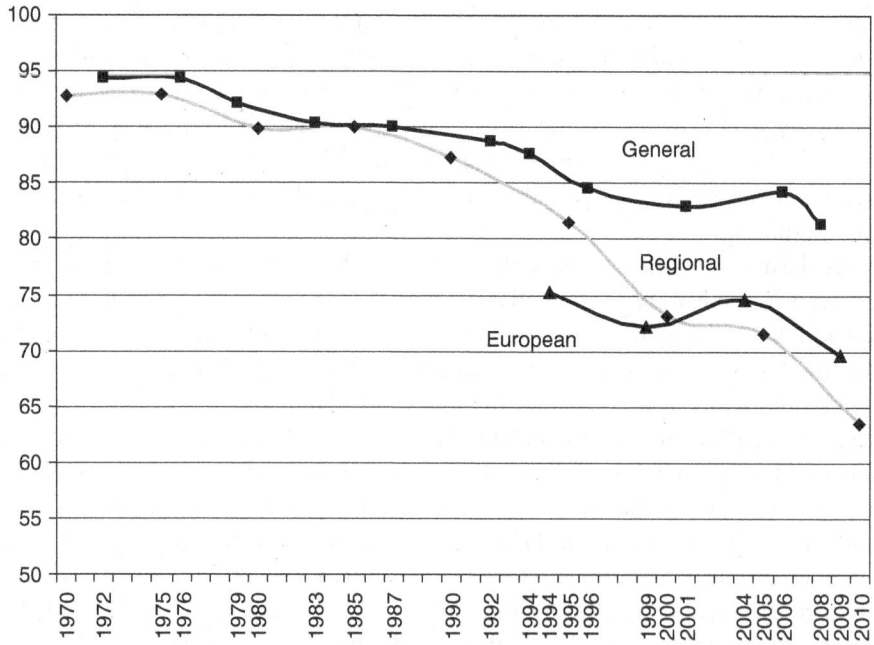

Figure 1 Turnout in Italy since 1970 for three different kinds of elections (for the 13 regions in which voting took place in 2010).
Source: Ministry of Interior, official data.

a democratic body that is ailing, abstentionism being the thermometer that's measuring its high temperature.

Who Won and Who Lost

Table 2 presents the electoral results for the proportional part of the vote: that is, the vote for parties and party lists. However, the first analysis of the vote should concern the winning coalition in each region, the one that was able to win the presidency and therefore the regional government, rather than the national vote of single parties. Before the elections, the centre-left governed in 11 regions and the centre-right in two. After the elections, seven regions became controlled by the centre-left and six by the centre-right. Therefore, the centre-right gained four regions (see Figure 2). We should also consider the fact that the six regions governed by the centre-right are more populous (and economically more important) than the seven governed by the centre-left (the population of the six centre-right regions is twice that of the seven centre-left regions). In this respect, the centre-right was clearly successful. In order to complete the national picture, it should be added that of the seven regions that did not vote in 2010, five are governed by the centre-right and just one by the centre-left (the remaining region is not controlled by either coalition; see note 1). Thus, the 2010 contests confirmed the centre-right's dominant position in the regions.

However, comparing the outcome of the recent elections with those of five years ago is not very useful for understanding the shifts that are taking place. Too many political

Table 2 Regional election of 2010: results of the vote to the party lists

	Per cent
Partito Democratico—Democratic Party—PD	26.1
Italia dei Valori—Italy of Values—IDV	7.3
Sinistra Ecologia e Libertà—Left Ecology Freedom—SEL	3.0
Federazione della Sinistra—Leftist Federation—FS	2.7
Partito Socialista Italiano—Italia Socialist Party—PSI	1.9
Verdi—Greens	0.7
Lista Bonino-Pannella—Radicals	0.5
Alleanza per l'Italia—Alliance for Italy	0.6
Personal lists of centre-left governors	1.9
Total centre left	**44.7**
Popolo della libertà—People of Freedom—PDL	26.8
Lega Nord—Northern League—LN	12.3
La destra—The Right	0.7
Personal Lists of centre-right governors	7.8
Total centre right	**47.6**
Unione di Centro—Union of the Centre—UDC	5.6
Movimento a 5 Stelle—Five Star Movement	1.8
Others	0.3
Total	100.0

Source: www.Repubblica.it

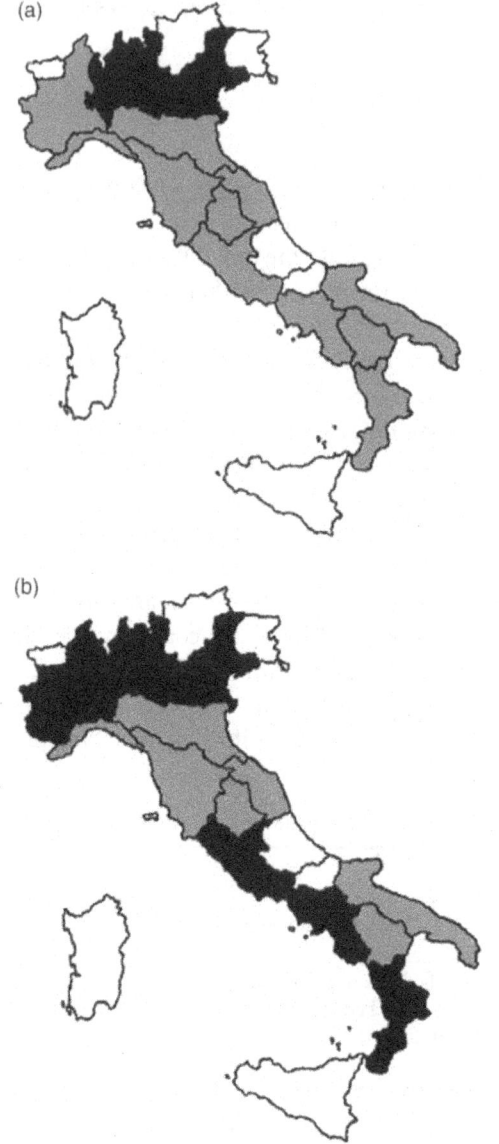

Figure 2 Regions governed by the centre-left and the centre-right before and after the 2010 elections. (a) Italian regional elections 2005. (b) Italian regional elections 2010.
Legend: white = regions with no elections in 2010; gray = regions with a centre-left majority; black = regions with a centre-right majority.

and electoral events happened in Italy between 2005 and 2010. We passed from a favourable situation for the centre-left in 2005 to a situation of stalemate between the two political camps in the general election the following year, followed by two clear victories for the centre-right in the 2008 general election and the European elections in 2009. Therefore, it would seem reasonable to compare these regional elections with the elections for the European Parliament in 2009. It is true that these are different kinds of elections, but they are a better comparison if we want to analyse the changes that are taking place in the country *today*. Before the elections, the left's expectations were not entirely negative. As has already been mentioned, the centre-left held 11 regions against two for the centre-right, but it was known that this situation could not be repeated and that Campania and Calabria would undoubtedly be added to the two already in the hands of the centre-right (Lombardy and the Veneto). So, a result of nine to four was possible, and this would have been interpreted as a success for the left, a kind of about-turn in the tendency underway following their burning defeat in 2008–9. However, two very important regions were in the balance: Piedmont and Lazio. It was clear to everyone that the result in these two regions would symbolise the elections politically: whoever took them would legitimately have been able to crown themselves the winners. Hearts were beating fast at the election counts. The result remained in the balance up until the last seat: but in the end both were won by the centre-right.[7]

Other factors should also be taken into consideration. In 2009, Berlusconi was in the middle of his honeymoon with the electorate (after having become prime minister again when he won the general election in 2008). The European election of 2009 took place after a successful year when he had removed the rubbish from Naples and acted as 'rescuer' in the aftermath of the Aquila earthquake. But in the nine months between the 2009 and 2010 elections, his image had been greatly damaged by personal scandals, and major tensions had emerged inside his party, the PDL. In addition, the government was grappling with the most serious post-war world economic crisis. Finally, these were mid-term elections, which normally favour the opposition: a few days before, in the regional elections in nearby France, Nicholas Sarkozy lost every region, except Alsace, to the opposition.

There were, therefore, many reasons why the opposition party could expect a good result. It was not to be. In the end, the PD's percentage of valid votes was substantially the same as in 2009 (26.1 per cent, up 0.6 percentage points). But it should be remembered that 2009 was electorally a particularly negative year for the PD, which in the European elections received one of the lowest percentages in its electoral history (Figure 3).[8] The party did not slip further but there was no sign of a revival. For this reason, for the PD the result can only be described as disappointing.

We cannot say that Belusconi's party, the PDL, did well electorally. From Figure 3 we can see that it fell almost six percentage points compared with 2009, going from 35.3 per cent in 2009 to 29.6 per cent, historically the lowest level ever for this party or for the two parties that had formed the PDL in 2008 (Forza Italia and Alleanza Nazionale). Frankly, it was a defeat. But this defeat was greatly compensated politically by the success of its ally, the LN. This is the only major party whose percentage of the vote increased, going from 11.3 per cent to 12.3 per cent between 2009 and 2010, thus securing its third consecutive electoral advance and obtaining its highest vote since 1994.

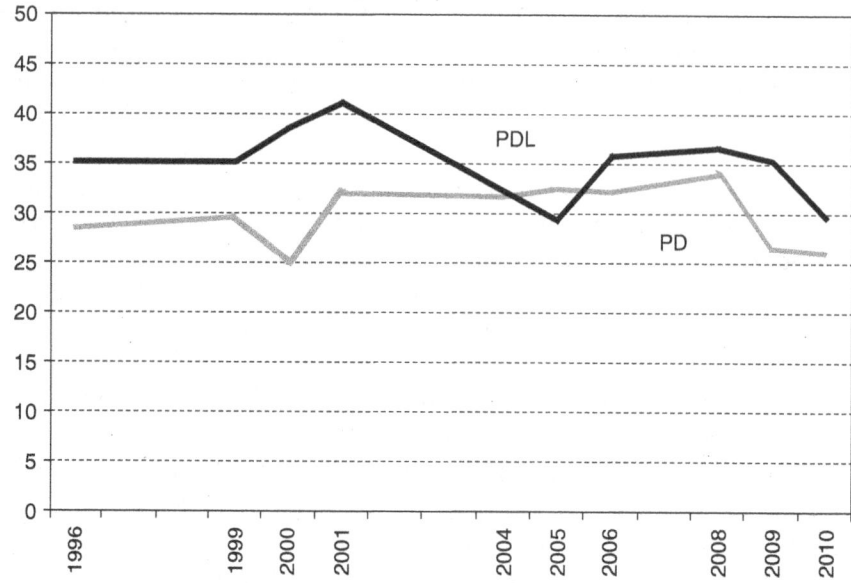

Figure 3 Votes for the two main parties (or for the parties that formed them) from 1996 to 2010 (for the 13 regions in which voting took place in 2010).
Note: See Table 1 for the kind of election.
Source: Ministry of Interior, official data.

The centre-right coalition's success (even if it was thanks to the LN) and the consequent winning of four new regions (above all the two that were uncertain until the last minute) were the distinguishing characteristics of these elections. As the chief editor of the daily newspaper *La Repubblica* wrote, 'The symbolic effect of Lazio and Piedmont, which changed political hands, swings the electoral balance towards Berlusconi, who went into these elections weakened and came out strengthened: everything else is just idle talk' (Mauro 2010). Thus, Berlusconi won these elections, not as leader of the PDL but as head of the governing coalition. The day after the elections the Italian newspaper *Corriere della Sera* correctly had the headline, 'Berlusconi and the Northern League win'.

The 'Northern Derby'

These elections were also a contest within the centre-right, between the LN and the PDL in the richest parts of the country—the three regions in the north.[9] In 2005 the centre-right had won in Veneto and Lombardy (the only two regions that it won in that year): in Veneto the PDL came slightly above the LN while in Lombardy the margin of victory for the PDL was larger. The question mark was not over who would win (there was no doubt that the centre-right would). The issue was whether the LN would overtake the PDL in Veneto and how close behind them it would come in Lombardy. Even though they are closely allied, the PDL and the LN openly challenge each other in the north of Italy, and at stake was political hegemony in the most modern, most European, most industrialised and richest parts of the country. In Piedmont (the third region in the sub-Alpine north), on the other hand, the contest between centre-right and centre-left was completely open: the outgoing governor was from the centre-left and the centre-right had entrusted a supporter of the LN with the job of challenging her. There is no doubt that a victory for the LN candidate would have strengthened the party in the whole of the north.

The results favoured the LN in all three situations mentioned. In Veneto it outclassed the PDL, becoming by a long way the biggest party with 35 per cent of the votes compared with 25 per cent for the PDL (while in the previous regional elections of 2005 the LN got only 16 per cent of the vote in this region). In Lombardy, the LN did not overtake the PDL, but halved the gap between them (which was 11.2 points in 2005, falling to 5.6 in 2010). And in Piedmont the centre-right candidate from the LN, Roberto Cota, won the difficult contest for the governorship, taking the region from the centre-left who had governed there for the previous five years. We should also add that in the other big region of the Po valley, Emilia-Romagna, traditionally a stronghold of the Communist Party and later of the centre-left (one of the 'red' regions), the LN went from 4.8 per cent in the 2005 regional elections to 13.3 per cent, almost tripling its electoral support in five years.

The clear consequence of all of this—together with the above mentioned considerable fall in support for the PDL—is a rebalancing (in favour of the Lega Nord) between the two main parties of the coalition. From Figure 4 we can see that in 2005, 16 out of 100 votes for the centre-right were votes for the LN while in 2010 the LN's electoral weight within the coalition doubled (to more than 31 per cent).

This redefining of the balance between the PDL and the LN has another consequence: the 'southernisation' of the PDL. If the PDL loses votes to the LN in the north, the 'northern' part of the party is weakened.

The Ambitions of the Centre

In the elections, an important match was also being played in the political centre. In Italy the debate over which electoral system to adopt is still open. From 1948 to 1993 the electoral system was based on a strictly proportional law which greatly helped the Christian Democrats, a typically centrist party, to hold power in a stable way. In 1993, following a referendum, the system was almost completely overturned when a mainly majoritarian electoral law was passed, upsetting the political landscape (with its main consequence the disappearance of the Christian Democrats). Then in 2005 the Berlusconi government reintroduced the proportional system but with a majority bonus, with the aim of forcing the parties to form coalitions (the formation of a bipolar rather than biparty system, with a centre-left and a centre-right pole).

Emerging from this bipolar system in 2008, when the two big parties—PDL and PD—were formed, was the centrist party UDC, which did not want to be imprisoned in a PDL led by Berlusconi. The UDC, previously a loyal ally of Berlusconi, began to go

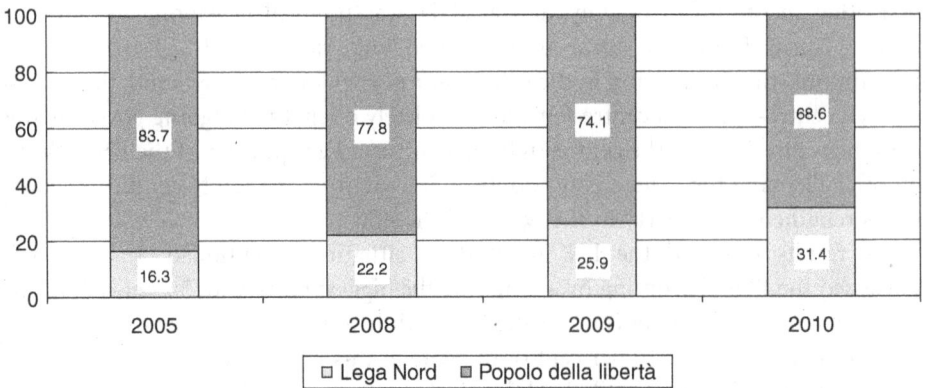

Figure 4 Distribution between the PDL and the LN of 100 votes for the centre-right coalition from 2005 to 2010 (for the 13 regions in which voting took place in 2010). *Source*: Ministry of Interior, official data.

it alone in elections, hoping to become a catalyst in the centre, should the electoral system once more move towards a proportional one. The advantages for a centre formation under a proportional system are clear: it would be in a position to influence the composition of the governing coalition. Furthermore, in Italy other political forces in addition to the UDC are in favour of moving towards a proportional electoral system (the model in this case is the German one), and this is an issue of bitter conflict inside the PD.

Against this background there was a clear interest in measuring the success of the UDC's new strategy. In 2010, the party made its flexibility as a centrist party clear for the first time, allying with the centre-left in four regions, with the centre-right in three and standing alone in the remaining six. Tired of conflict between pro- and anti-Berlusconi supporters, the party's plan was clearly one of attracting votes from a moderate electorate in the centre. Therefore, it was an interesting test, not only for the fate of the UDC itself, but also for understanding how far the bipolar system was consolidated in Italian culture and how much space there was for a centrist formation.

The result was clear: the UDC, which in the 2009 European elections obtained 6.2 per cent of the vote, now had 5.6 per cent (as always, the data refer to the 13 regions where voting took place in 2010). So, the improvement that its leaders expected did not take place. It should be added that compared with 2009 the party lost whether it ran alone or in alliance with the centre-left, while its vote remained unchanged (with a slight increase) where it was allied with the centre-right: this would signal that the heart of the UCD electorate beats more on the right than on the left. However, as has already been said, the point of this test was to understand whether the centrist strategy could pay off electorally, and the reply in the ballot boxes was negative. The party's oscillation between the two political poles brings with it the risk of losing its identity, and in the current political situation in Italy there appears to be little space between the centre-left and the centre-right.

The Unknown Area to the Left of the Democratic Party

The history of the Italian 'radical left' (or 'alternative left') is rather complicated. It was born at the end of the 1960s to the left of the communist and socialist parties and has been through 30 extremely difficult years of unity and splits. In the last few years it has been made up of two components. The first of these—let's call it 'radical left'—takes its inspiration from Marxism and is a direct descendant of the student movements of 1968. In 2006, it was still getting ten per cent of the vote, but in the 2008 elections (when it stood on the Sinistra Arcobaleno) it did not succeed in reaching the minimum four per cent threshold to enable it to enter parliament. This was almost a mortal defeat and was due to the fact that its electorate had not forgiven it for making life difficult for the Prodi government (the centre-left government from 2006 to 2008), and accused it of bringing about that government's fall, opening the way for Berlusconi's landslide victory in the 2008 elections.

In addition to this, there is the second component, the IDV, which was founded by Antonio di Pietro, a magistrate who played the role of principal prosecutor of Berlusconi in many of his trials, and who in 1998 abandoned the magistracy to go into politics. This party got by in the 2001–6 elections and managed with difficulty to enter Parliament in 2008 (4.4 per cent nationally), and subsequently had a big success in the 2009 European elections, doubling its vote (eight per cent nationally). This success was due to the disappearance of the radical left and its handing over of the anti-Berlusconi flag, which Di Pietro has waved at every opportunity. The question in the regional elections was how well an anti-Berlusconi would stance pay off. In other words, how much electoral support would a policy of full-frontal opposition to Berlusconi, including personal attacks, have?

In the 2010 regional elections the IDV did not do well compared with the European elections of 2009, falling back slightly. In the 13 regions where voting took place, the party had 7.8 per cent and now has seven per cent. Nor did the radical left—which stood as two separate groupings, the Left Federation and Freedom and Ecology Left— do well. Adding together their vote in the 13 regions under consideration, they got 7.3 per cent in 2009 and went down to 6.3 per cent in 2010.

But one other thing should be added, because one of the surprises of these elections was Beppe Grillo's Five Star Movement, a completely new political formation, founded by a showman. Beppe Grillo is a comic actor and, for some time now, a political activist, whose internet blog is one of the most visited in Italy and is in seventh place in the 2009 Forbes world ranking. He is a promoter of a discussion forum with thousands of members commonly known as 'Grillini' or 'friends of Beppe Grillo', has inspired numerous civic lists that carry his name and in October 2009 was behind the creation of a real national political movement, the Five Star Movement.

Ignored by the traditional media and with few economic resources, Beppe Grillo and his movement relied on the internet to spread their political programme, to mobilise voters and to recruit candidates (mainly 20- and 30-year-old social networkers). The result was that 60,000 people signed up. In the 2010 regional elections the movement only stood in five regions but had a completely unexpected success: an average vote of 3.7 per cent, with a highest vote of seven per cent in Emilia-Romagna (and 9.3 per cent in the city of Bologna). In addition, it won four regional council seats, two in Piedmont and two in Emilia-Romagna.

Beppe Grillo does not fit into any of the traditional political schemas, attacking the PDL and the PD equally violently and declaring that he is 'neither right nor left, but forward'. He has two main political proposals, one anarchic and one ecological. Above all, he has made his own the theme of popular distrust of traditional politics, its rites, its privileges and its protagonists discredited by scandals and corruption, among both the governing majority and the opposition. Discontent in Italy has reached extremely high levels. In this sense, Beppe Grillo's movement represents a last refuge for the disillusioned, offering electors (above all, young voters) the opportunity to cast a protest vote. Without this option, many of those who voted for the Five Star Movement probably would not have turned out. Secondly, Beppe Grillo has been able to pick up the ecological banner that had been left on the ground for some time by all of the other parties. He appeals to Italians who cycle, who want greener and cleaner air, who are concerned about the greenhouse effect, who buy fair-trade products, who want to recycle rubbish, who do not want their cities to be concrete jungles and who want environmentally clean transport. It is not a coincidence that in the Val di Susa in Piedmont, where for some time a struggle has been carried out against the building of a high speed train network, his movement won around 30 per cent of votes. However, at the moment it is not clear whether this political movement will be able to consolidate itself and become a stable presence on the Italian political scene.

Conclusion

Berlusconi has been the inspiration behind the Italian bipolar system for over 15 years. In every election, political coalitions have been formed around him and each electoral contest has been turned into a referendum on him personally. Berlusconi himself has personalised every election, even turning local elections with little national relevance into a test of himself, as, for example, in the regional elections in Abruzzo in 2008 and in Sardinia in 2009. And every time Berlusconi has championed an aggressive and bitter electoral campaign, completely centred on the charismatic relationship between the leader and the masses and intolerant of the mediating institutions that are the life blood of a democracy. Thus, he has all the classic features of a populist leader.

Berlusconi entered the 2010 regional elections in obvious difficulty. He seemed weakened personally by sexual scandals; weakened as prime minister because the government's Civil Protection Department—in charge of assistance in case of disasters—which should be the archetype of a can-do government, was immersed in corruption; weakened as party leader by the mess that the PDL made of the provincial lists in Rome (which led to the PDL list being excluded), and by the internal conflict that was behind that. Above all, these elections were a golden opportunity for the opposition because they were mid-term and, moreover, local (normally, the left in Italy does better in local elections than in national ones, thanks to its tradition of good local administration).

Despite all of this, the centre-right managed to conquer four regions and the PD achieved the same disastrous result it had in the European elections nine months before. So, did Berlusconi also win these elections? We can answer this question with a 'yes', while adding, however, that he won them as head of a government and head of a coalition but *not* as a party leader. As a well-known political commentator wrote in *Corriere della Sera* on the day after the elections, 'Berlusconi the Prime Minister has many more reasons to smile than Berlusconi leader of the PDL' (Panebianco 2010).

The PDL is a party in difficulty and the success of the LN accentuates this. It is in crisis for three reasons. First of all, the fusion between the two organisations that formed the party in 2008, Forza Italia and Alleanza Nazionale, appears not to have succeeded, and the continuing conflict between Berlusconi and Fini (previously leader of Alleanza Nazionale and now president of the lower chamber) bears witness to this. Secondly, the party's electoral support has greatly weakened. As we saw in Figure 3, between the elections of 2006/2008/2009 and those of 2010, the PDL lost between five and six percentage points. The crisis in its relationship with its electorate seems even more serious if we look at absolute votes, taking abstentions into account: between 2005 and 2010, the PDL lost over one million votes, and this figure reaches four million if we compare 2010 with 2008. Finally, the PDL is in crisis because in Northern Italy—the richest part of the country—it is losing out to the LN. We only have to consider the fact that two of the sub-Alpine regions—Piedmont and the Veneto—are now governed by the LN and in Italy you cannot run the country if you do not control the north.

The future of Italian politics seems unclear. Italy is at the highest point in the bipolar contest, but at the same time at the lowest point regarding confidence in institutions, and the collapse in electoral turnout is a symptom of this. The future of the PDL is completely uncertain. The party is still a 'plastic party', with few structures, and is held together only by Berlusconi's leadership.[10] Nobody can tell what will happen when Berlusconi inevitably leaves politics (we should not forget that in 2010 he is 74 years old).

The future of the LN is also very uncertain. Like other right-wing populist parties in Europe, it was born as a populist, xenophobic, anti-European and anti-modern movement. Will it be transformed as a consequence of its electoral support and the responsibility of government? And, if so, how will this happen?

Another question concerns where the PD is going. Today it is like a dazed fighter who is cornered in the ring, waiting for his opponent's blows and only capable of defending himself. Two years after its foundation, and following two changes of general secretary, this is, to say the least, an uncomfortable situation. Will it manage to find a leadership capable of giving it an identity and a programme, and of taking the situation inside the party in hand and silencing internal disputes? These are three big question marks and nobody knows the answers at the moment due to the instability of the Italian political scene.

Acknowledgements

I would like to thank Gianluca Passarelli for the help given in the data analysis and all the researchers of the Istituto Cattaneo for the stimulating discussions in the aftermath of the vote.

Notes

[1] The other seven regions held elections on different dates between 2005 and 2010. The centre-right won in Abruzzo, Molise, Sicily, Friuli-Venezia Giulia and Sardinia; the local autonomists supported by the centre-left won in Trentino-Alto Adige, and in Valle d'Aosta victory went to the Union Valdotaine, which is not connected to any of the main national coalitions.
[2] It should be added that since 1999 every region has been able to draw up its own statutes and its own electoral law. However, at the time of the 2010 elections, only seven regions had passed their own electoral law (Baldi & Tronconi 2010) and, in any case, these regional laws have not substantially modified the points made in (a) and (b) above, which are the key features of the electoral system.
[3] It should be remembered that both these parties were formed just before the 2008 general election: the PDL as the result of a fusion between Forza Italia (Berlusconi's party) and Alleanza Nazionale (National Alliance, which came from the neo-fascist MSI); the PD from a fusion between the Democratici di Sinistra (Left Democrats [DS], formerly the Communist Party) with the Margherita (Daisy, from the left wing of the Christian Democrats) (Corbetta 2009).
[4] For a more in-depth look at the 'Berlusconi phenomenon', see, among others, Ginsborg (2006) and Stille (2006). For an analysis of Berlusconi's entry into politics and his first electoral success, see Katz and Ignazi (1996).
[5] To update the reader, we would add that at the moment of writing (July 2010) none of the three proposals has yet completed its passage through parliament.
[6] In Italy, the high turnout in elections for the whole post-war period up until the end of the 1970s was due to the big contrast between the Partito Comunista and Democrazia Cristiana, which drew politics to the attention of many Italians, and the social roots these parties had, widely spread out through local party branches, which could mobilise electors when elections took place. (On Italian political culture in the 1950s and 1960s see Galli and Prandi [1970].)
[7] The victory of the centre-right in Piedmont was very narrow (47.3 per cent for the centre-right and 46.9 per cent for the centre-left, the difference being the equivalent of just 9,000 votes); in Lazio, the difference was slightly bigger: 51.1 per cent for the centre-right and 48.3 per cent for the centre-left.
[8] As already stated, both the PD and the PDL were formed just before the 2008 elections. In Figure 3, the percentages before 2008 refer to the parties that fused to make the PD and PDL.
[9] For a recent analysis of the LN and its local roots, see Cento Bull (2009).
[10] On Berlusconi and his party, see Maraffi (1995) for the genesis of Forza Italia and Raniolo (2006) for the more recent years.

References

Baldi, B. & Tronconi, F. (eds) (2010) *Le elezioni regionali del 2010. Politica nazionale, territorio e specificità locale*, Istituto Cattaneo, Bologna.
Cento Bull, A. (2009) 'Lega Nord: a case of simulative politics?', *South European Society and Politics*, vol. 14, no. 2, pp. 129–146.

Corbetta, P. (2009) 'Chronicle of a victory foretold: the 13–14 April general elections', in *Italian Politics. Governing Fear*, eds G. Baldini & A. Cento Bull, Berghahn Books, New York, pp. 59–80.

Di Virgilio, A. (2005) 'The Italian regional elections of April 2005: does the triumph of the Union signal the end of the Berlusconi era?', *South European Society and Politics*, vol. 10, no. 3, pp. 477–490.

Galli, G. & Prandi, A. (1970) *Patterns of Political Participation in Italy*, Yale University Press, New Haven.

Ginsborg, P. (2006) *Silvio Berlusconi: Television, Power and Patrimony*, Verso, London.

Gundle, S. (2010) 'Berlusconi, sex and the avoidance of a media scandal', in *Italian Politics. Managing Uncertainty*, eds M. Giuliani & E. Jones, Berghahn Books, New York.

Katz, R. S. & Ignazi, P. (eds) (1996) *Italian Politics. The Year of the Tycoon*, Westview Press, Boulder, CO.

Maraffi, M. (1995) 'Forza Italia: apparato personale e comitati elettorali', in *La politica italiana*, ed. G. Pasquino, Laterza, Rome, pp. 247–259.

Mauro, E. (2010) 'La partita da giocare', *La Repubblica*, 31 March, p. 1.

Newell, J. L. (2000) *Parties and Democracy in Italy*, Ashgate, Aldershot, UK.

Panebianco, A. (2010) 'Popolare e borghese', *Corriere della Sera*, 31 March, p. 1.

Raniolo, F. (2006) 'Forza Italia: a leader with a party', *South European Society and Politics*, vol. 11, nos. 3–4, pp. 439–455.

Sorgi, M. (2010) 'E' stata la campagna peggiore', *La Stampa*, 27 March, p. 1.

Stille, A. (2006) *Citizen Berlusconi*, Garzanti, Milano.

Vespa, B. (2010) 'La svolta di Silvio: senza rancori dopo il trionfo', *Il Resto del Carlino*, 1 April, p. 6.

Piergiorgio Corbetta is Professor of Methodology of Social Research at the University of Bologna. His main research interests include methodology of social research, statistics applied to social research, political participation and electoral studies. He is one of the founders, in the 1990s, of the ITANES project (Italian National Election Studies), a research programme aimed to survey Italian electoral behaviour and political attitudes at each political election.

The Turkish Cypriot Presidential Election of April 2010: Normalisation of Politics

Sait Akşit

The Turkish Cypriot presidential election of 18 April 2010 attracted extensive international interest because of its expected impact on the prospect for a Cyprus solution. The election of National Unity Party leader and serving Prime Minister, Derviş Eroğlu, in the first round was not a surprise. The main factors accounting for Eroğlu's victory were the state of play regarding Turkish Cypriot relations with the EU, deadlock in the negotiations on the Cyprus question and debate over domestic concerns. This article argues that the 2010 election meant the normalisation of Turkish Cypriot politics, indicating the need to focus on domestic concerns and ending the CTP/Talat interlude of 2003–10. The results do not support a move in public opinion away from a search for a solution.

The citizens of the 'Turkish Republic of Northern Cyprus' ('TRNC'), approximately 164,000 voters, went to the polls to elect their president on 18 April 2010. The election, which received extensive international press coverage, was significant as it had important implications for the continuing process of negotiations between the Turkish and Greek Cypriot communities on the island in the search for a federal solution to the longstanding conflict. The talks on the Cyprus question were going through a period of renewed hope following the failure of the comprehensive settlement plan drawn up by United Nations (UN) Secretary General Kofi Annan and the impasse that followed the 2004 referenda.

The result of the election was not a surprise for many: Dr Derviş Eroğlu, the leader of the right-wing National Unity Party (*Ulusal Birlik Partisi* – UBP) and Prime Minister since 2009, was elected as the third president of the 'TRNC' in the first round, running against the incumbent President, Mehmet Ali Talat. When compared with the pro-solution Talat, Eroğlu was known for his hard-line nationalist position, traditionally arguing for a two-state solution which envisages the independence of the 'TRNC' as an end point in itself.

The Eroğlu victory, following UBP's victory in the April 2009 legislative elections over Talat's former party, the Republican Turkish Party/United Forces (*Cumhuriyetçi Türk Partisi-Birleşik Güçler* – CTP/BG), was a reconfirmation that the extraordinary period in Turkish Cypriot politics was over. This period had been shaped by Cyprus's EU membership, Turkey's candidacy and developing relations with the EU, the euphoria around the prospect for a resolution of the Cyprus problem through the Annan Plan and the consequences of these developments for Turkish Cypriot politics. The 2010 presidential election took place at a time when the post-Annan Plan euphoria had faded away and attempts at overcoming the Turkish Cypriots' international isolation faced a stalemate, leading to frustration in Turkish Cypriot society. Political attention was increasingly focused on domestic issues and on how to restructure Turkish Cypriot society and politics. The economic crises since 2007 made restructuring urgent so that Turkish Cypriot society could achieve a viable political and economic system in the new situation in which it found itself. As such, it could be argued that the 2010 election meant the normalisation of Turkish Cypriot politics, indicating the need to focus on issues of domestic concern and ending the CTP/Talat interlude, which had begun with Talat's election as Prime Minister in 2003.

What factors account for Eroğlu's success? Should we consider the outcome as an individual or a party success? What implications does the presidential election have for Turkish Cypriot politics? Does the result indicate more of a general change in the political climate, a change in public opinion following the shift away from the status quo/right in the early 2000s? The answers should be sought in the interplay of international aspects and domestic political/economic dimensions of Turkish Cypriot politics.

This article continues with a brief background to the election, providing a short account of recent developments on the Cyprus question, the state of play regarding relations with the European Union, and the record of Talat and CTP/BG in power. Then, the article describes the role of the President in the 'TRNC' and presents details of the 2010 candidates and campaign, before proceeding to analyse the results. The article concludes with an assessment of likely future prospects based on the election results.

Background to the Election

The decades-long Cyprus problem is a result of inter-ethnic conflict between the two communities on the island—the Turkish and Greek Cypriot communities—who are co-founders of the 1960 Republic of Cyprus. The Republic was formed under the guarantorship of Great Britain, Turkey and Greece as a bi-communal republic based on a power-sharing mechanism (see Çarkoğlu and Sözen 2004, pp. 123–125). The system collapsed in 1963 with the outbreak of inter-communal violence, leading to the formation of a separate Turkish Cypriot administration. A coup engineered by the Greek junta in July 1974 led to Turkish military intervention, resulting in the current territorial division of the island. The 'Turkish Republic of Northern Cyprus', declared in 1983, is the last of a sequence of governing structures established by the Turkish Cypriot community. In contrast to the internationally recognised *de jure* state of the whole island—the Republic of Cyprus, which is administered by the Greek Cypriots—the 'TRNC' is not internationally recognised, except by Turkey. However, it exercises de facto sovereignty over the northern part of the island.

One of the important points to make here is the difference in interpretation of the two communities on the island regarding the starting point for defending their position on the Cyprus question. While the Turkish Cypriots take the 1960 accords as their basis, the Greek Cypriots focus on the 1974 intervention by Turkey. Various attempts at resolving the Cyprus question through the inter-communal talks which have been conducted since 1968 have failed to produce a compromise solution. The most comprehensive settlement plan to date remains that devised by the then UN Secretary General, Kofi Annan, which aimed to find a solution to the conflict before Cyprus's accession to the European Union on 1 May 2004. In the simultaneous referenda held on the two parts of the divided island on 24 April 2004, the plan was approved by the Turkish Cypriots but rejected after the Greek Cypriot 'no'. Yet, the conjuncture that led to the development of the plan had important implications for Turkish Cypriot politics.

The process of Cyprus's EU membership was one of the important factors influencing Turkish Cypriot politics through detailed negotiations between the two communities, with the involvement and increasing pressure of the guarantors, including Turkey, along a tight schedule and a clear set of points. The other significant factor was change in Turkey following the rise to power of the Justice and Development Party (*Adalet ve Kalkınma Partisi* – AKP) in November 2002. On the one hand, AKP was keen to reconsider Turkey's foreign policy priorities and to attempt to solve longstanding disputes, including the Cyprus question. On the other, the Cyprus question was one of the thresholds set by the EU for the start of Turkey's accession negotiations by 2004. The AKP government, which aimed to start Turkey's accession negotiations, assumed a position in favour of resolving the conflict by taking the Annan Plan as the basis of negotiations. It was aggressive, positioning itself against those who supported the 'status quo' on the island, took initiatives and based its policy on a win–win approach and on 'being one step ahead' of the Greek/Greek Cypriot approach.

These developments and the economic crisis of the early 2000s were instrumental in the emergence of an alternative to the existing power in the 'TRNC'. The status quo in Turkish Cypriot politics was associated with the right wing and personified by the 'TRNC' President since 1976, Rauf Denktaş, who was largely perceived by AKP as well as the Turkish Cypriot left as an intransigent and uncompromising nationalist leader whose position on the Cyprus question endangered Turkey's relations with the EU and its prospects of opening accession negotiations. The left-wing opposition skilfully capitalised on the perception of Turkish Cypriot society that a solution and EU membership would be the best answers in order to overcome the dissatisfaction and frustration with the socioeconomic difficulties in the 'TRNC'. The Turkish Cypriot left moderated its policies and moved towards the centre to appeal to business circles, right-wing voters and 'TRNC' citizens who had been born in Turkey. Overlapping with the AKP stance and rhetoric on the Cyprus question, which pledged to change the status quo, the left wing advocated change and progress. The AKP government in Turkey, aiming to sideline Denktaş as well as the ruling UBP which opposed the Annan Plan, favoured and supported the cause of left-wing parties in the 'TRNC', thus tilting the balance in Turkish Cypriot politics.

In this context, the left-wing CTP and Talat emerged as a serious alternative and later came to dominate the political scene with the shift in public opinion away from the status quo/right. The change in the Turkish Cypriot political climate could be observed in the increased vote share received by CTP and Talat. The CTP vote increased from a mere 13.4 per cent in the 1998 legislative elections to 35.2 per cent in 2003 and 44.5 per cent in 2005. In 2005, Talat was elected as the second president of the 'TRNC', receiving an overwhelming 55.6 per cent of the vote as compared with 10 per cent in the preceding presidential election in 2000 (see Table 1).

The focal point of CTP's political and economic aims was its European project: the integration of Turkish Cypriot society with the EU. Following the failure of a compromise solution, establishing direct trade links with the EU and unhindered financial aid became central to overcoming the international isolation faced by Turkish Cypriot society and achieving economic development and prosperity (see also Sözen 2009, p. 347). The EU Commission's immediate attempt to fulfil its pre-referenda promises to end the international isolation of the Turkish Cypriots by drafting two important regulations on trade and aid strengthened CTP's position. However, the problems in getting these regulations approved and the intra-EU struggle over them led to Turkish Cypriot disappointment with the EU.

The Green Line Regulation, approved on 29 April 2004 and dealing with the movement of persons and goods across the line that separates the communities on the island, remained very limited. The aid regulation was only approved after two years, on 27 March 2006, and promises on direct trade could not be fulfilled, due largely to the Greek Cypriot blockade in the EU Council. Despite renewed hopes for a solution with the February 2008 election of Demetris Christofias, the leader of the Cypriot communist party and a long-time friend and comrade of Talat, as the President of the Republic of Cyprus (see Christophorou 2008), the Greek Cypriots maintained their tough stance on the EU's Turkish Cypriot policy. The most recent EU attempt to establish direct trade links had occurred in early March 2010, just before the presidential election, with the European Parliament's initiative to assign a rapporteur to assess the new circumstances and possibilities of establishing direct trade links with the Turkish Cypriots following the entry into force of the Lisbon Treaty. The first parliamentary discussion on the issue was due to take place the day after the election, on 19 April 2010.

Table 1 Results of the 2010, 2005 and 2000 Turkish Cypriot Presidential Elections

2010		2005		2000*	
Turnout rate: 76.4 per cent		Turnout rate: 69.6 per cent		Turnout rate: 81.0 per cent	
Candidate	Vote share (%)	Candidate	Vote share (%)	Candidate	Vote share (%)
Derviş Eroğlu (UBP)	50.4	Mehmet Ali Talat (CTP)	55.6	Rauf R. Denktaş (Independent)	43.7
Mehmet Ali Talat (Independent)	42.9	Derviş Eroğlu (UBP)	22.7	Derviş Eroğlu (UBP)	30.1
Tahsin Ertuğruloğlu (Independent)	3.8	Mustafa Şenol Arabacıoğlu (DP)	13.2	Mustafa Akıncı (TKP)	11.7
Zeki Beşiktepeli (Independent)	1.6	Nuri Çevikel (YP)	4.8	Mehmet Ali Talat (CTP)	10.0
Mustafa Kemal Tümkan (Independent)	0.8	Zeki Beşiktepeli (Independent)	1.7	Arif Hasan Tahsin Desem (YBH)	2.6
Arif Salih Kırdağ (Independent)	0.4	Hüseyin Angolemli (TKP)	1.1	Şener Levent (Independent)	0.9
Ayhan Kaymak (Independent)	0.1	Zehra Cengiz (KSP)	0.5	Turgut Afşaroğlu (Independent)	0.6
		Arif Salih Kırdağ (Independent)	0.3	Ayhan Kaymak (Independent)	0.4
		Ayhan Kaymak (Independent)	0.1		

Source: High Electoral Council of the 'TRNC', http://ysk.mahkemeler.net.
Notes: *Rauf R. Denktaş was declared president as Derviş Eroğlu withdrew before the second round of elections was held. UBP: National Unity Party (*Ulusal Birlik Partisi*); CTP: Republican Turkish Party (*Cumhuriyetçi Türk Partisi*); DP: Democratic Party (*Demokrat Parti*); YP: New Party (*Yeni Parti*); TKP: Communal Liberation Party (*Toplumcu Kurtuluş Partisi*); KSP: Cyprus Socialist Party (*Kıbrıs Sosyalist Partisi*); YBH: Patriotic Union Movement (*Yurtsever Birlik Hareketi*).

Indeed, the positive conjuncture and the change in the political climate had led to a boom in the Turkish Cypriot economy between 2004 and 2007, despite the failure of the Annan Plan. Housing and investments in the tourism sector, taking the rules and regulations of the Annan Plan as the basis, formed the backbone of the economic development process. However, stagnation set in from 2007 onwards and was exacerbated by the global economic crisis. CTP was perceived by many voters as mismanaging the economic development process. Economic gains were distributed through wage increases and benefits for civil servants and workers, reflecting the governing party's ideological stance, while the government resorted to classical methods of increasing prices of goods and services in trying to overcome the difficulties (Sözen 2009, p. 339). Although there were attempts to reform the system, these remained limited, failing to match CTP's rhetoric on change and progress. As a result, CTP had shrunk to its traditional vote base in the 2009 legislative elections (see Table 2).

The 2010 Contest

The Rules of the Game

The 'TRNC' is a parliamentary system within which the government acts as the real executive power. The President of the 'TRNC' has a symbolic role with limited executive powers. The limited executive powers of the President are defined in accordance with the constitution and laws. The President, as the head of state, first and foremost, represents the unity and integrity of the State and the community. He should act independently, above and beyond political parties, to ensure respect for the Constitution of the Republic, the carrying out of public affairs in an uninterrupted and orderly manner and the continuity of the State. His executive powers confer on him the rights to appoint the prime minister, to entrust the prime minister with the duty to form the Council of Ministers, and to appoint the ministers on the proposal of the prime minister. In circumstances under which he considers it necessary, or at the request of the Prime Minister, he may preside over the Council of Ministers, albeit

Table 2 Results of the 2009 Turkish Cypriot Legislative Election across Districts

District	UBP	CTP/BG	DP	TDP	ÖRP	BKP	HİS
Lefkoşa	43.5	29.0	11.0	8.6	3.4	3.8	0.7
Gazimağusa	41.5	30.7	9.9	6.6	9.7	1.2	0.4
Girne	48.8	29.8	9.8	3.8	5,4	2.1	0.3
Güzelyurt	49.5	28.8	9.5	5.7	4.4	1.7	0.4
İskele	41.2	24.2	15.1	4.1	14.1	0.9	0.4
Total	44.0	29.4	10.6	6.9	6.2	2.4	0.5

Source: High Electoral Council of the 'TRNC', http://ysk.mahkemeler.net.
Notes: TDP (*Toplumcu Demokrasi Partisi* – Communal Democracy Party); ÖRP (*Özgürlük ve Reform Partisi* – Freedom and Reform Party); BKP (*Birleşik Kıbrıs Partisi* – United Cyprus Party); HİS (*Halk için Siyaset Partisi* – Politics for People Party).

without any voting rights. He also exercises powers in the promulgation of laws which are enacted by the Assembly and in the appointment of high-ranking public personnel, such as the president and judges of the Supreme Court. The President may only be replaced by the President of the Assembly upon his absence from work or incapacity to perform his duties.

The President is elected by universal suffrage for a period of five years. Almost any citizen of the 'TRNC' who is aged 35 or older and holds a higher education degree can run for the presidency. According to the electoral code, a candidate must obtain over 50 per cent of the total number of valid votes cast in order to be elected in the first round. If none of the candidates manages to obtain this absolute majority, a second round takes place after seven days between the two candidates who obtain the greatest number of votes. In the second round, the candidate who receives the highest number of votes cast becomes the President of the 'TRNC'. The constitution places no limits on the number of times a person can be re-elected as president.

Although the President of the 'TRNC' has only a symbolic role with regard to domestic politics, he is regarded by the UN and the international community as the 'community leader' of the Turkish Cypriots. As such, he is the main negotiator for the Turkish Cypriot community under the UN-sponsored peace talks. The post is also rather significant as the President acts as the main figure in directing the 'TRNC's' foreign policy, in coordination with Turkish officials.

The Candidates

A total of eight candidates officially applied to the High Electoral Council to run for the April 2010 election. The only female candidate, Serap Tezcan, was rejected on the grounds that she did not possess the qualifications to become president, due to the fact that she had psychological problems. One of the important events of the early stage of the campaign was the appeal against the candidacy of the incumbent President, Mehmet Ali Talat. The appeal was lodged by three citizens from the conservative wing, Vedat Çelik, Kamil Özkaloğlu and Vural Türkmen, on the grounds that Talat's rhetoric and initiatives contravened the second and third articles of the 'TRNC' constitution, creating concerns over the integrity and sovereignty of the 'TRNC' and the right to self-determination of the Turkish Cypriot people. The appeal was certainly related to the debate around the issues of single sovereignty and single citizenship as components of a possible federal solution, which the right-wing opinion makers argued was a concession given by Talat (see Zaman 2010). Ultimately, however, the appeal against Talat was rejected by the High Electoral Council of the 'TRNC', as Talat's candidacy was considered in line with the requirements of the constitution and the electoral law.

In the end, seven candidates ran for election on 18 April 2010. Table 3 summarises some basic information on the candidates. The number of candidates notwithstanding, the election was dominated by Eroğlu and Talat as the two most likely contenders. Tahsin Ertuğruloğlu and Zeki Beşiktepeli were seen as candidates who could possibly tilt the balance between Eroğlu and Talat by attracting rightist and leftist voters,

Table 3 Candidates Competing in the 2010 Turkish Cypriot Presidential Election (From Left to Right on the Ideological Spectrum)

Candidates	Zeki Beşiktepeli	Ayhan Kaymak	Mehmet Ali Talat	Arif Salih Kırdağ	Derviş Eroğlu	Mustafa Kemal Tümkan	Tahsin Ertuğruloğlu
Party affiliation	Independent	Independent	Independent	Independent	UBP	Independent	Independent
Political ideology	Leftist	Centre-left	Centre-left	Centre-right	Centre-right	Centre-right	Centre-right
Policy on the Cyprus issue	United Cyprus	Pro-federation	Pro-federation	Confederation	Pro-two-state solution*	Pro-two-state solution	Pro-two-state solution
Number of votes received**	1,967	168	52,294	520	61,422	964	4,647
Percentage of votes received**	1.6	0.1	42.9	0.4	50.4	0.8	3.8

Source: ** High Electoral Council of the 'TRNC', http://ysk.mahkemeler.net.
Notes: *Although Derviş Eroğlu, Mustafa Kemal Tümkan and Tahsin Ertuğruloğlu traditionally support a two-state position, during the election campaign they declared their intention to continue the ongoing process of peace negotiations aiming at federation.

respectively, who were dissatisfied with the performance of these two candidates. Both Eroğlu and Talat had the concrete support of a major political party, UBP for Eroğlu and CTP/BG for Talat, and a group of small parties. In Turkish Cypriot politics, the support of a major political party is important for electoral success. Generally, political parties consider nominating a party candidate prior to entering into an alliance, and usually party leaders or senior political figures are nominated as candidates of major political parties in Turkish Cypriot politics. In 2010, in contrast to many of the previous elections, Dr Derviş Eroğlu, the prime minister, ran as the only candidate who was affiliated with a party. Talat preferred to run as an independent rather than a CTP candidate, trying to appeal to a wider audience.

Dr Derviş Eroğlu, a 72-year-old medical doctor and a conservative veteran, had been involved in Turkish Cypriot politics since UBP was first founded in 1975. He was elected to parliament in 1976 and assumed various posts within the party. He was Minister for Education, Culture, Youth and Sports in the first UBP government in 1976–77 and UBP provincial chairman in Gazimağusa between 1977 and 1983. He became the leader of the party in 1983. He served as the prime minister from 1983 to 1993 and again from 1996 to 2003. Despite the fact that he was not considered a charismatic leader, Eroğlu dominated the party until he retired in 2006. However, the party subsequently failed to produce a strong leader and Eroğlu returned in November 2008 to lead UBP in the April 2009 legislative elections, in which he was elected Prime Minister.

Traditionally, Eroğlu has been known for his preference for a two-state solution, believing in the sovereignty of the 'TRNC' and the Turkish Cypriot people. He is perceived to possess an uncompromising stance on the Cyprus issue, accepting Turkey's 1974 intervention as a solution to the problem. Eroğlu, alongside former president, Rauf Denktaş, advocated a 'no' to the Annan Plan and opposed various steps taken during the Talat period, such as the establishment of the Immovable Property Commission set up in 2005 to address Greek Cypriot claims relating to abandoned properties in northern Cyprus.

Mehmet Ali Talat, the incumbent President, had been involved in Turkish Cypriot politics since 1977. He assumed various roles within the leftist CTP and, following the general elections of December 1993, served as the National Education and Culture Minister and Minister of State and Deputy Prime Minister in the DP–CTP coalition governments. In 1996, he was elected as the leader of CTP, which he transformed into a social democratic party. Talat emerged as an important political figure in the wake of a series of protests against President Denktaş in 2002 and 2003, by advocating change, promising a solution (as opposed to the nationalist, status quo stance) and membership in the European Union under a unified Cyprus. Under Talat's leadership, CTP joined forces with liberal business and civil society circles to become CTP/BG, leaning towards the centre/centre-left. Subsequently, Talat came to dominate Turkish Cypriot politics with his party's victory in the 2003 legislative elections (see Çarkoğlu and Sözen 2004).

Tahsin Ertuğruloğlu was a former Minister of Foreign Affairs, UBP leader from 2006 to 2008, and an active UBP parliamentarian, who initially supported Eroğlu's candidacy. In early March 2010, he declared that he would run in the presidential election following a series of meetings with Turkish President, Abdullah Gül and Prime Minister, Recep Tayip Erdoğan, and a meeting with Eroğlu in which he demanded a guarantee that he would become prime minister if Eroğlu was elected president. Given these circumstances, his declaration created controversy in Turkish Cypriot politics and was perceived by right-wing voters as an instance of indirect intervention by AKP to weaken Eroğlu.

Zeki Beşiktepeli, on the other hand, could potentially negatively influence support for Talat by attracting leftist votes dissatisfied with the latter's performance. A Moscow-educated academic, Beşiktepeli was an important figure in the leftist Jasmine Movement for a united Cyprus and a former board member of BKP (*Birleşik Kıbrıs Partisi* – United Cyprus Party) which officially supported Talat for the presidency in the 2010 contest.

The other three candidates remained marginal, without a party base or any significant support, and lacked clearly identified and detailed election programmes. Ayhan Kaymak was a former head manager of a state cooperative, PEYAK, who emphasised the importance of equal rights for the Turkish Cypriot people. Arif Salih Kırdağ worked independently in agriculture and trade and argued for a Cyprus solution based on a loose confederal structure. Finally, Mustafa Kemal Tümkan was a former military officer whose ideal was a sovereign independent 'TRNC'.

The Campaign

According to the electoral code, the formal campaigning period for the 18 April 2010 presidential election began on 23 March 2010. However, informal visits to regions were initiated well before this date. Given that the race essentially turned into a competition between two candidates, parties and interest groups largely grouped around Eroğlu on the right and Talat on the left. Eroğlu enjoyed the support of UBP (which had polled 44.0 per cent in the 2009 legislative elections), the centre-right DP (*Demokrat Parti* – Democratic Party, 10.6 per cent in 2009), the rightist HİS (*Halk için Siyaset Partisi* – Politics for People Party, 0.5 per cent), the rightist MAP (*Milliyetçi Adalet Partisi* – Nationalist Justice Party), business circles, and civil society organisations such as associations of retired military personnel. Talat, on the other hand, received support from his former party, the centre-left CTP/BG (with 29.4 per cent in the 2009 legislative elections), the left of centre TDP (*Toplumcu Demokrasi Partisi* – Communal Democracy Party with 6.9 per cent in 2009), CTP's former coalition partner, the right of centre ÖRP (*Özgürlük ve Reform Partisi* – Freedom and Reform Party, 6.2 per cent), the leftist BKP (2.4 per cent), some business circles, and civil society organisations, especially trade unions.

The most important aspect of these groupings was the active support of DP and the Denktaş family for Eroğlu. This was not an easy coalition to put together. DP was formed in 1992 by nine UBP parliamentarians—close to former president of the 'TRNC', Rauf Denktaş—who resigned following an inter-party struggle over discontent with the way Eroğlu ruled. The move in 1992 was read by Eroğlu as an attempt by Denktaş to end his leadership of UBP and soon developed into a personal rivalry. Ever since, UBP/Eroğlu and DP/Denktaş have not supported each other, even on policy issues where they shared similar viewpoints.

Eroğlu entered the campaign using the slogan, 'There is a difference! People are behind it!'('*Fark Var! Arkasında Halk Var!*'). His aim was to underline popular frustration and disappointment with Talat's inability to achieve a breakthrough in the post-Annan Plan period and his detachment from society, especially in respect of domestic developments. Talat was criticised for not being transparent about and not communicating the developments in the talks.[1] Eroğlu pledged to create a difference, a courageous stance towards a just and sustainable solution together with the people. This intent was reinforced by appeals to establish a national council involving people from different backgrounds as advisers in the negotiations and to inform the public on a regular basis. Eroğlu repeatedly emphasised that he would continue the negotiations without any preconditions. This was the most important sign of moderation in his stance. However, his messages were mixed. While declaring that he would not be the person to leave the negotiations table, he vowed to defend the 'interests of sovereign Turkish Cypriots' (Özerkan 2010), implying the continuing existence of the 'TRNC' as a state and the guarantorship of Turkey. His approach was indeed reminiscent of the hard-line, status quo approach, reflecting the UBP approach towards a two-state solution (see Sözen 2009, p. 342).

This nationalist tone was also reflected in the feeling of pride in the 'TRNC', a point of criticism directed to Talat concerning his reactions to the declaration of 'TRNC's' independence. In a recently published book, Talat openly stated that he had opposed the support given to the 1983 proclamation of the 'TRNC' by his party, declaring that he felt sad and had cried right after the declaration, believing this was a wrong political manoeuvre for the Turkish Cypriot cause (see Güven 2009, pp. 41–50). Another dimension of criticism concerned Talat's perceived failure to supervise his former party with regard to socioeconomic developments. Eroğlu underlined that he would do his part in supporting and supervising the government in overcoming socioeconomic problems as well as supporting initiatives for the universities, tourism, foreign investments and cooperation with Turkey in transporting water, electrical power and natural gas to Cyprus.

Talat, on the other hand, focused his campaign on anti-nationalist rhetoric as well as on domestic issues. His main slogan, 'Either Yesterday or the World' ('*Ya Dün Ya Dünya*'), appealed to the electorate to choose between the past and the future, between isolation from and integration with the world. As such, he associated yesterday with nationalist policies and backwardness, accusing Eroğlu and Rauf Denktaş of being responsible for the difficulties Turkish Cypriots currently faced as they were responsible for the fact that the Republic of Cyprus had become a member of the EU without a resolution to the problem. The left perceived the uncompromising attitude of the right-wing leaders as the most important stumbling block in reaching a deal, which led to mounting pressure on the Turkish side, thus increasing the isolation of the Turkish Cypriot society. In trying to counter criticisms of his position on the

'TRNC', Talat maintained there was no dilemma between the 'TRNC' and a reunified Cyprus, declaring that the choice was rather between a compromise solution and isolation (Özerkan 2010).

Talat presented himself as the leader who symbolised the integration of Turkish Cypriots with the world, supported by slogans such as 'If Talat is in, I am in! Because he is connecting me with the world/Europe/Turkey' ('*Talat varsa ben de varım! Çünkü beni dünyaya/Avrupa'ya/Türkiye'ye bağlıyor*'). Talat argued that the constructive approach adopted by CTP, that is, as a party in favour of a settlement of the conflict, had changed the international community's perception of Turkish Cypriot policy in a positive way, leading to an acceptance of Turkish Cypriot leadership by world leaders. In support of this, he listed the international figures whom he had met during his presidency, including UK Prime Minister, Gordon Brown; United States Secretaries of State, Colin Powell, Condoleezza Rice and Hillary Clinton; and a number of Foreign Ministers of EU member states. He argued that his stance had strengthened the 'TRNC' internationally, especially given the fact that some of the meetings had taken place in the Presidential Palace of the 'TRNC', such as the visits by British Foreign Secretary, Jack Straw, on 26 January 2006, President of the European Commission, José Manuel Barroso, on 25 June 2009, and UN Secretary General, Ban Ki-moon, on 1 February 2010. He also emphasised the establishment of a working relationship with the EU, which had paved the way for EU financial assistance under various programmes. He argued that these steps were made possible through a convergence of interests with Turkey on the need to solve the Cyprus question, integration into the EU and opening to a globalised world. Thus, he emphasised, he acted with the people for the people by presenting himself as a link between the internationally isolated Turkish Cypriot society and the world.

In this respect, one of the important aspects with regard to Talat's campaign was his attempt to show the Turkish Cypriot society the progress achieved in the negotiation. Talat held a press conference to publicise the achievements (see Kıbrıspostası 2010a), which he also used extensively in his election brochure. He claimed there was a possibility of solving the problem in 18 months. This move aimed to persuade the Turkish Cypriots to keep their hopes for a solution alive and to stick with him. Talat also outlined an economic vision, a lesser dimension of his campaign, advocating the development of initiatives to encourage specialisation in agriculture, alternative tourism, women entrepreneurs, entertainment and administrative restructuring.

As the elections approached, Talat pursued a more aggressive rhetoric, arguing that Eroğlu lacked the necessary leadership characteristics and vision. He presented himself as the sole redress for negotiations in the name of Turkish Cypriots. This line reflected his uncertainty concerning his possibilities of re-election, given the results of public opinion polls. As early as November 2009, pre-election polls suggested that Eroğlu was leading against Talat (Kıbrıs 2009). From January 2010, there was a proliferation of polls showing the same trend. In the later stages of the election campaign, the Eroğlu side used the polls to put pressure on Talat by predicting that there would be a 10 to 15 per cent difference between the two candidates and that Eroğlu would win the elections in the first round.

Talat, indeed, seemed to be reluctant to run for the presidency given the results of the public opinion polls and delayed the official announcement of his candidacy until 6 March 2010. During the later stages of his campaign, Talat preferred not to publish any polls, arguing that he felt change as he visited villages and contacted people. Talat perceived the support of the international community as another opportunity to strengthen his chances of winning the election. There were indeed indications of support. Some influential actors, such as the International Crisis Group, argued that Talat's re-election was the only way to an easy and quick deal on a federal state, implicitly signifying that the election of Eroğlu could lead to the failure of the negotiation process.[2] In addition, many reports indicated indirect support. The EU initiative on direct trade and the ECHR decision on the Immovable Property Commission in early March 2010 were read by the right wing as attempts to strengthen Talat's argument that his approach was yielding positive results. The ECHR decision recognised the Immovable Property Commission set up by the 'TRNC' in 2005 as an effective domestic remedy for claims relating to abandoned Greek Cypriot properties in northern Cyprus. This move was considered by Talat's supporters as significant in terms of creating an opening on the property issue.

The perceived Turkish support, on the other hand, was a little mixed. Statements by Turkish Prime Minister Erdoğan and Foreign Minister Davutoğlu on the need to continue a constructive approach were interpreted by media close to the AKP government as indications of implicit support for Talat (see Yanatma 2010). Indeed, *Zaman*, a leading Turkish daily with good connections with the ruling AKP, published an opinion poll on 11 April claiming Talat was closing the gap with Eroğlu and that he could manage to win the elections (Özkaya 2010).

Talat employed a different PR strategy from Eroğlu. He used the media extensively as well as holding public meetings, public demonstrations holding banners on major roundabouts, and village visits. He appeared on various TV programmes, both national and international, and called on Eroğlu for a live televised debate, thinking he would be able to gain the upper hand regarding the debate on the state of play in the negotiations and thus influence public opinion to his advantage through his charisma and ability to address people. However, Eroğlu refused to take part in such a debate. Instead he participated in a limited number of TV appearances, while largely organising his campaign around public meetings and village visits, as he had done in the April 2009 legislative elections (see Sözen 2009, p. 342). The two leaders appeared together only on the election programme of the official Turkish Cypriot television channel, BRT, where each candidate presented his programmes and positions through a monologue.

The campaign programmes of the minor candidates remained limited in nature, due to lack of finance. These candidates only took part in radio and television programmes and paid visits to villages, but did not stage any public meetings. According to reports, the electoral spending by Ertuğruloğlu was the highest among the five candidates, amounting to around €100,000–120,000 (Kıbrıs 2010). The financing of campaign activities by the other four candidates amounted to an average of €3500 each, compared with Talat's expenses of around €800,000 (Kıbrıspostası 2010d).

The slogans of these minor candidates included a dose of criticism for both Eroğlu and Talat. Tahsin Ertuğruloğlu advocated 'Starting from Scratch' ('*Sil baştan.*'), blaming Eroğlu for assuming a dynastic approach in UBP and Talat for not paying due attention to the interests of the Turkish Cypriots. Beşiktepeli used the slogan 'We will hear our voice not from Çankaya, but from Dikilitaş'[3] ('*Çankaya'dan değil dikili taştan sesimizi dünyaya duyuracağız.*'), arguing for full independence of Turkish Cypriot politics from Ankara. Kaymak's slogan was 'I am looking for a sane person' ('*Aklı başında insan arıyorum*'), following Diogenes of Sinope's search for an honest man and largely emphasising dishonesty in Turkish Cypriot politics. Kırdağ declared 'Justice to replace lies, for freedom, to find a Cyprus solution by electing a courageous Turkish Cypriot' ('*Yalan dolanın bittiği yerde adalet için.*'), arguing that Talat has not been honest and courageous enough. Tümkan's slogan was 'Perfect Merging' ('*Kusursuz birleşme.*'), emphasising sovereignty, statehood and equality with the Greek Cypriots as the basis for a perfect solution.

Despite the tension that built up between the two major candidates, no major incidents occurred during the campaign period or on Election Day. There were only rare attacks on the banners—attacks which Talat supporters argued were used as part of the pressure mechanism of the Eroğlu side.

Explaining the Results

Among the 164,072 registered voters, 125,294 (76.37 per cent) turned out to vote in the 2010 presidential election. This remains the second lowest turnout in a presidential election in the history of the 'TRNC'.[4] Although a second round between Eroğlu and Talat seemed a quite likely outcome during most of the counting process, Eroğlu incrementally increased his share to 50.4 per cent of the total votes cast, compared with 22.7 per cent in 2005. Talat received 42.9 per cent, faring poorly compared with his 55.6 per cent in 2005. Eroğlu became the third president of the 'TRNC', following Rauf Denktaş and Mehmet Ali Talat.

A clear victory for Eroğlu, the election success can certainly be attributed to his party, UBP, and the collaboration of the right wing behind Eroğlu. In the three previous presidential elections in which he had participated, his vote share was between 22 and 30 per cent of votes cast, even following strong performances by UBP. In 2010, it was important that, first, UBP remained intact in support of Eroğlu following the controversial candidacy of Ertuğruloğlu. Second, the party presented Eroğlu as the most important candidate on the right and facilitated the active support of DP and the Denktaş family, which proved to be crucial in achieving Eroğlu's electoral success. This ensured a support base resulting in an outcome that presented parallels in terms of party support received based on the results of 2009 legislative elections and the vote share obtained by Eroğlu (see Table 2 and Table 4).

A quick look at the figures in Table 2 and Table 4 suggests that political trends paralleled the electoral tendencies of the April 2009 legislative elections with variations at the regional level. Eroğlu built upon the success of his party in the legislative

Table 4 Results of the 2010 Turkish Cypriot Presidential Election across Districts

District	Number of Votes Cast	Derviş Eroğlu	Mehmet Ali Talat	Tahsin Ertuğruloğlu	Zeki Beşiktepeli	Mustafa Kemal Tümkan	Arif Salih Kırdağ	Ayhan Kaymak
Lefkoşa	39,055	44.0	47.2	5.5	2.2	0.5	0.5	0.1
Gazimağusa	33,293	53.0	41.4	3.1	1.0	0.9	0.4	0.2
Girne	23,298	50.8	43.2	3.0	1.9	0.7	0.3	0.1
Güzelyurt	16,371	52.5	42.0	2.3	1.6	1.1	0.4	0.1
İskele	13,277	59.3	34.1	4.1	0.8	1.1	0.5	0.1
Total	125,294	50.4	42.9	3.8	1.6	0.8	0.4	0.1

Source: High Electoral Council of the 'TRNC', http://ysk.mahkemeler.net

elections and enjoyed the support of smaller parties. Collaboration with the DP and the Denktaş family resulted in remarkable differences in favour of Eroğlu in regions of Gazimağusa and especially İskele, where UBP recorded its lowest vote shares in 2009 (respectively, 41.5 and 41.2 per cent). These regions are known for the high proportion of 'TRNC' citizens who are settlers from Turkey, with a tendency to vote for right-wing parties (see Hatay 2007, p. 68 and Çarkoğlu and Sözen 2004, p. 133). The left-wing CTP and Talat have generally fared poorly, especially in İskele—with only 24.2 per cent for CTP in the 2009 legislative elections and 34.1 per cent for Talat in the 2010 presidential elections. One of the reasons for this tendency is the failure of the left before the early 2000s to reach out politically to the 'TRNC' citizens in these regions who were born in Turkey.[5] Despite an increase in the vote shares of the left-wing parties in these regions in the last decade, the 2010 presidential elections confirmed the tendency of high support levels for the right. On the other hand, Eroğlu was not able to fully capitalise on the right-wing support in the capital, Lefkoşa, where Talat secured the lead and Ertuğruloğlu was successful in obtaining 5.5 per cent of the votes cast. The tendency in Girne and Güzelyurt regions paralleled the overall outcome, repeating the strong standing by UBP in the 2009 legislative elections.

The main factors leading to such an outcome can be interlinked and explained under three main headings: the state of play regarding the relations of Turkish Cypriot society with the EU; the Cyprus question and Talat's record; and domestic political and economic issues.

As mentioned above, the rise of CTP and Talat to power and their dominance in 2003–10 was very much related to and built around their European project. The EU's failure to meet its pre-Annan Plan referenda promises, resulting in policy outcomes which fell short of Turkish Cypriot expectations, put the European project of CTP and Talat into difficulty. The promises given by the EU to Turkish Cypriots were either delayed in being fulfilled or failed to meet demands to overcome the international isolation of Turkish Cypriot society. At the same time, following its 2004 Enlargement, the EU continuously demanded that Turkey open its sea and air ports to Greek Cypriot vessels through the extension of the Turkish Customs Union to the new member states including the Republic of Cyprus. This EU attitude led to a perception of EU ineffectiveness and submission to Greek Cypriot policy. In turn, this led to resentment and disappointment among different segments of Turkish Cypriot society (see EurActiv 2009, Star 2009, and Özgür 2010). The latest EU initiative regarding direct trade came at a very late stage and lacked a concrete foundation, thus failing to provide a positive signal concerning EU policy towards the Turkish Cypriots. In fact, in the eyes of the Turkish Cypriots, the EU had lost its privileged position as an actor who could contribute to the resolution of the problem and/or help end or ease the isolation faced. As a result, the EU factor indeed had a negative connotation for Talat.

The state of play with regard to the Cyprus question was a focal point for Talat in his election campaign. During his 1 April 2010 press conference on the course of talks, Talat highlighted progress achieved on three of the six main issues: governance and power-sharing, the EU and economic matters.[6] He also emphasised that the two leaders had generated a total of 31 'convergence papers' as a result of the 71 meetings that they had held since September 2008, a first in the negotiations on the conflict. However, there was no progress on sensitive issues of territory, property, security and guarantees or on establishing the agreement on the settlement as part of EU primary law (Kıbrıspostası 2010b, 2010c). These, coupled with the Greek Cypriot attitude in the last few months prior to the elections, strengthened the hand of the right wing. Manifestations of the Greek Cypriot attitude included President Christofias's unwillingness to hold a joint press conference despite repeated calls by Talat to do so, the Greek Cypriot parliamentary decision of 19 February 2010 stating that there should be no provisions for guarantors or guarantees in a unified Cyprus, which is a member state of the EU, and the statement by Greek Cypriot government spokesman, Stephanos Stephanou, that the government would take 'all necessary steps to deal with any moves to bring back the issue regarding the direct trade with the Turkish occupied areas of the Republic of Cyprus' (Cyprus News Agency 2010). These all created question marks concerning the flexibility and cooperation of the Greek Cypriot leadership and meant any progress in the talks had limited impact on the course of the elections. The Greek Cypriot approach certainly weakened Talat's standing, strengthening the right-wing rhetoric.

One of the most important variables in explaining the outcome of the 2010 presidential election—and one which depicts normalisation in Turkish Cypriot politics—is the re-emergence of domestic issues as a determining factor. As mentioned earlier, both Eroğlu and Talat referred to domestic issues in their campaigns, despite the limited executive powers of the president. Indeed, with the exceptions of the legislative and presidential elections of 2003 and 2005, domestic issues and ideological differences have always been important in Turkish Cypriot presidential election campaigns. The 2003 and 2005 elections were fought along political differences on the Cyprus problem and EU integration. However, with the economic crisis of 2007 these issues began to lose salience and the economic situation rose to prominence (see European Commission 2010, p. 6). Lack of a breakthrough on international isolation and deadlock on integration with the EU played a role, to an extent, in CTP's failure to meet its promise of change. However, mismanagement of the economic growth of 2004–07, limited attempts to reform the economic and political structures and the inability to establish a working relationship between the state and civil society—i.e. the trade unions—and, indeed, a disconnection between Talat and CTP proved to be crucial in affecting Talat's possibilities of re-election. In fact, Talat, in a way, acknowledged this and his failure to deal with domestic policy matters by promising that, if re-elected, in the future he would be more involved in a supervisory position and, if needed, would take corrective measures on a legitimate basis.

All in all, these factors, indeed, led to estrangement between CTP–Talat and the business circles/civil society and, coupled with the global economic crisis, meant the loss of liberal and right-wing voters who had departed from their tradition and unorthodoxly voted for CTP and Talat in the 2003 and 2005 elections (see Sözen 2009, p. 347). The result was Eroğlu's victory.

Conclusions and Prospects

The April 2010 presidential elections in the 'TRNC' marked the end of the Talat (and CTP) interlude in Turkish Cypriot politics during the extraordinary period from 2003 to 2010. It was not a surprise for many to see Eroğlu win in the first round of elections. The main factors accounting for Eroğlu's victory were the EU's ineffectiveness in fulfilling its promises to the Turkish Cypriots, the inability of Talat and CTP to overcome international isolation, the deadlock in the negotiations for a compromise solution to the Cyprus problem, the inflexible Greek Cypriot attitude with respect to both the negotiations process and the EU policy towards the Turkish Cypriot society and, indeed, CTP mismanagement of domestic issues and Talat's failure to supervise CTP. In fact, one of the significant aspects of the outcome, and normalisation in Turkish Cypriot politics, was the dominance of domestic issues and ideological differences as an important determinant, unlike the 2003 and 2005 elections, which were largely determined by a divide on European integration and the Cyprus problem.

The outcome can certainly be considered as the success of UBP rather than a personal success for Eroğlu. UBP was successful in remaining unified in support of Eroğlu following the controversial candidacy of former UBP leader and parliamentarian, Ertuğruloğlu. Its presentation of Eroğlu as the most important candidate on the right facilitated the active support of right-wing parties and figures, which proved to be crucial in achieving Eroğlu's electoral success. The process and outcome of the 2010 presidential election turned into a competition between two camps, reflecting continuity with the previous elections in the 2000s towards the development of a political system within which two major parties dominate, one on each side of the political spectrum, with minor parties scattered along the left and right political continuum.

However, such a development does not support the argument that there has been a move in public opinion away from the desire for a compromise solution. There was a growing perception among the electorate that Eroğlu would not be able to follow a drastically different stance leading the Turkish Cypriot community away from a search for a solution. Indeed, Eroğlu moderated his policy approach on the Cyprus question in order to regain the right-wing voters who had voted for Talat in the 2005 presidential election. Both during the campaign and right after winning the election, Eroğlu declared his intention of working with goodwill for a solution that takes the Turkish Cypriot community's rights into account. Eroğlu supported his campaign rhetoric by immediately sending a letter to UN Secretary General, Ban Ki-moon, calling for the negotiations to continue from where they had left off. He also established a core negotiating team and a 'negotiations advisory council' in May 2010 including various names from across the political spectrum of northern Cyprus, confirming his attempts to establish a constructive attitude in this early phase of his presidency.

Eroğlu's moderate approach also aimed not to estrange the ruling AKP government in Turkey. He was presented as being at odds with AKP, which was considered to be more supportive of Talat despite rhetorically being indifferent. It is important to note that no Turkish Cypriot president or ruling party can afford to come into conflict with the Turkish government, on which it is dependent diplomatically and economically. The sidelining of Rauf Denktaş is still fresh in the minds of the Turkish Cypriot elite. Yet, Turkey's approach on the Cyprus question and the state of Turkey–EU relations will show whether Eroğlu's initial approach was 'tactical' in nature or a sincere attempt to solve the conflict by involving various domestic actors.

Notes

[1] Indeed, in an interview with the author, former President Mehmet Ali Talat argued that he preferred not to communicate details of the talks in order not to single out and politicise issues and polarise public opinion (Mehmet Ali Talat, Lefkoşa, 17 March 2011, interview by the author).
[2] See for example Akyel and Pope 2010. The international community had in fact begun to talk about the possibility of partition of the island if the process of negotiations between Talat and Christofias failed. See for example Pope 2009.
[3] Çankaya is a district of Ankara, Turkey which hosts the main state institutions. Dikilitaş is the Turkish for the Venetian Column that marks the centre of Nicosia.
[4] The turnout rates for the previous presidential elections were: 85.7 per cent in 1985; 93.5 per cent in 1990; 85.1 per cent in the first round and 80.1 per cent in the second round in 1995; 81.0 per cent in 2000; and 69.6 per cent in 2005.
[5] See Hatay 2007 for a demographic analysis of the 'TRNC' population and for a detailed analysis of the voting behaviour of 'Turkish settlers' in the 'TRNC'.
[6] Talat and Christofias established six working groups on the main issues to be negotiated in April 2008 following the election of the Greek Cypriot leader. These are (1) governance and power-sharing, (2) territory, (3) EU matters, (4) economic matters, (5) property, and (6) security and guarantees.

References

Akyel, D. & Pope, H. (2010) 'The Lisbon Treaty shines a ray of hope on Cyprus, solving the EU–Turkey–Cyprus-triangle', Commentary, International Crisis Group, 15 April, available online at: http://www.crisisgroup.org/en/regions/europe/turkey-cyprus/cyprus/pope-akyel-the-lisbon-treaty-shines-a-ray-of-hope-on-cyprus.aspx

Christophorou, C. (2008) 'A new communist surprise—what's next? Presidential elections in the Republic of Cyprus, February 2008', *South European Society and Politics*, vol. 13, no. 2, pp. 217–235.
Cyprus News Agency (2010) 'Government—direct trade', 10 April, available online at: http://www.hri.org/news /cyprus/cna/2010/10-04-02.cna.html
Çarkoğlu, A. & Sözen, A. (2004) 'The Turkish Cypriot general elections of December 2003: setting the stage for resolving the Cyprus conflict?', *South European Society & Politics*, vol. 9, no. 3, pp. 122–136.
EurActiv (2009) 'Erçakıca: "AB'nin Kıbrıs sorununun çözümünde etkili bir rol oynama olanağı kalmadı"' ['Erçakıca: there remains no possibility for the EU to play a role in the resolution of the Cyprus problem'], 27 June, available online at: http://www.euractiv.com.tr/abnin-gelecegi/article/ercakca-abnin-kibris-sorununun-couzmunde -etkili-bir-rol-oynama-olanagi-kalmadi-006178
European Commission (2010) 'Eurobarometer 74: public opinion in the European Union: national report, Turkish Cypriot community', Autumn, available online at: http://ec.europa.eu/public_opinion/archives/eb/eb74/eb74_en.htm
Güven, E. (2009) *ADAM: Talat'ın Kıbrıs'ı, Söyleşi* [The Island: Talat's Cyprus], Doğan Kitap, İstanbul.
Hatay, M. (2005) 'Beyond numbers: an inquiry into the political integration of the Turkish "settlers" in northern Cyprus', *PRIO Report*, 4, Oslo/Nicosia, available online at: http://www.prio.no/Research-and-Publications/Publication/?oid=168905
Hatay, M. (2007) 'Is the Turkish Cypriot population shrinking? An overview of the ethno-demography of Cyprus in the light of the preliminary results of the 2006 Turkish-Cypriot census', *PRIO Report*, 2, Nicosia, available online at: http://www.prio.no/Research-and-Publications/Publication/?oid=180037
Kıbrıs (2009) 'Eroğlu %36 Talat %31, 4', 7 November.
Kıbrıs (2010) 'Ertuğruloğlu 200 bin TL'yi aştı' [Ertuğruloğlu has spent over 200 thousand Turkish Liras], 22 April.
Kıbrıspostası (2010a) 'İşte Talat'ın tam konuşma metni' [Here is the full text of Talat's speech], 1 April.
Kıbrıspostası (2010b) 'Eroğlu Talat'ın açıklamalarını yorumladı' [Eroğlu commented on Talat's statements], 1 April.
Kıbrıspostası (2010c) 'Serdar Denktaş "güney Kıbrıs Mehmet Ali Talat'ı, Mehmet Ali Denktaş yaptı"' [Serdar Denktaş: south Cyprus turned Mehmet Ali Talat into Mehmet Ali Denktaş], 1 April.
Kıbrıspostası (2010d) '2. Cumhurbaşkanı Talat'ın seçim harcamalarının kaynağı açıklandı' [The source of second president Talat's election expenditures are publicised], 8 June.
Özerkan, F. (2010) 'Top candidates battle to end in tough Turkish Cyprus elections', *Hürriyet Daily News*, 16 April.
Özgür, B. (2010) 'Cumhurbaşkanlığı seçiminde AB'nin rolü' ['The role of EU in the presidential election'], *Yenidüzen*, 31 March.
Özkaya, T. (2010) 'KKTC'de seçim yarışı kızıştı; Talat, Eroğlu ile farkı kapatıyor' [The election race in the TRNC heats up: Talat closes on Eroğlu], *Zaman*, 11 April.
Pope, H. (2009) 'Cyprus: reunification or partition?', International Crisis Group, Europe Report No 201, 30 September, available online at: http://www.crisisgroup.org/~/media/Files/europe/201_cyprus___reunification_or_partition.pdf
Sözen, A. (2009) 'The Turkish Cypriot legislative election of April 2009: towards the "last roll of the dice" in the Cyprus conflict?', *South European Society and Politics*, vol. 14, no. 3, pp. 337–350.

Star (2009) 'Denktaş: AB Rum'a, CTP, AB'ye teslim' [Denktaş: EU submitted to Greek Cypriots, CTP to EU'], 17 March.
Yanatma, S. (2010) 'KKTC'de kıran kırana seçimde Talat umutlu' ['Talat hopeful in the savagely contested election in the TRNC'], *Zaman*, 17 April.
Zaman (2010) 'Talat: tek egemenlik taviz ise, bu tavizi onlar verdi' ['Talat: if single sovereignty is a concession, this concession was given away by them'], 12 April.

Sait Akşit (PhD Middle East Technical University) is an Assistant Professor at Gediz University, İzmir, Turkey. His recent publications include 'The Turkish Parliamentary Elite and the EU: Mapping out Attitudes on the European Union', *South European Society and Politics*, 2011, vol. 16, no. 3, pp. 395–407 (with Ö. Şenyuva and I. Gürleyen) and *Turkey Watch: EU Member States' Perceptions On Turkey's Accession to the EU* (co-edited with Ö. Şenyuva and Ç. Üstün) (Ankara: Zeplin İletişim, 2009).

The Eurozone's First Post-bailout Election: The 2010 Local Government Contest in Greece

Susannah Verney

An apparent case of Greek exceptionalism, the 2010 local government election, held six months after the European Union (EU)/International Monetary Fund (IMF) bailout in the context of an explicit prime-ministerial pledge to call general elections if the outcome was deemed unsatisfactory, did not lead to the downfall of the incumbent government. Instead the socialists remained first party. Investigating this puzzle, the article examines how party strategies were shaped by the dynamics of a two-round contest fought at the sub-national level and shows that the split around the EU/IMF Memorandum of Understanding did not emerge as a new political cleavage. Assessing the results, it concludes that the main electoral verdict did not concern the future of the bailout but the legitimacy of the political system, which was in a state of deepening crisis.

Under other circumstances, the Greek electoral contest of 7 and 14 November 2010 would have attracted some national interest as the first local government election following major territorial restructuring. Nevertheless, falling at an early stage of the national electoral cycle, only 13 months after a sweeping socialist victory, the local elections would normally have had essentially local impact. But due to the eurozone crisis, this sub-national election in a relatively small European state acquired international significance. Its outcome was anxiously watched for its implications for the balance of national political forces and the stability of the central government. It was feared that the potential repercussions of the local election results could include the destabilisation of the euro, the money markets and even the global financial system.

Six months earlier, Greece had become the first eurozone recipient of a bailout from the European Union (EU) and the International Monetary Fund (IMF), accompanied by a programme of economic austerity and structural reform. The bailout had been agreed to avert a Greek sovereign debt default whose reverberations threatened to trigger a new deepening of the international economic crisis, following the precedent of the Lehman Brothers collapse two years earlier. The local government elections were widely regarded as the first post-bailout test of the Greek government's popularity and, by extension, of the legitimacy and sustainability of the Greek reform programme. When they occurred it was already becoming clear that further eurozone bailouts would follow. The Irish agreement was signed on 29 November, just two weeks after the second round of the Greek election, while the Portuguese bailout followed five months later in May 2011.

During the Greek election campaign, the key question was whether the local government poll would turn into a referendum on the Memorandum of Understanding with the EU and IMF. The official opposition certainly tried to give the contest such a character. Three weeks before polling day, Prime Minister George Papandreou accepted the challenge and, in a 135-minute interview shown live on all major TV channels, promised that an unsatisfactory result for his party would be followed by immediate parliamentary elections (Papandreou 2010). The announcement caused some consternation among Greece's international creditors, given that all but one of the opposition parties had voted against the Memorandum.

In the end, this election did not precipitate a new deepening of the national and international crisis. There was no change of government and no threat to the international bailout deal. Another year was to pass before the government of PASOK (Πανελλήνιο Σοσιαλιστικό Κίνημα – Panhellenic Socialist Movement) imploded under the pressures of administering the tough austerity and reform programme. This makes Greece an interesting exception. Within a few months, both the Irish and Portuguese governments were swept from power following their own EU/IMF bailouts. In contrast, Greece in 2010 appears to be a case of 'the dog that does not bark': a post-bailout election where the incumbent government declared victory.

Investigating this puzzle is the goal of this article. It begins by presenting the background to the elections before sketching the nature of the 2010 local government reform and the dynamics of Greek local government elections. Next, it examines the election campaign and the extent to which it was shaped by the Memorandum debate, before presenting the results and assessing their implications.

Economic Shock

For the overwhelming majority of Greeks, the advent of the national economic crisis and especially the realisation of its extent came as a major shock. For almost a decade, Greece's growth rates had averaged four per cent a year, making it for some years the eurozone leader. Visual symbols such as the Athens Metro and the new Athens airport, both opened in the run-up to the 2004 Olympic Games, exuded a new national self-confidence and reflected the changing image of a country once regarded as Europe's poor relation.

While the country continued to have a high public debt, the cost of financing it decreased with the introduction of the single currency. Government bond markets tended to assess the level of credit risk in the eurozone countries as almost identical. But with the outbreak of the international economic crisis, financial markets began to reassess comparative sovereign credit risk and to adjust lending rates accordingly. The rising cost of money meant that suddenly a level of public debt a little below 100 per cent of gross domestic product (GDP)—as Greece had had consistently throughout the 1990s and early 2000s—was no longer sustainable.

In January 2009, the government of ND (Νέα Δημοκρατία – New Democracy) revised its forecast of the annual budget deficit to 3.7 per cent of GDP, above the eurozone's three per cent criterion. As a result, in April Greece entered the eurozone excessive deficit procedure. In October the ND government was due to report to the European Commission on its performance in restraining the deficit. Instead it called early elections for 4 October, only two years into its four-year term. During the campaign, ND confessed that the deficit might actually be six per cent rather than the 3.7 per cent previously announced.[1] PASOK, then the official opposition, responded that the real deficit figure could be nearer eight per cent—but still campaigned on the slogan 'The money's there' (τα λεφτά υπάρχουν), suggesting that ND's promised austerity programme would not be necessary. Days after the election, the new PASOK government announced that the real deficit figure was likely to be around 12.5 per cent of GDP (*Financial Times*, 20 October 2009). Meanwhile, the national debt was re-estimated at 112 per cent of GDP, twice the eurozone's reference rate.

There followed a dizzying seven months of sovereign credit rating downgrades and spiralling debt-servicing costs, with interest rates on Greek debt repeatedly setting and then breaking new eurozone records. A country that had so recently seemed to be heading for a new prosperity now faced imminent bankruptcy. The government responded with a series of painful measures including public sector wage cuts, a rise in the pensionable age, a range of indirect tax rises and a one-off levy on higher incomes. The financial markets remained unconvinced. After a protracted and reluctant discussion on eurozone emergency aid, Greece was put on joint EU/IMF life support. The 2 May agreement for a €110 billion loan was accompanied by a Memorandum of Understanding detailing extensive deficit-cutting measures and economic reforms.[2]

Thus in autumn 2010 Greek society was in a state of shock. Public sector employees had seen their pay reduced by around 20 per cent, many categories of the self-employed felt threatened by the planned opening up of their professions, while the pension reform passed in the summer was driving unprecedented numbers into immediate and unplanned early retirement in order to avoid subsequent pension losses. The European Commission's autumn 2010 forecast projected the unemployment rate for the year at 12.5 per cent, a big jump from 7.7 per cent just two years earlier in 2008 (European Commission 2010b p.89). The austerity measures generated strong protests (see Psimitis 2010), including a series of one-day general strikes. These were accompanied by mass demonstrations which often turned violent, notably on 3 May when three bank employees died in a fire-bombing as Parliament discussed the EU/IMF bailout package.

Thus the Greek local government elections of November 2010 followed a year in which many Greeks had seen the abrupt overturning of the personal economic assumptions on which their lives were based. This was also a period of national humiliation, with the country's sovereign credit rating officially downgraded to junk, constant speculation about possible Greek expulsion from the eurozone, and derogatory comment in the international press inflaming opinion among a public suddenly precipitated from prosperity to economic insecurity. This suggested fertile soil for the expression of political discontent, especially given the political malaise that pre-dated the economic crisis.

Political Malaise

That all was not well in Greece came to world attention in a spectacular manner in December 2008. The police killing of a 15-year-old, followed by an attempt to defame the dead child, triggered a spontaneous and inchoate youth revolt, with the country convulsed by riots for several weeks.[3] The protests were not only directed against an established pattern of police brutality. Underlying the collective rage was a deep frustration at the injustice of a corrupt and clientelist system offering a lack of economic prospects for new labour market entrants. Despite Greece's growing prosperity, the graduates of the '700 euro generation' could expect salaries below a living wage and insecure employment conditions without full social insurance rights, often on short-term contracts in the public sector.

As Kevin Featherstone (2009, p. 3) notes, Greece had become 'a blocked society', suffering from an inability to 'process competing social demands to satisfy rising expectations'. Governing elites, operating on a clientelist basis, showed a lack of leadership, a reluctance to confront vested interests, and an inability to promote a strategy of reform. The system was blatantly unfair, with official tolerance of systematic tax evasion keeping state revenue low and the cost of (low-quality) public goods unevenly distributed.

As December 2008 so graphically illustrated, the years leading up to the economic crisis saw a rapid decline in the legitimacy of the political system. Endemic corruption, linked to close identification of the governing party with the state machine, had been the major factor behind the socialists' 2004 election defeat after 11 years in power. Hopes this would change with a new government were rapidly disappointed. New Democracy's period in power (2004–09) saw repeated government corruption scandals while a climate of immunity meant those involved escaped prosecution.

Electoral Volatility

Growing popular dissatisfaction with the political system was already being manifested in electoral behaviour before the economic crisis. The first signal was a significant drop in electoral turnout as shown in Table 1. Six months after the riots, the June 2009 European Parliament elections were marked by a shock 47.5 per cent abstention rate. This was considerably less than the EU average of 57 per cent and also below the symbolic 50 per cent level regarded as signalling the lack of legitimacy of a political system. Nevertheless, for Greece with its long tradition of high turnout, this level of non-participation was unprecedented. While the parliamentary elections four months later did not see a repeat of abstention at this level, turnout still decreased by over three per cent of the electorate compared with the previous parliamentary poll in 2007.

Table 1 Abstention in National and European Elections in Greece, 2000–09 (per cent)

National parliamentary elections				European elections	
2009	2007	2004	2000	2009	2004
29.1	25.9	23.5	25.0	47.5	36.8

A second indication of discontent was the decline in two-party domination. During the previous three decades, Greece had one of the most solid two-party systems in Western Europe and, apart from a few months in 1989–90, had consistently produced one-party majority governments. In the nine parliamentary elections from 1981 to 2004, there was only one occasion (in 1996) when the combined vote share of PASOK and ND fell below 80 per cent, while in six elections it topped 85 per cent. Thus, when following a change to a more proportional electoral law, the symbolic 80 per cent barrier was marginally breached in 2007 (see Table 2), some analysts began excitedly to predict the decline of the two-party system. While at the time this seemed far-fetched, the 80 per cent barrier was further eroded in 2009, due to the dramatic fall in support for ND registered in that election.

Table 2 Combined Vote Share (per cent) of the Two Major Parties in National and European Elections, 2000–09

National parliamentary elections				European elections	
2009	2007	2004	2000	2009	2004
77.4	79.9	85.9	86.5	68.6	77.0

At the same time, support for PASOK and ND was showing a new volatility, with sharp swings between the two parties. In 2007, PASOK, with 38.1 per cent of the vote, recorded its worst parliamentary election result since the 1970s. Just two years later, the party swept back to power with an unprecedented 10.4 per cent lead over ND. The latter, having won a second term with a scarcely reduced majority in 2007, now saw its electoral support plummet by over eight per cent, resulting in its lowest vote and seat share since the party's foundation in 1974. New Democracy's defeat was followed by a leadership contest and a significant shift to the right under a new leader, Andonis Samaras, who rapidly moved the party away from the centre ground that it had previously aimed to occupy.

Meanwhile, the rising protest vote meant that in 2009 small party support had risen to 22.6 per cent compared with 13.5 per cent in 2000. One of the main beneficiaries was the radical right-wing populist party, LAOS (Λαϊκός Ορθόδοξος Συναγερμός – Popular Orthodox Rally), which entered Parliament in 2007 with 3.8 per cent of the vote and ten seats, rising to 5.6 per cent and 15 seats in 2009. A second new player was the Eco-Greens (Οικολόγοι-Πράσινοι), who won their first European Parliament seat in 2009 and narrowly failed to cross the three per cent threshold for national parliamentary representation a few months later. Meanwhile, the combined votes of the two other parliamentary parties, KKE (Κομμουνιστικό Κόμμα Ελλάδας – the Communist Party of Greece) and SYRIZA (Συνασπισμός Ριζοσπαστικής Αριστεράς – Coalition of the Radical Left), had risen by over 50 per cent between 2000 and 2007 (from 8.7 to 13.2 per cent). Nevertheless, the party system at this point continued to be dominated by two leading protagonists flanked by four bit-players, as indicated in Table 3.

Table 3 Support for Main Parties in Greek National Parliamentary Elections, 2000–09 (per cent)

Party	2009	2007	2004	2000
PASOK	43.9	38.1	40.6	43.8
ND	33.5	41.8	45.4	42.7
KKE	7.5	8.2	5.9	5.5
LAOS	5.6	3.8	2.2	–
SYRIZA	4.6	5.0	3.3	3.2
Eco-Greens	2.5	1.0	–	–

The Memorandum Vote and the Party System

Into this already volatile party landscape came the economic crisis and the issue of the EU/IMF bailout. The parliamentary vote on the Memorandum of Understanding on 6 May produced a strange realignment of ideological forces. It did not follow either the left–right cleavage or a division between protest parties and parties of government. The radical right LAOS, hoping to establish itself as a responsible party of power, joined the governing socialists in supporting ratification. The centre-right ND—despite having campaigned on a tough austerity platform in 2009—lined up with the communists and the radical left SYRIZA in opposition. New Democracy's stance, decided just one day before the vote, meant that—in contrast to the consensus among the three main parties in Portugal the following year—the Greek loan and accompanying reform programme became an object of intense interparty competition.

The Memorandum vote also generated intra-party tensions. Some socialist MPs were reluctant to support the neoliberal prescriptions of the EU/IMF austerity programme while a number of their ND colleagues were reluctant to vote down the loan package and accompanying reform programme at a time of national crisis. In both cases, a strong party whip averted a potentially larger rebellion. However, one ND and three PASOK MPs were immediately expelled from their parties after voting against their respective party lines. They included former ND foreign minister and 2009 leadership contender Dora Bakogianni, the daughter of a previous ND prime minister who remained the party's honorary president. Meanwhile, in June, four MPs broke away from the radical left SYRIZA to form DIMAR (Δημοκρατική Αριστερά – Democratic Left). The split was not due to the EU/IMF bailout, which DIMAR also opposed, but had been a long time coming. Those who left represented a distinct intra-party faction opposed to SYRIZA's increasingly radical and movement-based turn and growing Euroscepticism. The foundation of DIMAR increased to seven the number of significant parties, i.e. those holding national or European Parliament seats.

The local government elections thus took place within a party system exhibiting a new fluidity. The question was how all this would play out in an election at the sub-national level. Adding to the uncertainty was the fact that the latter had just undergone extensive territorial restructuring, including the introduction of a brand new tier of local government.

The Local Government Arena

Until the 1990s, Greece, with a population of 10.3 million, had 5,825 local government units, including 4,580 with less than 1,000 inhabitants each while only 134 had a population of over 10,000.[4] The overwhelming majority of these dwarf units were obviously too small to provide significant services for their citizens. In 1994 a second tier of local government was introduced at the level of the 54 prefectures (νομοί), while in 1998 first-tier local government was regrouped into 1,033 units. Ten years later, there was a broad consensus that local government was still too fragmented. The Kallikrates reform, named after one of the architects of the Parthenon and passed into law in May 2010, further consolidated first-tier local government into 325 units. Each of the islands, for example, constituted a single municipality. The 13 regions (περιφέρειες), originally created in the mid-1980s as administrative units for the purposes of EU development programmes, now replaced the prefectures as the site of second-tier local government.

It was this new territorial structure of 325 municipalities and 13 regions which was to provide the arena for the eurozone's first post-bailout election. An important consequence was that the 2010 election results were not directly comparable with those of the previous sub-national elections. With the exception of a few major municipalities, all the units had changed. This enhanced the tendency for analysts to treat the first post-bailout election as a national contest, drawing comparisons with the 2009 parliamentary election rather than the previous local government election of 2006.

Dynamics of Local Government Elections

A major criticism of Kallikrates concerned its retention of the 'winner-takes-all' electoral system. The winner is the electoral list gaining a majority of 50 per cent + 1 of the votes,[5] if necessary on a second Sunday run-off between the two leading contenders. The selection of councillors is determined by a preference cross system. The winning list is allocated 60 per cent of council seats, leaving the remaining 40 per cent to be shared out among all the other lists. This super-safe majority eliminates the need for consensus- and majority-building, as mayors are essentially able to do whatever they please in the face of a weak and fragmented opposition. This undoubtedly contributes to municipal corruption, as mayors have no problem in passing spending plans, however dubious, through a council that they control.

The system obviously encourages confrontational contests, given the importance of coming first and the fact there is no need for post-electoral accommodation. It also means any coalitions should preferably be built pre- rather than post-election. Minor parties that run alone may become significant arbiters of the second Sunday outcome by encouraging their voters to support one of the two leading contenders. However, they are destined to play only a marginal post-electoral role, owing to the small number of council seats they will receive and the impossibility of even a united opposition being able to defeat the mayor's camp in council votes.

Because first-tier local government elections traditionally took place in such small units, they inevitably acquired a strong local character with personalities often playing a stronger role than party affiliation. This was enhanced by a Greek singularity: the legal prohibition in the Municipal Code on political parties contesting local government elections, a relic of the period of political demobilisation after the 1940s Civil War. Of course, in practice parties continue to participate in local government elections despite the ban, but not under their own party names and banners. Instead, officially these are contests among local lists, running under a locally specific name and built around the personality of the candidate mayor and the latter's chosen municipal councillors. This has made first-tier local government elections rather hard to follow without extensive knowledge of the particular political constellation represented by the lists in each locality. It also makes a national balance-sheet of party losses and gains virtually impossible to calculate.[6]

Instead, the focus has always been on the three largest municipalities of Athens, Thessaloniki and Piraeus, regarded as a barometer of the parties' support at national level. Here, the elections have more clearly assumed the form of a contest among national political parties (running under different names but immediately recognisable) and often choosing star party cadres as candidates. In a historic victory in 1986, ND won all three municipalities, partly due to followers of small left-wing parties not following the tradition of turning out on the second Sunday to vote against the right. Ever since, both Athens and Thessaloniki had remained bastions of the right, with an uninterrupted succession of ND mayors for 24 years, while Piraeus had changed hands several times and currently had a PASOK incumbent.

In the second-tier elections, as in the three large municipalities, the national parties behind each locally named list have been very visible. Thus, in contrast to the municipalities, at the second tier it has been possible to make a nationwide assessment based on simple numerical superiority, i.e. which party wins most units. In 2006 this was ND, with 30 of the 55 prefectures.

However, the 2010 regional reform added another key indicator—victory in Attica. Far and away the country's largest region, Attica, including Athens and Piraeus and covering five parliamentary constituencies,[7] had 2.7 million registered voters in 2010—around 27 per cent of the total. As noted by leading electoral analyst Ilias Nikolakopoulos, in parliamentary elections 'the tradition of the 35-year post-dictatorship period is that Attica is the barometer of electoral trends, as the party which predominates here is always the ultimate election winner' (Nikolakopoulos 2010a). Attica is also the region where the smaller parties elect a significant proportion of their MPs, gaining a higher vote share than their national averages. The contest in Attica has thus gained both symbolic and substantive significance, making the outcome there, alongside the three major municipalities, one of the most important measures of success in this election.

The Campaign

The Two Main Parties

In fact, the election in Attica—contested by ten candidate lists, all of which were to win representation on the Regional Council[8]—suggested both a party system under stress and a potentially strong anti-Memorandum dynamic. The fragmentation was mainly focused on the left of the political spectrum, with eight lists covering the space from the centre- to the far left. New Democracy and all seven lists to the left of PASOK ran on an anti-Memorandum platform. The extent of the challenge to the socialists was underlined by the presence of two lists headed by PASOK dissidents. National Council member Alexis Mitropoulos was the official SYRIZA candidate while MP Giannis Dimaras, expelled in May for opposing the Memorandum, ran as an independent.

Meanwhile, ND faced its own internal dissent over the Memorandum. In Crete, Dora Bakogianni, testing the waters for a new centre-right party, backed an independent candidate, thus splitting the right-wing vote and ensuring a PASOK victory in the region. The campaign period saw considerable friction with Bakogianni's supporters within ND, including the expulsion of one of the party's Members of the European Parliament in September and a very public break with the honorary president in October. It seemed likely that an unfavourable outcome in the November election could produce a direct challenge to Samaras's leadership.

Both main parties were also challenged by rebel lists based on local antipathies or the rejection of a candidate imposed centrally against the wishes of local party supporters. Those with prospects of entering the second round included a LAOS-backed former ND MP in the Piraeus municipality and a PASOK National Council member in the Ionian Islands region.

These challenges led the two main parties to adopt somewhat different strategies. Given the 'winner-takes-all' electoral law, the first key question in Greek sub-national elections concerns the formation of first-round alliances. The usual practice of both major parties has been to run alone except in areas where they seem unlikely to win without first-round allies. The second strategic choice is whether to fight the elections as second-order national contests around national issues or as local contests around local issues. In the 2010 elections, these choices gained a new dimension due to the new split around the Memorandum.

PASOK's original preference was to fight this contest as a local government election. It seems the socialists originally planned to centre their campaign on their flagship Kallikrates reform, hoping to stimulate interest in the election of the first regional secretaries, described, with some exaggeration, as '13 little prime ministers'. However, Papandreou had to backtrack on his promise to run top-rank cadres in the regions when a number of leading government members publicly declined to run, unwilling to risk defeat in the uncertain post-Memorandum climate. The party's ultimate choices—middle-ranking rather than frontline cadres—significantly reduced the excitement level around the regional elections.

Also indicative of the climate was Papandreou's personal decision, against the entrenched resistance of the party machine, not to run party candidates in the traditionally conservative Peloponnese region and the two largest municipalities. In all three cases, not running party cadres was a prudent tactic, potentially reducing the direct damage to the governing party in the case of a likely defeat. In the Peloponnese, the socialists rather controversially joined the radical right LAOS in supporting a former ND minister. This was the only significant alliance between the two Memorandum-supporting parties and was motivated by the predominantly right-wing electoral arithmetic of this region. In Athens, PASOK accepted a DIMAR proposal to support the independent candidacy of the Greek Ombudsman, Georgios Kaminis, in alliance with the Eco-Greens. In Thessaloniki, PASOK again joined DIMAR in supporting businessman and municipal councillor Giannis Boutaris, who had won 16 per cent of the vote running as an independent in 2006. As the Eco-Greens also opposed the bailout, these high-profile alliances (repeated in a number of smaller municipalities) cut across the Memorandum/anti-Memorandum divide.

In contrast, ND, seeking to recover from its devastating parliamentary election defeat in 2009, attempted to elevate the Memorandum/anti-Memorandum divide into a new political cleavage. This strategy promised second-round success along the lines of 1986 if left-wing voters could be induced to vote for anti-Memorandum ND—or at least not to vote for pro-Memorandum socialists. Samaras's earlier claim that without the Memorandum, he could eliminate the national budget deficit in two years

(Samaras 2010) was somewhat watered down during the campaign. Nevertheless, the ND line, ignoring the previous government's share of responsibility for the state of the economy, blamed the international bailout on PASOK's post-October 2009 mismanagement and claimed that an alternative policy mix could rapidly resolve Greece's problems. However, the second theme of ND's campaign—an attempt to repatriate LAOS voters through an anti-immigrant discourse—emphasised ND's differences with the left-wing anti-bailout parties. Nor was the party's alliance policy aligned with its anti-Memorandum strategy. In the high-profile contests in the 13 regions and three main municipalities, ND made five alliances[9]—all with LAOS.

New Democracy's anti-Memorandum strategy seemed to backfire when the electorate found its left-wing proponents more convincing. One month before the elections, Dimaras in Attica threatened to become the nemesis of both main parties. Opinion polls predicted he would exclude ND from the second round and then win an easy victory over PASOK in a Memorandum-centred run-off. Such an outcome in the country's crucial first region would not only have undermined the legitimacy of the government and the bailout policy. It would also have damaged ND and Samaras, as the weak party candidate running third in the polls had been his personal choice.

The threat was averted when PASOK switched to a more aggressive strategy, accepting ND's challenge and rebaptising the elections as a referendum on government policy. In his 25 October TV interview, Papandreou backed his call for general elections in the case of defeat by adopting a line of active support for the Memorandum based around the slogan 'Either we change or we sink' (Αλλάζουμε ή βουλιάζουμε) (Papandreou 2010). Meanwhile, media revelations about secret contacts between Dimaras and ND discredited the former among left-wing voters, leading to a rapid drop in his opinion poll ratings. Once these tactics paid off and the first round was safely over, PASOK switched back to emphasising the local government character of the elections—a line more conducive to second-round victory, especially in the municipalities.

The Other Political Forces

For the KKE, these elections saw the transfer to the sub-national level of the strategy of glorious isolation pursued nationally since the early 1990s. The KKE incorporated its opposition to the EU/IMF bailout into its existing anti-system strategy which classed all the other political forces as capitalist sellouts. Thus, for the communists the anti-Memorandum line did not imply any kind of political realignment but simply reinforced the one cleavage that mattered: that between the communists and everyone else. Hence, definitively turning its back on the post-war tradition of municipal communism, in 2010 the KKE decided it would not form any alliances or support any independent candidates. In the first round it ran its own cadres everywhere, with all its regional and municipal lists sharing the same title, Popular Rally (Λαϊκή Συσπείρωση) to increase their visibility. In the second round, the KKE instructed its followers to cast a blank or spoiled ballot everywhere, regardless of local conditions.[10]

The radical right LAOS had been a significant winner in the 2009 parliamentary election, when it became the first breakaway from one of the two main parties to achieve a second parliamentary term. The party's subsequent goal was to be accepted as a potential government partner. A proposal, made in April, for an alliance with ND in all 13 regions was rejected without discussion. However, subsequent alliances with ND in four regions and with PASOK in one offered the radical right legitimacy and a potential share in the exercise of regional power. In terms of campaign strategy, the party was at rather a disadvantage. Unable to fight on an anti-Memorandum ticket after voting for the bailout, LAOS also found it hard to run convincing campaigns on local issues due to the weakness of its local party machine. This reflected the party's strong reliance on the tele-persona of its leader rather than on traditional grassroots organisation. It was rather striking that in two regions the country's fourth largest party could not find a candidate to support. In the major municipal elections, LAOS supported the incumbent ND mayor in Athens, an ND rebel in Piraeus and an independent candidate in Thessaloniki. Elsewhere, LAOS's municipal presence was minimal.

SYRIZA, with a declining vote share in 2009, faced a serious internal challenge on two fronts. In addition to the scission with DIMAR, a long-running power struggle between SYRIZA's present and former presidents now reached a climax when former party leader Alekos Alavanos ran as an independent in Attica, supported by some of the more radical SYRIZA groupuscules. SYRIZA's opposition to the Memorandum reinforced its earlier rejection of any alliance with PASOK. Hence, it refused to join the municipal coalitions attempting to overturn the right-wing fiefs in Athens and Thessaloniki. However, these elections saw SYRIZA start to shift away from its long-term demand for the creation of a 'third pole' with the KKE to counterbalance the two main parties—an alliance that the communists had consistently rejected. Instead, SYRIZA began a new attempt to rally a broad anti-Memorandum front—exclusively on the left. This included a number of local alliances with the Eco-Greens and even with the breakaway DIMAR. Above all, however, the party shifted its attention to its right and began appealing to disaffected PASOK supporters, most notably through the Mitropoulos candidacy in Attica.

DIMAR, although formed only five months before the elections, represented the established 'renewal left' brand, dating back to the foundation of the Greek Eurocommunist party in 1968. This explains why this new party was able to establish an organisation in every prefecture by early autumn and to run lists in nine of the 13 regions in November (in three cases allied with the Eco-Greens). Strongly believing in institutional participation and aiming to participate in the exercise of power, at the municipal level DIMAR wherever possible pursued a strategy of alliances with parties on the left (PASOK, SYRIZA, Eco-Greens), determined by local conditions and not by its opposition to the Memorandum. In Athens, the small DIMAR became a major player, making the game-changing proposal for the Greek Ombudsman to run as an independent and building the three-party coalition with PASOK and the Eco-Greens in support. In Thessaloniki, the party was instrumental in promoting the Boutaris coalition through an early announcement of support which ruled out success for a separate PASOK candidacy.

The Eco-Greens, one year after winning their first European Parliament seat, hoped to consolidate their position on the Greek political scene by acquiring a local government presence. The party ran alone in eight regions and two of the big municipalities. When building alliances, the Eco-Greens' basic choice, like that of DIMAR, was to seek allies on the left without reference to the Memorandum, in this case with the aim of promoting Green politics. Thus, the Eco-Greens allied with DIMAR in three regions, SYRIZA in two and PASOK–DIMAR in Athens, while their other municipal alliances also entailed permutations of these three parties. In Thessaloniki, the party formally supported the Boutaris candidacy in the second round.

Consequences

One of the keys to understanding this election, therefore, is the dynamic of a two-round process fought at the sub-national level, with all this implied in terms of alliance-building. Of the five significant parties that opposed the Memorandum, only two, ND and the KKE, made this a central axis of nationally shaped campaigns. However, while ND proposed a different variation of the neoliberal policy recipe, the KKE rejected capitalist economics altogether. This led the two parties to very different evaluations of where the Memorandum/anti-Memorandum cleavage lay, with the KKE's rigid 'go-it-alone' strategy ruling out any possibility of even a tacit second-round alliance. Meanwhile, the six significant parties that did participate in alliances respected the left–right cleavage, only crossed in the rather exceptional case of the PASOK–LAOS partnership in the Peloponnese. In contrast, five of the six parties made choices crossing the Memorandum/anti-Memorandum divide. These alliance strategies clearly undermined the potential anti-Memorandum dynamic of this election.

The Results

Party Winners and Losers

Following the first round of the elections on 7 November, Prime Minister Papandreou declared that the people had given his party a mandate to continue until the end of its four-year term in 2013. This was a highly questionable assumption. Nevertheless, PASOK had emerged from the first electoral round with its legitimacy intact, having avoided the kind of defeat that would have made its hold on national power untenable. Especially important were the exclusion from the second round of the main anti-Memorandum challenger, Dimaras, in Attica, as well as of the PASOK rebel in the Ionian Islands and the reasonable results obtained by the candidates PASOK backed in Athens and Thessaloniki. After the second round a week later, the socialists were able to claim victory, having backed the winning candidates in eight of the 13 regions and two of the three main municipalities. These included three of the four major contests:

the flagship region of Attica and the two former right-wing bastions of Athens and Thessaloniki, with only Piraeus going to ND. Elsewhere, the newspaper *Ta Nea* (15 November 2010) estimated that PASOK had won 185 of the 325 municipalities, including all the winning lists in which the socialists allied with other parties. While the socialists' support had clearly declined since the previous year's landslide parliamentary election victory, PASOK retained its position as first party and Papandreou was strengthened when his personal gambles in Athens, Thessaloniki and the Peloponnese all paid off.

However, PASOK was not the only party to proclaim victory.[11] After the first round, ND party leader Samaras declared that 'never has an opposition party achieved such a total comeback on such a scale in just one year' (*Ta Nea*, 9 November 2010). His triumphalism was based on the regional vote, where ND emerged as first party in 32 of the 54 prefectures (*Eleftheros Typos*, 16 November 2010)—a curious measure of success when the prefectures no longer functioned as an independent level of local government. As with PASOK, the sense of elation was partly due to the worst case scenarios not materialising, thanks to the second-round exclusion of Dimaras and the party rebel in Piraeus. While Dora Bakogianni's success in relegating ND to third place in Crete opened the way for the foundation of her new centre-right party just six days later, Crete was the only regional contest in which ND did not come first or second. The following week, ND's hopes of second-round victory on the basis of its anti-Memorandum platform did not materialise at either regional or municipal level. The party won only five regions and, according to a calculation in *Ta Nea* (15 November 2010), 85 municipalities, just over a quarter of the total. The defeats in Athens and Thessaloniki were historic, although Thessaloniki—the chief election night thriller—was lost by only 329 votes and impressions were somewhat mitigated by victory in Piraeus. Nevertheless, although ND was still well behind PASOK in terms of support, the party had avoided a defeat commensurate with 2009. With its vote shares suggesting the party had begun its recovery from its 2009 nadir, Samaras was able to consolidate both his leadership and his anti-Memorandum strategy.

The KKE, clearly benefiting from the anti-Memorandum protest vote, reinforced its position as the country's third political force and increased its lead over the other minor players. The communist vote reached double figures in six regions[12] and two of the main municipalities. The KKE dominated the space to the left of PASOK with a vote share at least double that of SYRIZA in ten regions and all three main municipalities. Thus, the KKE had been successful in terms of recording a strong party presence—without this rise being on a scale to threaten the two-party system. Paradoxically, the KKE was simultaneously a loser, as its increased vote was accompanied by declining political influence. The party's 'no alliance' policy led to its exclusion from the second round in every region and all but two municipalities. In the end, the KKE elected only one mayor (in the Attica municipality of Petroupolis) and, owing to the electoral law, significantly fewer municipal councillors than its vote share warranted.

The radical right LAOS, although participating in three winning regional lists (two with ND and one with PASOK), emerged weakened from this election. In all five regions where it ran its own candidates, its vote share dropped compared with the 2009 parliamentary election. This loss of dynamism in a period when protest parties could be expected to flourish was widely attributed to the party's pro-Memorandum stance. It may also have been influenced by its limited investment in sub-national politics. The party's failure at the regional level was compounded by its unsuccessful choices in the three main municipalities. The ND rebel supported by LAOS in Piraeus failed to enter the second round while its candidate in Thessaloniki won only half of LAOS's 2006 vote share. The defeat of the ND–LAOS candidate in Athens left the party without a municipal councillor in the country's capital.

SYRIZA's regional vote, above three per cent everywhere, indicated a support level that would allow its return to Parliament, confirming the party would survive the split with DIMAR. But this was not a breakthrough election for SYRIZA: the KKE was considerably more successful in harnessing the protest vote. In Attica, the alliance with PASOK rebels had been expected to bring a result in double figures. Instead, SYRIZA came sixth with 6.2 per cent, its vote actually falling compared with 2009. SYRIZA had not established its appeal among disaffected PASOK voters, who preferred the PASOK rebel Dimaras. The Attica contest, however, resolved the power struggle between SYRIZA's current and former leaders in favour of the former. Alavanos, after a picturesque campaign including pledges to ban EU and IMF representatives from the buildings of the regional administration, polled only 2.2 per cent, the lowest of all ten candidates. At the municipal level, according to the party newspaper (*Avghi*, 16 November 2010), SYRIZA participated in nine winning lists, including the country's fifth municipality, Patras, the traditional KKE stronghold of Ikaria and five Attica municipalities. However, compared with 2006, SYRIZA's vote fell by almost half in Athens and a quarter in Thessaloniki, under pressure from the successful PASOK–DIMAR–Eco-Green alliances.

DIMAR before these elections had been labouring under a serious disadvantage. With only four MPs rather than the required ten, it was not recognised as a party by Parliament, limiting its possibility of parliamentary intervention and hence its impact. This was reflected in the regional elections where DIMAR emerged as a rather minor player. Its vote share, ranging from 1.5 to 4.0 per cent, suggested it might have difficulty in passing the parliamentary threshold in a general election. At the municipal level, however, the picture was very different. DIMAR's role in shaping the winning coalitions in Athens and Thessaloniki put the party on the political map, bringing increased media attention and local government influence out of all proportion to its vote share. In Athens alone, the party elected eight municipal councillors, four of whom became deputy mayors. DIMAR also participated in winning lists in three other important urban centres, Patras, Volos and Ioannina, and a number of other municipalities, including Nikaia, where a DIMAR cadre was elected mayor. Due to its second-round participation, this small party elected significantly more municipal councillors nationwide than the KKE.

The Eco-Greens, by their own estimates, elected 18–20 local government representatives (Eco-Greens 2010a). At the regional level, the Greens performed rather better than DIMAR, exceeding three per cent of the vote in six of the eight regions they contested independently. It seemed this small party might finally hope to enter Parliament at the next general election. At the municipal level, the Eco-Greens claimed that 18 mayors had been elected with their support (Eco-Greens 2010b), although this included cases of second-round support such as Thessaloniki. Weak party organisation, limiting the necessary mobilisation of preference crosses for its candidates, meant these alliances produced only two Eco-Green municipal councillors, including one in Athens. The Eco-Greens also elected five councillors in municipalities that the party contested independently. While they thus acquired a local government presence, the Eco-Greens were far from becoming a significant force.

From examining the performance of the six significant parties, it might seem that the elections essentially left intact the balance of forces within a system based on two major protagonists flanked by minor players. The two major parties had emerged in first and second place in 12 of the 13 regional contests (Crete being the only exception), with all rebel ballots excluded from the second-round regional run-offs. Anti-Memorandum protest had been primarily channelled into rising communist support that did not translate into council seats or threaten the two-party hegemony. The remaining anti-Memorandum forces were fragmented and hovering at or below the three per cent margin for parliamentary survival. But this does not give the true picture of the election result, which in fact, suggested a dramatic deepening of the country's political malaise.

Systemic Strains

The rise in abstention in 2010, as shown in Table 4, exceeded the shock increase in the 2009 Euro-election. At both levels of local government, second-round participation fell below the 50 per cent level regarded as crucial for system legitimacy. In the 11 regions that went to a second round, participation only marginally exceeded 50 per cent in five. At the municipal level, particularly striking was the 66 per cent abstention rate in Athens and Piraeus, while there were two cases (Lemnos and Konitsa) where it was over 70 per cent. In addition, in Athens, Piraeus and six regions, the proportion of second-round blank or spoiled ballots was over 10 per cent of votes cast, reaching

Table 4 Abstention Rates (per cent) in Greek Local Government (LG) Elections, 2002, 2006 and 2010

Type of election	2010	2006	2002
First-tier LG – first round	39.0	27.6	27.4
First-tier LG – second round	50.8	35.5	30.6
Second-tier LG – first round	39.0	27.6	27.3
Second-tier LG – second round	53.9	44.4	33.5

16 per cent in Attica. This meant that in Attica only 35.4 per cent of the registered electorate cast valid ballots in the second round.[13]

The second significant warning signal concerned the stability of the two-party system. As Table 5 shows, in ten regional contests the combined first-round vote of the lists backed by ND and PASOK exceeded 70 per cent.[14] But in three cases the presence of a strong party rebel significantly reduced the combined PASOK–ND support for the two main parties. The most striking example occurred in Attica, where the joint PASOK–ND score fell below 45 per cent. This very substantial drop compared with both the 2009 parliamentary elections (68.3 per cent) and the 2006 Athens–Piraeus 'super-prefecture' result (77.9 per cent) was by no means all absorbed by the 16 per cent of the vote gained by Dimaras. While in 2010 Attica appeared an exception compared with the other regions, such fragmentation of preferences in the region regarded as the national weathervane, as shown in Table 6, was a worrying omen for the future.

The Attica message was reinforced by a number of municipalities where the official candidate of one of the two main parties was excluded from the second round (e.g. ND in the fourth- and fifth-largest municipalities, Herakleion and Patras, or PASOK in Alexandroupolis and Lesvos), received a vote share marking a historic low for the area (e.g. ND in its historic heartland, Serres, or PASOK in Peristeri, one of the largest municipalities) or suffered an unexpected second-round defeat (e.g. PASOK in Patras, ND in Zographou).

Exemplifying such surprise outcomes were the three main municipalities. Not only did all three change hands, confounding predictions at the outset of the campaign, but also in all three cases the second round overturned the first-round result. A detailed analysis of the vote in Athens (Koustenis 2011) concluded that the election in the capital resulted in a radical change of the electoral map, due to the breaking down of

Table 5 Combined Vote Share (per cent) of the Two Major Parties in the First Round of the 2010 Greek Regional Elections

Region	Winning party	PASOK–ND combined vote share
Western Macedonia	ND	84.7
Epirus	ND–LAOS	83.5*
Eastern Macedonia & Thrace	PASOK	82.9
Peloponnese*	PASOK–LAOS	82.6
South Aegean*	PASOK	82.0
North Aegean	PASOK	74.6
Central Greece	PASOK	74.2
Central Macedonia	ND	73.9
Thessaly	ND	73.5
Western Greece	PASOK	73.0
Crete	PASOK	65.2
Ionian Islands*	ND	56.0
Attica	PASOK	44.8

* Includes LAOS.

Table 6 The 2010 First-Round Result in Attica Compared with 2009 Parliamentary and 2006 Local Government Elections (per cent)

Party (candidate)	2010 Regional elections first round	2009 Parliamentary elections	2006 Prefecture elections* first round
PASOK (Sgouros)	24.1	40.3	41.3
ND (Kikilias)	20.7	28.0	36.6
PASOK dissident (Dimaras)	16.0	–	–
KKE (Paphilis)	14.4	10.2	10.4
LAOS (Georgiadis)	6.6	7.5	3.8
SYRIZA (Mitropoulos)	6.2	6.8	5.7
Eco-Greens (Diakos)	4.0	4.0	–
DIMAR (Psarianos)	3.8	–	–
ANTARSYA (Hagios)	2.3	–	–
METOPO (Alavanos)	2.2	–	–

* The 2006 result is from the Athens–Piraeus 'super-prefecture'.

political affiliations across the ideological spectrum. This weakening of former allegiances seems to have been a national trend.

A further indication of this was the surprising performance by two extra-parliamentary parties on the political extremes. ANDARSYA (Αντικαπιταλιστική Αριστερή Συνεργασία για την Ανατροπή – Anticapitalist Left Collaboration for the Overthrow) received approximately 100,000 votes, four times its share in the 2009 parliamentary election (Nikolakopoulos 2010b). Running candidates in 11 regions, it won a seat in seven and elected a councillor in 12 municipalities. Particular shock was caused by the election of an Athens city councillor by the neonazi Chryssi Avghi (Χρυσή Αυγή – Golden Dawn), responsible for multiple violent attacks on immigrants, whose 0.29 per cent vote in 2009 had suggested its appeal was limited to the lunatic fringe. The success of these two parties provided an early warning of the potential impact of the economic crisis on the party system. It suggested that in future the protest vote would not necessarily be channelled through traditional outlets, such as the KKE, but might seek new and more dangerous means of expression.

Assessing the Outcome

That the eurozone's first post-bailout election did not turn into a vote against the Memorandum may be partly explained by a number of mitigating factors. The first was the socialists' recent return to power. Before 2004 PASOK had formed the government for 19 of the previous 23 years and bore the responsibility for the poor state of public finance in that period. But because the party was in opposition in 2004–09, it was not associated with the debt and deficit explosion of that period which left ND seriously discredited. A year after the government change, Papandreou's claim that ND had abandoned ship when faced with the economic crisis, leaving PASOK with 'a bomb ready to explode' (Papandreou 2010), could still evoke a sympathetic response. Arguably, the focal point of disaffection at this point was less the bailout than the economic crisis that led to it—and here the socialists did not bear sole responsibility. This differentiated Greece from both Portugal and Ireland, where the governments that negotiated the bailouts had been in power for several years.

Secondly, in autumn 2010 the austerity programme had only recently begun to bite. The official picture of Greece's economic prospects remained relatively upbeat. The European Commission's spring 2010 forecast predicted a three per cent drop in GDP for the year but only a 0.5 per cent decline for 2011, suggesting recession would be shortlived (European Commission 2010a, p. 90).[15] The EU/IMF agreement for a three-year support programme was based on the assumption that the economy would start to grow again in 2012, with Greece expected to be able to return to the market for loan finance from 2012 and to start repaying the bailout loan the following year. In 2010 the official message to the Greek people was that the country's economic difficulties were an interlude: a case of short-term pain for long-term gain.

Supporting this view, in the early weeks of the local election campaign, the Greek press reported a number of statements by leading EU politicians suggesting that after the bailout Greece was now on the right track.[16] While these remarks may have been motivated by the desire to inhibit crisis contagion to the rest of the eurozone periphery, they conveyed a climate of relative confidence in the Greek economy—certainly in comparison with the international lambasting that was to follow from spring 2011. It was not until shortly before the election that a shadow was cast over this picture, when it became known that Eurostat was reassessing the 2009 deficit upwards.[17] However, this news came fairly late in the day and does not appear to have had a significant impact on the campaign.[18]

Thirdly, despite popular rage at the austerity programme, there was considerable hope at this point that the crisis might bring catharsis after the seemingly endless stream of political scandals and act as a motor for long-overdue political and economic reform, finally bringing a rupture with the corrupt and clientelist state. This encouraged support for PASOK, despite its clientelist past, as the party that had agreed to the EU/IMF reform programme and undertaken to implement it.

Besides these factors, the other crucial point—so obvious it might be overlooked—was that, at the end of the day, these were local government elections. Even in the first round, the contest only revolved around national issues to a limited extent. Even more in the second round, when Papandreou had already ruled out a new parliamentary poll, voters knew their actual choice concerned their new local government authorities. This was especially apparent at municipal level.

It is characteristic that in all three major municipalities, the contests were essentially fought and won around the issue of which list should run the city. In Athens a major issue was the impact of undocumented immigration and the ghettoisation of the historic city centre. In Thessaloniki, the election acquired a culture wars dimension, with the ultra-conservative Bishop publicly campaigning against the socially liberal and anti-nationalist Boutaris.[19] In Piraeus, an important factor was the intra-PASOK feuding between supporters of the incumbent mayor and the candidate who replaced him. But the key issue in all three cities was corruption. The question of corruption, already central in the downfall of both the previous PASOK and ND governments, rose still higher on the public agenda with the economic crisis and primarily burdened the party previously in power. Concerns with their growing unpopularity led both PASOK in Piraeus and ND in Thessaloniki to replace their incumbent mayors with new candidates before the election[20] but without the desired effect. The result in all three cities was the ousting of the incumbents in a vote directed against the status quo—whichever of the two major parties this represented.

Commenting on the election result, the IMF Director, Dominique Strauss-Kahn, declared it showed the acquiescence of the Greek people to the EU/IMF bailout (*Ta Nea*, 16 November 2011). This interpretation, like Papandreou's declaration that the electorate had renewed his mandate, assumed that this contest had functioned purely as a second-order national election, centred exclusively on the government's handling of the economic crisis and not even concerned with the broader question of how the crisis had arisen in the first place. The preceding analysis suggests this was not the case. That Greek politics had not restructured around the Memorandum/anti-Memorandum split was made very apparent in Attica. While anti-Memorandum candidates took 69 per cent of the first-round vote, PASOK won the second round with an almost six per cent lead over ND, indicating the traditional left–right cleavage had prevailed over divisions around the Memorandum. In reality, the electoral verdict did not primarily concern the bailout but the credibility of the political system that had led the Greeks into economic crisis, including those who handled power at the local level. Its basic outcome was an alarming message of growing alienation, increased electoral volatility and declining political legitimacy.

Notes

[1] The admission was made by the Minister of Finance in an interview with Bloomberg; see *Eleftherotypia*, online edition, 17 September 2010, http://www.enet.gr/?i=news.el.article&id=83449
[2] For the text of the Greek Memorandum, see http://peter.fleissner.org/Transform/MoU.pdf
[3] For participant voices, see Schwarz, Sagris and Void Network (2010); for analyses, Economides and Monastiriotis (2009) and Karamichas (2009).
[4] Figures from Hlepas and Getimis (2011).
[5] Reduced to 42 per cent +1 under the 1998 Capodistrias reform, but re-established at 50 per cent + 1 under Kallikrates.
[6] The problem is compounded by the fact that the Ministry of the Interior does not record the party support base of self-declared independent candidates in the official results.
[7] Athens A and B, Piraeus A and B and 'the rest of Attica'.
[8] Compared with five seat-winning lists in the Athens–Piraeus 'super-prefecture' in 2006.
[9] In Athens and the regions of Epirus, Ionian Islands and North and South Aegean.
[10] For an interesting analysis of KKE strategy in these elections, see Eleftheriou (2011).
[11] The analysis that follows is based on the detailed election results available on the Ministry of the Interior site at: http://ekloges-prev.singularlogic.eu/dn2010/public/

[12] In two regions, North Aegean and Ionian Islands, the KKE polled over 15 per cent.
[13] Valid votes of 988,972 cf. 2,792,102 registered voters.
[14] In three cases, one of the lists was also backed by LAOS. In all three, the combined vote exceeded 80 per cent, suggesting that even without LAOS, joint PASOK–ND support would still have exceeded 70 per cent.
[15] The European Commission's autumn forecast was more pessimistic. For example, it suggested a 3.0 per cent decline in GDP in 2011 (European Commission 2010b, p. 89), which was still far from the reality of 6.9 per cent. However, the autumn forecast was published on 29 November and hence did not influence the climate of the local government elections.
[16] For example: 'Rehn: Bravo to you . . . Schauble: We will get paid!' (*Eleftherotypia*, 27 August 2010) and the characteristically entitled 'From Anathema to Bravo' (*To Vima*, 10 October 2010). There was even a report that some leading international banks were now recommending their customers buy Greek government bonds (*Ta Nea*, 21 September 2010).
[17] See www.bloomberg.com for 6 October 2010.
[18] Eurostat announced the official revision of the 2009 deficit to 15.4 per cent on 15 November, the day after the second electoral round. See http://www.bbc.co.uk/news/business-11755320
[19] One of the campaign's more colourful moments occurred when, the day after Boutaris had compared him to the mujaheddin, the Bishop told him publicly, in front of the Prime Minister, that 'As long as I live, you will not see inside the municipality'. See *To Vima*, 31 October 2010. The failure of the Orthodox Church, despite its active intervention, to achieve the election of its preferred candidate in Thessaloniki was another interesting indication of the weakening of traditional ties.
[20] This was ruled out in Athens when the incumbent mayor announced his early candidacy with the support of LAOS—making it unlikely ND could win the municipality if it ran another candidate against him.

References

Eco-Greens (2010a) Press release, 24 November, available online at: www.ecogreens-gr.org

Eco-Greens (2010b) 'Απόφαση για τα αποτελέσματα των αυτοδιοικητικών εκλογών' [Decision on the local election results], 24 November, available online at: www.ecogreens-gr.org

Economides, S. & Monastiriotis, V. (eds) (2009) *The Return of Street Politics? Essays on the December riots in Greece*, available online at: www2.lse.ac.uk/europeanInstitute/research/hellenicObservatory/pdf/Various/Greek_Riots_09_FINAL.pdf

Eleftheriou, K. (2011) 'Κομματική στρατηγική, οργανωτική αλλαγή και εκλογική κινητοποίηση: το ΚΚΕ στις αυτοδιοικητικές εκλογές του 2010' [Party strategy, organisational change and electoral mobilisation: the CPG in the local government elections of 2010], *Elliniki Epitheorisi Politikis Epistimis*, no. 37, pp. 69–97.

European Commission (2010a) 'European economic forecast – spring 2010', *European Economy*, no. 2, available online at: http://ec.europa.eu/economy_finance/publications/european_economy/2010/pdf/ee-2010-2_en.pdf

European Commission (2010b) 'European economic forecast – autumn 2010', *European Economy*, no. 7, available online at: http://ec.europa.eu/economy_finance/publications/european_economy/jj2010/pdf/ee-2010-7_en.pdf

Featherstone, K. (2009) 'Street protests in "une société bloquée"', in *The Return of Street Politics? Essays on the December Riots in Greece*, eds S. Economides & V. Monastiriotis, available online at:

www2.lse.ac.uk/europeanInstitute/research/hellenicObservatory/pdf/Various/Greek_Riots_09_FINAL.pdf

Hlepas, N. & Getimis, P. (2011) 'Impacts of local government reforms in Greece: an interim assessment', *Local Government Studies*, vol. 37, no. 5, pp. 517–532.

Karamichas, J. (2009) 'The December 2008 riots in Greece', *Social Movement Studies*, vol. 8, no. 3, pp. 289–293.

Koustenis, P. (2011) 'Δημοτικές εκλογές 2010 στην Αθήνα: ΛΑ.Ο.Σ. ή Κολωνάκι' [Municipal elections 2010 in Athens: LAOS or Kolonaki], *Ελληνική Επιθεώρηση Πολιτικής Επιστήμης*, no. 37, pp. 41–68.

Nikolakopoulos, I. (2010a) 'Η μάχη του Καλλικράτη: περιφέρεια Αττικής' [The battle for Kallikrates: the Attica region], *Ta Nea* [The News], 5 November, p. 12.

Nikolakopoulos, I. (2010b) 'Ραγισμένο οικοδόμημα το πολιτικό σύστημα' [The political system is a cracked edifice], *Ta Nea*, 13–14 November, pp. 16–17.

Papandreou, G. (2010) TV interview, 25 October, video and full text available online at: http://www.primeminister.gov.gr/2010/10/25/3405

Psimitis, M. (2010) 'The protest cycle of spring 2010 in Greece', *Social Movement Studies*, vol. 10, no. 2, pp. 191–197.

Samaras, A. (2010) Speech 'Zappeion I', 7 July 2010, available online at: http://www.nd.gr/web/proedros/press//journal_content/56_INSTANCE_Rb5c/36615/61160

Schwarz, A., Sagris, T. & Void Network (2010) *We Are an Image from the Future: The Greek Revolt of December 2008*, A.K. Press, Edinburgh.

Susannah Verney teaches at the University of Athens. She is one of the two Editors of *South European Society and Politics* (with Anna Bosco) and a former Associate Editor of *The Journal of Modern Greek Studies*. Her recent publications include two edited volumes published by Routledge: *Euroscepticism in Southern Europe: A Diachronic Perspective (2011)* and *Turkey's Road to European Union Membership: National Identity and Political Change* (co-edited with K. Ifantis, 2009).

The 2010 Regional Election in Catalonia: A Multilevel Account in an Age of Economic Crisis

Guillem Rico

This paper examines the context, actors, campaign, and results of the Catalan election of 2010, which took place in a context of economic recession and growing political discontent. I argue that certain circumstances concurred in this particular contest to enhance the influence of factors pertaining to the first-order (i.e. national) arena as compared with the influence of second-order (i.e. region specific) factors. As a result, regional incumbent support was found to be largely driven by evaluations of national incumbent performance, which worked against the tripartite coalition government.

The ninth election to the Catalan regional parliament, held on 28 November 2010 amid rampant economic recession and growing political discontent, brought about the return of the centre-right nationalists to power after seven years 'in the wilderness' (as they used to refer to their rare stay in opposition), thus putting an end to the left-wing, three-party coalition government, characterised, until its very last moment, by heated debate over reform of the Statute of Autonomy, the regional charter governing all aspects of political life in autonomous communities.

The formation, in 2003, of the three-party government (popularly known as *tripartit*, or 'tripartite') signified a 'landmark change in the Catalan political landscape', as it signalled the first alternation in the Generalitat de Catalunya (the Catalan regional government) since the centre-right, moderate nationalist Convergència i Unió (CiU, Convergence and Union) took office after the inaugural election of 1980 (Davis 2004). Comprised of the social-democratic and premiership-holding Partit dels Socialistes de Catalunya (PSC, Catalan Socialists' Party), the left-wing, pro-independence nationalist *Esquerra Republicana de Catalunya* (ERC, Republican Left of Catalonia), and the eco-socialist, post-communist Iniciativa per Catalunya Verds–Esquerra Unida i Alternativa (ICV, Initiative for Catalonia Greens–United and Alternative Left), the tripartite alliance proved unstable during its first term, which was mostly devoted to the statute's controversial reform. Although internal conflicts persisted, the government coalition managed to survive until the end of its second term. Two events captured the public's attention in the run-up to the election: (1) the critical situation of the national economy, which motivated the Spanish government, led by the minority Partido Socialista Obrero Español (PSOE, Spanish Socialist Workers' Party) to take drastic, unpopular measures to cut public spending and propose ambitious labour-market reforms; and (2) the cuts and interpretive restrictions imposed on the painfully reformed statute by the Constitutional Court after the conservative Partido Popular (PP, Popular Party), the main national opposition party, challenged the regional charter's constitutionality.

This paper examines the background to and results of the 2010 regional election in Catalonia and explores the reasons for decay in the tripartite's support. As a second-order election, though one of a very special character, interpretations must take into account the multilevel nature of the contest (Reif & Schmitt 1980). I contend that certain circumstances coalesced to boost the influence of factors pertaining to the first-order arena vis-à-vis the influence of region-specific factors. An argument will be made that, as a consequence of economic pessimism and increasing political dissatisfaction, and by way of the perceptual connection that voters established between the two levels of government, regional incumbent support was driven to a large extent by evaluations of national incumbent performance.

The rest of this paper is structured as follows: first, I describe the general context in which the election took place. Next, the main political contenders are portrayed and their campaign strategies outlined. The third section briefly summarises the election's results. In the fourth section, I review key patterns of voting behaviour in Catalonia and examine factors that may account for recent trends in party support. I also report the results, largely consistent with the above expectations, of an individual-level analysis of incumbent support. I conclude by discussing the main findings and their implications.

The Context

The second tripartite government—this time under the presidency of the newly elected leader of the PSC, José Montilla—was established in November 2006 with the objective of developing the recently reformed Statute of Autonomy and with the declared intention of avoiding the public disagreements that had frequently emerged among coalition members during the preceding three years and that ultimately caused the early end of their first term. Indeed, the government oversaw an intense and rather successful period of legislative activity, managing to pass a good many laws envisaged in the statute and on other relevant matters—most prominently the Education Law. It also reached a new financing agreement with the central government that substantially improved the amount of resources to be allocated to the Catalan government, although it did not meet statutory provisions. Yet, the image of disunion and lack of common direction persisted, with coalition partners recurrently making contradictory statements on government actions and voicing non-trivial policy discrepancies. A sense of political instability, in addition to other factors, such as a decrease in voter turnout rates, continued to feed a perception of growing disaffection among Catalan citizens, which had already brought about a lively public debate during the final stages of the previous term (see Vallès 2008).

However, the election of 2010 was to be marked by two issues fairly beyond the direct control of the tripartite. First and foremost was the economy. The global financial crisis, coupled with the collapse of the national housing bubble, caused Spain severe economic hardship. After 15 years of continuous growth, the country officially entered recession at the end of 2008. With an unemployment rate of around 20 per cent (the highest in the Eurozone, more than double the European Union [EU] average) and a massive budget deficit, and under the threatening menace of economic intervention after the Greek debt crisis, Spain's Socialist government faced increasing pressure from the markets and the EU to take resolute action. In May 2010, Prime Minister José Luis Rodríguez Zapatero, who was admittedly late in recognising the seriousness of the economic situation, introduced an unprecedented programme of cuts in public spending, intended to reduce the deficit. The austerity package, which included a five per cent wage cut for civil servants and the freeze of all but the smallest pensions, suggested a radical turn in the government's social policies. Shortly thereafter, in a further attempt to revive the economy and calm the markets, the government passed the reform of labour laws. Major trade unions responded by calling for a general strike, the first in eight years, which took place just months before the regional election. Meanwhile, the popularity of the Socialist government and its prime minister entered a steady decline as the public's confidence in the country's economic situation plummeted to its lowest point in recent history.

The other major event with potential consequences for the election was the Constitutional Court's ruling on the Statute of Autonomy. A modified regional charter had been approved in 2006 after long and exhausting negotiations between Catalan parties and parties in the national congress, mainly the PSOE. Recognising the singularity and national status of Catalonia, the new text sought to significantly advance the region's self-government. Shaped as an actual constitution, its main goals were: (1) to consolidate and shield the region's level of competences; (2) to redefine Catalonia's relationship with Spain's central government, mainly through the establishment of bilateral relations and the participation of the Catalan government in Spanish institutions and decisions that affected the regional competences; (3) to achieve fairer sharing of financial resources; and (4) to elevate to statutory rank the linguistic policy previously established by ordinary laws (Barceló, Bernardí & Vintró

2010). The ambitious bill encountered fierce opposition from the PP, whose leaders believed that the new statute might eventually undermine national unity. Hence, once ratified, the PP parliamentary group in the lower house challenged the constitutionality of the bill's statutory provisions. Other, more specific appeals were filed by the Spanish Ombudsman and various autonomous communities.

For the first time since the establishment of democracy in Spain, the Constitutional Court had to deal with a dispute over the statute of an autonomous community that had acceded to full autonomy via the accelerated procedure devised in the Spanish constitution for 'historical communities' and that, by law, had been submitted to referendum after being approved by regional and national legislatures. The judges, repeatedly subjected to pressure from both sides and themselves split into left and right wings of roughly equal sizes, found it difficult and extremely time-consuming to reach a decision. However, it soon became apparent that the Court was not going to ratify the constitutionality of the whole statute and that significant parts of it might be suspended. After months of anticipation, recurrent press leaks, and tense political debate, the judges finally announced, in June of 2010, their decision on the appeal initiated by the PP, with their full judgment to be released a few days later. At first glance, the statute did not appear to be seriously damaged, as only 14 of its more than 200 articles were deemed not in accordance with the constitution, while 27 were imposed an interpretation in conformity with it; most of the disputes in the appeal were rejected. Indeed, the Court refrained from overturning numerous articles. Instead, it produced an extensive and largely interpretive judgment, but, in doing so, it ended up seriously narrowing the reading of substantial parts of the law, to the extent that it often thwarted the intentions of the parties behind the bill. Core elements of long-established regional policies were affected, such as those dealing with the use of the Catalan language as the vehicular language in Catalonian education. Symbolic issues, such as the (legally inconsequential) reference to Catalonia as a 'nation' in the charter preamble, were also affected.

The Court's decision was received with outrage by the majority of Catalan political forces, which interpreted it as restrictive and manipulative and even as a step back in the process of territorial decentralisation. On 10 July, hundreds of thousands of protesters marched against the ruling in the streets of Barcelona, under the slogan 'We are a nation. We decide.' The demonstration was supported by the PSC, CiU, ERC, ICV, and a whole host of social and cultural organisations and prominent public figures—including President Montilla.

This was the last unitary act to be taken by the political parties that seven years earlier had joined efforts to reform the statute. From then on, they openly pursued divergent strategies on the territorial issue, as, in fact, had been the case since the Spanish parliament passed the new regional charter. In this new situation, it seemed advisable for parties to momentarily push the matter into the background. For one thing, there was a perception that the political tension unleashed had been harmful for the actors involved and fatiguing for the public, which, for the most part, appeared to be concerned chiefly about the economic crisis. Survey data collected before the election show that only 13 per cent of respondents mentioned either self-government or the related issue of regional funding as one of the region's two most important problems, while unemployment or the economy was named by 90 per cent.[1] Furthermore, the situation at the central level had reached a kind of deadlock that prevented parties from delineating their strategies. In the absence of formal institutions of intergovernmental relations, the territorial model's evolution has been negotiated mainly through bilateral agreements between the major state-wide parties or between these and non-state-wide parties, in exchange for support in the Spanish parliament (Muro 2009). By the time of the Catalan election, the popularity of Zapatero's government was at its lowest level since the Socialists returned to power in 2004, and the PP had clearly taken the lead in the polls. This set the stage for significant alterations to the political picture after the upcoming general election, which was to be held in a little over a year. All of the above might explain why the statute affair and the debate on self-government played a diminished role during the campaign.

The Parties and the Campaign

The 2010 election campaign was characterised by low intensity. The result was a foregone conclusion, and only some specifics remained unknown. Well in advance of the contest, the polls predicted a certain win for CiU, and it was assumed that the main opposition party would return to power, although it was not clear if it would require parliamentary support from other forces. On the other hand, the re-formation of a tripartite government was deemed unfeasible, as all forecasts pointed to a pronounced decrease in support for its members. Aware of the downward trend in sympathy for the alliance among voters, the two main partners in the alliance, the PSC and ERC, openly ruled out the possibility of repeating the tripartite formula after the election, even in the unlikely event that they could gather a sufficient number of seats. Hence, the campaign lacked the uncertainty and excitement that had characterised recent contests.

In view of election forecasts, CiU dismissed any possibility of joining a post-electoral alliance to get into office, and its leading candidate, Artur Mas, asked voters to grant the party a sufficient majority to govern on its own. The nationalists' campaign aimed at gathering the support of disillusioned tripartite voters by projecting an image of unity, responsibility, and good sense that stood in contrast with the impression of confusion and endless quarrelling that the incumbent coalition presented. Consequently, its campaign message emphasised its status as a virtual governing party, focusing on the economic crisis and the steps necessary to reduce public spending, while announcing the abolition of some of the most unpopular measures taken by the tripartite, such as the inheritance tax and speed limits on the highway access to Barcelona.

A smart intersection between concern for the economy and the party's natural accent on the centre–periphery dimension, CiU's major proposal was its pledge to negotiate a new financing system for the region. The imbalance between Catalonia's contributions to tax revenue and public funds received from the state—a negative difference that, according to official estimates, might amount to between 6.4 and 8.7 per cent of Catalonia's gross domestic product (Instituto de Estudios Fiscales 2008)—has often been seen as an unfair burden on the economic growth of the region, whose public deficit is currently the second highest of all autonomous communities. Indeed, the fiscal imbalance has become one of the main arguments used by Catalan political elites to advocate for greater autonomy or straight secession. CiU aspired to a financing system similar to the ones applied in the Basque provinces and Navarre (known as *concierto* and *convenio*, respectively). On the basis of historic rights (*fueros*) acknowledged in the constitution, these regions are granted large taxation powers, to the extent that they are responsible for the legislation and collection of most taxes, with some minor restrictions, while the state receives an annual quota in payment for the public services that it still provides in those territories. By contrast, under the common financing system applicable to other communities, regional budgets depend, for the most part, on the transfer of funds from the state, which retains control over taxation. Moderate nationalists envisioned a scenario in which a significantly higher level of financial autonomy would be negotiated, in exchange for parliamentary support of a minority government in Madrid. The particulars of the projected scheme, though, were never specified, beyond a general reference to the *foral* system. The proposal nonetheless allowed CiU to send the message that their national objectives transcended those of the new regional charter and the Spanish constitution, but that their intention in the short term, after the traumatic experience of statutory reform, was to revisit the strategy of bilateral negotiation that former Catalan president Jordi Pujol had sought rather successfully before the arrival of the tripartite government.

Members of the incumbent coalition faced the campaign from a more defensive stance. Two terms in office had eroded not only the basis of the coalition, but also the parties' internal unity. More than ever, the statutory process and its aftermath made apparent the tension between the Socialists' allegiance to the PSOE and its constituency, on the one hand, and their historical commitment to the advancement of self-government in Catalonia, on the other. Prominent Socialists voiced the need to reinforce their party's independence from its state-wide counterpart, mainly by challenging group discipline in the national congress or even forming their own parliamentary group—as, in fact, they had done during their first (1977–79) and second (1979–82) legislative terms. Both its partners in government and CiU visibly encouraged movements in this direction, in order to increase pressure on the central government to accept their demands. At the same time, the PSOE was glad to see the PSC moving away from ERC's radical nationalists—as alliance with ERC was perceived as harmful to the PSC's competition with the rising PP for the national vote—and sympathised with the idea of CiU returning to power, since this would add moderate nationalists to their list of potential allies for a minority government in Madrid. During the campaign, the PSC stuck with the new statute while trying to restore the parts that were cut by the Constitutional Court ruling—a moderate stance that sought to highlight the 'radicalisation' of the moderate nationalists and the Socialists' dissociation from ERC.

All in all, the PSC projected an impression of weakness and confusion. Unresolved issues within the party may have further weakened the authority of its leader, whose image had always paled in comparison with that of Pasqual Maragall, his immediate predecessor. Shortly before the election, Montilla announced that he would not run again for the presidency of the Generalitat, thus paving the way for a change in the party's direction.

The experience of governing proved to be much more devastating for ERC. As the flagship of the heterogeneous, convulsive Catalan secessionist movement, ERC sparked much controversy when it made the pragmatic decision to join the tripartite coalition. Against the will of some significant sectors, the major sponsor of the alliance, ERC leader Josep-Lluís Carod-Rovira, had advocated for a gradual path to independence and greater emphasis on the party's leftist element. The serious setback suffered in the general election of 2008, when ERC lost more than half its seats in the lower house of parliament, eventually unleashed the internal divisions that had barely been contained during the preceding years, leaving the leadership to reshuffle and change its policies. After a stormy congress, Carod-Rovira was marginalised in the party's central office, and a new leader, Joan Puigcercós, replaced his moderate strategy with a more aggressive secessionist platform. Other party figures who had levelled harsh criticism at Carod-Rovira's pragmatic line left the alliance soon afterwards. Joan Carretero, a former minister in the first tripartite administration, founded a new party, Reagrupament Independentista (RI, Pro-Independence Regrouping). Another candidate for ERC's leadership, Uriel Bertran, joined Solidaritat Catalana per la Independència (SI, Catalan Solidarity for Independence), the new secessionist party led by Joan Laporta.

A newcomer to politics, Laporta had acquired great notoriety as the president of Barcelona's football club (arguably the most prominent social institution in Catalonia and a deeply felt symbol of Catalan culture and identity) during its most successful era to date. Indeed, according to survey data collected prior to the contest, his name recognition was the same as that of CiU's leader and only below that of President Montilla, hence surpassing the candidates of all other parties already with seats in the regional parliament.[2] SI formed just a few months before the election as a coalition of ideologically diverse parties that had as their common purpose the formation of a Catalan state. The party's rhetoric focused almost exclusively on economic matters: Secession would put an end to 'fiscal plundering' and leave the region in a better position to overcome the crisis. Secession was the single issue in SI's legislative agenda, and it made its commitment to a unilateral declaration of independence the sine qua non requirement for its parliamentary support. In view of their similar interests and the uncertainty of their getting representation, RI and SI considered the possibility of forming an electoral alliance but eventually failed to reach an agreement.

Meanwhile, the separatist movement, which appeared to be on the rise, showed further signs of vitality.[3] Between September 2009 and June 2010, hundreds of small to mid-sized municipalities held informal, non-binding independence referendums arranged by civic organisations and generally supported by ERC, but also by local party representatives from Convergència Democràtica de Catalunya (CDC, Democratic Convergence of Catalonia, the main partner in the CiU coalition) and ICV. In this increasingly competitive context, ERC campaigned on an overtly pro-independence platform and sought to capitalise on the mobilisation of the secessionist camp by standing up for calls for a regional referendum to be held during the following term, while also advocating for a new financing arrangement along the lines of systems used in the *foral* regions.

ICV remained the most passionate champion of the tripartite's governance legacy, as well as the only one of its members to advocate for its continuity in the future, even if its experience in office had not been devoid of problems and controversy. In 2006, the eco-socialists took charge of the Department of the Interior, becoming responsible for the security policy of the Catalan government in a critical stage in the territorial deployment of the regional police. This represented a risky challenge for a party that had a known pacifist standing but was willing to prove its capability in a crucial area and present itself as something more than a fringe force. Indeed, ICV's innovative policies encountered fierce criticism from the opposition, damaging the reputation of Joan Saura, the party leader responsible for the Department of the Interior, who later announced that he would not run for election. Headed by Joan Herrera, a younger but experienced leader who, until then, had served as the party's representative in the lower house of the national parliament, ICV's campaign was mainly devoted to discussing proposals meant to counter the social consequences of the recession.

There were also significant changes at the top of the PP's list, as Alicia Sánchez Camacho had been recently put in charge of regional direction, thus ending a series of disagreements with the party's central office. Without setting aside their rhetoric in defence of Spanish identity and against Catalan nationalism—visible, for instance, in their advocacy for parents' right to choose the vehicular language used in their children's schools, as well as in their stated intention to repeal the recently approved law to ban bullfighting in Catalonia—the conservatives prioritised the adoption of the liberal recipe for economic recovery and the implementation of a tough policy to fight illegal immigration. Their discourse on the latter issue, heavily criticised for linking immigrants to delinquency, was often interpreted as an effort to take advantage of public fears in the context of rising economic insecurity. It also came shortly after several Catalan city councils were the first in Spain to ban the burqa, the niqab, and other face-covering garments in public buildings. The populist Plataforma per Catalunya (PxC, Platform for Catalonia), a xenophobic, radical-right party, had real chances of attaining representation in the Catalan parliament, after some notable success in the two preceding local elections (see Pardos-Prado & Molins 2009).

The young Ciutadans–Partido de la Ciudadanía (C-PC, Citizens, Party of Citizenship), born in the wake of the polarisation along the centre–periphery cleavage as an instrument to counter the nationalism of the Catalan political establishment, wanted to consolidate its support and at least maintain the representation it had obtained in 2006 (Lago, Montero & Torcal 2007; Pallarés & Muñoz 2008). C-PC had experienced internal difficulties during its first years in office, particularly after an erratic decision to run for the European Parliament as part of a right-wing Eurosceptic alliance caused two of its three representatives in the Catalan chamber to leave the party. By the time of the election, though, Albert Rivera's C-PC had already regained internal unity. Their message revolved around the 'excesses' of the linguistic policies undertaken by the tripartite and its predecessors to promote the use of Catalan in education and commerce, while persistently putting the spotlight on the recently revealed corruption cases involving both CiU and PSC members.

The Results

In spite of politicians' publicised fears of yet another episode of voter demobilisation, abstention decreased by three points in the 2010 election, compared with 2006, reaching a level of 41.2 per cent (see Table 1). The fact that turnout grew moderately as competitiveness decreased gives us a hint of the importance of national-level factors in the election. More than to features specific to the regional context, the slight fall in abstention may have responded to rising dissatisfaction with the national political situation caused by the economic crisis. Previous work on electoral participation in Spain has consistently found that increases in the aggregate level of dissatisfaction tend to result in higher turnout rates, suggesting that political and economic crises mobilise discontent voters to punish incumbents' poor performance to a greater extent than they have an alienating effect in segments of the electorate (Boix & Riba 2000; Font & Rico 2005).

Results, for the most part, confirmed expectations. All three incumbents experienced a decline in support, in both absolute and relative numbers. With a loss of more than

Table 1 Results of the 2010 and 2006 Regional Elections and the 2008 General Election in Catalonia

	2010 regional election			2006 regional election			2008 general election		
	Votes	%	Seats	Votes	%	Seats	Votes	%	Seats
CiU	1,202,830	38.4	62	935,756	31.5	48	779,425	20.9	10
PSC	575,233	18.4	28	796,173	26.8	37	1,689,911	45.4	25
PP	387,066	12.4	18	316,222	10.7	14	610,473	16.4	8
ICV–EUiA	230,824	7.4	10	282,693	9.5	12	183,338	4.9	1
ERC	219,173	7.0	10	416,355	14.0	21	291,532	7.8	3
C-PC	106,154	3.4	3	89,840	3.0	3	27,512	0.7	
SI	102,921	3.3	4						
Other	214,444	6.9		71,251	2.4		83,956	2.3	
Blank	91,631	2.9		60,244	2.0		57,274	1.5	
Null	22,354	0.7		13,574	0.5		19,939	0.5	
Abstention	2,211,058	41.2		2,339,166	44.0		1,581,549	29.7	
Total	5,363,688		135	5,321,274		135	5,324,909		47

Source: Departament de Governació i Relacions Institucionals (Generalitat de Catalunya) and Ministerio del Interior.

200,000 votes and nine seats in parliament, the Socialists' share sank below one-fifth—their lowest level ever in Catalonia. Though ERC's decline was similar in proportion, the mechanics of the electoral law produced a more devastating effect on its parliamentary representation. ERC's loss was particularly pronounced in the less-populated territories where it has traditionally obtained better results—the three districts of smaller magnitude that, due to the malapportionment of the electoral system, get a surplus of representation compared with the province of Barcelona. The number of seats occupied by the radical nationalists was more than halved, ERC becoming not the third, but the fifth, political force in the region. Compared with that of its coalition partners, ICV's marginal decrease in support, as well as its loss of two seats, was received as good news in party headquarters.

The tripartite's collapse accentuated CiU's sense of victory. Indeed, the moderate nationalists' advantage over the Socialists was larger than in any previous election. Although they remained six seats away from an absolute majority, their share of the vote returned to pre-tripartite levels, and the unequivocal defeat of the incumbent forces secured them a safe return to power after seven years in the wilderness. The other opposition parties had reasons to rejoice, too. By attaining representation and climbing to third place, the PP was able to recover a long-awaited position of influence in Catalan politics and feed expectations that if it could replicate the rising trend at the national level it could return to central government. C-PC, with consolidated support, managed to maintain representation—thus providing further evidence for the argument that there was a niche in the Catalan electorate that traditional parties had failed to fill.

One of the election's biggest surprises was the arrival in parliament of the pro-independence SI. It even surpassed C-PC in number of seats, despite the latter obtaining a slightly higher share of the vote, by virtue of the disproportionate weight of the Girona district, where the separatists performed best. For the second consecutive time, a new party entered the Catalan parliament, thus raising to seven the total number of parties with seats in the chamber. On top of that, the 2010 election confirmed the momentum experienced by new and small contenders in the regional electoral arena. Although it did not meet expectations, RI fared quite well in some areas, and the radical-right PxC obtained remarkable results, ending as the most successful party not voted into parliament. Indeed, the supply of political candidates was unprecedented in this race, with as many as 39 parties competing in at least one district (the previous record was 23). More significantly, popular support for extra-parliamentary parties increased from 5.4 per cent to 6.9 per cent (from 2.4 to 3.2 per cent, if we exclude the new parties that won seats for the first time), the largest proportion since the inaugural election of 1980.

These figures highlight a recent trend of electoral unsteadiness which, though it so far has been restricted to a minor segment of voters, requires at least some tentative explanation. Several interpretations suggest themselves. To begin, C-PC's successful attempt to get representation may have had a pull effect, as it proved to potential contenders, as well as voters themselves, that new parties have a real chance of entering parliament. Given the combination of a moderately large chamber (135 seats), a low number of districts (four, their magnitude currently ranging from 15 to 85), and a low legal threshold (three per cent at the district level), the electoral system used in the Catalan regional elections produces fairly proportional outcomes and favours the representation of small parties. In 2006, C-PC only needed to gather 3.5 per cent of the vote to win three seats in Barcelona; in 2010, SI managed to get the same number with a share of just three per cent and had enough, with 4.8 per cent of the vote, to win one seat in Girona.

More substantively, it must be pointed out that the newly elected parties (C-PC and SI) are located at opposite extremes of the territorial/identity issue, which clearly suggests that polarisation along this dimension—which commenced following the controversial second administration of José María Aznar and the formation of the tripartite government and was later fuelled by debate on the reform of the regional charter and eventually by the Constitutional Court's ruling—fostered the fragmentation of the political field on each side. This was particularly the case in the separatists' camp, where ERC had to face increasing competition from two emerging parties.

On the other hand, new parties, by their very nature, tend to display an anti-establishment attitude. In spite of their obvious differences, traces of anti-party rhetoric are clearly discernible in the discourse of both C-PC and SI, as well as in that of many of the minor candidates who failed to get representation. Their increased support thus suggests a growing sense of discontent with traditional parties among the Catalan public. The rise of the blank vote provides further evidence of this trend. In 2010, voters cast more than 90,000 blank ballots, 2.9 per cent of the valid vote, which again marks an all-time high and corroborates a pattern that was already visible in the previous election. Null votes were also on the rise, peaking at 0.7 per cent of ballots cast. The recent wave of protest voting may be due to factors specific to the regional arena, such as traditional parties' failure to meet some of the most salient demands of the Catalan electorate, as suggested by Lago, Montero, and Torcal (2007). It may reflect, at the same time, a more diffuse trend of growing disaffection with established political institutions, as has been detected in most contemporary democracies (Vallès 2008). Finally, it can be argued that concern about the economy and corresponding dissatisfaction with the central government's response to the crisis have reinforced, in the context of a 'second-order' arena, a tendency towards manifest protest in response to national-level events. It is to an examination of the importance of the latter factor that I turn in the next section.

A Multilevel Account

How can we explain the changes observed in voting patterns? In particular, what factors account for the tripartite's defeat and the subsequent upsurge of the moderate nationalists? And what do the results of the 2010 race tell us, from the wider perspective of previous research, about electoral competition and voter behaviour in

Catalonia? At face value, the long process of statutory reform and its later consequences, which became the most salient and controversial issues under the tripartite's rule, may have played a major role in the election's outcome. Notwithstanding the likely influence of that, however, regional elections are generally better understood as the confluence of circumstances at various levels of government. National forces, in particular, seem to have had a larger impact than in preceding elections, triggering underlying and ongoing regional dynamics.

Electoral competition in Catalonia is structured along a left–right dimension, which is the basic dimension of competition at the state level, and a centre–periphery or national identity dimension, which, to a varying degree, is specific to some Spanish regions. These cross-cutting dimensions organise voters' basic political orientations and behaviours, while giving rise to a remarkably distinctive party system, which is significantly more fragmented than the one in place at the national level, as the two largest state-wide forces, the Socialists and the conservatives, must compete with non-state-wide parties, with special emphasis on territorial issues (Font, Pallarés & Serra 1999; Pallarés & Keating 2003). Further, the Socialists are represented by the PSC (a party on its own, federated to the PSOE but traditionally more receptive to regionalist demands than its national counterpart) and have CiU as their main contender, while the PP stands as a minor alternative. Regular differences are observed in electoral results at different levels of government, as seen in Figure 1. Non-state-wide parties perform systematically better in regional elections than they do in general elections. This is certainly the case for the main Catalan nationalist forces, CiU and ERC, but the same pattern is also visible in C-PC's short history at the polls (see Table 1). By contrast, national elections appear to be a more favourable environment for the two largest state-wide parties. As a result, the Socialists have obtained a plurality of the votes in every national election since 1977, while CiU has led the PSC in all regional elections, except in 1999, when it got a majority of seats but lagged behind, by a short margin, in popular support.

These systematic differences have been explained as the result of two related processes. On the one hand, some parties happen to be more severely affected by so-called 'differential abstention', that is, the lower turnout rates registered in regional elections than in national elections, a phenomenon that arises with remarkable strength in Catalonia (Font, Contreras & Rico 1998; Riba 2000). State-wide parties, particularly the PSC, have more difficulty mobilising support for these elections than for general elections. On the other hand, research has detected that a noticeable proportion of voters shift their support between national and regional elections, opting for state-wide parties in the former and non-state-wide alternatives in the latter. The parties most affected by this 'dual voting' behaviour are the PSC and the PP, which lose some of their voters to CiU and, to a lesser extent, ERC (Font & Montero 1991; Riba 2000).

It has been argued that the comparative advantage of non-state-wide (specifically nationalist and regionalist) parties in regional elections stems, in part, from their ability to present themselves as better instruments for channelling the region's

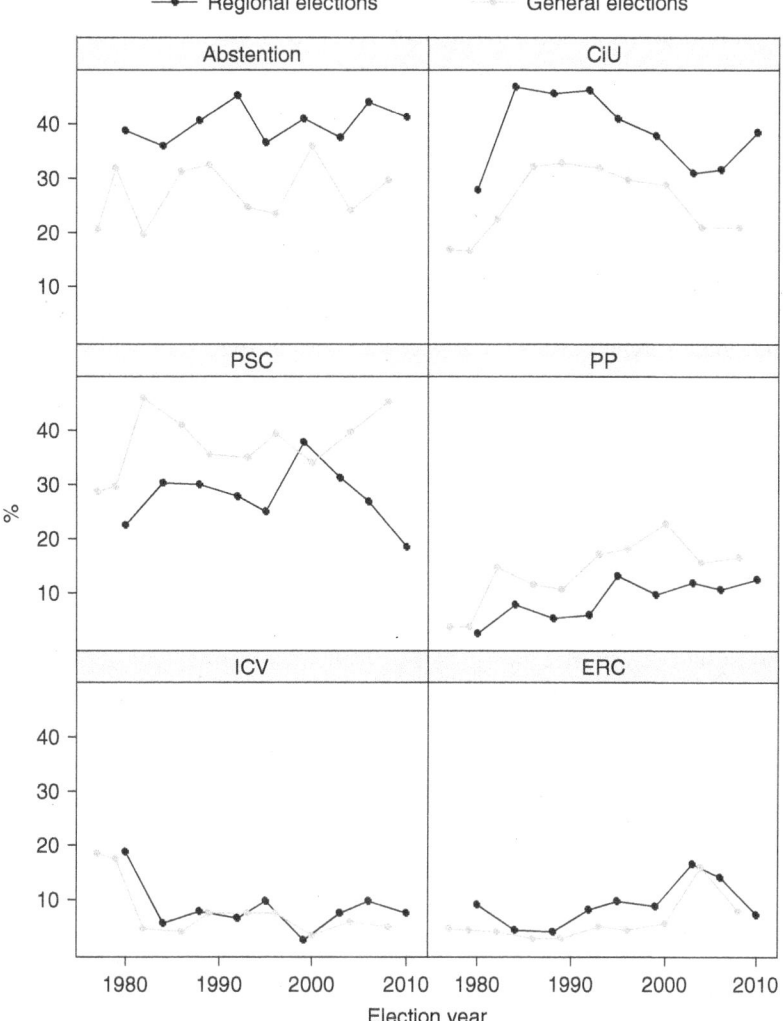

Figure 1 Evolution of electoral abstention and party vote shares in regional and general elections in Catalonia.
Source: Departament de Governació i Relacions Institucionals (Generalitat de Catalunya) and Ministerio del Interior.

demands and promoting its interests (Pallarés, Montero & Llera 1997). Indeed, their very origin is linked to their identification with the region and their recognition and defence of its singular identity, and they can also claim, more convincingly than statewide parties, their independence from any organisation based outside the regional territory. CiU is the party that has most successfully cultivated its image as a champion of the Catalan cause and benefited from this image in elections. Under the leadership of Jordi Pujol, the president of the Generalitat from 1980 to 2003, the moderate nationalists managed to obtain valuable advances in regional autonomy, in exchange for their support in the national parliament. As noted above, the gradual definition of the Spanish territorial model has, to a significant extent, depended on political agreements reached in a multilevel setting that often involves non-state-wide parties. The noticeable role that CiU, by virtue of its pivotal ability to build parliamentary majorities in Madrid, played in such agreements undoubtedly won the nationalists important symbolic rewards from the Catalan electorate.

However, CiU's image suffered after the dramatic turn that occurred during its last term in office, when the absolute majority that the PP attained in Madrid allowed it to do without the support that CiU had provided between 1996 and 2000, while the nationalists had to rely on the conservatives to sustain their minority government in the regional chamber. Released from dependence on the CiU, Aznar's second government developed a marked nationalistic profile, announcing its resolve to bring the devolution process to a halt after the transfers already agreed upon had been completed, voicing recurrent criticism of the peripheral nationalists' demands, and heightening its defence of Spanish identity (Santamaría 2004). Compelled to mute its disagreement, CiU's image as the advocate of regional interests gradually eroded. Meanwhile, the coalition of left-wing parties emerged as a viable alternative and challenged the moderate nationalists' reputation with its plan to reform the statute, which was publicly supported by the PSOE's leader. As seen in Table 2, the percentage of voters naming CiU as the party that best defends the interests of Catalonia remained well above that of any other political force during the 1990s; while it enjoyed an advantageous position vis-à-vis the party in central government, its authority started to decrease towards the turn of the century, as circumstances changed, and continued falling throughout the tripartite era. By contrast, the coalition's partners, chiefly ERC and, later, the PSC, improved their respective territorial standings, albeit to a more limited extent than CiU's diminished. The data for 2010, collected just before the November election, show a trend reversal. This time, the PSC and ERC experienced a sharp decline that by no means resulted in significant gains by CiU or any other party—which indicates that the party system, as a whole, was perceived as less capable of defending the region's interests than it had been previously. According to these data,

Table 2 Party that Best Defends the Interests of Catalonia, 1992–2010 (per cent)

	1992	1999	2001	2003	2006	2010
CiU	47	47	42	36	28	30
PSC	15	16	17	17	22	13
ERC	8	7	12	13	16	11
PP	1	3	3	5	3	3
ICV	4	3	2	5	5	4
C-PC						2
Observations	2,470	3,590	2,777	3,571	1,986	2,966

Source: CIS surveys no. 2033, 2373, 2410, 2543, 2656, and 2852.

then, the process that led to the tripartite government, statute reform, and the Court's ruling left the territorial images of the coalition partners much as they were before it all began. On the other hand, CiU's image was seriously damaged, and even though the party managed to recover the level of electoral support that it enjoyed in 1999, voters' confidence in its ability to push regional interests, if still unmatched, remained far below what it had been in prior years.

As I suggested above, there are reasons to think that, alongside regional dynamics, factors operating at the national level had a profound effect on the vote, to the extent that they may have acted as a catalyst for the influence of variables located on a more specific level. The subordination of second-order elections to the situation in the national arena is a well-established assumption of the second-order election model (Reif & Schmitt 1980; van der Eijk & Franklin 1996), and previous research has confirmed its validity for the analysis of regional elections in Spain (Pallarés 2008). However, scholars have also found that, as in fact is the case at hand, some of the model's predictions can be disrupted under certain circumstances—namely, the presence of a strong territorial dimension of political competition and the existence of relevant non-state-wide parties (Jeffery & Hough 2003; Pallarés & Keating 2003; Wyn Jones & Scully 2006). Yet, the influence of the situation in the first-order arena is not necessarily a fixed trait of a given regional setting, but can be enhanced (or depressed) as the result of changes in political context.

At the time of the 2010 election, several factors converged to heighten the ascendancy of first-order factors. First, the country was going through an economic recession that had devastating consequences and whose end was not foreseen in the near future. As shown in Figure 2, evaluations of the national economic situation were almost unanimously negative, as those perceiving it as 'bad' or 'very bad' surpassed those perceiving it as 'good' or 'very good' by more than 70 percentage points.[4] Given that the responsibility for major macroeconomic policy decisions is ascribed to the central government, it can be deduced that this state of affairs naturally directed the electorate's attention towards national-level politics. Second, the Socialists held the premiership of both the central government and the Generalitat. A number of studies have found that the effects of central government approval extend to the party of the incumbent at other levels of governance (e.g., Simon, Ostrom & Marra 1991; Tufte 1975; for the Spanish case, see Aguilar & Sánchez-Cuenca 2007), and research on United States (US) elections provides some evidence that national factors are enhanced in elections involving in-party incumbents, that is, incumbents of the central government's party (Hibbing & Alford 1981; Koch 2000). Further, after approval of the statute reform produced tensions between the PSC and the PSOE, the latter brought about Pasqual Maragall's replacement as leader of the Catalan Socialists by José Montilla, who, since 2004, had served as minister of industry in the Zapatero administration and was considered closer to the Spanish Socialists. By the same token, the tripartite alliance in Catalonia may have worked to the disadvantage of ERC and ICV, who, for a substantial part of the term, had also provided parliamentary support to the PSOE in Madrid. Indeed, Figure 2 shows that Catalan voters' evaluations of the

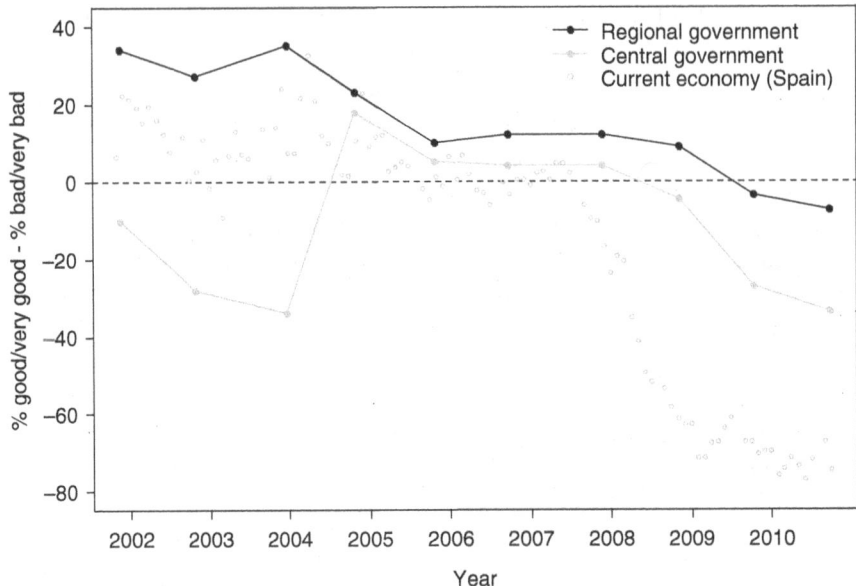

Figure 2 Evaluations of the regional and central governments in Catalonia and perceptions of the current economy in Spain.
Source: Annual ICPS opinion surveys (government evaluations) and monthly surveys of the CIS (perceptions of the economy).

regional and central governments, which had followed different paths while CiU was in power, became closely linked when the Socialists took control of both executives. The chart also suggests that economic perceptions affected approval at both levels, though the harm done by the failing economy to national incumbents was considerably higher than the harm done to regional incumbents. As a matter of fact, just before the election, opinions on national performance were much more negative than opinions on regional performance—26 points more negative, according to our index, a far from negligible difference that would have affected the final outcome, depending on the importance attached to each dimension in voters' decisions. Finally, it must be noted that the 2010 election was the first to be held after the central government announced its package of cost-cutting measures and unveiled the no-less-controversial labour market reform plan that led to the September general strike. The forthcoming general election was still distant, and hence the regional contest became a strategic opportunity for disappointed voters to voice their disagreement in protest at the incumbent's policy to address the crisis.

The public's attention, then, was focused on the first-order arena, and a connection could be easily established between the Socialist administration and the Catalan government. Consequently, it can be reasonably expected that, in this particular election, evaluations of the central government had as much of an impact on voters' support of Catalan incumbents as did evaluations of the regional government.

Extending this rationale, by contrast, we should expect the influence of central government approval to be outweighed by the influence of regional government approval in other regional elections, such as the immediately preceding race of 2006, where some, but not all, of the same favourable circumstances concurred.

In order to test this assertion empirically, a series of simple models of government support in the 2006 and 2010 regional elections were estimated. I draw on individual-level data from two surveys conducted by the Institut de Ciències Polítiques i Socials (ICPS), both with regionally representative samples, shortly before the respective election.[5] Two models are estimated for each year. In the first, the dependent variable is vote intention, coded 1 if the respondent intended to vote for one of the incumbent parties (the PSC, ERC, or ICV), 0 if the respondent were going to vote for any other party. In the second model, the dependent variable is defection from the tripartite, coded 1 if the respondent voted for one of the coalition members in the previous regional election but did not intend to do the same in 2010 (either because they were going to support another party or because they intended to abstain), 0 if the respondent maintained their support for any of the incumbent parties.[6] The same four factors are included in each model: evaluations of the regional and central government performance, measured on a five-point scale, ranging from 'very bad' to 'very good'; a dummy variable indicating the party viewed as best defending the interests of Catalans, scored 1 if the respondent named any of the tripartite partners, 0 otherwise; and self-placement on an 11-point left–right scale. All predictors are re-scaled to range from 0 to 1. Government evaluation and party 'territorial' image should display a positive relationship with incumbent voting and a negative relationship with incumbent defection. According to my hypothesis, central government approval is expected to have a higher impact in the 2010 model than in the 2006 model. Similarly, the impact of regional government approval is expected to decrease in 2010 compared with the previous election. Since ideology is the element that distinguished the tripartite from the main opposition parties, left–right placement ought to have a positive impact on the first set of models and a negative impact on the second.

The results of the analysis, reported in Table 3, provide strong support for the hypothesis. Looking first at the voting models, central government performance has a significant impact in the 2010 election, but not in the 2006 election. Somehow surprisingly, the opposite is true for regional government evaluations: estimates show no effect at all on vote intention in 2010 and a positive effect in the preceding election. These results are replicated when defection is used as the dependent variable; that is, only central government approval is found to affect the probability of defection from the tripartite in 2010, while only regional government approval influences it in 2006. The effects predicted by the models are sizeable. Holding all other variables at their mean values, the probability of voting for the incumbent parties in 2010 increases from 18 per cent, if central government performance is judged to be 'very bad', to 88 per cent, if it is considered 'very good', while the probability of defection from the tripartite is 56 per cent when voters give central government the lowest rating and only two per cent when they give it the highest. The predicted impact of Catalan

Table 3 Determinants of Incumbent Vote and Defection in the 2006 and 2010 Regional Elections

	Vote for incumbent		Defection from incumbent	
	2010	2006	2010	2006
Left–right ideology	−5.34***	−6.58***	3.10***	5.11***
	(0.58)	(0.69)	(0.80)	(1.22)
Party best defends Catalan interests	2.91***	3.23***	−2.35***	−3.38***
	(0.21)	(0.22)	(0.26)	(0.43)
Catalan government evaluation	−0.08	1.09+	−0.34	−2.71**
	(0.54)	(0.58)	(0.72)	(1.00)
Central government evaluation	3.49***	0.71	−4.37***	1.06
	(0.55)	(0.55)	(0.79)	(0.99)
Constant	−0.51+	0.74+	0.85*	−1.68**
	(0.30)	(0.38)	(0.37)	(0.60)
Likelihood Ratio χ^2 (4 d.f.)	625.283***	718.133***	207.532***	145.06***
Pseudo R^2	0.45	0.54	0.32	0.40
Observations	922	1,018	475	603

Note: Logit regression coefficients, with standard errors in parentheses.
$^+ p < 0.1$, $^* p < 0.05$, $^{**} p < 0.01$, $^{***} p < 0.001$.
Source: ICPS 2006 and 2010 surveys.

government evaluations in the 2006 elections is also substantial, though more limited, as it produces a maximum difference of 20 percentage points in the probability of voting for the tripartite and a maximum difference of eight points in the probability of defection. Finally, the coefficients for ideology and territorial party image are in the expected direction. There is some indication that, even if both factors remain highly consequential, their effect was slightly reduced in 2010, which tends to confirm the idea that political context and short-term considerations played an exceptional role in this election.[7]

Conclusions

CiU's leader, Artur Mas, was elected president of the Catalan government with the help of the Socialists' abstention on a second ballot in parliament. As envisaged during the election campaign, the centre-right nationalists did not forge an enduring deal to support their minority government in the chamber, but tried to enact policies by way of alternative agreements with opposition parties. For some, electoral failure had visible effects. José Montilla, who had already stepped down as PSC's leader, resigned his seat in parliament, while Joan Puigcercós was forced to rule out running for ERC's leadership in the upcoming party congress. Hence, in the short term, the parties' ability to develop effective opposition seems compromised until internal divisions are overcome and reshuffling is completed. In the longer run, though, the evolution of political competition in Catalonia will hardly be defined until the situation in the national arena becomes clearer over the next few years. Once in office, Mas revealingly expressed his hope that the PP would not win a majority in the upcoming general election, adding that only a PSOE reaction could prevent that from happening (*La Vanguardia* 2010). Certainly, the dynamics of Catalan politics cannot be fully comprehended unless their multilevel character is taken into account.

In this paper, I have argued that the substantial decrease in support for the incumbent coalition that led CiU back to power was, to a large extent, a consequence of the situation in the first-order arena. As shown in the analysis of the tripartite vote, the effect of central government evaluations in 2010, unlike in the previous election, clearly outweighed the effect of regional government evaluations. This somehow implies that the public's discontent with national incumbents would not have been so detrimental for the tripartite had voters attached the same weight to first-order considerations as they had in 2006. On the other hand, the survey data examined suggest that CiU's decline, which also began as the consequence of a particular multilevel configuration, was accompanied by the erosion of its image as the party best defending the region's interests—a dimension on which traditionally lay much of the party's differential advantage in regional elections. Although the nationalists recently recovered some ground on this territorial dimension, they still remain far from the position they enjoyed before the tripartite governments. Again, the extent to which they can rebuild that image will likely depend on the shape of the next national government.

The analysis presented in this paper has unveiled stark differences in the weight of national and regional performance evaluations across consecutive elections to the Catalan parliament. The conclusion can therefore be drawn that the second-order nature of regional elections may be enhanced when certain conditions are met in both the regional and national arenas. It was suggested that national factors played a greater role in the 2010 election by virtue of the concurrence of the same party at both offices and, crucially, as a consequence of the critical situation of the economy, which directed the public's attention to central government performance. Stated differently, one may infer that the relatively calm economy surrounding the 2006 election, coupled with the heated debate on the statute, helped to heighten the relevance of arena-specific factors. The current study, however, was restricted to two elections. Further research will be required in order to better identify and calibrate the impact of contextual variables on the relative weight that voters attach to their evaluation of central and regional governments in subnational elections.

Acknowledgements

The author would like to thank Agustí Bosch, the editors, and an anonymous referee for their helpful suggestions on the manuscript. This work was supported in part by a postdoctoral mobility grant from the Ministerio de Ciencia e Innovación/Fulbright (ref. 2008-0708).

Notes

[1] Respondents were asked to state what they believed to be the first and second most important problems in Catalonia at the time of the survey. These data come from pre-electoral survey no. 2582, conducted in October 2010 by the Centro de Investigaciones Sociológicas (CIS) ($N = 2,966$).

[2] The percentage of respondents professing to be *unaware* of each of the candidates is: José Montilla, 6; Joan Laporta, 14; Artur Mas, 17; Joan Puigcercós, 34; Alicia Sánchez Camacho, 43; Joan Herrera, 47; Albert Rivera, 55; Joan Carretero, 59. See survey information in note 5.

[3] The quarterly telephone surveys of the Centre d'Estudis d'Opinió point to a steady increase in the proportion of respondents naming 'an independent state' as their preferred territorial scheme, a shift from 14 per cent in October 2006 to 25 per cent in October 2010. The yearly face-to-face surveys undertaken by the ICPS show an increase from 18 to 23 per cent for the same period.

[4] Data on attitudes towards the economy come from national (not regional) representative surveys, which are available on a more regular basis. No relevant differences were observed when compared with the results of similar questions in regional surveys. 'Neither good nor bad' responses are not included in the index.

[5] The surveys were conducted in September–October 2006 ($N = 2,000$) and September 2010 ($N = 2,000$).

[6] Note that respondents may have changed their votes within the tripartite (e.g., by supporting the PSC in one election and ICV in the other one). Such cases are considered not defections, but instances of loyalty to the tripartite coalition.

[7] The substantive results of the analysis are highly robust to alternative specifications. For example, one may suspect that the influence of regional government evaluations is being captured by the party image variable. Indeed, party images do mediate some of the influence of regional government evaluations, but this nonetheless stands significantly below that of national incumbent approval if the party image is removed from the 2010 model. It may also be argued that the strong correlation between regional and national performance evaluations biases the results. Yet, the correlation never moves beyond 0.65, which should be considered an acceptable level of collinearity, and even if evaluations are entered separately, the effect of national performance tends to be higher than the effect of regional performance in 2010, while the reverse is true in 2006. The main substantive results also stand when other control variables—such as generic party sympathy, evaluations of both the Catalan and Spanish presidents, and preferences over government composition (single-party vs. coalition)—are added to the models. Interestingly, the influence of judgments of Prime Minister Zapatero is visible higher in 2010 than it is in 2006, thus following the same trend observed in the impact of central government performance. Finally, diagnostic tests show that the findings cannot be ascribed exclusively to the Socialist vote, which arguably is the most prone to encourage voters' connection across levels of government, but extend to the minor members of the tripartite coalition. When PSC voters are dropped from the models, central government performance still has a greater influence in 2010 than it does in the previous election, while the reverse is true for of regional government performance.

References

Aguilar, P. & Sánchez-Cuenca, I. (2007) '¿Gestión o representación? Los determinantes del voto en contextos políticos complejos', *Revista Española de Investigaciones Sociológicas*, no. 117, pp. 61–86.

Barceló, M., Bernadí, X. & Vintró, J. (2010) 'Balance y perspectivas', *Revista Catalana de Dret Públic*, available online at: http://www10.gencat.net/eapc_revistadret/recursos_interes/especial%20estatut/ca_ese/es

Boix, C. & Riba, C. (2000) 'Las bases sociales y políticas de la abstención en las elecciones generales españolas: recursos individuales, movilización estratégica e instituciones electorales', *Revista Española de Investigaciones Sociológicas*, no. 90, pp. 95–128.

Davis, A. (2004) 'The November 2003 elections in Catalonia: a landmark change in the Catalan political landscape', *South European Society & Politics*, vol. 9, no. 3, pp. 137–148.

Font, J. & Montero, J. M. (1991) 'El voto dual en Cataluña: lealtad y transferencia de votos en las elecciones autonómicas', *Revista de Estudios Políticos*, no. 73, pp. 7–34.

Font, J. & Rico, G. (2005) 'Learning to vote: changing patterns of voter drop-off in Spain', paper presented at the annual conference of the American Political Science Association, Washington, 1–4 September.

Font, J., Contreras, J. & Rico, G. (1998) *L'abstenció en les eleccions al Parlament de Catalunya: diagnòstic i propostes*, Editorial Mediterrània, Barcelona.

Font, J., Pallarés, F. & Serra, J. (1999) 'El comportament electoral dels catalans: factors i pautes', in *Eleccions i Comportament Electoral a Catalunya, 1989–1999*, eds M. R. Virós, J. M. Vallès, F. Pallarés, J. Font & R. M. Canal, Editorial Mediterrània, Barcelona, pp. 171–206.

Hibbing, J. R. & Alford, J. R. (1981) 'The electoral impact of economic conditions: who is held responsible?', *American Journal of Political Science*, vol. 25, no. 3, pp. 423–439.

Instituto de Estudios Fiscales (2008) 'Las balanzas fiscales de las CC.AA españolas con las AA. Públicas centrales 2005', available online at: http://www.meh.es/Documentacion/Publico/GabineteMinistro/Varios/BalanzasFiscalesCCAA.pdf

Jeffery, C. & Hough, D. (2003) 'Regional elections in multi-level systems', *European Urban and Regional Studies*, vol. 10, no. 3, pp. 199–212.

Koch, J. W. (2000) 'Candidate status, presidential approval, and voting for US senator', *Electoral Studies*, vol. 19, no. 4, pp. 479–492.

Lago, I., Montero, J. R. & Torcal, M. (2007) 'The 2006 regional election in Catalonia: exit, voice, and electoral market failures', *South European Society & Politics*, vol. 12, no. 2, pp. 221–235.

Muro, D. (2009) 'Territorial accommodation, party politics, and statute reform in Spain', *South European Society & Politics*, vol. 14, no. 4, pp. 453–468.

Pallarés, F. (ed.) (2008) *Elecciones autonómicas y locales 2007*, CIS, Madrid.

Pallarés, F. & Keating, M. (2003) 'Multi-level electoral competition: regional elections and party systems in Spain', *European Urban and Regional Studies*, vol. 10, no. 3, pp. 239–255.

Pallarés, F. & Muñoz, J. (2008) 'The autonomous elections of 1 November 2006 in Catalonia', *Regional and Federal Studies*, vol. 18, no. 4, pp. 449–464.

Pallarés, F., Montero, J. R. & Llera, F. J. (1997) 'Non state-wide parties in Spain: an attitudinal study of nationalism and regionalism', *Publius*, vol. 27, no. 4, pp. 135–169.

Pardos-Prado, S. & Molins, J. (2009) 'The emergence of right-wing radicalism at the local level in Spain: the Catalan case', *International Journal of Iberian Studies*, vol. 22, no. 3, pp. 201–218.

Reif, K. & Schmitt, H. (1980) 'Nine second-order national elections: a conceptual framework for the analysis of European election results', *European Journal of Political Research*, vol. 8, no. 1, pp. 3–44.

Riba, C. (2000) 'Voto dual y abstención diferencial: un estudio sobre el comportamiento electoral en Cataluña', *Revista Española de Investigaciones Sociológicas*, no. 91, pp. 59–88.

Santamaría, J. (2004) 'El azar y el contexto: las elecciones generales de 2004', *Claves de Razón Práctica*, no. 146, pp. 28–43.

Simon, D. M., Ostrom, C. W. & Marra, R. F. (1991) 'The president, referendum voting, and subnational elections in the United States', *American Political Science Review*, vol. 85, no. 4, pp. 1177–1192.

Tufte, E. R. (1975) 'Determinants of the outcomes of midterm congressional elections', *American Political Science Review*, vol. 69, no. 3, pp. 812–826.

Vallès, J. M. (2008) *Actituds polítiques i comportament electoral a Catalunya: materials per a un debat social*, Generalitat de Catalunya (Departament d'Interior, Relacions Institucionals i Participació), Barcelona.

Van der Eijk, C. & Franklin, M. (eds) (1996) *Choosing Europe? The European Electorate and National Politics in the Face of Union*, University of Michigan Press, Ann Arbor.

La Vanguardia (2010) 'Dios no quiera que el PP saque mayoría absoluta', 25–26 December.

Wyn Jones, R. & Scully, R. (2006) 'Devolution and electoral politics in Scotland and Wales', *Publius*, vol. 36, no. 1, pp. 115–134.

Guillem Rico received his PhD from Universitat Autònoma de Barcelona and is currently a researcher at the Department of Political and Social Sciences of Universitat Pompeu Fabra. His research interests include voting behaviour and political leadership. He is the author of *Líderes políticos, opinión pública y comportamiento electoral en España* (CIS, 2009).

The 2011 Portuguese Presidential Elections: Incumbency Advantage in Semi-presidentialism?

Carlos Jalali

The 2011 Portuguese presidential election resulted in a comfortable victory for the incumbent president, Cavaco Silva, an outcome consistent with the notion of substantial incumbency advantages. However, as this article demonstrates, the Portuguese case is part of a broader pattern, with semi-presidentialism in post-war Western Europe generating a considerable pro-incumbency bias in presidential elections. Using the Portuguese elections as a case study, it is found that this advantage derives not only from the direct benefits of holding office, but also from an indirect effect of incumbency on the quality of challengers. In particular, the average quality of challengers is significantly lower in elections with an incumbent than in open-seat contests.

On a cursory reading, the most recent Portuguese presidential election appears to be a rather uneventful plebiscite, with the incumbent Cavaco Silva being comfortably re-elected in the first ballot, as widely forecast. However, a closer examination of the 23 January vote suggests it merits further scrutiny. In particular, the election result was consistent with the notion of substantial incumbency advantages in Portuguese presidential elections. Indeed, all previous incumbents were also comfortably re-elected throughout the democratic period.

As this article will demonstrate, these effects are not exclusive to Portugal. Examining all post-war elections contested by an incumbent president in present-day semi-presidential countries of Western Europe, the re-election rate of sitting presidents is in excess of 97 per cent, a proportion that is comparable to the incumbent re-election rates of the US Congress.

Within this comparative context of a high re-election rate of incumbents, the Portuguese case emerges as a particularly salient and interesting case. This article thus considers the potential lessons of the most recent presidential elections in Portugal for our understanding of this—as yet largely unexplored—pattern of a pro-incumbent bias in semi-presidential elections. As will be shown, the Portuguese case is largely consistent with contemporary research on incumbency advantage. Presidents certainly derive direct benefits from holding office, notably in terms of visibility and valence advantages. However, the indirect effect of incumbency on challenger quality—an increasingly salient aspect of incumbency advantage in the American case—appears to be at least as relevant, if not more so. Not only did the 2011 elections present, on average, weaker challengers than the 2006 open seat contest, but that pattern is also evident across previous presidential elections in Portugal. Overall, then, the Portuguese case suggests that the mechanisms of the pro-incumbency bias in semi-presidentialism may resemble those found in the US case.

The Advantages of Incumbency

The literature on the advantages of incumbency is extensive. It largely derives from the empirical pattern of American legislative elections, where the proportion of incumbents winning re-election has consistently exceeded 90 per cent since the 1950s, and been close to the ceiling of 100 per cent since the late 1990s (Friedman & Holden 2009, pp. 593–594). There is also evidence of a considerable advantage to incumbency in presidential elections, even if falling short of US Congress proportions. Thus, Mayhew (2008, p. 213) finds evidence of such a pro-incumbency bias in US presidential elections in the period of 1788 to 2004, with two-thirds of all incumbents gaining re-election. This compares with a partisan re-election rate of 50 per cent when the incumbent president was not running. Likewise, Jones (2004, p. 81)—analysing presidential elections in 50 countries, presidential and semi-presidential combined, since the 1940s—finds incumbents to have been re-elected in 81 per cent of the elections they contested.

Of course, all this discussion begs the question of what exactly is incumbency advantage. As Mayhew (2008, p. 205) explains, the term can be read as a statistical pattern whereby 'candidates running again as incumbents perform better in elections than … candidates not holding that status'; or it can be interpreted as an explanatory variable for this pattern, with incumbency advantage the answer to '*why* candidates already holding office run better in elections'. This latter interpretation is clearly of greater relevance. However, it too begs an obvious question: if incumbency does generate this pattern, then what is it about incumbency that generates these effects?

The abundant literature on incumbency has sought to break down the mechanics of incumbency advantage, taking in a wide range of possible factors. Following Cox & Katz (1996), we can distinguish between direct and indirect effects of incumbency. The direct effects pertain to the specific benefits of holding office. These include aspects such as greater visibility (Erikson 1971), potentially accentuated by the expansion of television (Prior 2006). Likewise, incumbency has been associated with greater fund-raising (Levitt & Wolfram 1997, p. 46), of particular importance in American elections. Last but not least, the direct effects pertain to incumbents' valence advantage. As Mayhew (2008, pp. 215–216) puts it:

> In the line of prerogatives, incumbent presidents can choose when and if to make speeches, break ribbons, sign bills, issue executive orders, send off cruise missiles, hand out ice during Florida hurricanes (as George W. Bush did in 2004), and engage in many other kinds of possibly vote-winning behaviour ... lacking to challenger candidates.

The indirect effects are generally associated with candidate quality, both of the incumbent and her/his challengers (Cox & Katz 1996, pp. 482–483). In particular, it posits that incumbents will face 'low quality' challengers, based on the assumption that incumbents are more formidable candidates than their open-seat counterparts (Levitt & Wolfram 1997). This leads 'high quality' challengers not to contest incumbents, opting rather for open-seat contests, leaving incumbents to face lower quality opponents (Levitt & Wolfram 1997). In other words, it leaves 'only patsies to take on most incumbents seeking re-election' (Cox & Katz 1996, p. 482), thus increasing the chances of the latter's success.

This indirect effect is not unconditional. Rather, as Cox & Katz (1996, p. 483) point out, it depends on candidate quality being relevant for voters' choices—if voting is a 'choice between parties rather than a choice between individual candidates' then challenger quality becomes irrelevant. Cox & Katz (1996, p. 483) dub this the 'quality effect': the more candidate characteristics matter for voting behaviour, the stronger the 'scare-off effect' on potential challengers, deterring them from contesting incumbents.

Interestingly, the current balance of research on incumbency advantages—in the US case, at least—tends to identify candidate quality as the main explanatory factor for rising incumbency success. As Levitt & Wolfram (1997, p. 57) put it—in a study assessing the relative impact of the direct advantages of holding office and the indirect benefits in terms of candidate quality—'Virtually all of the growth in the incumbency advantage since the 1960s appears to be attributable to a reduction in the relative quality of challengers'. This conclusion is consistent with other studies that take into account the direct and indirect effects of incumbency, such as Cox & Katz (1996), or those that examine candidate quality more specifically (Bond, Covington & Fleisher 1985; Krasno & Green 1988).

While the literature on incumbency advantage is extensive, it is also largely unbalanced. One glaring omission is the assessment of the effects of incumbency in the direct presidential elections of semi-presidentialism. This omission is glaring for two reasons. First, and obviously, because there is virtually no work on incumbency advantages in semi-presidential regimes.[1] Second, and more importantly, these presidential elections tend to fit rather well with much of the existing theory on incumbency advantages, especially with regard to the indirect candidate quality dimension.

As highlighted above, the effect of candidate quality on incumbency will be stronger the more personal traits of candidates impact on voting behaviour. In the case of presidential elections in semi-presidential regimes, the impact of personal candidate qualities on voting behaviour is likely to be correlated to the powers and executive role of a president (Magalhães 2007, pp. 281–284). Thus, it is likely to be weaker in countries where the chief executive is (usually) the president, such as France; and stronger where the president plays a less substantial role. Using Wu's (2011) typology of operational sub-types of semi-presidentialism, the expectation is that voting choice in semi-presidential regimes that are quasi-parliamentary in terms of functioning will be more centred on candidate traits than those sub-types that imply greater presidential power.

The existing evidence, albeit not extensive, is generally consistent with this expectation. In quasi-parliamentary cases—be it those where the president is an entirely ceremonial role as in Ireland or somewhat more relevant as in Portugal—the presidential elections do tend to place a premium on personal characteristics as compared with legislative elections, even if they fall short of being mere 'popularity contests' (van der Brug, van der Eijk & Marsh 2000; Magalhães 2007). In cases where the president plays a more salient role, such as France, other factors—such as ideology, partisanship or economic voting—play a considerable role in voting behaviour, potentially more so than in legislative elections (Fleury & Lewis-Beck 1993; Lewis-Beck & Nadeau 2000, p. 178; Lewis-Beck & Stegmaier 2000).

This suggests that the extent to which semi-presidential elections are prone to quality effects is likely to be correlated with the degree of presidential power. Examining West European semi-presidentialism, the expectation is for presidential elections to be particularly prone to a pro-incumbent bias. Indeed, looking at Wu's (2011) classification of semi-presidential countries by sub-type—classified on a four-point scale, where 1 represents low presidential powers ('quasi-parliamentarism') and 4 depicts the cases of most extensive presidential powers ('presidential supremacy')—we find the average for West European semi-presidential regimes to be 1.5 and the mode equal to 1. In the remainder of this article, we briefly assess to what extent this expectation is corroborated in West European semi-presidentialism generally and in the Portuguese case specifically.

The Pattern in European Semi-presidentialism: The Incumbent Generally Wins

A full and detailed examination of incumbency advantage in semi-presidentialism is beyond the scope of this article. Rather, our goal is a more modest one: to provide an exploratory analysis of incumbency advantages in post-war West European semi-presidential countries, and then to analyse the 2011 Portuguese presidential election as a case-study of incumbency advantage, against the backdrop both of the theory on pro-incumbent biases and of the empirical pattern of advantage of presidents seeking re-election in West European countries.

Table 1 details the pattern of incumbent re-election rates since 1945 for all West European countries that have semi-presidentialism. In terms of the classification of semi-presidentialism, we use the list of countries identified in Wu's (2011) comprehensive study, which also coincides with other classifications of semi-presidential countries.[2]

Table 1 Re-election of Presidents in West European Semi-presidential Regimes, 1945–2011

	Post-war popular elections with eligible incumbent	Incumbent re-elected	Incumbent defeated	Incumbent did not run (incumbent barred[1])	Running incumbent re-election rate[2] (%)	Eligible incumbent re-election rate[3] (%)
Austria	11	5	0	6 (5)	100	83
Finland	11[4]	7	0	4[5] (1)	90	70
France	8	3	1[6] (Giscard, 1981)	4 (3)	75	60
Iceland	17[7]	13	0	4 (1)	100	81
Ireland	11[8]	4	0	7 (4)	100	57
Portugal	7	4	0	3 (3)	100	100
Total	65	36	1	28 (17)	97	71

Notes:
[1] In parentheses is the number of incumbents that were barred from running in presidential elections. Incumbents are considered barred from running if they reached term limits, were impeached or died whilst in office.
[2] Proportion of running incumbents who were re-elected.
[3] Proportion of incumbents that were eligible to run and were re-elected.
[4] This count starts with the 1950 presidential elections. Paasiviki was elected in 1946 by Parliament, and ran (successfully) for President in the 1950 presidential elections. This also excludes the third term extension of Kekkonen (1973), as it was voted by Parliament. It does, however, include the 1982 election as a case of re-election. Following Kekkonen's resignation, Koivisto was acting President from October 1981 until the elections of January 1982, in which he ran.
[5] This includes Paasiviki in 1956, when for all intents he did not run for re-election.
[6] This does not include Alain Poher, who ran against Pompidou in the June 1969 presidential election. Poher was acting President following De Gaulle's resignation in late April. He is not included here as an incumbent as his time in office was very brief and coincided with the campaign for the presidential election (De Gaulle resigned on 28 April 1969; the first ballot of the election took place little over a month later, on 1 June 1969).
[7] Björnsson was elected President by Parliament in 1944. He was re-elected (unopposed) in the 1945 popular elections. As such, this last election is included.
[8] This includes the second Irish presidential election of 1945, which the outgoing President, Douglas Hyde, did not contest.

We by-and-large exclude the inaugural elections of semi-presidentialism as these generally do not have an incumbent candidate. However, in practice some inaugural elections did include a pre-existing incumbent president running (e.g. de Gaulle in 1965)—such instances are accounted for and noted in the table.

We assess incumbent re-election rates in two different ways. First, we examine how many incumbents ran and were re-elected. While this is a very standard measure of incumbency advantage, it is also potentially a misleading one: incumbents that face a likely defeat may simply choose not to run for re-election, thus biasing the re-election rate (Stone, Fulton, Maestas & Maisel 2010). Thus, we also take into account the cases where incumbents opted not to run for re-election even though they were eligible to do so. We compute this as the difference between incumbents who did not run and those who were barred from doing so, using a very stringent criterion for the latter.

Incumbents are thus considered barred from running if they reached term limits, were impeached or died whilst in office. This is a very stringent criterion, as a number of presidents did not seek re-election on very genuine health grounds. In the Finnish case, where term limits were introduced only in 1991, the only candidate barred from running by our criteria was Koivisto in 1994, due to term limits. Yet at least one further president—Kekkonen—resigned for health reasons and was terminally ill at the time of the re-election he did not contest. Nevertheless, we adopt this stringent criterion given the obvious difficulty in assessing whether incumbents' health was truly impeditive of running for president. In Iceland, where there are no term limits, the only president that meets our criterion for ineligibility was Björnsson, having died in office in 1952. However, all evidence suggests that his three successors who opted not to run again—Ásgeirsson in 1968; Eldjárn in 1980; and Finnbogadóttir in 1996—did so out of office fatigue rather than a fear of impending defeat, having always been always comfortably re-elected (often unopposed). Finally, we consider presidents who resigned the office but were alive—such as De Gaulle in 1969, Ó Dálaigh in 1976 or Mary Robinson in 1997—as eligible. Again, this is a very strict criterion for ineligibility, as presidents who resign are generally legally barred from running. However, we count resigning presidents as eligible as they chose to resign, and it was this endogenous option that made them ineligible (as opposed to cases of impeachment, for instance).

So what can we discern from the West European case? First, there is a strong pro-incumbency bias for incumbents who run for re-election. On average, in a total of 65 elections, over 97 per cent of incumbents who contested elections were re-elected. This re-election rate is comparable to American Congress rates, and is higher than both the American presidency rate provided by Mayhew and the presidential elections analysed by Jones. Indeed, the mode is for running incumbents *always* to be re-elected. The re-election rate is inevitably lower if we consider incumbents who were eligible to run rather than those who did actually seek re-election. Nevertheless, it remains very high, with over 70 per cent of eligible incumbents achieving re-election. This is all the more striking when we take into account the very strict criterion for ineligibility adopted here.

How does Portugal fare in this comparative backdrop? As Table 1 highlights, all incumbents who ran for re-election in Portugal succeeded. However, this is hardly a surprising result given this is the modal outcome in European semi-presidentialism. Where the Portuguese case becomes more interesting is when we consider the final column of Table 1. Portugal stands out as the one case where eligible incumbents have always been re-elected in Western Europe. Moreover, this perfect re-election rate cannot be dismissed as an artefact of Portugal's comparatively late adoption of semi-presidentialism. Indeed, by 2011, the current Portuguese democracy has held as many direct presidential elections as Fifth Republic France. Within this context, Portugal emerges as a particularly salient case of incumbency advantage. In a sense, while eligible incumbents are *generally* re-elected in Europe, in Portugal they have *always* been re-elected, a pattern that was reaffirmed in the 2011 presidential election.

The 2011 Portuguese Presidential Election: Confirming the Rule

The 2011 election resulted in a comfortable victory for the incumbent President, Cavaco Silva, with 53.1 per cent of the vote, well ahead of his main challenger, Manuel Alegre (19.7 per cent of the vote) and the other four candidates, Fernando Nobre (14 per cent), Francisco Lopes (7 per cent), José Manuel Coelho (4.5 per cent) and Defensor Moura (1.6 per cent). Cavaco Silva thus won his second and final term[3] without needing a second round, given the majority-runoff electoral system used in Portugal's presidential elections. The election—where voters aged 18 and above can vote—was marked by a high level of abstention, with an official turnout rate of 46.4 per cent.

In this section we analyse the 2011 Portuguese presidential election in greater detail, to assess what insight it provides into the pro-incumbency bias generally found in Western Europe. We begin by analysing the candidates and the campaign of this election, followed by a brief assessment of the election results. We then examine to what extent the theoretical explanations for incumbency advantages are applicable to the Portuguese case. This preliminary assessment—which includes, where relevant, a longitudinal perspective—suggests a challenger 'scare-off effect' as well as a valence advantage for incumbents.

Candidates and Campaign

The presidential elections of January 2011 were contested by six candidates. The incumbent president was Aníbal Cavaco Silva, an Economics Professor who was previously Portugal's longest serving prime minister in democracy, from 1985 to 1995, when he led the centre-right PSD (Partido Social Democrata, Social Democratic Party). Cavaco Silva was the frontrunner throughout the campaign, with polls consistently giving him strong majorities.[4] As in 2006, Cavaco Silva was backed by the two main parties of the right, his own PSD and the smaller right-wing CDS-PP (CDS-Partido Popular, CDS-Popular Party[5]).

As in 2006, Cavaco kept his partisan supporters at some distance, seeking to maintain his carefully cultivated 'above party' image. However, on this occasion Cavaco was more accommodating of the PSD and CDS-PP. While in 2006 the involvement of the then leaders of PSD and CDS-PP was limited to attending campaign events, in 2011 both party leaders were invited to give speeches in Cavaco Silva campaign rallies. On the one hand, this greater party involvement may be partly explained by the need for mobilisation on the part of the Cavaco Silva campaign. With polls putting him very comfortably ahead and an election that was expected to have a low turnout, activating the party networks became an important way of ensuring Cavaco Silva's likely supporters came out to vote come election day. On the other hand, it might also have reflected broader trends in Portuguese politics. At the time of the 2006 presidential elections, the Socialists were less than one year into their first single-party majority and comfortably led in the polls.[6] If he was elected, Cavaco would have to cohabit with a strong Socialist government for the majority of his first term. In 2011, the situation had dramatically changed. While the Socialist Party remained in power, it now governed with a parliamentary minority that was increasingly unpopular as a result of rising unemployment and slow economic growth, with polls placing it well behind the PSD in terms of voting intentions.[7]

Cavaco Silva's opponents came mostly from the left. The main challenger was Manuel Alegre—a historic member of the PS (Partido Socialista, Socialist Party), described in a Wikileak as 'the old lion' of the Portuguese left (Simas 2010). An ally of Soares in the revolutionary period of 1974–75 against the Communist Party and the extreme left—a period that defined the enduring division on the Portuguese left between the Socialists and the parties to its left—Alegre became the Socialist Party's leftist critical conscience as the party took over power from the mid-1990s.[8] Thus, Alegre presented a motion in the 1999 party congress, which was very critical of the leadership and government of then party leader and prime minister António Guterres (Lisi 2009, pp. 164–165).

If anything, Alegre's internal opposition became even more vocal during José Sócrates' leadership of the Socialist Party, against whom Alegre lost the 2004 internal election for the party leadership. The most salient aspect of Alegre's dissonance with the party leadership was the 2006 presidential election, which he contested without his party's support and against the Socialists' endorsed candidate, Soares. Alegre was to come in second in these presidential elections, obtaining some 20.7 per cent of the vote and over a million votes, substantially outpolling Soares despite the lack of party backing. Alegre's internal dissidence was to continue beyond 2006, forming an internal tendency in 2008 ('*Opinião Socialista*'—'Socialist Opinion') and remaining a vocal critic of the Sócrates government's policies (Lisi 2010, pp. 382, 387).

Alegre's stance inevitably caused internal frictions within the PS. While he was able to gain the Socialist Party's backing for the 2011 presidential elections, he did so with reservations in segments of his own party (Jornal de Notícias 2010), critical not only of his decision to run against the party's endorsed candidate in 2006, but also—and perhaps even more so—of his positions regarding the PS government. Indeed, as late as November 2008 Alegre was strongly criticised by party leader and prime minister José Sócrates, who stated that 'Manuel Alegre is always willing to say everyone is right, except the government and the PS' (Expresso 2008). The party's reservations were reflected also in the somewhat belated decision to back Alegre—the PS voted to support Alegre in late May, more than four months after Alegre had announced his intention to run again for the presidency.

In the end, however, the PS had little choice but to back Alegre, even if grudgingly. Alegre launched his 2011 bid with the memory of his 2006 result—and the heavy defeat of the official PS candidate—still very much in Socialist minds. Alegre could legitimately claim to be the best candidate to defeat Cavaco; and with no party heavyweight willing to run, supporting Alegre became the least-bad option for Sócrates, preferable to presenting a weak candidate (and risk a demoralising heavy defeat as in 2006) or even no candidate at all (which might be understood as tacit support for Cavaco Silva, with whom relations had become increasingly frayed since 2008). Additionally, backing Alegre would—at least temporarily—quell his criticisms of the government, a not unwelcome respite for the increasingly besieged Sócrates executive.

This delayed decision of the PS contrasted with the other party endorsement that Alegre received from the BE (Bloco de Esquerda, Left Bloc), with the BE leader Francisco Louçã publicly announcing the party's support for Alegre little over a week after the candidate had made public his intention to run. While the Left Bloc's support came quickly, it was also not entirely unanimous within the BE (Coelho 2010). To a large extent, this opposition reflected the enduring divisions in the Portuguese left. For the critics of Bloc's choice of Alegre, this represented an unacceptable kowtowing to a Socialist Party that was not left-wing enough. At the same time, the joint support of PS and BE was welcomed in those segments of the Portuguese left that have sought to bridge these historic divisions and generate a rapprochement between the Socialists and the Left Bloc. Indeed, these segments previously organised the Forum of the Lefts (Fórum das Esquerdas) in 2008 and 2009, an initiative that inter alia brought together Alegre and Louçã.

The third party-backed challenger was Francisco Lopes. A Communist stalwart, Francisco Lopes was virtually unknown outside his party despite an important role within the party hierarchy, having been considered for the secretary-general position in 2004 (Público 2004). Close to the party's historic leader, Álvaro Cunhal, Francisco Lopes was generally considered to have sided with the internal wing that successfully defended Marxist-Leninist orthodoxy within the party in the 1990s and early 2000s, as the Portuguese Communists faced the fallout from the collapse of the Soviet Union. Francisco Lopes was backed by the Communist Party and its perennial ally in the CDU (Coligação Democrática Unitária, Unitary Democratic Coalition) alliance, the Greens.

The other three candidates did not have the backing of relevant political parties. The most notable was the party-unaffiliated Fernando Nobre, a doctor who rose to prominence as founder of a leading humanitarian NGO, AMI (Assistência Médica Internacional, International Medical Assistance). While being a non-partisan figure,

Fernando Nobre had not shied away from political involvement in the past. Politically, he was generally seen as being on the left[9]—having for instance backed the Left Bloc in the 2009 European and legislative elections, and supported Soares in the 2006 presidential elections—although he had in the past also backed the centre-right PSD of José Manuel Durão Barroso in the 2002 legislative elections.

The other two candidates were expected to be minor contenders. The first, Defensor Moura—a Socialist Party MP and former Mayor of the picturesque northern town of Viana do Castelo—justified his candidacy as a means of appealing to Socialist voters unhappy with Alegre. The second, José Manuel Coelho, was a former Communist affiliated at the time of the elections to a minor right-wing party, the PND (Partido da Nova Democracia, New Democracy Party). The PND arose from a split in the CDS-PP in the early 2000s, led by the former leader of the CDS-PP, Manuel Monteiro. While the party failed to make headway at national level, it proved more successful in the autonomous region of Madeira, where it elected a deputy to the regional assembly in the 2007 regional elections in a list that included José Manuel Coelho. The latter was to assume the position of deputy to the regional assembly in 2008, and his presidential bid aimed at regional objectives. Indeed, upon formalising his bid, the candidate stated that he had a 'regional message' and sought to 'bring attention to the situation ... in Madeira' (Diário IOL 2010).

The campaign was largely unengaging, with political commentators dubbing it one of the least interesting since democratisation. Portugal's most watched TV pundit, Marcelo Rebelo de Sousa, went so far as to say he could not recall such a 'dull, inhospitable and uninteresting campaign' (Lusa 2011). The campaign focused mostly on three issues. The most salient was an allegation of financial impropriety on the part of Cavaco Silva in his dealings with a private bank, the BPN (Banco Português de Negócios, Portuguese Business Bank). This bank, originally run by former ministers of Cavaco Silva, was nationalised in 2008 after a number of illegalities were detected. The campaign issue was the 140 per cent profit Cavaco Silva made when he bought and sold BPN shares in 2001–03, when he was not in public office. Cavaco Silva strenuously denied allegations of wrong-doing, claiming he was the victim of a smear campaign.

The second broad issue tied directly to Portugal's economic and public finance woes. On the one hand, all candidates discussed the rising interest rate on Portugal's sovereign debt and the rumours of an impending IMF bailout of Portugal, maintaining it should be avoided. Likewise, all candidates sought to position themselves as the defenders of those who have fared worse as a result of the economic crisis. While Alegre sought to introduce an ideological line—stating he would defend the welfare state and use presidential powers to protect the national health service and public schools—the campaign failed to generate major divisions, with all candidates focusing on uncontroversial pronouncements against poverty and social exclusion.

The third issue resulted from Cavaco Silva's robust criticism of the Sócrates government during the campaign, with the President inter alia stating that 'the right measures at the right time' had not been undertaken (Simas 2011) and disapproving of unpopular government measures such as wage cuts for public sector workers (Simas, Oliveira & Gomes 2011). Indeed, Cavaco Silva at one point went so far as to hint at a dissolution of parliament against the Sócrates government, by stating that he 'would use all his powers so … Portugal can find the right direction for the future …' (Económico 2011), although he later was to moderate this position by saying he had 'little appetite' for dissolving parliament (Sá 2011a). These statements by Cavaco drew strong criticism from his opponents, with Alegre coming out in defence of the government, while the other candidates argued that Cavaco was also responsible for the current situation given his background as both president and prime minister.

Results

The final election results are presented in Table 2. Unsurprisingly, Cavaco Silva was comfortably re-elected at the first ballot. However, his 53.1 per cent of the vote fell well short of earlier polls, and was also lower than the vote share of previous presidential incumbents on their re-election (the previous minimum was Sampaio in 2001, with 55.6 per cent of the vote). On the one hand, Cavaco Silva may have been penalised by a demobilisation of his potential supporters by the consistently strong leads in the polls. His result may also have been adversely affected by the allegations of impropriety over the so-called BPN affair. Indeed, despite Cavaco Silva's protestations of his innocence— and later refusal to discuss the issue—the BPN affair ended up dominating much of the campaign (Sá 2011b).

The election brought a heavy defeat for Alegre, who obtained 19.7 per cent of the vote—less than he had obtained in 2006, when he ran without party backing. On the other hand, independent and minor candidates polled strongly: Fernando Nobre obtained 14 per cent of the vote, while Coelho obtained a very surprising 4.5 per cent of the vote, well ahead of Defensor Moura (1.6 per cent). As for the Communist candidate, Francisco Lopes obtained 7.1 per cent of the vote, suggesting he was unable to go beyond the Communist faithful. Last but not least, the elections were marked by very low levels of electoral participation, with official turnout well below 50 per cent. While the real turnout is almost certain to be higher than the official turnout because of Portugal's chronically inflated voter registers, it is nevertheless a comparatively low turnout, beating the previous minimum official turnout of 2001, which stood at 49.7 per cent. Moreover, this low turnout was itself accentuated by an uncharacteristic poor organisation of the election process. In particular, prior to the election the voter registration details of thousands of voters were changed with no or insufficient information provided to them, thus potentially precluding many of them from voting (Correia 2011). By all accounts, the presidential election of 2011 was a low point in terms of electoral administration in Portugal, contrasting with the sound organisation of previous plebiscites.

It is hard not to read the election results as a sign of dissatisfaction with the main parties. Manuel Alegre's defeat was interpreted by several commentators as having

Table 2 Results of the 2011 Portuguese Presidential Election

	Votes	%	Vote share of supporting parliamentary parties in 2009 legislative elections (%)	Vote share of supporting parliamentary parties in 2011 legislative elections (%)
Cavaco Silva	2,209,227	53.1	39.5 (PSD 29.1, CDS-PP 10.4)	50.4 (PSD 38.7, CDS-PP 11.7)
Manuel Alegre	817,980	19.7	46.5 (PS 36.7, BE 9.8)	33.3 (PS 28.1, BE 5.2)
Fernando Nobre	583,582	14.0	–	–
Francisco Lopes	293,143	7.1	7.9 (CDU 7.9)	7.9 (CDU 7.9)
José Manuel Coelho	187,836	4.5	–	–
Defensor Moura	65,775	1.6	–	–
Blank + void ballots	274,306	6.2	–	–
Turnout (electorate)	4.431,849 (9,543,550)	46.4		

Sources: Presidential election—official results, published in Diário da República, 1.ª série—N.° 32—15 de Fevereiro de 2011, p. 819. Legislative elections – Comissão Nacional de Eleições.

been exacerbated by his attempt at reconciling the seemingly irreconcilable PS and BE under his candidacy (see for instance Martins 2011; or the quote attributed to Vitorino in Tavares 2011). Perhaps so, but equally it is worth noting that both the number and share of votes he obtained in 2011—with the backing of two parties—was below what he obtained in 2006, when he ran unsupported. This suggests Alegre was unable to mobilise his 2006 electorate—and if so, understandably, given that he had made his independence from political parties such a central element of his 2006 campaign.

Likewise, the results of Nobre and Coelho—not to mention the 6.2 per cent of blank and void ballots—are consistent with dissatisfaction with the main parties. Both candidates heavily criticised 'professional politicians' in their campaigns, with a discourse that not only bordered on the anti-systemic but often crossed that Rubicon. Indeed, Coelho was to label himself explicitly as an anti-system candidate (Coelho 2010). While Nobre was more cautious (declaring in a speech that he was 'neither 'of the system' nor 'anti-system'—Nobre 2010), his result was interpreted as deriving to a large extent from anti-party and anti-system protest voting (Cerdeira 2011). While the strong showing for independent candidates is not unprecedented, the anti-systemic component that emerged in 2011 was more salient than in previous elections. Although the independent candidates who did well in previous elections—Alegre in 2006 and, to a lesser extent, Maria de Lurdes Pintasilgo in 1986—sought to capitalise on dissatisfaction with parties, they certainly avoided tarring the entire political class with the same brush.

Visible Presidents, Uncontroversial Presidents: Direct Effects of Incumbency in the 2011 Portuguese Elections

As highlighted earlier, Portugal provides a salient case of incumbent re-election in presidential elections. The question that remains is to what extent existing theories of incumbent advantage help explain this Portuguese pattern—and, by extension, may potentially also be useful in explaining the high rate of incumbent re-election in European semi-presidential countries.

In terms of the direct effects of incumbency highlighted in the theory, some appear largely inapplicable to the Portuguese case. The greater fund-raising capacity of incumbents appears overstated, at least in the 2011 elections. As Table 3 indicates, the declared campaign budget of Cavaco Silva was lower in 2011, when he was an incumbent, than in 2006 when he was first elected. Additionally, the share of the budget that was obtained as donations and through fund-raising activities also fell in 2011 vis-à-vis 2006. Moreover, as Table 3 also indicates, this pattern is not explained by a lower campaign expenditure of his opponents in 2011 as compared with 2006. In the 2006 presidential elections, Cavaco Silva's campaign budget exceeded that of his main opponent, Soares, by a ratio of 1.25 euros for every euro of Soares's budget. In 2011, Cavaco Silva still outspent his main opponent (now Alegre), but the ratio was lower, at 1.12 euros for every euro spent by Alegre.

Table 3 Campaign Budget, 2006 and 2011 Presidential Elections

	2006		2011	
	Total campaign budget in €	Share of budget obtained from donations and fund-raising (%)	Total campaign budget in €	Share of budget obtained from donations and fund-raising (%)
Cavaco Silva	3,700,000	55	2,120,000	26
Manuel Alegre	1,500,000	40	1,900,000	3
Mário Soares	2,949,521	24	–	–
Jerónimo de Sousa	1,100,000	3	–	–
Francisco Louçã	546,948	10	–	–
Garcia Pereira	22,050	100		
Fernando Nobre			842,660	39
Francisco Lopes			800,000	2
J. M. Coelho			90,000	33
Defensor Moura			250,000	8

Source: Own calculations based on data of the *Entidade das Contas e Financiamentos Políticos* of the Portuguese Constitutional Court.

The more plausible direct effects pertain to visibility and valence advantages. On the one hand, presidents enjoy great visibility and can endogenously increase it through speeches and public statements, leading one author to describe presidential speeches as a 'a weapon of the president' (Barroso 1986, pp. 237–238). Moreover, presidents have cultivated a supra-partisan, 'above politics' stance—especially in their first term—that has proved very popular with the electorate (Jalali 2011, p. 161). At the same time, presidents can pick and choose their political fights, and generally circumscribe these to issues that are popular (Jalali 2011, p. 169). This pattern appears to be particularly evident in presidential first terms, a pattern that would further reinforce incumbency advantage. Indeed, presidents have by and large been much less conflictual in first terms than in second terms, as evidenced through the use of their veto and preventive review powers (Jalali 2011, p. 170). This pattern is consistent with Cavaco Silva's first term, with the president generally avoiding controversy, a pattern that he maintained during the 2011 election campaign. Indeed, even Cavaco Silva's more robust criticisms of the Sócrates government during the campaign were probably made easier by the government's unpopularity at the time.

Only Patsies Run? Indirect Effects of Incumbency Advantage in Portuguese Presidential Elections

The direct benefits of incumbency are of course only part of the story of incumbency advantage—indeed, as highlighted earlier, current research on the US case suggests they are perhaps the less relevant part of the story. In this section we explore the indirect effects of incumbency on challenger quality.

In order to assess this effect, we use three different measures. The first is based on Krasno & Green's (1988) eight-point index of candidate quality. As Krasno & Green (1988, p. 922) explain, this basically tallies up candidate characteristics that reflect 'quality', allowing a comparable measure of challenger quality, with quality defined here as 'the personal characteristics which contribute to the strength of a candidacy' (ibid., p. 921). As per Jacobson & Kernell (1983) and Krasno & Green (1988, p. 922), we also assume that a crucial difference between candidates is whether they have held political office or not. As such, following the Krasno & Green model, we also give challengers who have held political office a baseline quality rank of 4. The modifications that are made to the Krasno & Green index seek to adapt it to the context of the Portuguese presidential elections. Thus, the 'celebrity status' item is removed from the index—while relevant for US congressional races, it is unlikely to be a sign of quality for Portuguese presidential elections—while other items were adapted, yielding a seven-point scale. Figure 1 outlines how the challenger quality index was constructed for the Portuguese presidential elections.

We then use two simpler measures of challenger quality: first, whether the candidates were prime ministers (incumbent or previous); second, whether the candidates were party leaders (incumbent or previous). In their model, Krasno &

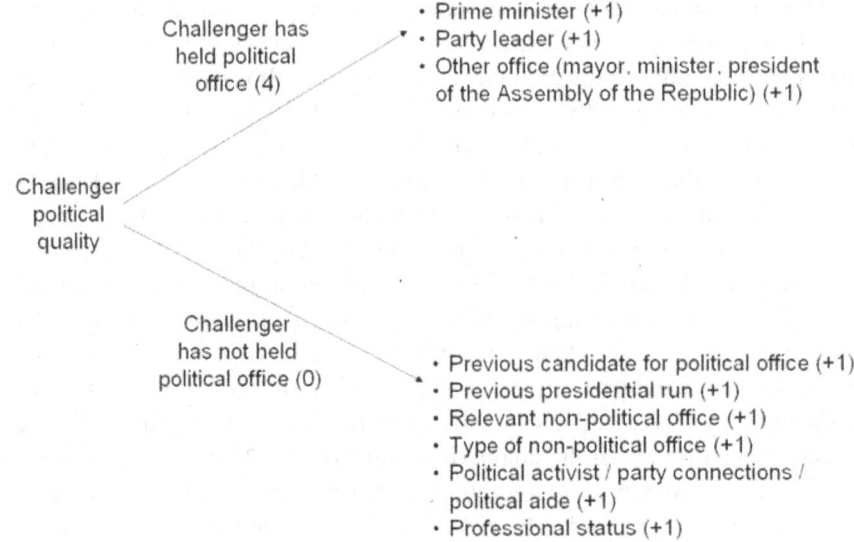

Figure 1 Challenger Quality Index. *Source*: Adapted from Krasno & Green (1988, p. 923).

Green separate two different elements of quality: first, attractiveness (education, occupation, fame, personality); and second, political skill, in terms of the 'ability to organize and conduct an effective campaign' (Krasno & Green 1988, p. 921). As they explain, elective office reflects well on both counts. With regard to attractiveness, it 'establishes one's occupational qualifications and furnishes a measure of celebrity'; with regard to political skill, 'having run successfully for office provides a candidate with the political connections so important to campaigning, as well as the political skills gained as a candidate' (Krasno & Green 1988, p. 922). While not necessarily elective offices in the terms defined by Krasno & Green, being a party leader or prime minister is consistent with the underlying logic. Achieving either position is an arduous task in any democracy, and will generate not only 'attractiveness' (visibility, name recognition, occupational qualification) but also substantial political skill (connections, political knowledge, campaigning experience).

Table 4 presents the comparison between the 2011 and 2006 presidential elections using the seven-point candidate quality index already presented. As can be seen, there was no drop in the quality of the runner-up in 2011 vis-à-vis 2006—for obvious reasons, as it was the same candidate, Manuel Alegre. However, there is a noticeable drop in terms of the average quality of challengers, statistically significant at the 0.079 level (Mann–Whitney test). Whereas in 2006 the losing candidates included a former prime minister and three incumbent party leaders, in 2011 there was a considerable drop in quality: indeed, at least two of the candidates—Defensor Moura and José Manuel Coelho—were relative unknowns prior to the election at national level, despite having held political office.

Table 4 Challenger Quality, 2006 and 2011 Presidential Elections

2011		2006	
Candidate	Quality score	Candidate	Quality score
Cavaco Silva (winner)	(incumbent)	Cavaco Silva (winner)	7 (PM; party leader; other office—minister)
Manuel Alegre	5 (other office—junior minister)	Alegre	5 (other office—junior minister)
Fernando Nobre	4 (relevant non-political office; type of non-political office; political activist; professional status)	Soares	7 (PM; party leader; other office—minister)
Defensor Moura	5 (other office—mayor)	Louçã	5 (party leader)
José Manuel Coelho	4 (political office only)	Jerónimo de Sousa	5 (party leader)
		Garcia Pereira	5 (party leader)
Average quality of defeated candidates	4.5	Average quality of defeated candidates	5.4

Source: Author's own elaboration.

In order to assess whether the 2011 election is part of a broader trend, we analyse the evolution of challenger quality in the preceding elections (Table 5). This analysis is carried out for the elections since 1986, excluding the first re-election of 1980. The reason for this exclusion is the 'implicit' military clause that resulted from Portugal's mode of transition, which determined that the first president would come from military ranks (Neto & Lobo 2009, p. 238). Indeed, of the ten candidates who contested the first two presidential elections of 1976 and 1980, only two were not military men, and these two were also the candidates least voted for in the elections they contested. Thus we restrict our analysis to the period post-1986, when the presidency became fully civilianised and incorporated into the party system (Neto & Lobo 2009, p. 251).

As the data indicate, the drop in candidate quality in 2011 is not an exception. Indeed, all elections with an incumbent candidate generated lower average challenger quality than the preceding open elections. On average, for the period 1986–2011, the average quality of defeated candidates in elections with an incumbent candidate was 4.6 in our seven-point index, against a mean of 5.6 when no incumbent ran, a difference that is statistically significant at the 0.007 level (Mann–Whitney test). This pattern is also confirmed when we look at simpler indicators of challenger quality. Thus, in the period 1986–2011, there were three elections contested by former prime ministers: 1986, 1996 and 2006. Unsurprisingly, these were the only elections with no incumbent candidate running. Likewise, these three elections were the only ones to be contested by former or incumbent party leaders—in the case of 2006 attracting four current or former party leaders.

Overall, then, the Portuguese case is very much consistent with the broader literature that ascribes incumbency advantages to the indirect effects it has on challenger quality. As the figures given indicate, the average quality of candidates is considerably lower when an incumbent is contesting elections. While our data do not allow us to assess the relative weight of the direct and indirect effects of incumbency, these results are certainly consistent with the latter playing an important role in the high re-election rate of Portuguese incumbents.

Conclusion

As this article has demonstrated, semi-presidentialism—in Europe, at least—tends to generate substantial advantages to incumbent presidents seeking re-election. Nowhere is this incumbency advantage more salient than in democratic Portugal, where all eligible incumbents have contested and been comfortably re-elected to the presidency, most recently in the 2011 presidential election. As this article has also shown, in the Portuguese case this pro-incumbent bias does not derive solely from the direct benefits of the presidential office, even if these are far from irrelevant. Rather, consistent with contemporary research on incumbency advantage, there appears to be a considerable effect of incumbency on challenger quality, with open-seat elections presenting a significantly higher quality of candidates than elections where the incumbent sought re-election.

Table 5 Challenger Quality, 1986–2001 Presidential Elections

2001 (incumbent running)		1996		1991 (incumbent running)		1986	
Candidate	Quality score	Candidate	Quality score	Candidate	Quality score	Candidate	Quality score
Jorge Sampaio (winner)	(incumbent)	Jorge Sampaio (winner)	6 (party leader; other office—Mayor)	Soares (incumbent)	(incumbent)		
Ferreira do Amaral	5 (other office—minister)	Cavaco Silva	7 (PM; party leader; other office—minister)	Basílio Horta	5 (other office—minister)	Freitas do Amaral	6 (party leader; other office—minister)
António Abreu	4 (political office only)			Carlos Carvalhas	5 (other office—minister)	Salgado Zenha	5 (other office—minister)
Fernando Rosas	4 (political office only)			Carlos Marques	4 (political office only)	Maria de Lurdes Pintasilgo	5 (PM)
Garcia Pereira	5 (party leader)						
Average quality of defeated candidates	4.5	Average quality of defeated candidates	7	Average quality of defeated candidates	4.7	Average quality of defeated candidates	5.3

Source: Author's own elaboration.

Inevitably this analysis is more an initial assessment of incumbency advantage in semi-presidentialism than a conclusive statement on the precise mechanisms that underlie the clear pro-incumbent bias here identified. Thus, future studies will be able to test the wider validity of the results for the Portuguese case that has been presented. Moreover, there remains scope for further assessment of the Portuguese case also, especially in terms of assessing the relative weight of the direct and indirect effects of incumbency.

Nevertheless, beyond what these results potentially tell us about incumbency advantage and about semi-presidentialism, they also have clear implications for the choices faced by voters in Portuguese presidential elections. On the one hand, open seat elections attract high-quality challengers and generate competitive elections. Yet on the other hand, voters' choices appear to be severely constrained by the supply of candidates in re-election years, generating uncompetitive elections and weak voter interest, reflected inter alia in low turnout levels. This inevitably has an adverse effect on the quality of democracy. This bipolar nature of presidential elections may be advantageous to political agents and result from their rational self-interest, as they seek to maximise their chance of election. However, by limiting the choice that voters have, this pattern does not appear to maximise collective benefits in terms of democratic choice and quality.

Notes

[1] For a rare exception, see Fortes & Magalhães (2005), which takes into account incumbency in its analysis of presidential elections as second-order elections in semi-presidentialism.
[2] See for instance Robert Elgie's: http://www.semipresidentialism.com/The_Semi-presidential_One/Blog/Entries/2007/12/30_Up-to-date_list_of_semi-presidential_countries.html
[3] Presidents are limited to two consecutive terms. They can seek a third term, so long as it is not consecutive.
[4] For an overview of polls from early 2010 to the eve of the election, see Pedro Magalhães excellent blog *Margens de Erro*, especially the following entry: http://margensdeerro.blogspot.com/2011/01/tendencias.html (consulted 20 April 2011).
[5] This party was originally CDS (Partido do Centro Democrático Social, Party of the Democratic Social Centre). In the mid-1990s it changed its official name to Partido Popular (Popular Party), albeit retaining CDS in its acronym, being formally registered as CDS-PP. In 2009, the party changed its official name to CDS-Partido Popular, with the acronym CDS-PP. However, while the CDS is part of the official party name, it now stands as a name on its own rather than as an acronym.
[6] The monthly *Eurosondagem* barometer gave the Socialists 43.3 per cent of voting intentions in January 2006, more than the PSD (33 per cent) and CDS-PP (7.7 per cent) combined.
[7] The *Eurosondagem* barometer of January 2011 gave the PSD 37.4 per cent and the CDS-PP 9.6 per cent of voting intentions, well ahead of the Socialists 30.3 per cent.
[8] The PS was absent from power from 1985 till 1995. Since 1995, it has governed for all but three years, from 1995 to 2002; and then from 2005 till June 2011.
[9] Indeed, in a recent television interview of 17 April 2011, Fernando Nobre stated that in social terms, in humanistic terms I am certainly a man of the left, available online at: http://www.youtube.com/watch?v=yLqOR3YXzdc&feature = related, minute 6:18-6:35

References

Barroso, J. D. (1986) 'Les conflits entre le Président portugais et la majorité parlementaire de 1979 à 1983', in *Les Régimes Semi-Présidentiels*, ed. M. Duverger, Presses Universitaires de France, Paris, pp. 237–254.
Bickers, K. N. & Stein, R. M. (1996) 'The electoral dynamics of the federal pork barrel', *American Journal of Political Science*, vol. 40, no. 4, pp. 1300–1326.
Bond, J. R., Covington, C. & Fleisher, R. (1985) 'Explaining challenger quality in congressional elections', *Journal of Politics*, vol. 47, no. 2, pp. 510–529.
Cerdeira, S. (2011) 'Resultados de Fernando Nobre e José Manuel Coelho são "voto de protesto" contra os partidos', I Online, 25 January.
Coelho, H. F. (2010) 'Alegre une críticos de Louçã no BE, Diário de Notícias', 27 August.
Coelho, J. M. (2010) '1 de Novembro de 2010: Coelho Anuncia Lançamento de Candidatura', available online at: http://coelhopresidente.wordpress.com/2010/11/01/coelho-candidato-a-presidente/
Correia, A. P. (2011) 'Eleitores foram obrigados a engrossar taxa de abstenção', Jornal de Notícias, 24 January.
Cox, G. W. & Katz, J. N. (1996) 'Why did the incumbency advantage in U.S. House elections grow?', *American Journal of Political Science*, vol. 40, no. 2, pp. 478–497.
Diário IOL. (2010) 'Tenho vontade de ganhar, mas vou perder por 10-0 ou 20-0', 23 December.
Económico. (2011) 'Cavaco: "Utilizarei os meus poderes para que Portugal encontre o rumo certo"', 13 January.
Erikson, R. S. (1971) 'The advantage of incumbency in congressional elections', *Polity*, vol. 3, no. 3, pp. 395–405.
Expresso. (2008) 'Sócrates critica Alegre', 12 November.
Fleury, C. J. & Lewis-Beck, M. S. (1993) 'Anchoring the French voter: ideology versus party', *Journal of Politics*, vol. 55, no. 4, pp. 1100–1109.
Fortes, B. G. & Magalhães, P. C. (2005) 'As eleições presidenciais em sistemas semipresidenciais: participação eleitoral e punição dos governos', *Análise Social*, vol. XL, no. 177, pp. 891–922.
Friedman, J. N. & Holden, R. T. (2009) 'The rising incumbent reelection rate: what's gerrymandering got to do with it?', *Journal of Politics*, vol. 71, no. 2, pp. 593–611.
Jacobson, G. C. & Kernell, S. (1983) *Strategy and Choice in Congressional Elections*, rev. 2nd ed., Yale University Press, New Haven.
Jalali, C. (2011) 'The president is not a passenger: Portugal's evolving semi-presidentialism', in *Semi-presidentialism and Democracy*, eds R. Elgie, S. Moestrup & Y. -S. Wu, Palgrave Macmillan, Houndmills, pp. 156–173.
Jones, M. P. (2004) 'Electoral institutions, social cleavages, and candidate competition in presidential elections', *Electoral Studies*, vol. 23, no. 1, pp. 73–106.
Jornal de Notícias. (2010) 'Vitalino Canas diz que Alegre "dividirá seriamente" o PS', 16 January.
Krasno, J. S. & Green, D. P. (1988) 'Preempting Quality Challengers in House Elections', *Journal of Politics*, vol. 50, no. 4, pp. 920–936.
Levitt, S. D. & Wolfram, C. D. (1997) 'Decomposing the sources of incumbency advantage in the U.S. House', *Legislative Studies Quarterly*, vol. 22, no. 1, pp. 45–60.
Lewis-Beck, M. S. & Nadeau, R. (2000) 'French electoral institutions and the economic vote', *Electoral Studies*, vol. 19, no. 2–3, pp. 171–182.
Lewis-Beck, M. S. & Stegmaier, M. (2000) 'Economic determinants of electoral outcomes', *Annual Review of Political Science*, vol. 3, no. 1, pp. 183–219.
Lisi, M. (2009) *A Arte de Ser Indispensável: Líder e Organização no Partido Socialista Português*, Imprensa de Ciências Sociais, Lisboa.
Lisi, M. (2010) 'The renewal of the socialist majority: the 2009 Portuguese legislative elections', *West European Politics*, vol. 33, no. 2, pp. 381–388.

Lusa News Agency. (2011) 'Rebelo de Sousa rejeita que intervenção do FMI signifique queda do Governo e critica Passos Coelho', 10 January.

Magalhães, P. C. (2007) 'What are (semi)presidential elections about? A case study of the Portuguese 2006 elections', *Journal of Elections, Public Opinion, Parties*, vol. 17, no. 3, pp. 263–291.

Martins, P., 'Alegre tacticismo ou como fazer a espargata', *Jornal de Notícias*, 4 January

Mayhew, D. R. (2008) 'Incumbency advantage in U.S. presidential elections: the historical record', *Political Science Quarterly*, vol. 123, pp. 201–228.

Neto, O. A. & Lobo, M. C. (2009) 'Portugal's semi-presidentialism (re)considered: an assessment of the president's role in the policy process, 1976–2006', *European Journal of Political Research*, vol. 48, no. 2, pp. 234–255.

Nobre, F. (2010) 'Discurso à Convenção Nacional', available online at: http://www.fernandonobre2011.com/como-recomecar-portugal/discursos-do-candidato/convenao-nacional.aspx

Prior, M. (2006) 'The incumbent in the living room: the rise of television and the incumbency advantage in U.S. House elections', *Journal of Politics*, vol. 68, no. 3, pp. 657–673.

Público. (2004) 'Quem é Quem no PCP?', 26 November.

Sá, P. (2011a) 'Cavaco com "pouco apetite" para usar a dissolução', *Diário de Notícias online*, 19 January.

Sá, P. (2011b) 'BPN ensombrou eleições e irritou o Presidente', *Diário de Notícias*, 14 April.

Simas, N. (2010) 'Adversários e partidos "suaves" com Cavaco', *Público*, 14 December.

Simas, N. (2011) 'Cavaco Silva aumenta as críticas e desafia Governo a explicar medidas de austeridade', *Público online*, 11 January.

Simas, N., Oliveira, M. J. & Gomes, M. (2011) 'Cavaco Silva critica cortes salariais e diz que também quer ver "privados" a pagar a crise', *Público*, 16 January.

Stone, W. J., Fulton, S. A., Maestas, C. D. & Maisel, L. S. (2010) 'Incumbency reconsidered: prospects, strategic retirement, and incumbent quality in U.S. House elections', *Journal of Politics*, vol. 72, no. 1, pp. 178–190.

Tavares, R. (2011) 'Solilóquio do perdedor', *Público*, 26 January.

Van der Brug, W., Van Der Eijk, C. & Marsh, M. (2000) 'Exploring uncharted territory: the Irish presidential election, 1997', *British Journal of Political Science*, vol. 30, no. 4, pp. 631–650.

Wu, Y.-S. (2011) 'Clustering of semi-presidentialism: a first cut', in *Semi-presidentialism and Democracy*, eds R. Elgie, S. Moestrup & Y.-S. Wu, Palgrave Macmillan, Houndmills, pp. 21–41.

Carlos Jalali is Assistant Professor and researcher at the Governance, Competitiveness and Public Policies Research Centre of the University of Aveiro. His research is on Portuguese political institutions, parties and electoral behaviour, published inter alia in *Party Politics* and *Journal of Political Marketing*. He is also the author of *Partidos e Democracia em Portugal, 1974-2005* (Imprensa de Ciências Sociais, 2007).

The Twilight of the Berlusconi Era: Local Elections and National Referendums in Italy, May and June 2011

Alessandro Chiaramonte and Roberto D'Alimonte

Following its victory in the spring 2008 general elections, the centre-right coalition led by Silvio Berlusconi formed a government that appeared to be the most cohesive in the history of the Second Republic. Three-and-a-half years later, in November 2011, Berlusconi was forced to resign, ending a long period in which he had dominated Italian politics. By analysing the 2008–11 political–economic cycle, with special attention to the local elections and the referendums of May and June 2011, we argue that the downfall of Berlusconi's government can be explained by the interplay of the international economic crisis, the scandals related to the prime minister's private life, the divisions of the parties of the centre-right and the shrinking of its parliamentary base.

On 12 November 2011 Silvio Berlusconi resigned as prime minister of Italy. A few days later Mario Monti, the former European Union (EU) commissioner, formed a new technocratic government supported by all the parties in parliament with the exception of the Northern League (Lega Nord, LN). Berlusconi did not resign because he had lost a vote of confidence. His majority simply faded away. A few days before his resignation the Chamber of Deputies had voted on a budget bill. Only 308 out of 630 deputies voted in favour. Berlusconi did not have to resign but he did. The vote showed that his government had become too fragile to be able to cope with Italy's growing economic and financial problems. It was the outcome of a process of progressive weakening of the unity of the centre-right bloc and of Berlusconi's leadership.

In the last general elections held in 2008 the centre-right coalition led by Berlusconi had won 344 seats (54.6 per cent) in the Chamber and 174 seats in the Senate (55.2 per cent). Following the election Berlusconi formed his fourth cabinet,[1] which consisted of only two parties, the People of Freedom (Popolo della libertà, PDL) and the LN. The PDL alone gained 37.4 per cent of the vote in the Chamber, more than any party since the Christian Democrats (DC) in 1979. On paper this was the most cohesive government coalition in the history of the Second Republic. Particularly, it is worth pointing out that it replaced the centre-left coalition led by Romano Prodi which had consisted of eight parties and lasted for only two years.[2] The two most important members of this coalition were the Left Democrats (Democratici di sinistra, DS) and the Daisy (La Margherita). The former was the largest successor of the Italian Communist Party and the latter was formed mainly by leftist Catholics. In 2007 these two parties merged into the Democratic Party (Partito democratico, PD). In 2008 the PD gained 33.2 per cent of the votes in the Chamber. Ever since it has been the most important opposition party.

The general expectation was that the new Berlusconi cabinet would be stable and durable. This was not the case. After the summer of 2010 support for his government started to weaken. At the parliamentary level the major blow came with the split of the PDL due to the defection of a group of deputies and senators led by Gianfranco Fini.[3] This left Berlusconi's government with a slim majority, particularly in the Chamber. At the electoral level his declining popularity became evident in the local elections and the referendums held, respectively, in May and June 2011. Their negative outcome for the parties in power revealed that the mood in the country was rapidly changing. Until then the governing coalition had been able to maintain more or less the same level of support as in the 2008 general election. This is shown by the results of the 2009 European elections and of the elections held in 2010 for the renewal of the regional governments. This was not the case in the following electoral round, which took place in the spring of 2011 with local elections and four referendums.

The 2011 local elections were held in 1,316 municipalities and 11 provinces. The four most important municipal tests were Milan, Naples, Turin and Bologna. The pattern of competition in these cities was similar to that on the national level, with a centre-right coalition facing a centre-left and a centrist coalition. The expectation was that the centre-right parties would not do very well across the board. Nonetheless they were expected to win at least in Milan and in Naples. Instead they lost in both cities. The loss of Milan, Berlusconi's hometown and a moderate stronghold, was particularly relevant, since the centre-left had never won in this city during the Second Republic. Overall the PDL and the LN did very poorly. The centre-right coalition won 40 out of the 133 larger municipalities, 15 fewer than in the previous elections, while the number of local administrations controlled by the centre-left increased from 76 up to 85.

Another setback for the Berlusconi government occurred a few weeks later with the vote on four referendums. Voters were asked to decide on the repeal of four existing laws approved by the Berlusconi governing coalition. The referendums were promoted by a variety of opposition groups. They dealt with the regulation of water utilities (two of them), the development of nuclear energy and the immunity of high government officials from appearing in court while in office (the so called 'legitimate impediment'). In all four cases the existing laws were repealed. Over 50 per cent of eligible voters participated. Approximately 95 per cent of them voted to repeal. It was a clear repudiation of government policies and a stunning defeat for Berlusconi.

How can we explain the erosion of the parliamentary and electoral support of the government? The split of the PDL is one reason. Along with it, two other factors played a significant role: the economic crisis and the scandals related to Berlusconi's private life. But their impact cannot be fully understood without placing them in a larger context. In the next section we will describe the 2008–11 political–economic cycle. Subsequently the focus will centre on the local elections and the referendums, the two political events that provided clear evidence of the declining popular support for the governing parties. In the last sections we will update the analysis covering the events leading to the fall of the Berlusconi government.

The Decline of Berlusconi's Fourth Government: Political Splits, Economic Crisis and Pretty Women

Since he entered politics in 1994, Berlusconi's goal was the unification of the Italian right, a goal that he had accomplished by 2001. This success was the basis of his leadership. Paradoxically the unity of the right started to unravel in 2008 after one of its greatest electoral victories. The merger of Berlusconi's Forza Italia (Go Italy!), and Fini's National Alliance (Alleanza nazionale, AN) to form the PDL was intended to strengthen the unity of the moderates. It had the opposite effect. The Centrist Union (Unione di Centro, UDC), another member of the centre-right, refused to join the new party and was forced out of the Berlusconi coalition that won the 2008 election.

In retrospect we can now say that this was the beginning of the end. Fini's split two years later was the second act of the dissolution of the right. The third act would be the separation between the PDL and the LN at the time of the formation of the Monti cabinet when the PDL voted in favour and the LN voted against. The dissolution of the unity of the Italian right is not the direct consequence of either the economic crisis or the sexual scandals. But these factors certainly contributed to it. At the same time if Berlusconi had been able to keep all the moderate parties together, as he did in the period 2001–08, the crisis and the scandals would have had less of an impact on his leadership and on his capacity to govern.

Certainly the scandals did not *cause* Berlusconi's resignation. In other countries this might have been the case. Not in Italy. They tarnished his image and his credibility but they had no direct impact on his tenure in office or on the stability of his cabinet. Even their effect on his popularity was not felt immediately. The first public revelations of Berlusconi's questionable private behaviour date back to April 2009. At that time Italy was already in the midst of a recession caused by the consequences of the international financial crisis. Yet, in the European election held in June 2009 the PDL got 35.3 per cent of the votes. Actually the combined electoral strength of the two major governing parties—PDL and LN—in 2009 was basically unchanged from 2008 (45.5 and 45.7 per cent, respectively). More or less the same can be said about the 2010 regional elections.

The role of the international financial crisis and its repercussions on the financing of Italy's huge public debt cannot be underestimated. There is no question that this factor, even more than the sexual scandals, did have a direct and significant impact on the stability of the cabinet. The progressive worsening of the crisis, as shown by the growing spread between Italian and German treasury bonds, raised increasing doubts about the ability of the government to take the necessary measures to regain investors' confidence. But, even so, would Berlusconi have resigned if he had still had a working parliamentary majority? It is, of course, impossible to say. What actually happened instead is that Berlusconi, in spite of mounting external pressure, gave no signs for months of his intention to quit. Eventually he asked for a vote of confidence and decided to resign only after he realised that his parliamentary majority had shrunk further, even though the opposition did not have enough votes to force him out. No single factor can explain this outcome. Berlusconi's fall is rather the result of the progressive dissolution of the centre-right bloc and of his leadership combined with the sexual scandals and the worsening economic crisis. This will be our argument in the following pages.

Silvio Berlusconi became prime minister of Italy for the fourth time on 8 May 2008 following his clear victory in the general elections held the month before (13–14 April). Soon after, his government had to face the most serious financial crisis of the post-1945 period. This caught Italy in a difficult situation. Since the early 1990s the country's gross national debt has been over 100 per cent of the gross domestic product (GDP). According to the Organisation for Economic Cooperation and Development (OECD),[4] in 2008 it was 114.7 per cent, the second highest debt-to-GDP ratio in the European Union (after Greece). The size of the debt represented a constraint on the capacity of the Berlusconi government to expand public expenditures or cut taxes to offset the impact of the economic and financial crisis. In spite of this constraint the deficit and the debt rose. However, if we compare Italy's fiscal performance with that of the other major EU countries, the increase of both the deficit and the debt has been the lowest. In fact, according to OECD, in 2008 the government deficit was 2.7 per cent. It went up to 5.4 per cent in 2009. In 2010 it dropped to 4.5 per cent and in 2011 to 3.6 per cent.[5] In this period of time only Germany did better. We can see the same trend with regard to the national debt. In Italy it increased by 13 percentage points between 2008 and 2011. In Spain, the United Kingdom and France it increased substantially more. However, one cannot neglect the fact that Italy's debt was much higher.

Italy's relative success in controlling its public finances was widely credited to the Minister of the Economy, Giulio Tremonti. He succeeded in holding the line against his colleagues in the spending ministries who criticised his strategy of across-the-board cuts and tight ceilings on outlays. The austerity policy championed by Tremonti caused tensions inside the cabinet but it did not destabilise it. The popularity ratings of the prime minister stayed over the 50 per cent threshold until the summer of 2009 when the effects of the financial crisis were already being felt (Figure 1).

This helps explain the outcome of the European elections held in 2009 and the regional elections in 2010 (Baldi & Tronconi 2010; Corbetta 2012). In both cases the

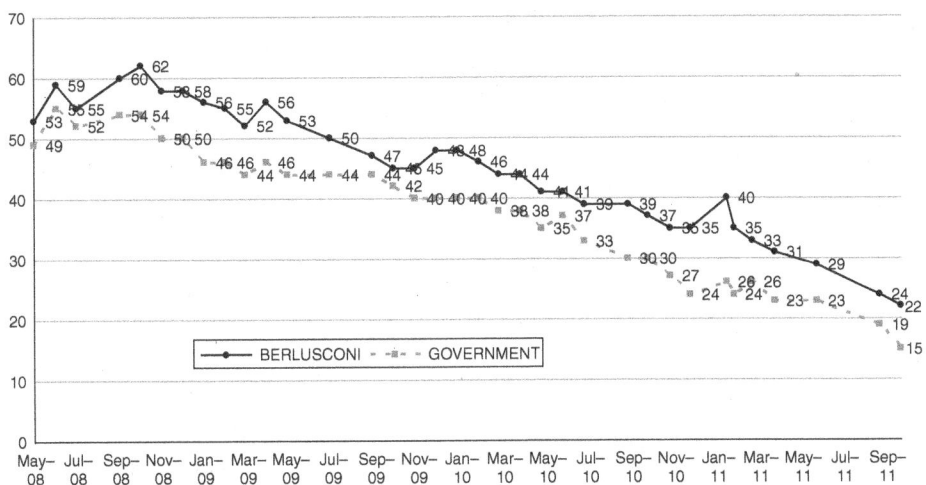

Figure 1 Popularity Ratings of Berlusconi and his Government. *Source:* IPR Marketing (2011).

centre-right coalition received a share of votes similar to that obtained in the general elections of 2008. This is most surprising, as it shows, on the one side, that the popular support for the government was still quite high two years after the outbreak of the financial crisis and, on the other side, that the opposition was not able to capitalise at all from it in spite of the fact that the economy had become the most salient issue in public debate.

By 2010, the general picture showed a puzzling contrast between a government whose electoral support was close to its 2008 peak and an economic situation that was getting worse and worse. Both in 2008 and in 2009 the GDP trend was negative (−1.3 per cent and −5.2 per cent, respectively) (see Table 1). The trend turned positive in 2010 but growth was only + 1.2 per cent, less than in the other major European economies with the exception of Spain. Unemployment rose from 6.1 per cent in 2007 to 8.4 per cent in 2010. Much worse are the figures for youth unemployment. By 2010 more than one in four young people between the age of 15 and 25 could not find a job; and in 2011 the youth unemployment rose to 28.6 per cent. Only in Spain, among the larger European democracies, was the figure worse.

The increase in unemployment did not correspond, however, to a similar increase in the number of strikes in the same period of time. Their number in 2010 was basically the same as in 2007, the year before the outbreak of the crisis. Workers' protest remained at normal levels.

The contrast between the poor state of the economy and the support enjoyed by the government is even more puzzling if we take into account the revelations concerning Berlusconi's scandalous personal life. On 27 April 2009, the major Italian newspapers reported the news that he had attended the birthday party of Noemi Letizia, an unknown 18-year-old girl outside Naples. The prime minister was unable to explain in

Table 1 Indicators of the Economic Crisis in Italy (2007–11)

Indicator	2007	2008	2009	2010	2011
GDP % change from previous year	+1.4	−1.3	−5.2	+1.2	+1.1*
Unemployment rate (%)	6.1	6.7	7.8	8.4	8.2*
Youth unemployment rate (%)	20.3	21.3	25.4	27.9	28.6*
CIG (million hours)	183.7	227.6	914.0	1,203.6	953.5
Strikes called (no.)	2,017	2,195	1,899	2,093	n.a.

Source: OECD for GDP; ISTAT (National Institute for Statistics) for the two unemployment rates; INPS (National Institute for Social Insurance) for CIG; Commissione di garanzia sciopero (2011, p. 54) for the number of strikes called.
Note: * Estimate; n.a. = not available.

a convincing fashion the reasons for being there. The following day *La Repubblica*, one of the most popular newspapers in the country, published on its front page a letter written by Berlusconi's wife, Veronica Lario, in which she denounced her husband's behaviour in explicit terms, referring to it as a 'malaise'. As we mentioned above, this had no impact on the performance of the governing parties in the European elections held in June.

How can we explain this puzzle? Here we can only formulate some hypotheses. First, the impact of the economic crisis on the labour force was mitigated by the widespread use of unemployment benefits.[6] The recurring theme in government communication was that no one would be left behind. Second, the opposition failed to propose a credible alternative. Actually its popularity remained consistently and significantly lower than that of the government. The plausible explanation is that the parties of the centre-left still suffered from the legacy of the Prodi cabinet that had governed the country between 2006 and 2008 and had been paralysed by internal dissent. Third, the government benefited from the perception that the origin of the crisis was not domestic but international and therefore it was not directly responsible for it. Actually, Berlusconi and Tremonti were very careful to point out that Italian public accounts were under control and that the Italian banking system had far fewer problems than in the rest of Europe and in the United States. This left the impression in public opinion that great sacrifices were not needed to tackle the consequences of the crisis.

The strategy of denying the existence of a serious problem for Italy worked for almost two years. In the spring of 2010, when the major rating agencies downgraded the Greek sovereign debt to the status of junk bonds, Berlusconi's popularity was still well over 40 per cent. Soon after, however, things started to change for the worse. Since then, with the exception of a short-lived upturn in December 2010, the popularity ratings of both the prime minister and the government declined dramatically. This was the result of a series of economic, political and personal factors which, taken together, undermined the strategy of denial which had worked well until then.

The perception (and the illusion) that Italy was insulated from the worst effects of the international financial turmoil was shattered when the prospects of a Greek default became real. All of a sudden Italian public finances started to be subject to a much closer scrutiny by the major international rating agencies and by the International Monetary Fund (IMF) and the EU. Until then the government's time frame for balancing the national budget was the 2014 fiscal year. From Berlusconi's point of view this deadline made a lot of sense politically, since general elections were due in the spring of 2013 and he did not want to run on a record of cuts in pension benefits and tax hikes. However, by the summer of 2010 he was no longer in full control of the agenda. Control had started to shift abroad. For the Italian government this was a turning point.

The time frame for balancing the budget had to be changed and the question of structural reforms for promoting growth became a hot issue. The first response was an economic package presented in parliament at the end of May 2010, which passed at the end of July. It did include important corrective measures (Gualmini & Pasotti 2011, p. 58), but the impression is that even at this time Berlusconi did not grasp all the implications of the rapidly changing international economic scenario. One is led to believe that, if he had, then the political upheaval that erupted in his party in the spring–summer of 2010 would have been avoided.

Gianfranco Fini has been the historical leader of AN, a party of the right which replaced the Italian Social Movement (Movimento Sociale Italiano, MSI) in the Second Republic. Since 1994 his party has been a member of every centre-right coalition formed by Berlusconi. Before the 2008 general elections Berlusconi proposed merging his party—FI—with AN to form the PDL. Fini accepted. The new party gained 37.4 per cent of the votes and 43.8 per cent of the seats in the lower Chamber. It was the largest party in the Italian parliament. When Berlusconi's fourth cabinet was formed, Fini preferred the position of president of the Chamber of Deputies to that of a government minister.

Personal relations between Berlusconi and Fini have never been smooth but until the summer of 2010 their alliance was never in question. This is why the growing criticism voiced by Fini over the actions of the government and the personal behaviour of its leader caught many by surprise. In April 2010 the dissent between the two leaders of the PDL came into the open at a meeting of the PDL directorate. The conflict escalated in the following months and reached its climax on 29 July when Fini was expelled from the PDL. The next day he formed new parliamentary groups in both the Chamber and the Senate called Future and Liberty for Italy (Futuro e libertà per l'Italia, FLI): 34 deputies and ten senators followed him (Hine & Vampa 2011).

The most plausible reason for the split was a mix of policy and personal motivations, on the one hand, and political miscalculations, on the other. For Fini, the creation of the PDL should have made him the second most important leader in the party and Berlusconi's legitimate heir. Instead, he found himself increasingly isolated within the PDL with no prospect of becoming its future leader. At the same time, however, the worsening of the economic crisis, the growing controversies over the government judicial initiatives and Berlusconi's private conduct offered him the opportunity to regain visibility and political autonomy. In all probability, he wanted to claim a greater role within the PDL and not to create a new party. However, Berlusconi's unwillingness to find a compromise led to the split (from Berlusconi's point of view) or the expulsion (from Fini's perspective). Both men miscalculated. Berlusconi did not anticipate correctly the cost of the split in terms of the number of defections and found himself with a razor-thin relative majority in the Chamber. Fini probably did not expect to be forced out of the party so abruptly.

The split of the major governing party created uncertainty over the stability of the cabinet with the final showdown on 14 December 2010. For months the opposition parties had wanted to table a motion of no confidence, but were persuaded to postpone it by the President of the Republic, Giorgio Napolitano. He wanted to see the approval of the finance bill for 2011 before the onset of a possible government crisis. The vote was finally scheduled in the Chamber of Deputies on 14 December. The final tally was 314 votes in favour of the government (out of 630), 311 against and two abstentions.[7] Since a simple majority is required, the fourth Berlusconi cabinet survived the test. But the Prime Minister found himself in the position of having to face growing economic and financial problems with a very slim and unstable parliamentary majority. Initially, his surprising victory boosted his popularity rating, but the effect did not last very long. To make things worse for him there were also new embarrassing revelations about his controversial private conduct.

The 'Rubygate' episode is the last in a sequence of sexual scandals involving Berlusconi. As in the case of Noemi Letizia, it had to do with an underage young woman whose real name is Karima El Marough. On 27 May 2010 she was arrested by the police in Milan on charges of theft. Berlusconi called the head of the Milan police and pressed for her release, claiming the girl was the niece of the then Egyptian President, Hosni Mubarak. In the following days it became clear that Ruby was part of a 'vast pimping network' of young women who were paid to attend 'bunga bunga' sex parties with the prime minister at his home. In January 2011, Berlusconi was placed under criminal investigation for allegedly having sex with an underage prostitute and for abuse of office relating to her release from detention. On 15 February 2011, a judge indicted him to stand trial.

By the spring of 2011, when local elections were scheduled, the popularity ratings of the government and the prime minister had reached new lows. The strategy of denial was no longer working. The outcome of the 2011 local elections and that of the following referendums would show that the governing parties had lost the support of important sectors of their electorate.

The 2011 Local Elections

On 15 and 16 May about 13 million Italians, roughly a quarter of the whole electoral body, were called to vote in municipal and provincial elections. In spite of their local character, they became a national test for Berlusconi and his government. The vote involved 1,316 municipalities with 10,925,391 registered voters and 11 provinces with 3,647,187 voters. In Table 2 we show the results by party and by coalition for the 133 municipalities with a population of at least 15,000 residents. The reason behind

Table 2 Aggregate Votes for Party Lists and Blocs in the 2011 Local Elections for a Total of 133 Municipalities and Comparison with the 2010 Regional Elections for a Subset of 118 Municipalities

Party lists and blocs	Total (133 municipalities) 2011 votes N	%	2011/2010 comparison (118 minicipalities) 2011 %	2010 %	Difference 2011/2010
PD (Democratic Party)	1,023,823	23.3	23.5	27.3	−3.9
IDV (Italy of Values)	163,346	3.7	3.7	7.5	−3.8
SEL (Left. Ecology. Liberty)	184,005	4.2	4.1	3.5	0.5
FDS (Federation of the Left)	105,816	2.4	2.4	2.7	−0.3
PS (Socialist Party)	51,788	1.2	1.2	0.3	0.9
Other centre-left lists	378,811	8.6	8.4	3.0	5.4
Centre-left total	*1,907,589*	*43.4*	*43.2*	*44.4*	*−1.2*
UDC (Centrist Union)	217,853	5.0	4.7	5.3	−0.6
FLI (Future and Liberty for Italy)	51,690	1.2	1.1	−	1.1
API (Alliance for Italy)	33,125	0.8	0.8	0.9	−0.1
Other Third Pole lists	135,667	3.1	3.3	0.2	3.1
Third Pole total	*438,335*	*10.0*	*9.9*	*6.4*	*3.5*
PDL (People of Freedom)	1,661,375	21.7	22.0	32.4	−10.4
LN (Northern League)	226,956	5.2	5.4	7.9	−2.6
La Destra (The Right)	23,489	0.5	0.5	0.6	−0.1
Other centre-right lists	459,354	10.5	10.1	4.5	5.6
Centre-right total	*951,576*	*37.8*	*38.0*	*45.5*	*−7.5*
Mov. 5 Stelle (5 Stars Movement)	130,550	3.0	3.1	2.5	0.6
Others	256,068	5.8	5.8	1.2	4.6
Total valid votes	4,393,917	100.0	100.0	100.0	0.0
Turnout rate		69.7	69.9	62.4	7.5

Source: Our own elaboration from Ministry of the Interior data.

this selection is that this threshold separates two arenas of competition characterised by different electoral systems. In the municipalities under 15,000 residents, the list with the plurality of votes wins two-thirds of the seats, while one-third of the seats are allocated proportionally among the remaining lists. The lists competing in these municipalities are often local ones, with no reference to national parties or coalitions. This is why we have excluded them from our analysis.

In the municipalities with at least 15,000 residents the electoral system combines a two-round majority formula for the direct election of the mayor and a proportional formula with a majority bonus for the election of the municipal council. The majority bonus is assigned to the list or coalition of lists supporting the winning candidate mayor.

In this arena the pattern of competition is often similar to the national one, particularly at the coalitional level. In fact, though local lists are almost always present, in many cases they are connected to one of the major national blocs. This is why it is possible to compare these local elections with those held the year before for the renewal of regional governments. Taken in isolation the 2011 results do not tell us much about the loss of support for the centre-right coalition but the comparison with 2010 is revealing. However, in order to proceed we had to do a further selection. In fact, not all the municipalities voting in 2011 voted also in 2010. Therefore our database includes only the 118 municipalities that voted in both elections. The voters involved in this subset are about nine million. For a correct interpretation of the results we must add that this set of 118 cases is not a national representative sample in terms of geography and demography. Among these municipalities the larger ones, especially in the north, are overrepresented.[8] However, as we are interested in electoral trends, this is not a serious problem.

Table 2 clearly shows the centre-right electoral defeat. In the regional elections of 2010 the Berlusconi coalition obtained 45.5 per cent of the votes in the 118 municipalities. A year later it was down to 38 per cent, a loss of 7.5 percentage points. The negative performance of the PDL stands out. Its share of the vote declined from 32.4 to 22.0 per cent. However, the real beneficiary of this loss was not the centre-left. The winners were the so-called 'Third Pole'—formed by the UDC, Fini's FLI and Alliance for Italy (Alleanza per l'Italia, API) and the minor lists (most of whom are local). The 'Third Pole' won 9.9 per cent of the votes compared with 6.4 per cent in 2010. The minor lists won 8.9 per cent, up from 3.7 per cent in 2010. In this group it is worth mentioning the performance of the list 5 Star Movement (Movimento 5 stelle), created by the popular comedian Beppe Grillo, which received 3.1 per cent of the votes.

For the centre-left these elections were a mixed success (Legnante 2012). The good news was that out of 133 municipalities it won 85, up from 76 in the previous elections, whereas the centre-right won 40, down from 55. But in terms of votes the centre-left parties did not make any gains. They actually lost some—down from 44.4 to 43.2 per cent—in spite of the significant decline of their main rival.

The centre-right losses are systematic but not uniform (Table 3). Territorial variations are significant and they help to identify the national factors behind the defeat of the governing coalition. To explore this we divided the country into three areas: North, Centre and South. In the North we have included the municipalities in the regions of Piemonte, Lombardia, Veneto and Liguria.

Table 3 Aggregate Percentage Votes for Blocs in the 2011 Local Elections by Geographical Area (Comparison with the Percentage Votes in the 2010 Regional Elections for 118 Municipalities)

Blocs	North (36)			Centre (21)			South (61)			Italy (118)		
	2011	2010	Diff.	2011	2010	Diff.	2011	2010	Diff.	2011	2010	Diff.
Centre-left	47.1	43.3	3.9	52.8	52.6	0.2	36.6	42.3	−5.7	43.2	44.4	−1.2
Third Pole	5.3	3.4	1.9	4.2	4.4	−0.2	15.8	9.8	6.0	9.9	6.4	3.5
Centre-right	39.2	49.4	−10.2	28.3	38.2	−9.9	40.5	44.9	−4.4	38.0	45.5	−7.5
Others	8.4	4.0	4.4	14.7	4.8	9.9	7.1	3.0	4.1	8.8	3.7	5.1

Source: Our own elaboration from Ministry of the Interior data.

The Centre includes Emilia-Romagna, Toscana, Marche and Umbria. As for the South the regions involved are Lazio, Campania, Basilicata, Puglia and Calabria.

The most interesting evidence regards the North. In 2010 in the 36 municipalities included in our set the centre-right was the largest coalition with 49.4 per cent of the votes, whereas the centre-left had 43.3 per cent. In 2011 the balance was reversed. The centre-left became the largest bloc with 47.1 vs. 39.2 per cent. In one year the centre-right in the North lost more than 10 percentage points and the centre-left gained 3.8. In the Centre the loss of the centre-right was the same as in the North, but the centre-left did not make any significant gains. In the South both major coalitions lost votes. Actually, here the centre-left lost more than the centre-right, which remained the largest coalition and increased its advantage over its main rival.[9]

These data suggest an explanation. The centre-right parties and candidates running in the local elections almost everywhere have paid a price for their association with the centre-right national government. The price turned out to be higher in the North and in the Centre, the most economically advanced areas of the country, because this was where the impact of the economic crisis was felt earlier and more intensely. In the South the crisis had an impact too, but less so because the economic system is less dynamic and therefore less responsive to the changes in the business cycle. The same pattern occurred at the end of the First Republic in 1992–93. At that time the Christian Democracy vote declined much faster in the North and in the Centre than in the South basically for the same reasons.

This interpretation is supported by the result of the election in Milan, which is the financial capital of the country and Berlusconi's hometown. Since 1993 Milan has been a stronghold of the parties of the centre-right. Here the centre-left has never won a mayoral election during the Second Republic. In 2006 Letizia Moratti, a member of Berlusconi's cabinet between 2001 and 2006, won the election on the first round with 52 per cent of the votes. She ran again in 2011 supported by the two major parties of the centre-right, PDL and LN. Her main rival was Giuliano Pisapia, a former MP elected with Communist Refoundation (Rifondazione comunista, PRC), a radical left-wing party. Though Pisapia was considered a left-wing moderate, his association with PRC made him an unlikely competitor in a city where the moderates have always dominated the political scene. Yet, he defeated the official candidate of the main centre-left party, the PD, in an open primary and then went on to beat the incumbent mayor.

From the beginning of the campaign the Milan election was treated as a crucial national test. Berlusconi himself reminded voters that he was 'always in the running'. He and Umberto Bossi, the leader of the LN, campaigned heavily in favour of Letizia Moratti. The confrontation turned ugly. Berlusconi resorted to old tactics that had worked in the past. He went as far as saying that those 'who vote for the left leave their brain at home' (Magri 2011). Contrary to general expectations, Letizia Moratti was forced into the runoff arriving in second with 41.6 per cent of the votes. Pisapia got 48 per cent. The result of the second ballot, held two weeks later, was even more surprising. Pisapia won with 55.1 per cent, Moratti scoring 44.9 per cent. Turnout in the two rounds was the same. Less than one per cent of moderate voters who abstained on the first ballot went to the polls in the second to prevent the victory of a 'communist'. Nor did the voters of third-party candidates rally in the second round to support the most moderate of the two contenders left in the field. An analysis of individual vote shifts at the precinct level shows that only 55 per cent of those who voted for the centrist candidate, Manfredi Palmeri, in the first round cast their ballot for Moratti in the second (Paparo & Cataldi 2011).

The victory of Pisapia in the financial capital of the country was a very serious blow for Berlusconi and his government. Losing Milan, after making this election a national test, clearly exposed how weak the centre-right coalition had become even in its own territory. There's no doubt that local factors did play a role in Moratti's defeat. She was not a popular candidate. Her record in office was considered negative. And she ran a bad campaign. That said, however, she would not have lost had she been supported by the same coalition that elected her in 2006 and if moderate voters had not defected. In this respect she was the most prominent victim of the divisions of the centre-right: the exit of the UDC from the national centre-right coalition in 2008 and the split of FLI from the PDL in 2010. Yet, Berlusconi expected that in Milan, as well as in other parts of the country, these divisions would not have an impact on the capacity of his candidates to win by holding on to moderate votes. The fact that this did not happen across the country, and particularly the fact that it did not happen in Milan, was a clear indication of the weakening of his coalition and of the waning of his leadership under the weight of the sexual scandals and the consequences of the economic crisis.

Naples was another major blow for Berlusconi. This election was considered just as symbolic as the one in Milan, albeit for different reasons. The outgoing administration of centre-left mayor Rosa Russo Jervolino, which had governed the city since 2001, was very unpopular due to its poor record on the most salient issue in Neapolitan politics: garbage collection. The centre-right coalition was therefore quite confident that his candidate, Giovanni Lettieri, the former president of Naples Business Conference, would easily win. Furthermore, the centre-left was badly divided and still reeling from the consequences of a primary election that was annulled because of electoral fraud. Its official candidate was Mario Morcone, who was supported by the largest party of the centre-left, the PD, and by Left, Ecology, Liberty (Sinistra, Ecologia, Libertà, SEL). The other centre-left candidate was Luigi De Magistris, a former prosecutor. He was supported by his own party, Italy of Values (Italia dei Valori, IDV), and a joint list of two parties of the extreme left. On paper he was the weakest of the three main candidates with no chance of getting to the second ballot. Yet he did. Morcone came in third and the runoff took place between Lettieri and De Magistris. De Magistris not only won but actually trounced Lettieri. The final tally was 65 per cent for De Magistris and 35 per cent for Berlusconi's candidate.

Such a defeat of the centre-right came as a complete surprise, as polls failed to assess correctly the fickle state of public opinion in the city. More than in other cases the outcome was a mix of local and national factors. De Magistris prevailed because he ran an effective grassroots campaign with a strong populist appeal and succeeded in coming across as an outsider with no responsibility for the garbage mess. This differentiated him from the failures of the centre-left mayor as well as those of the centre-right national government. The strong support Berlusconi gave to Lettieri did not help at all to mobilise moderate voters.[10] The analysis of individual vote shifts at the precinct level shows that one-third of those who had voted for Lettieri in the first round did not go to vote in the runoff (Paparo & Cataldi 2011). For Berlusconi, who never failed to remind Neapolitans of his role in helping their city with its garbage problems, it was a political and personal setback. Even in the volatile South the 'Berlusconi magic' was no longer effective.

Turin and Bologna complete the picture of the centre-right defeat. These were the other two major towns voting in this round of elections. Turin, the city of Fiat, and Bologna, which lies in the heart of the Italian 'red belt', had been ruled by the centre-left during the previous five years but the candidates of the coalition led by the PD were now new entries. Here the centre-right coalition did not really expect to win. Its goal was to force its opponents into a runoff. The presence of Grillo's candidates made this a likely prospect. They were expected to attract leftist voters, making the candidates of the centre-left bloc less competitive. In both cities the Grillo movement did well but Piero Fassino in Turin and Virginio Merola in Bologna, both members of the PD, won in the first round with, respectively, 56.7 per cent and 50.5 per cent of the votes.

The Popular Referendums

Just two weeks after the runoffs in the local elections, Italian citizens were called again to vote for a series of popular referendums (12–13 June). These referendums were promoted in order to repeal some controversial laws passed by the Berlusconi government. They represented therefore a new test for the popularity of Berlusconi and his cabinet, especially after the negative results of the previous round of local elections.

The four questions submitted to the voters addressed: (1) the private management of local water utilities; (2) the setting of a fair rate of return for private investments in water utilities; (3) the production of nuclear energy; (4) immunity for high government officials from appearing in court while in office (the so called 'legitimate impediment').

Under Italian law, referendums require more than half the electorate to vote to be binding. This quorum had not been reached in any of the six referendums held since 1997.[11] Given these facts, for the parties in favour of the existing laws the best strategy for preventing their repeal was to tell their voters not to show up at the polls. This was precisely what the parties of the Berlusconi coalition did. Moreover, the television networks under the direct or indirect control of the Italian prime minister almost ignored the ballot.

But in this case the strategy did not work. The turnout was quite high: 54.8 per cent. Excluding Italian citizens residing abroad, turnout actually reached 57 per cent. All the laws were repealed. On each of the four questions the percentage of votes in favour of repeal was overwhelming. It varied slightly between 94.1 and 95.8 per cent according to the specific question (see Table 4).

Table 4 Results of the Popular Referendums of 12 and 13 June 2011 (%)

Referendum	Turnout	Yes (repeal)	No (confirm)
Private management of water utilities	54.82	95.4	4.6
Return on investments for water utilities	54.83	95.8	4.2
Nuclear energy	54.79	94.1	5.9
Legitimate impediment	54.78	94.6	5.4

Source: Italian Ministry of the Interior.
Note: The figures shown in the table include both the Italian domestic constituency and the constituency of Italians residing abroad.

The outcome was a second crushing defeat for Berlusconi in less than one month. More than 25 million Italians voted 'Yes' to repeal laws proposed and backed by his government. The Fukushima accident, which occurred just before the date set for the referendum, played a major role in stirring emotions and fears over nuclear power and therefore in motivating people to vote. But also the referendums on the water utilities attracted a lot of attention. Many voters were afraid of what they perceived as a 'privatisation' of water services. Nonetheless, it is a fact that even the most politically sensitive among the four laws, i.e. the one on 'legitimate impediment', was repealed with an overwhelming majority. This was a particularly damaging setback for Berlusconi, who had championed the law. After its repeal he was left without a legal tool for delaying his trials. A lot of people who had followed him until then stayed home or voted against him. The negative outcome showed that he had lost touch with public opinion. In spite of the low profile that he tried to take during the campaign, the rejection of his policies was indeed a rejection of his leadership. Coming after the setback in the local elections, this was another clear sign of the erosion of his electoral support.

Comparing the results of these referendums with data from the 2006 and 2008 general elections gives a clear idea of the extent of Berlusconi's defeat. In June 2011 roughly 25 million Italians voted against Berlusconi's policies. In the 2006 and 2008 general elections the votes cast in favour of parties outside the centre-right perimeter were roughly 19 million. In these elections the turnout was, respectively, 83.6 per cent and 80.5 per cent. We need, of course, to be very cautious in comparing results from such different electoral arenas. In theory it is possible that different and partially non-overlapping segments of the electorate went to the polls. However, the figure of 19 million votes cast 'against' Berlusconi refers to elections in which the percentage of abstentions is not much higher than the percentage of chronic Italian non-voters—between 10 and 15 per cent of the overall electorate (Tuorto 2010).

It is, therefore, plausible to assume that a significant portion of the 25 million 'Yes' votes in the referendums were cast by voters who had voted for either Berlusconi's party or one of his allies in the last general election.[12] We don't know who they are and why they voted this way, nor we do know what their choices will be in the future. There is no doubt, however, that in these referendums they expressed their dissatisfaction with Berlusconi and with his policies. They did so without taking sides politically and without committing to a specific party choice. For incumbent governments referendums are a dangerous tool if they come at a time of declining popularity because they allow a degree of freedom that general elections don't. Voters feel free to support positions taken by parties they don't usually vote for because they do not consider their referendum vote an act of party endorsement. Berlusconi learned that lesson in 2011.

'That's All, Folks': The Fall

The results of the local elections and of the popular referendums set the stage for the final demise of the Berlusconi government. They further weakened the cohesion of the centre-right majority coalition by fostering increasing dissent and a number of defections in the ranks of the PDL parliamentary groups. In conjunction with this development, the Prime Minister's popularity rating and that of his government declined at a faster pace throughout the summer and the fall of 2011. As can be seen from Figure 1, in October the rating for the cabinet was less than 20 per cent and that for the Prime Minister just over that level. According to several polls conducted in November 2011, only 35–38 per cent of the respondents indicated their intention to vote for one of the parties of the centre-right coalition. The fragility of the government was evident.

Just a few weeks after the referendums, the Greek crisis worsened. The prospect of a Greek default led markets to reassess the risk on Italy's sovereign debt. The most sensitive indicator of such a risk is the difference in the interest paid on ten-year German bonds (Bund) and Italian bonds (Buoni del Tesoro Poliennali, BTP), the so-called 'spread BTP–Bund'.[13] From the introduction of the euro in 2001 to the end of 2009 the spread was under one per cent. Thanks to the common currency, Italy did not have to pay a significant premium to finance its government debt in spite of its size. In other words, investors did not consider Italy's debt a serious problem. During 2010 and up to June 2011 the spread did rise, but only marginally so. It never went over two per cent. This 'benign neglect' by the markets was the main reason why Berlusconi and Tremonti could continue to claim that Italy was better off than many of its partners.

As can be seen in Figure 2, the picture changed radically in the summer of 2011. At that time the spread started to grow dramatically. Suddenly it became clear that international markets started to consider Italian Treasury bonds a much riskier investment. This put the problem of financing the huge Italian national debt in a completely different light. Questions about Italy's capacity to sustain it in the long term started to be raised openly. The main argument was that without economic growth Italy would not be able to fulfil its obligations, with dramatic consequences not just for Italy but for the euro and the EU. Italy's borrowing costs were already very high as a percentage of its GDP. With escalating interest rates and no growth the sustainability of the debt would be highly problematic.

The sudden change at the international level regarding the perceived risk of investing in Italian public bonds caught the government by surprise. The intriguing question is that the fundamentals of the Italian economy had not changed in the last few months and yet the risk evaluation changed abruptly and dramatically. Undoubtedly the negative evolution of the Greek crisis was one reason. The decision

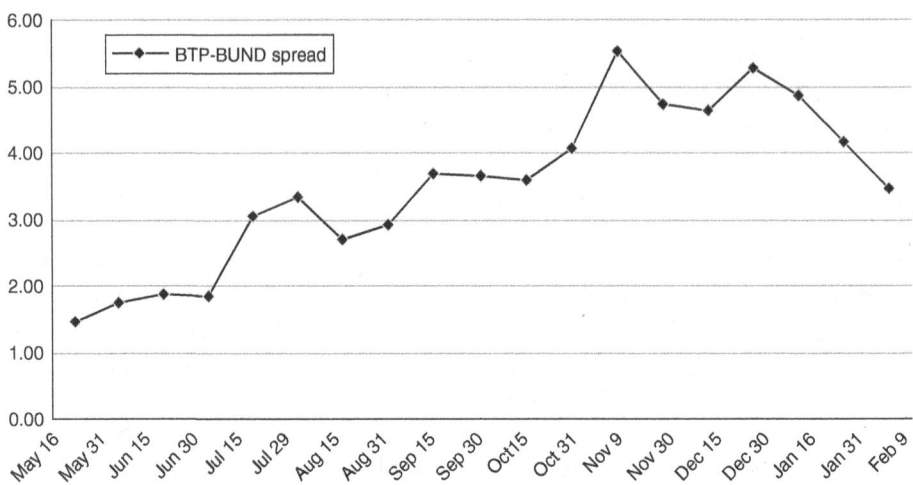

Figure 2 The BTP–Bund Spread (percentage points difference between BTP and BUND ten-year interest rates, May 2011 to February 2012). *Source*: Bloomberg (http://www.bloomberg.com/quote/!ITAGER10:IND/chart).

made at the EU level about the restructuring of Greek sovereign debt was a shock for investors. The very low recovery rates of private owners of that debt may have served as a wake-up call for holders of other peripheral sovereign bonds. But another important factor driving the change was the fragility of the Italian government. The combination of a large debt, low economic growth and a government with a weak parliamentary base made markets nervous and unwilling to lend more money except at higher premium. This in turn weakened the government further. It was a vicious circle that higher interest rates might not have been able to break. Actually, according to some analysts the higher the interests paid on the debt the higher the probability of a default due to the increasing uncertainty on its sustainability. That made the debt less, not more, attractive. 'Higher yields also cast doubt on the economic outlook, which not only intensifies doubts about the debt dynamics but also raises the prospect of political tensions' (Barclays Capital Economics Research 2011, p. 3)

This external shock forced the government to change its economic agenda during the summer of 2011. In July it passed an economic reform package covering the period 2011–14. The goal was to reach a balanced budget by the end of 2014. However, the fiscal adjustment was scaled in such a way that most of it was delayed after the election of 2013. In fact, the deficit correction was set at 2.1 billion euros for 2011, 5.6 billion for 2012, 24.4 billion for 2013 and 47.9 billion for 2014. A few days after the approval of this policy framework the government received an official letter from the European Central Bank signed by the outgoing president Jean-Claude Trichet and the incoming one Mario Draghi. The letter raised three major issues: (1) it explicitly stated that the July measures were not sufficient and that additional steps were needed; (2) it outlined a detailed agenda for the government including reforms aimed at promoting economic growth and ensuring the sustainability of public finances; (3) it set September 2011 as the deadline for the parliamentary approval of the required measures. As a response to this letter, the Berlusconi government was forced to introduce a new austerity package which was approved in parliament on 14 September. On the basis of the corrective measures included in this package the target for achieving a budget balance was updated to 2013.

Too little, too late. This seemed to have been the reaction of the markets to the economic measures passed in the hot summer of 2011. As can be seen in Figure 2, the BTP–Bund spread continued to rise dramatically. New measures were required. During the autumn a series of proposals were put forward with a major focus on pension reform. However, the opposition of the LN prevented any concrete action. Moreover, the conflict between the prime minister and minister of the Treasury Tremonti escalated, adding to the picture of a government paralysed by internal dissent. On 20 September, Standard & Poor's cut Italy's long-term debt rating from A+ to A, arguing specifically that the divisions within the government were exacerbating the weakness of the country's growth prospects (Jones 2012).

Under these conditions it became increasingly clear that it was impossible to pass a more aggressive plan for restoring the confidence of investors and international financial institutions. It was a combination of the low credibility of the prime minister, a weak parliamentary majority and divisions over policy. As in Greece implementation of the measures already taken became an issue in itself. There was a growing awareness that only a cabinet of national unity could change the course of events. Even within the ranks of the PDL the issue of a new government with a larger parliamentary base was openly debated.

This was the situation leading to the vote that took place in the Chamber of Deputies on 8 November on a budget bill. The bill itself was not very important but the vote was to ascertain whether Berlusconi still had a viable parliamentary majority on his side. Only 308 deputies of the centre-right coalition voted in favour while 321 did not vote. There was one abstention. The bill passed. But the vote showed unmistakably the fragility of the government's parliamentary base. The same day Berlusconi announced his intention to resign after the approval of the financial stability law for fiscal year 2012. He did so on 12 November. Street demonstrations greeted the event. *The Economist* (2011) saluted it with a cover page that anticipated the end of an era: 'That's all, folks.' Time will tell if the fall of Berlusconi's fourth cabinet will really mark the end of an era. For the time being we can say that it inaugurated an armistice among the major political parties.

Notes

[1] The three previous cabinets led by Berlusconi lasted from May to December 1994, from June 2001 to April 2005 and from April 2005 to May 2006.
[2] The number of ministers, vice-ministers and undersecretaries amounted to 102, the largest in the Second Republic. The ministers of the cabinet represented eight different parties, but if we consider also the vice-ministers and the undersecretaries the number of parties in the cabinet

increases to 12 (Chiaramonte 2007). This makes the second Prodi government one of the most fragmented in the world of contemporary democracies.

[3] Fini was (and still is) the president of the Chamber of Deputies. As the leader of AN, in March 2009 he led his party into a merger with FI, the party created by Berlusconi in 1994. The new party was named PDL and it included some other minor centre-right political groups.

[4] See http://www.oecd-ilibrary.org/economics/government-debt_gov-debt-table-en

[5] See http://www.oecd-ilibrary.org/economics/government-deficit_gov-dfct-table-en

[6] Here we refer especially to the 'Cassa integrazione guadagni' (CIG), the main tool for supporting workers laid off by industries that need to downsize their workforce. Redundant workers are not fired but 'temporarily' placed on the payrolls of the CIG. They continue to receive a percentage of their salaries until they are called back to work or are permanently laid off. As can be seen in Table 1, the number of hours paid by CIG increased exponentially between 2008 and 2009.

[7] In the Senate the vote was 162 in favour, 135 against and 11 abstentions.

[8] For more details on the representativeness of the 118 municipalities sample see De Lucia and Maggini (2011). In Italy the size of the municipality is strongly associated with voting behaviour, particularly in the north (small towns are the strongholds of the LN). In general, the larger the municipality the better for the centre-left. On this latter point see Emanuele (2011).

[9] The same results are obtained by Natale, Feltrin and Cristadoro (2011) using the larger set of 133 municipalities and comparing the local elections of 2011 with the European elections of 2009.

[10] On May 20 Berlusconi gave six interviews to radio and TV stations. They all had the same basic message. He pointed out the risks for the voters in Milan and Naples if the left-wing candidates won and strongly encouraged those who had abstained in the first round to go and vote in the second. The appeal had no effect in either city.

[11] The previous six referendums were held in 1997 (seven questions on various matters; turnout rate ranging from 30.0 to 30.3 per cent), in 1999 (one question on the parliamentary electoral law; 49.6 per cent), in 2000 (seven questions on various matters; 31.9 to 32.4 per cent), in 2003 (two questions, the first on the protection of workers from dismissal and the second on the construction of electricity networks; 25.7 per cent), in 2005 (four questions on assisted fertility; 25.6 to 25.7 per cent) and in 2009 (three questions on the parliamentary electoral law; 23.5 to 24.0 per cent).

[12] As shown by the results of a survey done a few days after the referendum, more than 25 per cent of the PDL voters and about 42 per cent of the LN voters went to the polls. The political dimension of the referendum was at least as important as the content of the specific questions (Carrozza 2012).

[13] The ten-year German Bund interest rate is considered a benchmark in Europe.

References

Baldi, B. & Tronconi, F. (eds) (2010) *Le elezioni regionali 2010. Politica nazionale, territorio e specificità locale*, Istituto Carlo Cattaneo, Bologna, pp. 257–274.

Barclays Capital Economics Research (2011) 'Can Italy save itself?', *Euro Themes*, 7 November.

Carrozza, C. (2012) 'I referendum del 2011. Una vittoria a metà', in *Politica in Italia. I fatti dell'anno e le interpretazioni. Edizione 2012*, eds A. Bosco & D. McDonnell, Il Mulino, Bologna.

Chiaramonte, A. (2007) 'Il nuovo sistema partitico italiano tra bipolarismo e frammentazione', in *Proporzionale ma non solo. Le elezioni politiche del 2006*, eds R. D'Alimonte & A. Chiaramonte, Il Mulino, Bologna, pp. 369–407.

Commissione di garanzia sciopero (2011) 'Relazione annuale 2011 sull'attività svolta nell'anno 2010', available online at: http://www.commissionegaranziasciopero.it

Corbetta, P. (2012) 'The 2010 regional elections in Italy: another referendum on Berlusconi?', *South European Society and Politics*, 17, no. 2, pp. 155–173.

De Lucia, F. & Maggini, N. (2011) 'Le elezioni amministrative del 2011: il voto per blocchi e per partiti', paper presented at 25th Convegno della Società Italiana di Scienza Politica, Palermo, 8–10 September.

Economist, The (2011) 'That's all, folks', 12 November.

Emanuele, V. (2011) 'Riscoprire il territorio: dimensione demografica dei comuni e comportamento elettorale in Italia', paper presented at 25th Convegno della Società Italiana di Scienza Politica, Palermo, 8–10 September.

Gualmini, E. & Pasotti, E. (2011) 'Introduzione. Molto rumore per nulla?', in *Politica in Italia. I fatti dell'anno e le interpretazioni. Edizione 2011*, eds E. Gualmini & E. Pasotti, Il Mulino, Bologna, pp. 47–67.

Hine, D. & Vampa, D. (2011) 'Un altro divorzio: Il Pdl nel 2010', in *Politica in Italia. I fatti dell'anno e le interpretazioni. Edizione 2011*, eds E. Gualmini & E. Pasotti, Il Mulino, Bologna, pp. 69–91.

IPR Marketing. (2011) 'La fiducia nel premier, nel governo e nei ministri del governo', available online at: www.sondaggipoliticoelettorali.it

Jones, E. (2012) 'La crisi del debito sovrano e la caduta di Silvio Berlusconi', in *Politica in Italia. I fatti dell'anno e le interpretazioni. Edizione 2012*, eds A. Bosco & D. McDonnell, Il Mulino, Bologna, pp. 181–200.

Legnante, G. (2012) 'Berlusconi ha perso. Ma chi ha vinto? Le elezioni comunali di maggio', in *Politica in Italia. I fatti dell'anno e le interpretazioni. Edizione 2012*, eds A. Bosco & D. McDonnell, Il Mulino, Bologna, pp. 123–140.

Magri, U. (2011) 'Berlusconi attacca: "solo chi è senza cervello vota la sinistra"', *La Stampa*, 26 May.

Natale, P., Feltrin, P. & Cristadoro, A. (2011) 'Amministrative 2011: cambia il vento?', *Polena*, vol. 8, no. 2, pp. 9–24.

Paparo, A. & Cataldi, M. (2011) 'Elettori in movimento a Milano e a Napoli', paper presented at 25th Convegno della Società Italiana di Scienza Politica, Palermo, 8–10 September.

Tuorto, D. (2010) 'La partecipazione al voto', in *Votare in Italia: 1968–2008. Dall'appartenenza alla scelta*, eds P. Bellucci & P. Segatti, Il Mulino, Bologna, pp. 53–79.

Alessandro Chiaramonte is Professor of Political Science at the University of Florence, where he teaches Italian and comparative politics. He is member of the Centro Italiano di Studi Elettorali (Italian Centre for Election Studies) and has published several articles and books on elections and electoral and party systems, both in Italy and in a comparative perspective.

Roberto D'Alimonte is Professor of Political Science at the Luiss Guido Carli University in Rome, where he teaches Italian politics. He also teaches European Integration and US–Italy relations at the Florence Campus of the New York University. He is the founder and Director of the Centro Italiano di Studi Elettorali (Italian Centre for Election Studies) and a commentator for *Il Sole24Ore*, Italy's leading financial newspaper.

In the Whirlwind of the Economic Crisis: Local and Regional Elections in Spain, May 2011

Belén Barreiro and Ignacio Sánchez-Cuenca

With an unemployment rate over 20 per cent and following the passage of an economic austerity plan and the Prime Minister's announcement that he would not be standing again, the local and regional elections of 22 May 2011 saw the incumbent Socialist Party obtain its worst results in the history of Spanish democracy and lose most of its municipal and regional power. In the Basque Country, Bildu, a coalition dominated by members of ETA's political wing, obtained very high popular support. We comment on the context, the campaign and the results of the elections and then discuss the extent to which the results are due to the economic crisis.

On 22 May 2011, local and regional elections were held in Spain. Local elections are nationwide and take place simultaneously all over the country. The local councillors of around 8,000 urban centres are chosen. In each municipality, the councillors elect the mayor. Regional elections took place in only 13 regions (out of 17), as Andalusia, Catalonia, Galicia and the Basque Country are special regions that have their own electoral cycle. Regions in Spain (called *Comunidades Autónomas*) have wide powers in matters such as education, health and other social policies. Although they do not have much tax power, their expenditure represents almost half of the country's total expenditure.

Local elections tend to be boring political events. However, in this case there were various elements that created some excitement. This election took place in the midst of a deep economic crisis and after the government was forced by the European Union to pass an austerity plan. In April, the Socialist Prime Minister, José Luis Rodríguez Zapatero, announced that he would not run for re-election in the next general election. Given his low popularity, his aim was to avoid being a deadweight for the party during the campaign. On 5 May, the Constitutional Court overruled the Supreme Court and decided that Bildu, a coalition featuring many members of the former Batasuna—the political wing of the terrorist organisation Euzkadi ta

Azkatasuna (ETA, Basque Homeland and Freedom)—could run in the election. On 12 May, an earthquake in Murcia disrupted the normal development of the campaign. And in the week before 22 May thousands of citizens, most of them young people, peacefully occupied the squares of many cities to protest against corruption, the electoral law, the ruling class and the effects of the crisis.

In this heavily loaded context, three results of the elections stand out. First, the incumbent Partido Socialista Obrero Español (PSOE, Spanish Socialist Workers' Party) obtained its worst results in the history of post-Franco democracy, which forecast defeat in the next general election. Secondly, there was a significant increase in protest voting (embodied in blank and non-valid voting), which is most likely due to the protest movement. And thirdly, Bildu obtained 25.4 per cent of the vote in the Basque Country, becoming the strongest political force in Gipuzkoa, one of the three Basque provinces.

The article is structured as follows. First, we introduce the context in which the elections took place: the crisis and the movement of the *indignados*. Second, we comment briefly on the electoral campaign. Third, we analyse in some detail the results of the local elections. Fourth, we focus on the results in the Basque Country, where Bildu obtained strong support. Fifth, we deal with the results of the regional elections. Finally, we conclude with a discussion about the weight of the economic crisis in the loss of popular support for the incumbent party.

Context: The Crisis and the *Indignados*

Spain was no exception from the effects of the international crisis. The crisis hit the country in the autumn of 2008, barely six months after the general election of March in which Zapatero was re-elected. The problem was aggravated by the collapse of the housing bubble, a problem that Spain shared with Ireland and the United Kingdom. Unemployment went from 8.3 per cent, a historical low, in 2007 to 20.1 per cent three years later, the highest in Europe. Spain was the country that created the most employment in Europe during the boom years, but it is also the one that destroyed the most jobs when the crisis arrived. The greater effects of the economic cycle compared with other European countries is a well-established pattern of the Spanish economy. In terms of growth, the country went into recession in 2009, with a negative growth of 3.7 per cent that year.

In the expansion years, Spanish governments very significantly reduced public debt, from 67 per cent of gross domestic product (GDP) in 1996 to only 36 per cent in 2007 (one of the lowest in Europe). With the crisis, it has increased to 61 per cent in 2010 (still below the European Union average). The fiscal situation was balanced before the crisis; in fact, there was a surplus of 1.9 per cent of GDP. The situation changed dramatically with the fall in revenues, which produced a deficit of 11.1 per cent of GDP in 2009.

The initial reaction of the government was to implement expansionary policies in order to reactivate demand. Low public debt and fiscal surplus led the government to launch one of the biggest stimulus plans in the Organisation for Economic

Cooperation and Development (OECD), amounting to four per cent of GDP in the years 2008 and 2009 (Oficina Económica del Presidente del Gobierno 2010, p. 41). However, the European debt crisis triggered by Greece frustrated the government's plans. With the premium risk of Spain's debt rising, the European Commission, the European Central Bank and pressure from the German government forced Spain to pass a fiscal contraction in exchange for European support for Spanish debt bonds. On 12 May 2010, the Prime Minister announced an austerity package consisting of an average reduction of five per cent in the income of civil servants, the freezing of pensions, a dramatic reduction in public investment, and the withdrawal of a number of social benefits (such as a €2,500 payment for the birth of a child). This was a profound shift in economic policy. The opposition party, the right-wing Partido Popular (PP, Popular Party), voted in Parliament against the adjustment package. Had it not been for the abstention of minority parties, the package would have been rejected, with unforeseeable consequences for the Spanish economy. The policy reversal of the government was followed by an express reform of the pension system and labour market reforms that lowered the severance payment of workers.

This new orientation of economic policy halted economic recovery, putting Spain on the verge of recession. The unions responded with a general strike on 29 September 2010, which was only a partial success. But the main reaction to the crisis came during the electoral campaign, when the movement of the so-called *indignados* (those who were indignant at the crisis and the political reaction to it) erupted. The movement was called '15 May' (15-M), because on that day of 2011 massive protest demonstrations, much larger than expected, took place in Madrid and other cities. Afterward, the participants occupied and camped in public squares and started to hold assemblies in which they denounced the ruling class and the effects of the crisis. They called for real democracy (as opposed to a merely formal one, based on periodic elections), demanded changes in the electoral law to end the dominion of the two big parties and complained about corruption. The movement was peaceful, not anti-system per se, with a strong emphasis on public deliberation and participation in public life.

A recent study, based on a sample of protesters in Salamanca, shows that most protesters are young people (between 19 and 30 years old), with higher education, leftists but not necessarily revolutionaries (their ideological mean is 2.8 on a 1–10 scale in which 1 is extreme left and 10 extreme right), and their main concerns are corruption, the electoral system (they denounce closed lists and too little proportionality) and the regulation and limitation of financial powers (Calvo, Gómez-Pastrana & Mena 2011).

The response by the state was one of tolerance, avoiding clashes between the police and the demonstrators. The camps were dismantled two weeks after the elections, the protestors showing clear signs of fatigue.

The Campaign

The campaign was a low-profile one. Slogans were as simplistic as usual, partisans attended rallies and politicians criticised each other. The PSOE tried to conduct a local campaign, avoiding national issues, particularly those related to the economic crisis of the country. Zapatero's early announcement that he would not run for re-election was aimed at preventing a campaign focused on him and his record, which was precisely the goal of the PP. The conservatives tried to frame the campaign in economic terms, talking about the unemployment rate, the deficit, and the lack of capacity of Zapatero to fix these problems. For the PP, the local elections were a kind of rehearsal for the general elections.

For a number of reasons, the dominant frame during the campaign was the national one, the economy and the government getting all the attention. Strangely enough, Zapatero, other top members of the government and the party participated in many of the rallies organised by the socialist party, contributing in this way to a national campaign rather than a local one.

But the key here was the emergence of the *indignados*, which had an immediate impact on the media and dominated the agenda. Their demands were certainly not local ones. In the survey carried out by Calvo, Gómez-Pastrana and Mena (2011), the goal of improving cities was the least important among all the goals mentioned in the questionnaire. The movement made the crisis particularly salient during the campaign.

Furthermore, the protest overshadowed the traditional electoral campaigns of the parties. The PSOE did not know how to react. There was some ambivalence: on the one hand, the party thought they had to listen to the movement's demands; but, on the other, the party was concerned about the image of the socialists as part of an establishment that was not responsive to the needs of those who were more severely hurt by the crisis. For the PP, it was simply confirmation that the government was unable to cope with the problems of the youth. The PP did not feel touched by the protest against corruption, despite the fact that some of the most egregious cases affected the right-wing party (more on this below).

Results in the Local Elections

Although fears of high abstention were echoed in the press during the campaign, under the assumption that the crisis would lead many demoralised voters to stay at home, the truth of the matter is that abstention was 34 per cent, the average for local elections in Spain, and somewhat lower than that of the 2007 local elections, 36 per cent (see Table 1). Probably the unexpected emergence of the *indignados*, and the prominence it gained during the campaign, helped to mobilise people who otherwise would not have gone to the polls. The *indignados* did not call for abstention.

The PSOE suffered a dramatic fall in electoral support, obtaining its worst result since 1977: 27.8 per cent of the vote. This means a loss of 7.1 percentage points compared with the previous local elections in 2007 and a loss of 16.1 per cent compared to the previous general election in 2008, when Zapatero was re-elected.

The difference between the PSOE and the PP was ten percentage points, much larger than in the previous three elections (see Table 1). The only precedents of such a margin

Table 1 Electoral Results of State-wide Parties in the Last Four Elections (per cent)

	2011 (local)	2007 (local)	2009 (European)	2008 (general)
PSOE	27.8	34.9	38.8	43.9
PP	37.5	35.6	42.1	39.9
IU	6.4	5.5	3.7	3.8
UPD	2.1	–	2.8	1.2
Abstention	33.8	36.0	55.1	26.1
Non-valid vote	1.7	1.2	0.6	0.6
Blank vote	2.5	1.9	1.4	1.1
Electoral census	35,655,630	35,153,523	35,492,567	35,073,179

Source: Ministerio del Interior (www.mir.es)
Note: Only nationwide parties are included. UPD did not exist in 2007.

are in the general election of 2000, when the PP won a majority in parliament, and in the local elections of 1995. Interestingly, though, the PP did not significantly increase its vote share, going from 35.6 per cent in 2007 to 37.5 per cent in 2011. The difference between the two parties is largely explained by the fall of the PSOE.

These results fit a pattern that has been well established since the mid 1990s. Broadly speaking, the ideological distribution of voters is not symmetric in Spain. There are more voters on the left than on the right. And their behaviour is different in each case. Whereas right-wing voters are very loyal to the PP and highly stable in their support, left-wing voters are more unpredictable, with waves of enthusiasm and despair (Sánchez-Cuenca 2009, p. 35). On top of that, there is only one nationwide party on the right, but two on the left, the PSOE and Izquierda Unida (IU, United Left, a coalition dominated by the Communist Party). This creates more volatility in the left bloc.

IU has increased its vote share somewhat, obtaining 6.4 per cent, which is not much compared with the 2007 local elections (5.5 per cent), but it is substantial if the reference level is that of the 2008 general elections, 3.8 per cent. IU tends to gain votes when the PSOE faces hard times.

A recently created party, Unión, Progreso y Democracia (UPD, Union, Progress and Democracy), obtained two per cent of the vote. The party ran for the first time in the general election of 2008, when it gained one MP, that of its leader, Rosa Díez. She is a former socialist politician who competed with Zapatero to be the general secretary of the PSOE in 2000. Ideologically, it is hard to say what its position is on socioeconomic issues. The party's main concerns are territorial decentralisation (it favours a recentralisation of powers) and terrorism (it fiercely opposes a negotiated settlement with ETA). The party is particularly strong in Madrid, where its vote share is almost seven per cent.

Lastly, a remarkable result of the local elections was a very significant increase in non-valid and blank votes (see Table 1), reaching a historical maximum of 4.2 per cent (1.7 per cent non-valid votes plus 2.5 per cent blank votes).[1] The sum of the two adds up to 973,518 votes, the fourth-biggest outcome after the PP, the PSOE and IU. This can be interpreted as a kind of protest voting by people who are dissatisfied with the existing parties or with the functioning of democracy more generally. Despite the lack of hard evidence, it seems natural to connect protest voting with the 15 May movement.[2] The movement had a strong anti-party component and developed a harsh critique of the Spanish institutional system. Given that they rejected abstaining in the polls, many of the protesters, most likely, opted for the non-valid or blank vote.

The PSOE's loss has not benefited any party in particular. A simple inspection of the aggregate flows of votes shows that the seven percentage points that the PSOE has lost must have gone in small portions to the PP, to IU, to small parties and to the protest vote. In fact, as Table 1 shows, results have changed only marginally for these parties; the exception is the PSOE. These vote transfers are probably not enough to account for all the electoral losses of the socialists. Even if the turnout level had been similar to that of 2007, it makes sense to suppose that the internal composition of abstention has changed, with a greater presence now of former socialist voters and a smaller one of right-wing voters. Otherwise, it is hard to understand where the lost socialist votes have gone.

The PSOE has suffered particularly in the big cities. In cities over 100,000 inhabitants, the vote share of the PSOE was 25.2 per cent, compared with 33.9 per cent in municipalities below 2,000 inhabitants. The PSOE has not won in any city over 175,000 inhabitants. The pattern is the opposite for the PP: the bigger the city, the greater the support. The 'ruralisation' of the vote and the decline among the urban middle classes had already happened in the final years of Felipe González's lengthy incumbency (1982–96). With the generational renovation of the party in 2000 and the choice of Zapatero as the new general secretary, the party was able to connect once again with the more dynamic segments of society, but after seven years of incumbency (2004–11), this connection is again seriously damaged.

There is an interesting contrast between the local elections of 2011 and those of 2007. In 2007 there was an unusual territorial variation in the vote. The PSOE increased its vote share in some regions and suffered losses in others, and the same held for the PP. In 2011, however, the fall of the PSOE and the rise of the PP was a common pattern in every Spanish region.

Local Elections in the Basque Country: The Case of Bildu

The 22 May elections produced far-reaching changes in the Basque Country which are quite unrelated to the electoral results in the rest of Spain. These changes have to do with the specific problem of terrorism in the Basque Country. As is well known, ETA has been involved in violence for the last four decades in that region, asking for independence from Spain and reunification of the Spanish and French Basque provinces in a single new state. At the time of the local elections, ETA was sustaining a truce: it had declared a unilateral truce in January 2011.

The political wing of ETA, which has adopted various names and is usually referred to as 'Batasuna', was banned after the law on parties was passed in 2001. Although it was able to circumvent the law by running under different labels, the authorities were able to prevent its participation in the regional elections of 2009, which was crucial because the socialists were able to form a minority regional government and bring an end to the nationalist hegemony of the Partido Nacionalista Vasco (PNV, Basque Nationalist Party) (de la Calle & Sánchez-Cuenca 2009).

The weakness of ETA, plus the ostracism of Batasuna, led the political leaders of the movement to rethink their relationship with the terrorist organisation. A process of ideological revision was undertaken. Being aware that the electoral fate of Batasuna is much brighter when ETA is inactive (as was demonstrated in 1998 when Batasuna obtained extraordinary results during ETA's truce), they eventually decided to play the political and institutional game even at the cost of distancing themselves from ETA and putting pressure on ETA to stop violence. They created a new party, Sortu, but the Supreme Court considered it to be the old Batasuna under a new guise and banned it. Batasuna brought the case to the Constitutional Court, which will make a ruling in coming months.

The movement, nevertheless, had an alternative plan, that of its people running as independents in the electoral lists of a new coalition, called Bildu, formed by these independents plus two minor splinter parties (one from the PNV and the other from IU). On 5 May, a very controversial ruling of the Constitutional Court established that Bildu should be allowed to run in the elections.

The results for Bildu were astonishing. As Table 2 shows, it secured the second-largest number of votes, 25.4 per cent, in the Basque Country, and became the first party in Gipuzkoa, with 34.6 per cent of the vote. This was far beyond the most optimistic expectations of the people in Batasuna. In 1998, when regional elections took place one month after ETA had declared a truce, Batasuna (under the name of 'Euskal Herritarrok') had obtained 17.9 per cent of the vote. The support for Bildu varies considerably depending on the size of the municipality. Thus, in villages with less than 2,000 inhabitants, Bildu gained 43.6 per cent of the vote, but only a mere 16.3 per cent in towns with more than 100,000 inhabitants.

The redoubtable success of Bildu was crucial in precipitating ETA's decision to stop violence. The wide popular support for the political strategy reinforced considerably the political wing vis-à-vis the military one. It showed to ETA that the future is

Table 2 Results of Local Elections in the Basque Country (per cent)

	Basque Country	Araba	Bizkaia	Gipuzkoa
PNV	30.5	22.5	37.4	21.0
Bildu	25.4	20.7	21.3	34.6
PSOE	16.3	16.2	15.5	17.8
PP	13.3	25.3	12.7	9.6
IU	3.2	3.5	3.4	2.6
Non-valid vote	1.4	2.2	1.3	1.1
Blank vote	2.2	2.5	2.0	2.3
Abstention	36.4	36.3	35.9	37.3
Census	1,099,921	157,334	593,077	349,510

Source: Ministerio del Interior (www.mir.es)

brighter with ballots than with bullets. ETA announced the 'definitive' end of violence on 20 October 2011.

Results in the Regional Elections

Regional elections were held simultaneously with the local ones in 13 of the 17 regions. Here, the change in the balance of power between the socialists and the conservatives was even more pronounced. Table 3 presents the variation in the vote share for the two main parties. Results are not entirely clear, due to the fact that in some regions there are strong regionalist parties. Nonetheless, the fall in electoral support for the PSOE relative to 2007 is apparent in all the regions, whereas the PP either expands or maintains its support (except in the two regions in which there were splits in the right, Asturias and Navarra).

During Zapatero's second term, which started in 2008, the PSOE lost power in the regional elections of Galicia (2009) and Catalonia (2010), became the incumbent in the Basque Country (2009) and retained a majority in Andalusia. As Table 3 shows, before the May 2011 elections the PSOE was in power, alone or in coalition, in six of the 13 regions in which elections were held. After the elections, the socialists are in

Table 3 Results of the Regional Elections (per cent)

	PSOE		PP		Incumbent[1]	
	2011	2007	2011	2007	2011	2007
Aragón	28	40	39	30	PP	PSOE
Asturias	29	41	19	41	Other[2]	PSOE
Baleares	21	27	46	45	PP	PSOE
Canarias	20	32	31	23	Other + PSOE[3]	Other + PP[3]
Cantabria	16	24	46	41	PP	Other + PSOE[4]
Castilla–León	29	37	51	49	PP	PP
Castilla–La Mancha	43	51	48	42	PP	PSOE
Extremadura	43	52	46	38	PP	PSOE
Madrid	26	33	51	53	PP	PP
Navarre	16	23	7	–[5]	Other + PSOE[5]	Other[5]
Murcia	23	31	58	58	PP	PP
Rioja	30	40	51	48	PP	PP
Valencia	27	33	48	51	PP	PP

Source: ABC at: http://www.abc.es/especiales/elecciones-municipales-autonomicas/2011/resultados/index.html

[1] It is not specified whether the incumbent was a majority, coalition or minority government. If PP or PSOE was the major partner in the coalition, they are simply referred to as the incumbent.
[2] In Asturias the PP suffered a split involving Francisco Álvarez-Cascos, the former vice-president in the government of José María Aznar. After 2007, he created a new party that won regional elections in 2011.
[3] In Canarias, the main incumbent party is CC (Canary Coalition), a regionalist party.
[4] In Cantabria, the main incumbent party was PRC (Regionalist Party of Cantabria).
[5] In Navarra, the PP did not run in 2007, establishing an alliance with the dominant regionalist party, UPN (Union of Navarre People). During the legislature, there was a breakdown between the PP and UPN. UPN won the elections in 2011 and coalesced with the PSOE.

opposition in four of the six and they have not regained any of the regions in which the PP was the incumbent. In Navarra, the socialists are the minor partner in a coalition government with the right-wing regionalist party Unión del Pueblo Navarro (UPN, Union of Navarre People). In the Canary Islands, the PSOE is the minor partner in a coalition government with Coalición Canaria (CC, Canary Coalition).

In regions such as Extremadura or Castilla-La Mancha, in which the PSOE has governed for the last 29 years, the PP is now in power. At the time of writing (October 2011), the only places where the socialists still rule are Andalusia (with a majority) and the Basque Country (in minority), two of the four regions that did not hold elections on 22 May. Yet, the prospects for the PSOE are rather bleak. In the local elections, the loss for the incumbent was eight percentage points in both regions. According to surveys, the PSOE is most likely to lose the regional elections in Andalusia in March 2012.

The PP has concentrated an unprecedented amount of power at the regional and local levels. Right now, it rules in most big cities and in 12 of the 17 regions. After obtaining a majority in the general election on 20 November 2011, the PP is a hegemonic force in Spanish politics.

Discussion: Is It All about the Crisis?

We shall discuss now the effects that the *indignados* and the economic crisis may have had on the results of the May elections. Regarding the *indignados*, it seems that the direct electoral impact of the movement was not very significant. As pointed out before, there was a considerable increase in protest voting, but that increase was less than three percentage points of the total vote. It is important to bear in mind that the *indignados* are not very representative of Spanish youth in general (see also Urquizu 2011, Table 4). The surveys of the Centro de Investigaciones Sociológicas (CIS) show that younger people are today more inclined towards the PP. For instance, in survey CIS survey no. 2,885 (April 2011), the lowest vote intention for the PSOE is among those who are under 34 years of age. In the younger voters, those who are 18–24 years old, the advantage for the PP over the PSOE is 11 points. Despite the crowds of youngsters in the streets, there is a conservative majority in this age group.

The effect of the movement was probably more substantial on the public agenda than on the electoral results.[3] Once the crisis dominated the campaign, the way was paved for punishment of the incumbent. In fact, local elections have been used in the past by the electorate to punish the incumbent. This was particularly obvious, for instance, in 1995, when the PSOE was in its twelfth year in power and the country was overcoming the economic crisis of 1992–93. On that occasion, the PP won by almost ten points. One year later, however, in the general elections of 1996, the difference between the two parties was only 1.2 points. It is tempting to assume that the results of the 2011 local elections can be interpreted in similar terms, as a punishment of the incumbent for the bad economic outcomes generated by the international crisis.

The vast majority of the electorate had rather negative views about government performance. Figure 1 shows how public opinion evolved during the whole Zapatero

Table 4 Five Indicators of the Capacity of Parties

	April 2009				April 2011			
	PSOE	PP	The same	Difference	PSOE	PP	The same	Difference
Party with better prepared people	25.9	25.2	48.9	0.7	34.8	46.9	18.4	−12.1
Party more divided and with greater internal conflict	13.8	55.0	31.2	41.2	34.7	29.2	36.2	5.5
Party more concerned about the issues that Spaniards really care about	32.8	26.4	40.8	6.4	44.5	39.2	16.2	5.3
Party more involved in cases of corruption	11.2	53.3	35.5	42.1	19.1	34.9	46.1	15.8
Party more dependent on big economic groups	12.2	33.6	54.1	21.4	23.5	32.8	43.7	9.3

Source: CIS survey no. 2,799 (April 2009) (*N* = 3,255) and no. 2,885 (April 2011) (*N* = 2,463).

Note: In CIS 2,799, the respondent was asked about these five statements separately for the two parties. For every question, there was a 1–4 scale. In CIS 2,885 the five statements were read and the respondent had to answer which of the two parties fitted the statement better (the answers may also be both parties or none of them). In order to compare answers, we have calculated in CIS 2,799 the percentage of respondents that gave higher scores to each party and we have compared these percentages with those of CIS 2,885.

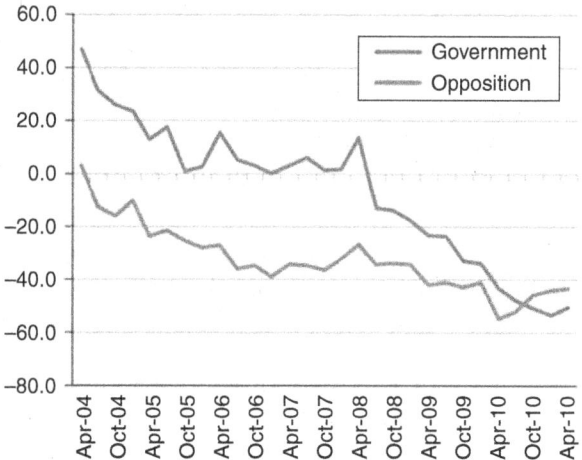

Figure 1 Evaluation of Government and Opposition (positive minus negative answers). *Source*: CIS, various years. *Note*: Each series represents the difference in the percentages of positive answers (values 1 and 2) and negative ones (3 and 4) in the original variable.

period. The deterioration is quite obvious. For many months, the only relief for the government was that public evaluation of the opposition was still lower, though this changed in October 2010 when the opposition gained advantage over the incumbent for the first time. It was the same with the popularity of Zapatero himself. During the crisis he has obtained the lowest popularity of any prime minister since 1977. It is true that the popularity of the opposition leader, Mariano Rajoy, was even worse, but in April 2011, for the first time, Rajoy was ahead of Zapatero, as can be seen in Figure 2.

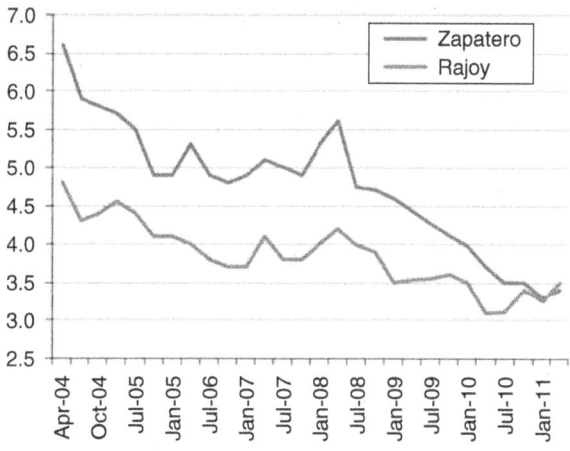

Figure 2 Mean Approval of Zapatero and Rajoy. *Source*: CIS and own elaboration. *Note*: Respondents were asked to value politicians on a 0–10 scale, where 0 is the lowest and 10 the highest evaluation.

The government has paid a high cost for the crisis not only in terms of electoral support, but also in terms of the perceptions citizens have about its capacity. Table 4 compares five indicators of party capacity in two moments of the crisis, April 2009, when Zapatero was defending a plan against the crisis based on fiscal expansion, with unemployment close to 18 per cent, and April 2011, almost one year after the adjustment plans had started and when unemployment was slightly over 21 per cent.[4] The erosion of the PSOE is spectacular: if we talk about how many well-prepared people the two parties have, the two parties were more or less equal in April 2011, but two years later the PP is ahead, 12 percentage points higher than the PSOE. Perceptions about divisions and internal conflicts have also worsened dramatically for the PSOE and have improved for the PP. People were also asked to what extent the parties are dependent on the support of large economic groups: it is remarkable that the percentage has doubled for PSOE after adopting neoliberal policies, going from 12 per cent in 2009 to 24 per cent two years later.

The fact that Zapatero denied or minimised the depth of the crisis in 2008 was fatal for his popularity. Also, his many failed predictions about the immediate recovery of the economy and employment cast doubt on his capacity to fight the crisis.

More specifically, various surveys of the CIS reveal that people think that the PP is better able to handle the economy than the PSOE. In October 2010, 34.9 per cent said that the PP was the party better prepared to deal with the economy, compared with 19.6 per cent who mentioned the PSOE.[5] The comparison regarding employment is very similar: 29.9 per cent named the PP, while 21 per cent named the PSOE.

That people used the vote on May 2011 to punish the incumbent is clearly borne out by the results of the regional elections. Table 5 shows data for the ten regions in which

Table 5 Regions Ruled by the PSOE or the PP

	Regional governmental approval (%)	Regional president's approval (%)	Electoral gains and losses (percentage points)	Incumbent re-election
Regions with PSOE incumbents			PSOE	
Aragón	−24.1	−17.0	−7.4	No
Asturias	−23.0	−16.4	−9.8	No
Extremadura	−5.6	+10.9	−6.2	No
Castile–La Mancha	+3.3	+18.2	−7.4	No
Baleares	−27.9	−16	−5.5	No
Mean	−13.05	+5.1	−7.1	
Regions with PP incumbents			PP	
Castilla–León	−16.7	−6.7	+1.9	Yes
Madrid	+2.7	+7.5	−2.2	Yes
Murcia	−12.1	+1.2	+0.5	Yes
Valencia	−8.7	−6.4	+0.2	Yes
Rioja	+16.7	+17.8	+2.7	Yes
Mean	−3.6	+2.68	+0.6	

Source: Calculations are based on the electoral results reported by the Ministerio del Interior (www.mir.es).

either the PSOE or the PP was the only incumbent or at least the major partner in a ruling coalition. This leaves out the Canary Islands, Navarra and Cantabria. Thus, we have five regions that were ruled by the PSOE in the period 2007–11 and five by the PP. The PSOE was not re-elected in any of its five, while the PP was re-elected in all of its five. In the five regions ruled by the PSOE, the party lost seven percentage points of vote share on average. In the five ruled by the PP, this party had a small average gain of 0.6 points.

The puzzle comes when we look at the columns of government and regional president approval (measured as positive minus negative responses). There seems to be no correspondence between the evaluation of government performance and electoral results. Take Castilla–La Mancha and Valencia. In Castilla–La Mancha the government approval rating was positive and even more so the regional president approval rating (indeed, it was the highest in Spain). However, the PSOE lost 7.4 points and the PP obtained a majority in this region. In Valencia, both the government and the regional president approval were negative. Moreover, the regional government in Valencia was involved in many scandals of corruption and illegal financing of the party. These scandals were in the headlines of national newspapers for months. Yet, the PP did not suffer any punishment in Valencia. In fact, it increased its vote by 0.2 per cent.

We interpret these surprising results as evidence that the electorate punished the PSOE regardless of the performance of the socialists in the region or the regional nature of the elections. The punishment was uniformly administered in all the socialist regions independently of the government and regional president approval ratings. And the performance and corruption scandals of some regional governments ruled by the PP were pardoned by the voters.

In sum, there is ground to conclude that many voters used the local and regional elections to punish the incumbent for the state of the economy. Moreover, there is a widely shared perception in Spanish public opinion that the PP is the party better prepared to deal with the economy than the PSOE, mainly due to Zapatero's initial denial of the severity of the crisis. The emergence of the *indignados* increased even more the saliency of economic issues during the electoral campaign, which focused more on broader issues than on local ones. At the end of the day, economic considerations trumped any other issue, including the important corruption scandals affecting the PP in various regions (Madrid, Murcia and Valencia). This pattern seems to be replicated in many other European countries where local and mid-term elections are being used by voters to punish governments.

Notes

[1] For a more detailed analysis of protest voting in the 22 May elections, see Jiménez (2011).
[2] However, as one reviewer pointed out, the blank vote was already quite high in the Catalan elections of 2010 (2.9 per cent), long before the *indignados* started their protests. This casts some doubt on the specific impact of the movement in the elections.

[3] For a more nuanced analysis, see Jiménez (2011). He finds some partial evidence that in those cities where protests were larger, protest voting was greater and the proportion of vote share going to the two big parties lower.
[4] The questions were the same; the answer option varied. We have homogeneised the variables to make them comparable: see the methodological note in Table 4.
[5] CIS, Survey no. 2,847 ($N = 2,475$), October 2010.

References

Calvo, K., Gómez-Pastrana, T. & Mena, L. (2011) '¿Quiénes son y qué reivindican?', *Zoom Político* (Fundación Alternativas), no. 4, pp. 4–17.

De la Calle, L. & Sánchez-Cuenca, I. (2009) 'The end of three decades of nationalist rule: the 2009 regional elections in the Basque Country', *South European Society and Politics*, vol. 14, no. 2, pp. 211–226.

Jiménez, M. (2011) '¿Influyó el 15M en las elecciones municipales?', *Zoom Político* (Fundación Alternativas), no. 4, pp. 18–28.

Oficina Económica del Presidente del Gobierno (2010) *Informe económico del Presidente del Gobierno 2010*, Ministerio de la Presidencia, Madrid.

Sánchez-Cuenca, I. (2009) 'Las elecciones de 2008: ideología, crispación y liderazgo', in *La España de Zapatero. Años de cambios, 2004–2008*, eds A. Bosco & I. Sánchez-Cuenca, Pablo Iglesias, Madrid, pp. 25–48.

Urquizu, I. (2011) 'El vuelco electoral del 22-M', *Claves de la Razón Práctica*, no. 214, pp. 14–23.

Belén Barreiro is the Director of the Laboratorio of Fundación Alternativas (Madrid). She is the former president of the CIS. Her areas of research are electoral behaviour, electoral campaigns and democratic theory.

Ignacio Sánchez-Cuenca is the Research Director and Professor of Political Science in the Center for Advanced Study in the Social Sciences, Juan March Institute (Madrid). He is also an associate professor of sociology at the Universidad Complutense (Madrid). His areas of research are political violence, democratic theory and electoral behaviour.

Disengaging Citizens: Parliamentary Elections in the Republic of Cyprus, 22 May 2011

Christophoros Christophorou

The chief characteristic of this election was the significant rise in abstention, suggesting citizens' disengagement. The loss of influence of political parties is related to a long-term cumulative effect of disappointment arising from missed opportunities, including Cyprus's entry into the European Union and domestic shifts in power. Political leaders failed to secure expected benefits and offer new prospects that could mobilise and sustain participation. The article examines the background, the campaign and the results of the 2011 parliamentary election and refers to the potential impact on resolution of the Cyprus question.

In the presidential system of the Republic of Cyprus, parliamentary elections are ranked second after the presidential contests and can induce no change of power. This is because governments are formed by the president of the Republic, who is elected for a five-year term, and do not need a vote of confidence in the House of Representatives. Hence, the main interest of legislative elections lies in the changing patterns of party support which they reveal and the impact of the electoral outcome on the handling of state affairs. The elections of 22 May 2011 offered an opportunity to rate more than three years of Cyprus's first ever government under a communist president, including its handling of the Cyprus Problem and the economic crisis, while party clientelism was another critical issue. Foreign diplomats were concerned about the possible impact of the elections on the negotiations for a solution to the Cyprus Problem, while the Cypriot political parties were worried about abstention. The significant fall in electoral turnout indicated an emerging crisis of the political system, in which past failures and lack of future prospects had led to citizen disengagement from politics.

The communist AKEL (Ανορθωτικό Κόμμα Εργαζόμενου Λαού – Progressive Party of the Working People), first party in the 2001 and 2006 parliamentary elections, fell to second place. Although the party's vote share actually rose, the total number of voters supporting AKEL declined. This reflected the big jump in abstention from 11.0

per cent in 2006 to 21.3 per cent in 2011. The centre-right DISY (Δημοκρατικός Συναγερμός – Democratic Rally) emerged as the first party, increasing not only its vote share but also its total votes, leaving the party leader in a good position to contest the presidential election of 2013. Another feature of this election was the surprise emergence of an extreme-right party running on an anti-immigrant platform, which, however, failed to win a parliamentary seat.

Background: Cyprus Stalemate and Economic Crisis

AKEL, after decades in opposition, decided in 1995 to claim government responsibilities. Following strategic alliances with DIKO (Δημοκρατικό Κόμμα – Democratic Party) and EDEK (Ενιαία Δημοκρατική Ένωση Κέντρου – Unified Democratic Union of the Centre), the party elected its secretary general, Christofias, as Speaker of Parliament in 2001. It also held five ministerial portfolios in the government of the previous president Tassos Papadopoulos, formed in 2003, but withdrew from the government in July 2007 in the run-up to the next presidential election. That election, in February 2008, saw a communist—Demetris Christofias, secretary general of AKEL—elected to the presidency for the first time in the island's history. Initially, the same three parties, DIKO, EDEK and AKEL, participated in the government as in the previous Papadopoulos presidency, but with a different political programme. However, EDEK withdrew from the coalition in February 2010 owing to disagreements about the Cyprus question.

Following his election in 2008, domestically the new president enjoyed support from large groups entertaining high expectations. His election was also welcomed by the European Union (EU), United Nations (UN) and all those in Cyprus and abroad who hoped for decisive steps for a solution and reunification of the island. Greek Cypriots expected even more from Demetris Christofias: that he would be a catalyst of unity, fulfil his promises for social justice and welfare and combat favouritism, the latter a major flaw in the Republic's life.

The warming up of relations with Western capitals, as well as with Israel, and the exchanges of visits between leaders, strengthening the Republic's international position, were also extended to Russia and China, and even to Cuba. Some developments deviating from or indicating reluctance to adopt EU policies caused internal frictions. A prominent example was the rejection by AKEL and the government of a resolution by the House of Representatives (February 2011) for Cyprus to join the North Atlantic Treaty Organisation's (NATO's) Partnership for Peace (PfP). AKEL voted against the Treaty of Lisbon in July 2008 without affecting the Treaty's ratification. On another front, the United States (US) viewed the new government and its relations with Havana, Moscow and Damascus with suspicion (*Phileleftheros* 2011a).

The Cyprus Question

However, after three years of Christofias's presidency, the Cyprus question seemed no closer to a solution. In 2003, movement across the line dividing the Greek Cypriot and

Turkish Cypriot communities had been permitted by the Turkish army for the first time since 1974. Meanwhile the promotion of a comprehensive UN proposal, the Annan Plan, had created hopes for a solution to the Cyprus Problem and an end to the division of the island, which dated back to summer 1974. A better future for all was expected within the EU, following accession in May 2004. Greek Cypriot rejection of the UN Plan in the April 2004 referendum was a source of subsequent strain in relations with the UN, Brussels and others, and deepened the gap with the Turkish Cypriots. Internally, deep divisions affected Greek Cypriot society, the media and the political forces, with the *nenekides*—those who had voted 'yes' to the Plan—ranged against the *ochides*, those who had opposed it.[1] The signs of division persisted in the form of splinter parties, in a conflictual political discourse, in media narratives and even in social relations.

Efforts for 'a Cyprus solution' brokered by Cypriots themselves had led to the opening of more crossing points across the Green Line and to full-fledged negotiations between President Christofias and the Turkish Cypriot leader, Mehmet Ali Talat, in September 2008. During the course of these negotiations, two significant legal cases with conflicting repercussions appeared further to complicate efforts for a solution. The decision of the European Court of Justice (ECJ) in the *Orams* case (April 2009) that court decisions in an EU member-state were enforceable by courts in other member states greatly increased the power of Cypriot courts. The verdict broadened the range of applicability of decisions by courts in the Republic of Cyprus on matters of importance to Greek Cypriots, such as on property in the areas under Turkish control in the northern part of the island. In March 2010, however, considerable Greek Cypriot disappointment was caused by a decision of the European Court of Human Rights (ECHR). The recognition of the Immovable Property Commission, established in the non-internationally recognised 'Turkish Republic of Northern Cyprus' ('TRNC'), as an acceptable and effective local remedy for settling property claims, forces Greek Cypriots to apply to a Commission they resent before filing claims with the ECHR. Some weeks later, the electoral defeat of Mehmet Ali Talat by Derviş Eroğlu (see the article by Akşit in this volume), regarded as a hardliner and not favoured by the Turkish government in Ankara, was seen as unfavourable to the course of the negotiations. Despite some progress in the latter, prospects for a breakthrough were not apparent. While blaming Ankara, some Greek Cypriots also considered that President Christofias was not daring enough to achieve real progress. Opinion polls suggested that few people believed a solution was coming. In a major opinion poll, conducted in February to March 2011, to the question 'Are we nearer a solution to the Cyprus Problem than last year?', 78 per cent replied 'no', compared with 56 per cent in 2006 (*Public Issue* 2011). Meanwhile at the international level scepticism returned.

The Economy

Without a solution to the island's division in sight, the economy emerged as a central problem. Having inherited important cash reserves, the government began its mandate by offering 'targeted' subsidies and allowances. Disadvantaged groups such as pensioners, refugees and young couples received assistance or housing. When the global economic crisis began, Cypriot officials initially foresaw no particular problems for the country's economy (see Besim & Mullen 2009). However, the limited effects obtained by injecting €1.4 billion, in the form of treasury bills, into the banking system simply showed that, in a crisis environment, the structural problems of the national finances needed radical, more complex and long-term actions. Its high deficit resulted in Cyprus being placed under the EU surveillance mechanism, while the rating agencies downgraded its economy and banks twice, in November 2010 and May 2011. Public spending and in particular the size of public sector salaries and pensions became issues of grave concern, for which the government sought solutions through a dialogue with social actors. In addition, the initially perceived vitality of the banking system appeared compromised by the exposure of Cypriot banks to the Greek economic crisis, through huge investments in Greece. At another level, unemployment increased from 3.5 per cent in June 2008 to 7.6 per cent three years later[2] while the price index rose from 106.78 in January 2009 to 117.04 in May 2011.[3] Unemployment among those aged under 25 years old was above 20 per cent.

Facing the crisis proved difficult as the President and AKEL were reluctant to adopt measures and policies they considered 'anti-popular' because they would erode workers' benefits. Instead, the government introduced a bill to increase corporate and property tax, which was rejected by parliament in July 2010.[4] It also took measures to stimulate private sector employment, while in the public sector it cut 1,000 posts and initiated negotiations for a zero salary increase for two years. Financial contributions by public sector employees and profit-making businesses to cover the public deficit were to be negotiated after the elections.

In other political areas, significant steps were taken towards the adoption of a comprehensive policy and coordinated action with Brussels on the very sensitive issue of undocumented migration. This did not avert criticism by individual deputies and parties seeking electoral gains, who made claims that were often unfounded or marked by racist intonations. Cases of involvement of the presidential palace and the office of the Secretary General of AKEL in favouritism and problematic presidential appointments to high posts inflicted a serious blow to the image of Christofias and the communists on the subject of meritocracy, which is a major issue for Greek Cypriot society. The work of the government was often hampered by the criticisms and diverging positions of its partner parties, which chose to vote with the opposition in parliament even on important issues, such as the budget, the economy and Cyprus joining the PfP. When EDEK quit the cabinet in February 2010, DIKO's party organs voted in favour of staying, without this ending divisions and strains.

The Campaign

Despite the high tension in the exchanges between politicians during the campaign, apathy and indifference seemed to prevail among large parts of the electorate.

Additionally, negative media reports about the work of parliament and the deputies were likely to affect popular trust in politics and the significance of elections. In this negative climate, advertisements on billboards, mostly by individual candidates, and an array of campaign activities were deployed. There was extensive use of new media, in particular of social networks (Karides 2011). While a newly approved ceiling of €30,000 for campaign expenses per candidate appeared quite high, it seemed nevertheless that some candidates breached it; however, no sanctions were expected against anyone, as effective auditing means were not provided for in the law.[5] Advertising in the press, radio and television was estimated to amount to €1,964,000, television attracting about 65 per cent and AKEL spending more than the other parties (*Phileleftheros* 2011b; *Politis* 2011). These figures represented only part of the cost, since expenses related to the internet, printed material, billboard advertising and other media were not listed. While official television advertising started only three weeks before polling day, from February onwards there were daily radio and television programmes on the elections.

In the political debate, the economy was a major issue and the main focus of interest of all political forces. Some opinion polls showed that the electorate was more concerned about the financial crisis than the Cyprus Problem, which was surprising, as usually nothing can be placed above this 'national problem' (*Public Issue* 2011). With regard to the latter, the debate centred on proposals made by the President, which entailed accepting a rotation of the presidency of the proposed Cypriot federation between Greek and Turkish Cypriots. Another proposal entailed 45,000 Turkish settlers being allowed to stay. Immigration, a rapidly emerging problem often connected with unemployment, was a subject not only of heated debates but also of demonstrations by various groups, against or in support of immigrants.

Signs that there would be very high abstention, in particular the higher rates among young voters, alarmed all parties. Appeals for participation, including by the President of the Republic, continued even on election day.

Political Actors Prepare for the Battle

The present party system, shaped after 1974, features a strong left–right cleavage that dates back to the 1940s. A second dividing line, cutting across party lines, concerns differences over the solution of the Cyprus Problem. The four main parties, AKEL, DIKO, DISY and EDEK, have had a continuous presence in Parliament, in which they were the only political forces represented until the 2001 elections. Subsequently, a new proportional system (adopted in 1996) enabled some new formations to enter parliament. Ten parties contested the 2011 elections: the six currently holding parliamentary seats and four small extra-parliamentary parties. The total number of candidates, including six independents, was 412.

AKEL has consistently promoted a conciliatory approach on the Cyprus Problem and rapprochement with Turkish Cypriots (despite failing to support the UN Plan in 2004, which caused serious strains within the party). Since participating in power,

AKEL as a party has hardly distinguished its policies and stances from those of the government, except on seminal issues where the party's ideologically grounded position conflicted with the government's unavoidable EU obligations, such as the vote against the Treaty of Lisbon. In the elections the party projected the government's role in defending the rights of the working classes and supporting those in need, in favour of the progress and development of all ('Στις 22 του Μάη απαντούμε: ΑΚΕΛ Ισχυρό, Δύναμη για το Λαό' – 'On 22 May we respond: A strong AKEL – Power to the People'). It presented its own history and achievements as a 'creative, constructive' force, also promoting its positions and the work it had done on the Cyprus Issue and the solution sought.

DISY, currently the other major party in the system, is the Greek Cypriot member of the European People's Party. Its founder Glafcos Clerides held the presidency of the Republic from 1993 to 2003. Without allies since 2003, the party has been struggling to regain contact with DIKO and EDEK, its potential future coalition partners. In spite of some contradictions in statements and positions by its leaders, DISY also favours a conciliatory approach on the Cyprus Problem and supported the Annan Plan. DISY's initial support for Christofias's handling of the Cyprus Problem was later withdrawn because 'the President failed to consult with or brief the party on important issues'. While DISY's main slogan presented it as a unifying and daring force ('Ενώνουμε Δυνάμεις' – 'We Unite Forces') and a source of hope, its campaign focused mainly on the economy. Rising prices, unemployment and businesses closing down were key issues in its discourse. Notably, DISY's two televised messages exclusively targeted the economic crisis.

DIKO, although electorally a small party, had held the presidency of the Republic (Spyros Kyprianou) from 1977 to 1988, with the support of AKEL and/or EDEK. The party supported a 'resounding no' to the UN Plan in 2004 and is seen as a hardliner on the Cyprus Problem. Since 2008, DIKO has experienced significant internal problems due to top-level dissent on the party policy towards the Cyprus Problem and on participation in the government. In the election campaign, DIKO targeted the economic crisis but also promoted its role as a moderate force, an alternative to polarisation between left and right. Through projecting its 'struggles, achievements and successes', it claimed to be a reliable force that could respond to challenges ('Δύναμη Ευθύνης, Δύναμη Προοπτικής' – 'A Responsible Force, a Force with a Vision'). It did not fail to recall its 'no' vote against the UN Plan, asking voters to 'say no to those that voted yes'.

EDEK, a member of the Party of European Socialists, had voted against the Annan Plan in 2004. While not officially opposing a federal solution, its political discourse on the Cyprus Problem is often veiled, calling for a change of course which would take advantage of Cyprus's status as an EU member. EDEK also focused its election campaign on the economy, stressing that 'the citizen should not pay for the government's policies'. Having left the government in 2010 over the Cyprus problem, it emphasised this issue more than the other parties, asking for the withdrawal of proposals made by President Christofias, in particular for a rotating presidency.

EVROKO (Ευρωπαϊκό Κόμμα – European Party), a right-wing party, was founded in 2005 by NEO (Νέοι Ορίζοντες – New Horizons), at the time the only political force against a federal solution, and dissidents from DISY. The party sustains opposition to a federation, favouring instead a vaguely defined 'European solution' to the Cyprus Problem. EVROKO supported none of the presidential candidates in 2008, and placed itself in opposition, maintaining a critical stance towards the government. In the election the party promoted its 'European Solution', economic progress for all and 'control over immigration', all under a general slogan of 'Αλλαγή Τώρα' (Change Now).

The Greens (Κίνημα Οικολόγων Περιβαλλοντιστών – Ecologists Environmentalists Movement) have held one parliamentary seat since 2001. The party focuses its activity on both the environment and the Cyprus Problem. On the latter it voted against the UN Plan in 2004 and has followed a critical stance against the policies and positions of the current government. Its discourse on a federal solution is veiled. In the election the Greens focused on the Cyprus Problem and various issues affecting daily life, including transport.

Among the four non-parliamentary formations that contested the elections, the most notable was ELAM (Εθνικό Λαϊκό Μέτωπο – National Popular Front), which is organised on the model of the Greek extreme anti-immigrant party Golden Dawn. It caused alarm in society with violent attacks against immigrants, Turkish Cypriots and opponents. On the Cyprus Problem, ELAM is clearly opposed to a federation. On its first electoral appearance, in the 2009 European elections the party had secured 0.22 per cent. The other three formations, all recently constituted and essentially personalistic parties, did not present full candidate lists.

In criticising the government on the economy, all parties except AKEL claimed that it had failed to assess the gravity of the problems, that it reacted too late and that it did not propose concrete and complete measures adequate to face the crisis. Arguments about the state of the economy and its future prospects were based on a selective choice of indicators in order to fit each party's objectives, projecting a favourable or a grey picture of the economy. This could hardly allow voters to assess the real state of the economy.

The Results

Rising Abstention

More than 531,000 citizens had the right to vote. Voting is compulsory in all electoral contests in the Republic of Cyprus. However, the provision of the law that those unjustifiably failing to vote could pay a fine of up to €342 has since 2001 not been implemented. After abstaining en masse (27.5 per cent) in the European election of 2004, voters had returned to the polls in the 2006 legislative and 2008 presidential elections (89 and 91 per cent, respectively). In 2011, however, participation fell far behind previous elections. With abstention at 21.3 per cent, this meant that more than 113,000 voters failed to go to the polls, up from 55,000 voters in 2006 (see Table 1). Abstention was clearly influenced by place of residence and constituency, with the lowest rate in small rural communities (up to 500 voters), then a gradual increase in big rural communities and in suburban areas and the highest abstention in towns (18.0 and 25.7 per cent, respectively). There was, however, a significant differentiation between towns and districts. Abstention in the capital Nicosia reached 28.2 per cent, with a similar trend in the suburbs (26 to 29 per cent), while in the second-largest city, Limassol, the rate was 25.4, with 23 to 24 per cent in the suburbs. Larnaca and Paphos followed with the lowest abstention rates, at 23.6 and 22.4 per cent, respectively. However, the increase in non-participation appears to be homogeneous for all cases: the abstention rate almost doubled compared with 2006, with the exception of Paphos and Limassol constituencies, where the increase was 57 and 80 per cent, respectively.

The extraordinary decline in turnout substantially modifies the perspective from which one can assess the election outcome and necessarily differentiates the final conclusions. It cannot be based on comparison of share of vote because abstention reveals a landscape where there is hardly any real winner. Even though some increased their share, the parties' overall and individual influence over the electorate and the society in general diminished substantially. This led some commentators to say that the real winner was abstention, the 'third-largest' political force. Seen in this light, how could any political party claim victory in a contest where, abruptly, such a significant proportion of the voters, in comparison with the recent past, alienated themselves from the electoral process?

Table 1 Share of Valid Vote and Parliamentary Seats in the 2011 and 2006 Legislative Elections

Political party	2011		2006		Difference 2011–2006	
	Vote (%)	Seats	Vote (%)	Seats	Vote (%)	Seats
DISY	34.3	20	30.3	18	+3.9	+2
AKEL	32.7	19	31.1	18	+1.5	+1
DIKO	15.8	9	17.9	11	−2.2	−2
EDEK	8.9	5	8.9	5	0	0
EVROKO	3.9	2	5.7	3	−1.9	−1
Greens	2.2	1	1.9	1	0.3	0
ELAM	1.1	0	–	–	–	–
Others	1.2	0	4.0	0	2.8	–
Total	100.00	56	100.00	56	–	–
Abstention	21.3	–	11.0	–	+10.3	–
Blank ballots	1.2	–	2.3	–	−1.1	–
Invalid ballots	2.1	–	3.3	–	−1.2	–

Source: Data compiled by the author from official election results available from Cyprus Press and Information Office, www.moi.gov.cy/moi/pio

Parties: Winners and Losers

Celebrations of 'a victorious' outcome started soon after the exit polls were released and in spite of the forecast high abstention rate. A cheerful atmosphere was staged by supporters of AKEL and DISY, both of which increased their vote share compared with 2006, but also by the leadership of DIKO, which had apparently lost more than two percentage points. A phenomenon noted in 2001 and 2006, whereby parties losing influence declared themselves winners, indicated a new criterion for assessing performance: parties compare their score with opinion polls during the campaign instead of with past election results.

A party's performance is usually assessed by changes in its vote share and number of seats. The fact, however, that its vote share refers to valid votes cast means that in cases where an abrupt change occurs in the abstention rate comparisons may be misleading. Valid votes in 2006 accounted for 84 per cent of the electorate and in 2011 were down to 76 per cent. Therefore, to assess the real variation rate, Table 2 shows each party's vote share as a proportion of the total electorate.

Table 2 Vote Share as a Proportion of Total Registered Voters, 2001–2011

POLITICAL PARTY	2011		2006		2001	
	TOTAL VOTES	VOTE SHARE (%)	TOTAL VOTES	VOTE SHARE (%)	TOTAL VOTES	VOTE SHARE (%)
DISY	138,682	26.1	127,776	25.5	139,732	29.9
AKEL	132,171	24.9	131,076	26.2	142,647	30.5
DIKO	63,763	12.0	75,458	15.1	60,977	13.0
EDEK	36,113	6.8	37,533	7.5	26,770	5.7
EVROKO*	15,711	3.0	24,196	4.8	21,194	4.5
ECOLOGISTS	8,960	1.7	8,193	1.6	8,128	1.7
ELAM	4,354	0.8	–	–	–	–
OTHERS	4,823	0.9	16,855	3.4	11,548	2.5
VALID VOTES	404,577	76.1	421,087	84.0	410,996	87.9
REGISTERED VOTERS	531,463	100.0	501,024	100.0	467,543	100.00

Source: Data compiled by the author from official election results available from Cyprus Press and Information Office, www.moi.gov.cy/moi/pio
*The 2001 vote share for EVROKO combines the vote of the founding party and an ally.

DISY was a winner in terms of vote share and seats, making it first party ahead of AKEL. Its vote share increased by four percentage points and the party gained two seats, taking it up to 20. If support is measured as a proportion of total registered voters, DISY and the Greens were the only parliamentary parties not to lose influence. However, DISY's gain—as shown in Table 2—was a meagre 0.6 per cent of the total electorate. In terms of geographical distribution, DISY became the most influential political force in the three largest constituencies and in Paphos, while it lagged 1.5 points behind AKEL in Larnaca. Its average score was higher than AKEL's except in the group of large rural communities, where it lagged behind by three points. Thus, DISY's average influence ranged between 34 and 35 per cent, except in the very small communities (32.5 per cent). It received 36.5 per cent in the capital Nicosia, 34.6 in Larnaca and 31.6 per cent in Limassol.

AKEL, although coming second to DISY, also increased its share of both votes (by 1.6 per cent) and seats (from 18 to 19). This performance, at a time when it was having to pay the political costs of the economic crisis, can be regarded as a success. However, as Table 2 shows, both the total number of party voters and AKEL's vote as a share of the total registered electorate had fallen in comparison with 2006. In terms of constituencies, AKEL performed best in Kyrenia, Nicosia and Famagusta,[6] made minor gains in Limassol, but suffered small losses in Larnaca and Paphos. In the urban centres, AKEL's vote declined in the towns of Larnaca and Limassol. The party's distribution of influence was uneven: its share was 24.6 per cent in small communities, 29.6 per cent in towns and 38.1 per cent in large rural communities. AKEL was head to head with DISY in Larnaca and Limassol (34.5 and 30.7 per cent), but lagged seven points behind in Nicosia.

DIKO lost 2.1 per cent of the total valid vote (down to 15.8 per cent) and two seats (down to nine). In terms of registered voters, the party lost more than 15 per cent of its electoral base. DIKO suffered significant losses (13 to 19 per cent) in all constituencies except Paphos (only one per cent) and Larnaca, where it increased its share by 36 per cent. The party made marginal gains in small communities, but declined significantly in urban and particularly suburban areas. After the election, DIKO's leader Marios Garoyian failed to be re-elected as House speaker, because one of the party's own MPs voted against him. The expulsion of the dissenter and the party's deputy chairman caused a new crisis threatening DIKO's cohesion.

EDEK equalled its 2006 vote score (8.9 per cent) and kept its five seats. This still meant a decline in the total number of voters for the party. EDEK lost in four constituencies and gained in two; its share increased by 25 per cent in Limassol and by 11 per cent in Paphos. Its main losses were in suburban areas of Nicosia and Larnaca, as well as in large rural communities. EDEK's unevenly distributed influence peaked in small communities (14.3 per cent), falling to 9.2 per cent in urban and 7.1 per cent in suburban areas. Thanks to tactical support by DISY and a DIKO dissenter, EDEK's leader gained the office of Speaker of the House of Representatives. As the second-highest state office—whose holder substitutes for the president of the Republic when necessary—this post offers prestige and power to the party.

EVROKO lost 1.9 percentage points of the total vote, down to 3.9 per cent. In terms of total votes, its loss was equivalent to 35 per cent of its 2006 electoral base. The party also lost one of its three seats. Its most severe losses were in Kyrenia and Limassol constituencies, where it declined by 50 and 42 per cent, respectively. EVROKO's substantial losses put its future in peril.

The Greens gained 0.3 per cent of valid votes and kept their single seat; they also increased their total number of voters compared with 2006. The Greens declined slightly in Larnaca but made minor gains elsewhere; their share in Nicosia increased by 25 per cent.

Among the non-parliamentary parties, the biggest surprise concerned the extreme-right ELAM, contesting its first parliamentary election. With a nationalist and racist discourse, ELAM secured 1.1 per cent, below the parliamentary threshold of 1.8 per cent but hardly negligible. Its highest score was in Paphos and in Nicosia (2.0 and 1.4 per cent, respectively).

In addition to the fact many of the parties saw their influence decline among the electorate as a whole, there was a considerable turnover of parliamentary personnel.

The 16 new faces in the House amounted to 28.5 per cent of the total. A number of long-established party officials and other notable incumbent deputies failed to be re-elected, often losing to journalists or other celebrities. The losers included the chairmen of labour and farmers' unions (AKEL), the parliamentary spokesperson of DISY (who had been regularly elected since 1991), the first vice-chairman of EDEK and both the current and the former deputy chairmen of DIKO.

Discussion and Conclusions

The 2011 legislative elections were expected to be a contest of normalisation. They came after the rupture vote of the 2004 Annan Plan referendum, when voters en masse did not follow their party lines, and the subsequent realignment noted in the 2004 European and the 2006 parliamentary elections. One indication of normalisation was the parties' votes shares in 2006 (Christophorou 2007). However, in 2011 further steps back to a pre-crisis balance did not take place. Instead, massive abstention gave the contest the feature of a new rupture, which needs an explanation.

The main question was abstention. The fact that going to the polls, along with being a civic duty, is mandatory by law in the Republic explains the high participation over the years; conversely, the fact that the authorities had taken no action against absentees since 2006 may have prompted higher abstention. Similarly, the decline of invalid and blank votes from 24,800 to 13,600 in 2011 suggests that voters wishing to avoid sanctions in the past used not to abstain and instead spoiled their vote, but that when they felt that they no longer risked sanctions if they abstained they stayed away. Thus, abstention rates were fed by former spoiled ballots. In addition, further loss of trust in politics weakened the value of the vote as a civic duty and increased abstention.

Changes have also been noted in citizens' relations with political parties and the mobilising power of ideological rhetoric, founded on the left–right cleavage. The increase of the swing vote in recent years shows that attachment to parties and ideology is declining (Christophorou 2008a; 2008b). The 2004 referendum further eroded the trust that voters with strong views on the Cyprus Problem had in their parties, alienating them. This led many voters either to switch their vote or to abstain.

Moreover, during the first decade of the twenty-first century a number of factors had sustained high voter mobilisation. These included the island's course towards EU accession, offering apparent prospects for a solution to the Cyprus Problem and for a better European future within the EU. Another factor was the hopes connected to shifts in power, with the election of Tassos Papadopoulos as president in 2003 and the election of a left-wing president in 2008. The reality in 2011 contrasted with the euphoria and hopes of the early 2000s. The two key factors were the serious economic crisis and the lack of a breakthrough towards a solution and reunification of Cyprus. With regard to the latter, the 2010 decision of the ECHR, disappointing the hopes of the 1974 refugees, caused additional disappointment and disaffection with politics. As a result of these factors, large groups of voters saw no meaning in the vote, as no concrete and convincing promise could be formulated. Politicians had failed to address the challenges and to capitalise on significant developments such as EU entry. Following successive alternations in power, including the election of the first communist president, no leadership appeared able to offer real vision to these groups. Thus, the big increase in abstention indicated a cumulative effect of disappointment arising with missed opportunities and the failure of political leadership.

In this climate DISY was able to become first party despite some weaknesses of its otherwise strong party machine. As an alternative to the governing parties, DISY attracted former DIKO and EVROKO voters. In contrast, AKEL paid the cost of the failures and weaknesses of the President and his government, although control of the spoils of power and the efficiency of the party machine helped it to limit its losses. The party's communication management showed little tolerance of criticism and dissenting views while often failing to publicise the government's achievements. Favouritism and unsuccessful appointments to key positions damaged the image of both the government and the party.

DIKO's participation in a government that had rather conciliatory views on the Cyprus Problem made the party's demanding positions sound unconvincing and alienated refugee voters in particular. Its internal battles also demobilised some of its voters. EDEK's criticism of a government in which it had participated for two years did not help the party. EVROKO suffered from organisational weaknesses. Meanwhile ELAM secured its main influence in areas with a high concentration of immigrants and higher rates of unemployment. It remains to be seen how this party will fare in a future electoral contest.

The outcome of the May 2011 elections suggested that the political system had reached a turning point following the alternation of political forces in power and their failure to seize opportunities related to promising developments in the 2000s. The low turnout, by Cypriot standards, indicated declining party influence among the electorate and society.

The governing coalition was reduced from 29 to 28 seats (out of 56), thus losing its one-seat majority. This was expected to increase the opposition's margin for bargaining over or rejecting bills proposed by the government. Under the presidential system, an occasional negative vote would not cause a government crisis. The election of the House speaker showed the potential for majorities based on circumstantial vote and expediency. It remains to be seen whether the state of the economy will lead the parties to adopt cooperative or confrontational approaches and what kind of coalitions may emerge in the run-up to the 2013 presidential election. Meanwhile, no major change is expected in the course of the talks on the Cyprus Problem. Neither an interruption of the talks nor a breakthrough seem likely.

Notes

[1] The names came from the Greek words for 'yes' (ναι) and 'no' (όχι).
[2] The data refer to April 2011, available online at: http://epp.eurostat.ec.europa.eu/portal/page/portal/product_details/dataset?p_product_code=UNE_RT_M, accessed 30 June 2011.

[3] Source: Statistics Service, Republic of Cyprus, available online at: http://www.mof.gov.cy/mof/cystat/statistics.nsf/index_en/index_en?OpenDocument, accessed 30 June 2011.
[4] The philosophy behind this was illustrated in the following statement by an AKEL spokesperson: 'We feel big and provocative wealth should play its part for the state to emerge from the crisis and we are truly saddened to see political parties identifying with big wealth instead of making sure that everyone assumes their share of responsibility for the financial crisis' (*Cyprus Mail*, 6 July 2010).
[5] The General Auditor wrote in a letter to the parliament and the Ministry of Interior that gaps and vagueness in the law made auditing a rather impossible task (*Phileleftheros*, 12 August 2011c, p. 17).
[6] The Republic is divided into six constituencies as prior to 1974 and displaced voters cast their vote for candidates of their constituency of origin.

References

Akşit, S. (2012) 'The Turkish Cypriot presidential election of April 2010: normalisation of politics', *South European Society and Politics*, vol. 17, no. 2, pp. 175–194.

Besim, M. & Mullen, F. (2009) 'Cyprus in the global financial crisis: how the lack of banking sophistication proved an advantage', *South European Society and Politics*, vol. 14, no. 1, pp. 87–101.

Christophorou, C. (2007) 'An old cleavage causes new divisions: parliamentary elections in the Republic of Cyprus, 21 May 2006', *South European Society and Politics*, vol. 12, no. 1, pp. 111–228.

Christophorou, C. (2008a) 'A new communist surprise: what's next? Presidential elections in Cyprus, February 2008', *South European Society & Politics*, vol. 13, no. 2, pp. 215–233.

Christophorou, C. (2008b) 'The evolution of Greek Cypriot party politics', in *The Government and Politics of Cyprus*, eds H. Faustmann & J. Ker-Lindsay, Peter Lang, Oxford, pp. 83–106.

Karides, N. (2011) 'A socially networked election', *In-depth*, vol. 8, no. 3, available online at: http://www.cceia.unic.ac.cy.

Phileleftheros. (2011a) 'Υπονόμευση Χριστόφια από τις ΗΠΑ' [Christofias undermined by the USA], 2 July, p. 5.

Phileleftheros. (2011b) 'Έφθασε σχεδόν τα 2 εκατ. η διαφήμιση' [Publicity almost reached two million euros], 27 May, p. 5.

Phileleftheros. (2011c) 'Παραμένουν μυστικές οι Χρηματοδοτήσεις' [Funding remains a secret], 11 August, p. 17.

Politis. (2011) 'ΑΚΕΛ – Πρώτο κόμμα στη δαπάνη' [AKEL – first party in spending], 27 May, p. 20

Public Issue. (2011) Opinion poll for RIK (Cyprus Radio Foundation), 14 March, available online at: http://www.publicissue.gr/wp-content/uploads/2011/03/15th-cyprus-20111.pdf

Christophoros Christophorou studied education in Cyprus and Paris and political science in Athens and Lille, where he obtained his PhD. He is an assistant professor at the University of Nicosia, and has extensively worked in media experts groups at the Council of Europe and other European organisations.

After the Bailout: Responsibility, Policy, and Valence in the Portuguese Legislative Election of June 2011

Pedro C. Magalhães

This article discusses the 2011 legislative election results in Portugal and the context in which they took place. After describing how the economic and financial crisis unfolded, leading to the European Union/International Monetary Fund bailout, it analyses the campaign strategies of the major parties. On the basis of a post-election survey, the article then discusses how successful these strategies were, and concludes by analysing the aftermath of the election in terms of government formation.

The results of the 5 June 2011 legislative elections in Portugal were awaited with some trepidation. After all, just a month earlier, Portugal had become the third Eurozone country—after Greece and Ireland—to negotiate a European Union (EU)/International Monetary Fund (IMF) bailout package (of €78 billion) in order to maintain its debt obligations in a context of deep economic and financial crisis. How was this going to play out in the election? What kind of government, in terms of composition and overall support, was likely to emerge?

Several conflicting hypotheses concerning the answers to these questions could be proposed at the time. On the one hand, there were reasons to expect an extremely severe punishment of the incumbent centre-left PS (Partido Socialista—Socialist Party). Just a few months earlier, following the Irish bailout, the traditionally dominant party in Ireland, Fianna Fáil, had experienced the most dramatic defeat in its history, dropping no less than 24 points in relation to the previous election and losing more than two-thirds of the seats it held in parliament. The main background conditions—elections after an EU/IMF bailout package negotiated in a context of recession, very high unemployment, and record levels of budget deficit and public debt—seemed similar to those now faced by the Portuguese Socialists. Furthermore, elections took place at a time when several observers were suggesting that, in times of economic crisis such as those faced in Europe, voters were starting to move away from left-wing parties,[1] in a pattern that does find some empirical support in the literature (Stevenson 2001; Kayser 2009).

On the other hand, there were also reasons to suppose that whatever punishment was in store for the incumbent Socialists might be mitigated by several factors. The current crisis, triggered by the 2008 liquidity shortfall in American banks, is a good example of how global economic and European political interdependence can take economic outcomes away from the control of domestic political authorities. There are good reasons to believe that voters' attribution of responsibility for the economy can be affected by these processes (Fernández-Albertos 2006; Hellwig & Samuels 2007), weakening the relationship between perceptions of the state of the economy and the vote. Besides, Portugal stands out as a case where public commitment to the role of the state in the economy, to public services, and to redistributive and egalitarian policies seems particularly strong in a comparative context (Vala 1993; Freire 2007 and 2009; Fishman 2011). Thus, it was reasonable to hypothesise that the kind of austerity policies advocated by the EU/IMF agreement and more strongly defended by the major opposition party, the centre-right PSD (Partido Social Democrata—Social Democratic Party) might result in a kind of 'policy-oriented' (rather than 'incumbent-oriented') economic voting (Kiewiet 1981), through which concerns with the consequences of austerity, particularly the rise in unemployment, might lead to increased support for the left-wing parties.

On election day, the Socialists were indeed roundly defeated, obtaining 28 per cent of the votes, a loss of more than eight points in relation to their 2009 score. The winner was the PSD, a member of the European People's Party and traditionally the dominant force on the Portuguese centre-right, with 39 per cent of the vote. And yet, at the same time, the elections brought nothing like the dramatic party system change experienced in Ireland. The Socialists remained the dominant force on the left, while the PSD's score was lower than its last electoral victory in 2002. So how should we interpret these results in light of the conflicting hypotheses set forth in the preceding paragraphs?

This article attempts to provide a first answer to this question. The next section describes the economic and political context of the elections and the main political players. This is followed by a discussion of the campaign and then of the results. Possible explanations are then proposed on the basis of a preliminary analysis of data from a post-election survey conducted in July 2011, and finally conclusions are presented.

The Economic and Political Background

In 2005, the Socialist Party, under the leadership of José Sócrates, a former minister in the Guterres cabinets in the 1990s and early 2000s, obtained a historic victory, achieving the Socialists' first ever absolute majority in the history of Portuguese democracy. The PS came to power with a commitment to fiscal consolidation and sweeping structural reforms in the economy and the state, after a period when, throughout the first half of the decade, there had been repeated breaches of the budget deficit threshold (3 per cent) established in the European Stability and Growth Pact. This included a record deficit of 6.1 per cent of GDP in 2005.

Until 2008, Portugal seemed indeed to be on a path towards fiscal consolidation, as the government brought the deficit down to 2.2 per cent of GDP by the end of that year. However, as in the rest of the Eurozone and beyond, the response of the Portuguese government to the liquidity shortfall in American banks in late 2008 and the global crisis it triggered was to engage in anti-cyclical policies (Torres 2009). These consisted of major public investments in the modernisation of schools and the energy and communications infrastructure, as well as enhanced social and unemployment protection. The eagerness with which the Socialist government seized upon the (rather short-lived) European consensus on how to address the crisis was probably not unrelated to the electoral calendar. After all, by September 2009 the PS would again face elections, this time rendered more difficult than anticipated by the declining popularity of the prime minister. José Sócrates had been beleaguered in the second half of his term by a succession of media reports on alleged (although never proven) frauds relating to the way he had obtained his university degree and to his involvement in a corruption case when he had been a minister in a previous Socialist cabinet. In 2009, the Portuguese economy contracted 2.9 per cent in real terms, rather less than the Eurozone average (-4.3 per cent), while real wages increased by more than three per cent, allowing the incumbent a cushion against the well-known effects of recession on the electoral fate of incumbents.

In the 2009 elections, despite considerable losses (a drop of 7.5 percentage points in the vote share and 24, or 10.5 per cent, of its parliamentary seats), the PS still managed to obtain a comfortable victory. It enjoyed a seven-point advantage over the major opposition party, the PSD. However, this time the PS lacked an absolute majority. Here again, the Portuguese party system was to display one of its more resilient features: the imbalance between the left and the right in terms of the potential for coalition-building. On the right of the political system, the PSD and the smaller conservative CDS-PP (Centro Democrático e Social–Partido Popular—Democratic Social Centre–Popular Party), also a member of the European People's Party (to which it was readmitted after a brief fling with Euroscepticism during the 1990s), are relatively close on most policy issues and have found it possible to coalesce on several occasions in the past, going as far back as 1979. To the left of the PS, however, we find two major parties. One is the CDU (Coligação Democrática Unitária—Communist Party/Greens Coalition), led by Jerónimo de Sousa, a member of the Communist Party since its clandestine era in the 1960s and an MP since the 1975 Constituent Assembly. The other is the left-libertarian BE (Bloco de Esquerda—Leftist Bloc), led by Francisco Louçã, a university professor and former leader of PSR, a Trotskyist party that merged with other left-wing forces to found BE in 1999. Overall, with few exceptions—which we will discuss later—the Socialists' policy positions, as measured, for example, by the policy proposals contained in party manifestos (Volkens et al. 2011), have become closer to the parties to their right than to those on their left, and remain very distant from those of the CDU or the BE on crucial issues of high politics, such as

European integration and defence. In other words, the potential for coalitions on the left is very small. Since 1974, there has never been a national-level coalition between the Socialists and the Communists. In 2009, once again, the Socialists opted to form a minority government.

In the meantime, however, Portugal's capacity to re-emerge unscathed from the anti-cyclical policies it had adopted during the first stage of the economic crisis was undermined by several fundamentals. The major part of the previous fiscal consolidation had been obtained on the side of revenue generation, through better collection enforcement and increased taxes, rather than from expenditure cuts and streamlining of the state apparatus. Furthermore, due to lack of competitiveness and low productivity, economic growth had remained comparatively sluggish: in 2007 GDP grew at a far from spectacular rate of 2.4 per cent, which was then followed by stagnation in 2008. On average, since 2005, real GDP growth in Portugal was about half the average of the EU27. The first signs of what was to come were already visible before the 2009 elections, as international rating agencies began downgrading the debt of most peripheral European countries, including Portugal. However, the pressures created by the electoral calendar, and what turned out to be the misguided perception that the European consensus would persist as the crisis mutated into a sovereign debt crisis, seem to have contributed, in different degrees, to preventing Portuguese policy-makers from seeing what some—including in the pages of this journal—were already able to foresee very early on. This was the fact that, 'even though EMU participation shelters its members from currency risk, it does not do so from credit risk' (Torres 2009, p. 65).

This only became painfully clear to all in the aftermath of the Greek crisis. The May 2010 EU/IMF package for Greece and the downgrade of its debt to 'junk' status was followed by rises in the spreads in the Irish, Spanish, and Portuguese sovereign bonds and further debt downgrades. With austerity policies in Portugal now seen as necessary to 'reassure the markets' and under increasing pressure from the EU, the PS minority government was forced to engage in negotiations with the opposition. The PSD was now led by Pedro Passos Coelho, an economist and businessman who had served as leader of the party's youth organisation back in the 1990s. Following a failed party leadership bid in 2008, he finally won new internal elections in March 2010 with more than 60 per cent of party delegates' votes, a reassuring contrast compared with the highly divided intraparty contest of 2008. Throughout 2010, the newly elected Passos Coelho faced a dilemma. Should he, however reluctantly, lend a hand to the government, presenting himself as a credible leader who was serious enough to place the interests of the nation first and foremost? Or should he completely avoid being held even partially accountable for the necessary measures? The answer throughout 2010 was the former. Following a first package in March 2010 (passed in parliament with PSD's abstention), two additional ones were passed during that year following negotiations between the PS and PSD and with the opposition of all the other parties in parliament. These successive packages focused on cutting public sector salaries and pensions, welfare benefits, and tax exemptions and privileges, together with increased taxation and accelerating privatisations.

However, by early 2011 domestic and international conditions had further deteriorated. The unemployment rate had reached 12 per cent, up from 7.6 in 2005. More pressingly, central government debt now reached 93 per cent of GDP, up from 71 per cent in 2005. The budget deficits of 2009 and 2010, close to 10 per cent of GDP, were the largest for 160 years.[2] The interest rate at which the Portuguese government was able to finance itself in the secondary markets surpassed seven per cent, the level that the government itself had declared, just a few months earlier, would make an EU/IMF bailout inevitable. In this context, the PS government proposed a new austerity package (the fourth), which was negotiated in Brussels and announced prior to any significant exchanges with the PSD. Its rejection, Prime Minister Sócrates warned, would be inevitably followed by his resignation and create a political crisis that would increase the likelihood of an EU/IMF bailout.

It was clear that, once more, all other opposition parties would vote against this new package, as they had before. But the crucial vote was again the PSD's. This time, buoyed by voting intention polls that gave the party its best result for a very long time and allegedly under considerable internal pressure to force elections, Passos Coelho opted to join the rest of the opposition parties in rejecting the package, arguing that the government's failure to engage the PSD in negotiations, the lack of emphasis on cutting expenditure, and the failed implementation of the previous packages approved in 2010 rendered the new one simply not credible. After the fourth package was rejected in parliament on 23 March, Sócrates indeed resigned, and elections were called for June 2011. However, on 6 April the Portuguese government was forced to recognise that it would not be able to meet its debt obligations before the elections and requested help from the EU and IMF. Negotiations were conducted directly with the government, but the PSD was also indirectly involved, given the EU's insistence that the agreement be signed by the three largest parties (the PS, the PSD, and the CDS-PP), i.e. those likely to be involved in any future government solution. The Memorandum of Agreement was completed in early May and subscribed by all three parties.

A controversy about the similarities and differences between the Memorandum and the rejected fourth package immediately followed. While the PS argued that the Memorandum was fundamentally based on the fourth package, adding a series of unnecessarily painful measures that could have been avoided had the PSD approved it and avoided the EU/IMF bailout,[3] the PSD described that notion as 'pure fantasy',[4] pointing to the unrealistic government projections and the insufficient emphasis on cutting expenditure in the government's fourth package. There was a kernel of truth in both positions. To be sure, the Memorandum reiterated many of the measures proposed in the package. But it was also a much more ambitious document. The massive 68-page Memorandum contained basically two kinds of measures: those aiming at fiscal consolidation and those aimed at addressing state and market inefficiencies, i.e. structural reforms. Among them, we can find projected cuts of about €200 million in education and €600 million in the National Health Service, as well as increases in co-payments in public health services; the full privatisation of transport, energy, communication, and insurance companies; a reduction of unemployment insurance benefits and severance payments, as well as a facilitation of dismissals; and a reduction in employers' social security contributions to boost competitiveness, to be compensated by an increase in indirect taxation.[5] In sum, the basic platform of any future government was now defined. Elections, however, were still a month away.

The Electoral Campaign

The campaign was totally dominated by two interrelated issues. The first was the question of who should be held responsible for the financial situation of the country and the ultimate need for EU/IMF intervention. The second concerned the kind of measures necessary to address the country's economic crisis and their likely consequences.

The PS's campaign discourse was, to some extent, an extension of its main discourse ever since the financial crisis unfolded: pointing out the factors that exonerated the government from major responsibility for that crisis. Throughout 2010, the government had explained how Portugal's increasingly unsustainable financial situation resulted from Greek contagion, the role of the unregulated financial markets, and the unfairness of the downgrades made by the rating agencies. There was certainly something to this argument, especially as indicators related to growth and exports showed that, by early 2010, some semblance of economic recovery might be taking place.[6] Now, following the PSD's rejection of the last austerity package, an additional actor was to blame: the PSD and Passos Coelho's 'immature' willingness to cause elections, which had contributed to 'throw the country into the arms of the IMF' and force the government to negotiate a bailout.[7]

In contrast, the PSD focused its campaign on turning the election into a basic judgement of the Socialist government's economic performance, stressing that the PS had been in power for the last six years (and 13 out of the previous 16 years, only interrupted by the short-lived PSD/CDS-PP coalition of 2002–05) and had failed to set the country on the path of economic growth and fiscal consolidation. All these exchanges took place on rather acrimonious terms, reaching an extreme point when a very prominent PSD politician accused Sócrates of being a 'compulsive liar' and compared the Socialist 'propaganda machine' to that of Nazi Germany.[8]

A second theme in the campaign, connected to the previous one but with deeper implications, concerned the economic and social policies espoused by the PSD. Back in April 2010, just after Passos Coelho had triumphed in the PSD's internal elections, he had announced that the party would propose a series of constitutional amendments generically designed, among other things, to 'reduce the role of the state in society' and 'increase people's ability to make choices in health and education'.[9]

The drafts discussed within the PSD and invariably made public in the following months included, among other things, eliminating the expression 'tend to be free of charge' with reference to the National Health Service; changing the 'fair cause' limitation on the dismissal of workers; and removing the state obligation to 'progressively make all levels of education free of charge'. Additional proposals emanating from PSD circles, such as 'delivering social benefits and subsidies in the form of vouchers'[10] or 'reducing the amount of pensions to be received in the future on the basis of past unemployment benefits'[11], reinforced the basic message. Finally, the PSD presented its electoral platform as bringing about a 'change of the current statist paradigm', blaming the PS for a 'mistaken model of development ... based on a continual increase in the weight and size of the State'.[12]

The PS's reaction from the very beginning was to seize upon this as an opportunity to depict the PSD as a party composed of 'conservatives' and 'neo-liberals' set on undoing the Portuguese welfare state.[13] Such discourse was to be employed up to election day, allowing the PS to describe the most unpopular austerity measures included in the EU/IMF Memorandum of Agreement as something the PSD had espoused and desired all along. During the campaign, Sócrates accused the PSD of 'ideological radicalism' and of attempting to destroy the National Health Service and public education system, shifting funds to the private sector.[14] In sum, while the PSD tried to use the election to legitimise a new 'economic paradigm' for Portugal while blaming the government for the economic situation, the PS attempted to turn it into a fight for the survival of the fundamental traits of Portuguese social welfare policies, which the PSD was supposedly set on destroying, a goal allegedly achieved by having forced the EU/IMF bailout.

The CDS-PP, led by Paulo Portas, the longest-serving leader among the five major parties, was clearly aligned with the PSD in attempting to hold the government accountable for the economic and financial situation, but was also more restrained in advancing an economic liberalisation platform, as befits a party whose electoral appeal is partially built on attracting different segments of the electorate that are dependent on government transfers, such as pensioners and farmers. Furthermore, throughout 2010, the CDS-PP had always opposed the packages negotiated between the PS and the PSD, and hoped to benefit from its consistent opposition to what were clearly rather unpopular measures.

For the parties on the left, CDU and BE, the agenda also seemed simple and consistent enough. It included a blanket rejection of the austerity policies explicitly or implicitly adopted in the EU/IMF Memorandum, the renegotiation of the debt, and higher taxes on personal fortunes and financial transactions. However, the BE's position was, from the start, somewhat more uncomfortable than that of the CDU. On the one hand, many of the banners that had contributed to BE's electoral rise— social issues such as abortion, gay marriage, and decriminalisation of drug use—had been taken over by the PS government itself, which had advanced a particularly progressive agenda in this regard under Sócrates's leadership. On the other hand, in the presidential elections held in January 2011 the BE had supported Manuel Alegre, the unsuccessful candidate who was also endorsed by the PS. In contrast to the Communists, who as always presented their own presidential candidate, the BE's failure to reactivate its relatively unanchored electoral basis with a candidate of its own and its counterproductive association with the Socialists in the presidential elections seemed to take their toll on public opinion. Polls on voting intention showed declining support for BE, beginning precisely from the period of the presidential election campaign.[15]

The Results

The first notable result of the election was the particularly low level of turnout. At 58 per cent, it was the lowest ever in the history of democratic legislative elections in the country. Portugal's turnout rates are noticeably lower than those of Spain, even though the Iberian countries share a similar length of democratic experience and a proportional-representation (PR) closed-list electoral system. However, it is also clear that the official Portuguese turnout figures are deflated by the apparent inability of the authorities to keep the electoral register updated, not taking full account of deceased voters and emigrants, who often remain registered in Portugal. In any case, there is little doubt that in 2011 turnout reached a historical low in Portugal, as can be seen in Figure 1.

The second notable result was, of course, the clear defeat of the PS. Opinion polls had shown the PSD ahead in voting intentions ever since June 2010, the party reaching its best score, with an average ten points' lead over the Socialists, around March 2011. However, the controversy around the rejection of the government's last austerity package seemed to take its toll, at least temporarily: although the PSD never ceased to be ahead in the polls, in April there was a visible decline in voting intentions for the Social Democrats and a corresponding rise for the PS, some analysts

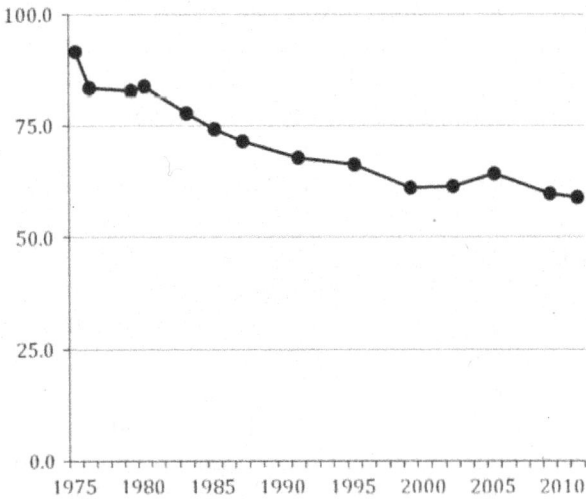

Figure 1 Turnout in Portuguese Legislative Elections (%). *Source*: Comissão Nacional de Eleições, available online at: http://eleicoes.cne.pt/sel_eleicoes.cfm?m=raster

suggesting the election could be a close call. It was only in the last two weeks of the campaign that the polls began to converge again on what was to be the final outcome. In the end, the Socialists lost more than eight per cent of the vote compared with the 2009 election, experiencing the second-largest negative vote swing in their history and their worst electoral score since 1987. As a result, on election night Sócrates resigned from the party's leadership and announced his withdrawal from active politics.

As can be seen in Table 1, the PSD obtained 38.7 per cent of the vote, more than ten points ahead of the Socialists, but nevertheless below the party's score in 2002, when it was led by José Manuel Barroso, later president of the European Commission. The CDS-PP, with 11.7 per cent of the vote, obtained its best score since 1983, albeit short of the very high expectations that it had entertained during the campaign. In any case, this result signals the ability of the CDS-PP to reverse the pattern of the late 1980s and early 1990s: the loss of 'tactical votes' to the PSD whenever the major party on the right won an election. The Communists of the CDU basically kept their 2009 score of 7.9 per cent, which in turn had represented a small but nevertheless relevant improvement vis-à-vis both the 2002 and 2005 elections. The resilience of the Communists contrasts with the notable decline of the BE, which up to 2012 had systematically increased its vote share ever since its first election in 1999, emerging as the Communists' main adversary on the left side of the party system. In the previous election, the BE had even managed to surpass the vote share of the Communist Party. This time, however, the BE dropped nearly five percentage points, spectacularly losing nearly half of its previous voters and revealing how politically and socially unanchored its electorate was in comparison with the Communist vote.

The electoral system, one of the least proportional among the PR systems in Europe—given the large number of small districts and the use of the d'Hondt method—gave its usual premium to the largest parties. That premium, however, was insufficient

Table 1 Vote Shares, Turnout, and Seat Shares, 2002–11 Elections (%, number of seats in parentheses)

	Votes				Seats			
	2002	2005	2009	2011	2002	2005	2009	2011
PSD	40.2	28.8	29.1	38.7	45.6 (105)	32.6 (75)	35.2 (81)	47.0 (108)
PS	37.8	45.0	36.6	28.1	41.7 (96)	52.6 (121)	42.2 (97)	32.1 (74)
CDS-PP	8.7	7.2	10.4	11.7	6.1 (14)	5.2 (12)	9.1 (21)	10.4 (24)
CDU	6.9	7.5	7.9	7.9	5.2 (12)	6.1 (14)	6.5 (15)	7.0 (16)
BE	2.7	6.4	9.8	5.2	1.3 (3)	3.4 (8)	7.0 (16)	3.5 (8)
Others	1.7	3.2	4.1	5.3				
Blank/void	2.0	1.9	2.1	3.1				
Turnout	61.5	64.3	59.7	58.0				

Source: Comissão Nacional de Eleições, available online at: http://eleicoes.cne.pt/sel_eleicoes.cfm?m=raster

for the PSD to reach an absolute majority. In the end, the Social Democrats obtained 47 per cent of the seats, which meant that, in order to form a majority cabinet, they were forced to seek a coalition. As for the Socialists, almost a third of the parliament remained in their hands, allowing them, in spite of a clear defeat, to remain second party and the dominant force on the left. Together, PSD and PS represent about 70 per cent of the vote and 80 per cent of MPs, similar to what had occurred in 2009. Party system fragmentation is the same as in the previous election: Laakso and Taagepera's (1979) effective number of parliamentary parties was about three in both the 2009 and 2011 elections.[16] This does confirm a historical trend away from the near two-party system that had appeared to be developing during the late 1980s and 1990s (Freire 2010; Magalhães 2011). But, having said that, party system fragmentation remains comparatively moderate and the major signs coming from the 2011 election in this respect are of continuity rather than change.

The Mechanics of Electoral Change

What explains these electoral results? A first important aspect concerns the mechanics of electoral change between 2009 to 2011, particularly concerning the losses experienced by the PS and the BE. Data collected in a July post-election survey conducted by the Portuguese Electoral Behaviour (CEP) project[17] suggest that demobilisation of previous PS voters played a very important role. Pre-election polls already showed a strong 'enthusiasm gap' between the PSD and PS electorates, the latter declaring they were 'certain to vote' at a consistently lower rate. The CEP post-electoral survey tends to confirm this. A vote-transfer matrix, based on vote recall in the latest (2011) and the preceding (2009) election, shows that while the PS lost only about ten per cent of its previous voters to the PSD, it lost more than 20 per cent to abstention. Similarly, when we look at party identification as declared by respondents in the 2011 CEP survey, close to one in four PS identifiers report having abstained, which is twice as high as the abstention rate among PSD identifiers.

The BE was even less capable than the PS of retaining its previous electorate. With the qualification that in this case we are dealing with small sub-samples and that previous election vote recall is a question certainly subject to considerable rationalisation on the part of voters, it is nevertheless interesting to note two features about declared former BE voters. On the one hand, about one in five reported having abstained this time, while the BE was seemingly unable to compensate such losses by attracting previous abstainers or new voters. On the other hand, the fickleness of the party's electoral base becomes evident when we notice that the party's major source of losses actually consisted of defections to parties other than the PS or PSD, including to smaller extra-parliamentary parties of the extreme left and, curiously, to the CDS-PP. It is worth remembering here that the BE's past electorate shared important socio-demographic features (higher levels of income and, especially, of education) with CDS-PP voters.

Responsibility for the Economy

The second important aspect of the election concerns responsibility for the economy. As we have seen, while one of the main features of the PSD's campaign discourse was an attempt to turn the election into a referendum on the socialist incumbency, the PS attempted precisely to deflect and diffuse responsibility for the economic crisis. There are good reasons to believe that voters might have had difficulties in assigning full responsibilities to the incumbent government for economic outcomes. On the one hand, the crisis had a clear global dimension, and the role of both international organisations and relatively impersonal market forces was evident. On the other hand, the PSD's early agreements with the PS and the breakdown of negotiations in early 2011 created a context where responsibility for both the difficult austerity measures and the EU/IMF intervention could be assigned to actors other than the PS and the government.

There were early signs that voters were indeed divided in this respect. When asked in 2010 in a Catholic University poll whom they should blame for the state of national economic affairs, only 21 per cent of respondents placed full and exclusive responsibility on the PS government and more than 25 per cent also blamed the international crisis or 'banks and financial institutions'.[18] In a new poll conducted just before the request for financial rescue was finally made,[19] less than half the electorate blamed the PS government for the likely need for foreign support, while the remaining voters accused the PSD, the President of the Republic, the international crisis, or even the EU.

The data collected by the CEP July post-election survey confirms the importance of this aspect of the campaign debates. There was little variation in voters' perception of the state of the economy: 86 per cent described it as 'bad' or 'very bad' while 94 per cent believed that it had become 'worse' or 'much worse' during the previous year. But this also meant that a lot might hinge on who or what should be held accountable for this. In fact, as Figure 2 shows, Portuguese voters were less than unified in assigning credit or blame for the state of the economy. While 65 per cent of respondents held the government 'very' or 'extremely responsible', close to or above 50 per cent of voters also held 'the international economic situation', 'the banks', or even the 'rating agencies' equally accountable. Meanwhile, about a third of voters found 'the opposition' to be 'very' or 'extremely responsible'. Similar results were evoked by a question about whom to hold accountable for the need for a EU/IMF bailout.

Initial cross-tabulations on the basis of the CEP survey, as shown in Table 2, suggest a correlation between the attribution of responsibility and vote choice. Among respondents who held the government 'very' or 'extremely responsible' for the economy, the PSD scored very high and the PS very low. However, among respondents who, regardless of their view concerning governmental accountability, tended to hold other agents responsible for the state of the economy,[20] the PS performed somewhat better. Meanwhile, the PS dominated overwhelmingly among the small segment

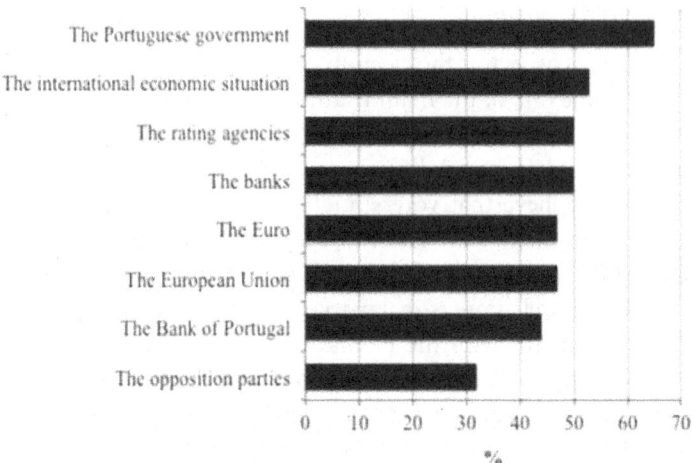

Figure 2 Shares of Survey Respondents Holding Each Agent 'Very' or 'Extremely' Responsible for the Country's Economic Situation (%). *Source*: CEP survey, July 2011.

(about eight per cent of the sample) of those who exonerated the government and blamed other agents. Of course, future studies will have to examine the causal relationship here and the extent to which party identification was itself determinant in shaping perceptions of economic responsibility.

Policy Issues or Valence?

A third important aspect of the election was the extent to which the PSD was willing to present a rather openly 'liberal' (for some, 'neo-liberal') and pro-austerity discourse

Table 2 Vote Shares According to Perceived Responsibility for Economic Crisis (column percentages)

	Government 'very' or 'extremely' responsible	Other agents highly responsible	Government not 'very' or 'extremely' responsible and other agents highly responsible
Among reported voters			
PSD	44	37	25
PS	19	28	51
Others/blank/void	37	35	24
Total	100	100	100
Whole sample			
PSD	25	20	16
PS	10	16	34
Others/blank/void	21	20	17
Did not vote	44	44	33
Total	100	100	100

Source: CEP survey, July 2011.

vis-à-vis the role of the state in the economy, while the PS attempted to define a vote for the PSD as a vote against social rights and the welfare state. The PSD's strategy seemed dangerous. In terms of ideological self-placement, while Portuguese voters tend to position themselves slightly left-of-centre, they have increasingly perceived the PSD as a rightist party, closer to the CDS-PP than to either the PS or the median voter (Freire 2009, p. 190; 2010, p. 598). Besides, in terms of issue positions, Portuguese voters have displayed leftist positions on most issues related to the economy or to the state's role in society (Vala 1993; Freire 2007 and 2009), and such positions seem to have been consequential for voting behaviour, at least in the 2005 elections and the then defeat of the PSD (Freire 2009).

The Social Democrats' clear triumph in 2011 could be interpreted as a sign that the policy preferences of the Portuguese electorate have moved away from leftist positions and in defence of economic liberalism and austerity policies. However, there is no evidence of this having occurred. Asked in the CEP July 2011 survey whether they favoured privatisation of public companies, private responsibility for pension schemes, and private control of education or health services, voters tended to express a rejection of these positions similar to the findings of the previous 2005 and 2009 post-election surveys (Figure 3). Considering that we are dealing with three different elections, with two different winners, and similar surveys in terms of their timing and methodology, this absence of change becomes particularly credible.

On the other hand, it is not clear either that the Socialists were able to capitalise on these policy preferences. Issue positions seem to be generally weak predictors of

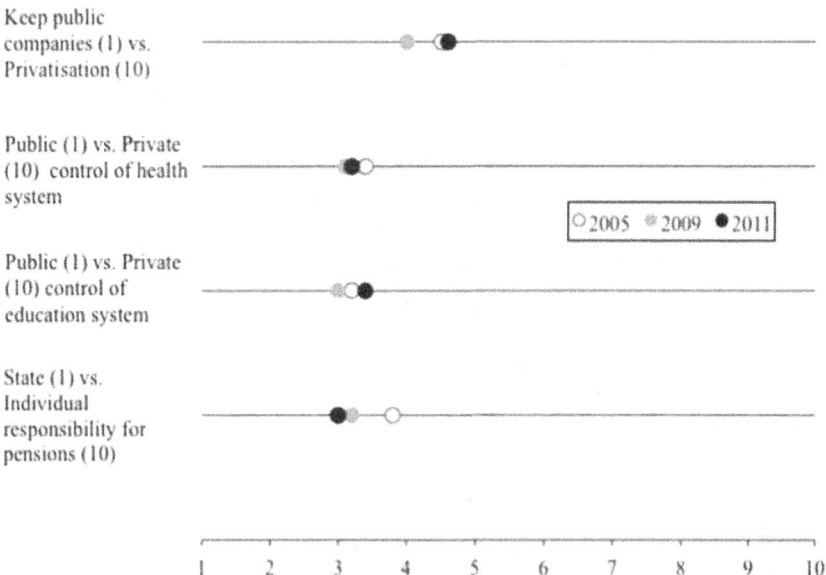

Figure 3 Mean Placements of the Electorate in Ten-Point Issue Position Scales in Three Post-election Surveys. *Source*: CEP surveys of 2005, 2009, and 2011.

Table 3 Rank Correlation (tau-c) between Issue Positions and Voting Recall for PS (0) or PSD (1) in Three Elections

	2005	2009	2010
Keep public companies (1) vs. privatisation (10)	0.14***	0.01	0.14**
Public (1) vs. private control of health system (10)	0.15***	0.12	0.03
Public (1) vs. private control of education system (10)	0.13***	0.07	0.05
State (1) vs. individual responsibility for pensions (10)	0.07*	0.06	−0.09

* $p < 0.05$; ** $p < 0.01$; *** $p < 0.001$.
Source: CEP surveys of 2005, 2009, and 2011.

vote choices in Portugal, but in 2011 they were even less consequential than usual. As Table 3 shows, although voters' positions on privatisation remained (weakly) related to the choice between the PS and the PSD, the remaining issues simply failed to drive any sort of wedge between PS and PSD voters. In fact, there was an even weaker association between issue positions and vote choices than in 2009.

This contrasts very clearly with the importance of variables related to a valence model of electoral choice (Clarke et al. 2004 and 2009), i.e. based on 'retrospective evaluations rooted in the performance of governing and opposition parties in delivering on the issues which voters care about' (Clarke et al. 2009, p. 50). The survey asked voters to evaluate government performance on a four-point scale (from 1 'very bad' to 4 'very good') both overall and on several valence issues. Here it became clear that the Socialists fought the election from a very weak position. Overwhelming majorities of respondents (ranging from 65 to 80 per cent) rated the Sócrates government as 'bad' or 'very bad'. Table 4 displays measures of association between those evaluations and the vote for the incumbent. As we can see, those evaluations are invariably much more strongly associated with vote choices than the policy positions analysed in Table 3, suggesting it was the general picture of the incumbent government's performance, rather than the policy positions or the austerity and anti-austerity discourses adopted by the two main parties, which played the major role.

Again, future studies on the 2011 elections will certainly be able to disentangle in greater detail and rigour, using multivariate analyses, the extent to which voting

Table 4 Rank correlation (Tau-c) between valence evaluations and voting recall in 2011

	PS (1) vs. PSD (0)	PS (1) vs. Others (0)
Government performance (overall)	0.60***	0.53***
Economy and finances	0.45***	0.38***
Education	0.48***	0.38***
Health	0.48***	0.42***
Employment and social security	0.44***	0.38***
Justice and public safety	0.46***	0.41***

* $p < 0.05$; ** $p < 0.01$; *** $p < 0.001$.
Source: CEP 2011 survey.

behaviour was affected by voters' policy positions or by valence issues. But there are good reasons to assume that the context in which the elections took place made the effects of policy positions even less relevant than usual. First, since 2005, the Socialists had been increasingly perceived by voters as moving away from the left and towards the centre (Freire 2010, pp. 595–598). This meant the PS faced a serious credibility problem when it attempted to frame the election as a choice between 'neo-liberal austerity' and 'the defence of the welfare state'. Second, this was compounded by the fact that most of the campaign took place *after* the bailout agreement between the PS government, the EU, and the IMF, which was also subscribed by the PSD and the CDS-PP. Most of the Memorandum measures imply a further rolling-back of the role of the state and further market-oriented liberalisation. In other words, the economic policy endorsed by the PSD and criticised by the Socialists during the 2011 campaign was, in fact, the basic platform that all viable government parties had already committed to implement. In this particularly acute context of policy convergence, it is little wonder that most voters felt that PS's campaign discourse was not credible and that the election or the choice between the PS and the PSD was not really about these issues. In fact, in the July 2011 survey, only seven per cent of respondents agreed that the election was really about 'the survival of the welfare state', as the PS attempted to frame it.

Government Formation

The new PSD/CDS-PP government took office less than three weeks after the election. By Portuguese standards, this was a comparatively short period of government formation. Speed was necessitated by the urgency of the measures agreed with the EU and IMF. During the campaign, there had been allusions to the possibility of a grand coalition of the PSD and PS. This would have constituted a revival of the 'Central Bloc' that had led the country during the period of the previous IMF agreement in 1983–85. However, it was never a real possibility. On the one hand, the level of opposition hostility to Sócrates in the last few years of his government and the personal acrimony in his relations with successive PSD leaders seemed to rule out such a coalition if he had remained PS's leader. On the other hand, his departure made a grand coalition impossible too, by opening a process of leadership selection in the PS, involving primary elections and a party congress. This left the PSD without an interlocutor with whom to negotiate a coalition within the tight time frame dictated by the bailout agreement.

The new government, with 12 ministers including the prime minister, and 35 'junior ministers' (*secretários de estado*), is the smallest cabinet since 1985 and significantly smaller than the historical average of 56 cabinet members, including both ministers and junior ministers. A total of 18 cabinet members—more than one-third of the total—are 'independents', that is, unaffiliated to either party. This is the highest number ever, if we discount the 'presidential initiative' cabinets in the 1970s. However, this is also far from a new trend in Portuguese politics. Since 1976, the average proportion of independents in cabinet has been 25 per cent and they represented nearly a third of the 2005–09 Sócrates cabinet. The importance of the cabinet 'independents' is a pattern shared with Spain, setting these two countries apart from most European democracies (Pinto & Almeida 2009). This trend is rather symptomatic of how depleted party organisations in Portugal have become of competent cadres, of the perceived need to insulate governments from pressures from party organisations, and of the level of hostility towards parties which prime ministers intuit in public opinion. However, it also incurs the danger of recruiting politically inexperienced ministers with little clout within parties, making them more dependent on direct support from the prime minister and thus increasing the latter's authority in the cabinet.

While the CDS-PP controls about one-fifth of the MPs supporting the coalition in parliament, cabinet members affiliated to the party represent a quarter of the total (and one-third of the non-independents). While CDS-PP party leader, Paulo Portas, has become the minister of foreign affairs, one of the most crucial aspects of Portuguese external relations in the next few years, i.e. the relationship with the IMF and EU and the monitoring of the implementation of the Memorandum measures, has been assigned to a structure led by a junior minister (a former PSD minister) who reports directly to the prime minister. In the case of another significant CDS-PP portfolio, Social Security, the minister in charge has ceded important competences to the Ministry of Economy and is joined by a PSD political heavyweight as a 'junior minister', who, again, responds directly to Prime Minister Passos Coelho. In sum, the cabinet and most of its relevant political and economic coordination portfolios are firmly under the control of the PSD.

Conclusion

In the 2011 election, the incumbent Socialists' strategy to resist their inevitable electoral punishment was twofold: framing the crisis as a systemic event in which many forces and agents, including the opposition itself, were not devoid of blame, and depicting the EU/IMF bailout as something the PSD had desired all along in order to adopt its preferred 'neo-liberal' austerity policies, which threatened the survival of fundamental public services and transferred resources to private economic interests. As it happened, most voters did seem, in general, to cast a wide net when thinking about what had led Portugal to its present economic situation, and that did seem to play a role in mitigating, to some extent, vote transfers from the PS to the PSD. However, the PS's perceived centrist shift during its tenure in office and the particular circumstances of the election undermined the credibility of the second part of their electoral message. The Socialists were unable to disentangle themselves from a bailout agreement their own government had negotiated and signed, and which made policies of austerity, privatisation, and market liberalisation faits accomplis from the voters' point of view. As a result, economic policy issue positions seem to have been rendered mostly irrelevant for vote choices and failed to result in any visible benefits for the PS. In contrast, valence issues prevailed.

In the 2011 elections, Portuguese voters were basically unwilling to renew their trust in a PS government that most saw now as fundamentally incompetent in dealing with the problems voters cared about, and they did so either by demobilising or by shifting their support to the main alternative, the PSD. The latter's victory does not seem to have resulted from any significant shifts in the policy preferences of the electorate, supporting (or, for that matter, rejecting) austerity policies. First, those preferences counted for little in voters' choices. Second, Portuguese voters remained, in the aggregate, firmly on the side of scepticism vis-à-vis austerity and the role of private initiative in the economy and in social policies.

Acknowledgements

Several segments of this article were previously published in the blog *The Monkey Cage* (www.themonkeycage.org), in two posts entitled 'June 2011 Portuguese Parliamentary Elections: Pre-Election Report' (available online at: http://alturl.com/5rvho) and '2011 Portuguese Parliamentary Election: Post-Election Report' (available online at: http://alturl.com/kboak). I thank both the editors of the blog and of the journal for permission to reprint them here. Part of this article was written while I was Luso-American Development Foundation Visiting Professor at the Department of Government of Georgetown University. I wish to thank the Luso-American Development Foundation for their support.

Notes

[1] 'Europe's left: left out', *The Economist*, 7 June 2011, available online at: http://www.economist.com/node/21518773

[2] Bank of Portugal, *Main Economic Indicators*, available online at: http://www.bportugal.pt/en-US/Pages/inicio.aspx.

[3] 'Acordo entre troika e Governo desenvolve PEC 4, diz Teixeira dos Santos', *Actualidades*, 5 May 2011, available online at: http://noticias.portugalmail.pt/artigo/20110505/acordo-entre-troika-e-governo-desenvolve-pec-4-diz-teixeira-dos-santos

[4] 'Ideia de que PEC IV esteve na origem do acordo é "pura fantasia"', *Jornal I*, 4 May 2011, available online at: http://www1.ionline.pt/conteudo/120998-ideia-que-pec-iv-esteve-na-origem-do-acordo-e-pura-fantasia

[5] The English versions of the memorandum and accompanying documents are available online at: http://alturl.com/bxv7c. For an analysis of the document, see 'Memorandum of economic and financial policies: 11 perspectives', available online at: http://alturl.com/fzv36.

[6] See R. Fishman, 'Portugal's unnecessary bailout', *New York Times*, 12 April 2011, available at: http://alturl.com/q5483

[7] E. Miranda, 'Sócrates acusa PSD de querer FMI e crise política,' *Jornal de Negócios*, 15 March 2011, available at: http://alturl.com/sycmj

[8] 'Catroga compara Sócrates a Hitler', *Expresso*, 11 May, 2011, available at: http://aeiou.expresso.pt/catroga-compara-socrates-a-hitler=f648180.

[9] P. Pires and S. Marques, 'Vamos rever a Constituição e vamos revê-la depressa', *TVI*, 11 April 2010, available at: http://alturl.com/a2jrd

[10] 'Vice do PSD quer benefícios sociais atribuídos em cartão de débito', *Diário Económico*, 19 April 2011, available at: http://alturl.com/p2r5i

[11] 'Mais Sociedade provoca polémica ao ligar reforma e subsídio desemprego', *Sol*, 27 April 2011, available online at: http://alturl.com/odese
[12] 'Passos Coelho quer "mudar actual paradigma estatizante"', *Diário de Notícias*, 29 March 2011, available online at: http://alturl.com/ywd3j
[13] Leonete Botelho and Nuno Simas, 'Assis abre jornadas do PS com críticas à proposta de revisão constitucional do PSD', *Público*, 5 July 2010, available online at: http://alturl.com/ytedk
[14] See 'Sócrates acusa PSD de querer "destruir o Serviço Nacional de Saúde"', *Jornal de Notícias*, 7 May 2011, available online at: http://alturl.com/kghe7; and Carla Soares, 'Sócrates acusa PSD de querer desviar verbas da escola pública para a privada', *Jornal de Notícias*, May 8th, 2011, available online at: http://alturl.com/drjot
[15] The blog *Margens de erro* (http://www.margensdeerro.blogspot.com) kept an updated register of all polls published during the campaign. For the decline of the BE, see: http://margensdeerro.blogspot.com/2011/06/alegrebloco.html
[16] Laakso and Taagepera's formula for effective number of parties is

$$N = 1/\sum_{i=1}^{n} p_i^2$$

where n is the number of parties with at least a seat and p is the proportion of seats.
[17] The CEP project was coordinated by Marina Costa Lobo and Pedro Magalhães at the Institute of Social Sciences of the University of Lisbon (ICS-UL). It was a Computer Assisted Personal Interviewing survey of registered voters conducted in continental Portugal, executed by TNS Euroteste, $N=1000$, stratified by region and size of locality, with fieldwork between 8 and 28 July 2011, and a 62 per cent response rate. All results weighted by actual election results.
[18] Poll results available online at: http://alturl.com/je5t3
[19] Available online at: http://alturl.com/734s8
[20] I computed an average score, from 1 (not responsible at all) to 5 (extremely responsible), of responsibility awarded to agents other than the government. Voters above the median value of this variable see other agents as 'highly responsible'.

References

Clarke, H. D., Sanders, D., Stewart, M. C. & Whiteley, P. F. (2004) *Political Choice in Britain*, Oxford University Press, Oxford.
Clarke, H. D., Sanders, D., Stewart, M. C. & Whiteley, P. F. (2009) *Performance Politics and the British Voters*, Cambridge University Press, Cambridge, UK.
Fernández-Albertos, J. (2006) 'Does internationalisation blur responsibility? Economic voting and economic openness in 15 European countries', *West European Politics*, vol. 29, no. 1, pp. 28–46.
Fishman, R. (2011) 'Democratic practice after the revolution: the case of Portugal and beyond', *Politics & Society*, vol. 39, no. 2, pp. 233–267.
Freire, A. (2007) 'Issue voting in Portugal', in *Portugal at the Polls*, eds A. Freire, M. Costa Lobo & P. C. Magalhães, Lexington Books, Lanham, MD, pp. 101–124.
Freire, A. (2009) 'Valores, temas e voto em Portugal, 2005 e 2006: analisando velhas questões com nova evidência', in *As Eleições Legislativas e Presidenciais, 2005–2006*, eds M. Costa Lobo & P. C. Magalhães, Imprensa de Ciências Sociais, Lisbon, pp. 183–224.
Freire, A. (2010) 'A new era in democratic Portugal? The 2009 European, legislative and local elections', *South European Society and Politics*, vol. 15, no. 4, pp. 593–613.

Hellwig, T. & Samuels, D. (2007) 'Voting in open economies: the electoral consequences of globalisation', *Comparative Political Studies*, vol. 40, no. 3, pp. 283–306.

Kayser, M. (2009) 'Partisan waves: international business cycles and electoral choice', *American Journal of Political Science*, vol. 53, no. 4, pp. 950–970.

Kiewiet, D. R. (1981) 'Policy-oriented voting in response to economic issues', *American Political Science Review*, vol. 75, no. 2, pp. 448–459.

Laakso, M. & Taagepera, R. (1979) '"Effective" number of parties: a measure with application to West Europe', *Comparative Political Studies*, vol. 12, no. 1, pp. 3–27.

Magalhães, P. C. (2011) 'Elections, parties and policy-making institutions in democratic Portugal', in *Contemporary Portugal: Politics, Society, and Culture*, ed. A. C. Pinto, Social Science Monographs, New York, pp. 224–248.

Pinto, A. C. & Almeida, P. T. (2009) 'The primacy of "independents"', in *The Selection of Ministers in Europe: Hiring and Firing*, eds K. Dowing & P. Dumont, Routledge, Abingdon, UK, pp. 147–158.

Stevenson, R. T. (2001) 'The economy and policy mood: a fundamental dynamic of democratic politics?', *American Journal of Political Science*, vol. 45, no. 3, pp. 620–633.

Torres, F. (2009) 'Back to external pressure: policy responses to the financial crisis in Portugal', *South European Society and Politics*, vol. 14, no. 1, pp. 55–70.

Vala, J. (1993) 'Valores socio-políticos', in *Portugal: Valores Europeus, Identidade Cultural*, ed. L. de França, Instituto de Estudos para o Desenvolvimento, Lisbon, pp. 221–259.

Volkens, A., Lacewell, O., Lehmann, P., Regel, S., Schultze, H. & Werner, A. (2011) *The Manifesto Data Collection*, Manifesto Project (MRG/CMP/MARPOR), Wissenschaftszentrum Berlin für Sozialforschung (WZB), Berlin.

Pedro C. Magalhães is a researcher at the Institute of Social Sciences of the University of Lisbon and since 2002 has been one of the coordinators of the Portuguese Election Study. His work has been published in journals such as *American Journal of Political Science*, *Electoral Behavior*, *West European Politics*, *Comparative Politics*, and *Public Choice*, and in edited volumes published by Oxford University Press, Routledge, Westview Press and others.

No Crisis, No Change: The Third AKP Victory in the June 2011 Parliamentary Elections in Turkey

Senem Aydın-Düzgit

Amidst debates over a new constitution and increasing tensions over the Kurdish issue, the June 2011 parliamentary elections were considered crucial for the fate of democratic consolidation in Turkey. The article first discusses the background of the general elections, providing an account of the main political developments since the July 2007 general elections. After a discussion of the election campaign, the results of the parliamentary elections are presented. The article concludes by discussing the implications of the election results for democratic consolidation in Turkey under the Justice and Development Party's (AKP's) third term of single-party rule.

The Turkish general elections were held on 12 June 2011. Unlike the previous general elections of 22 July 2007, this was not an early election and the campaign period was not focused on the nature of the regime, but mainly on the economy, provision of services, values and the Kurdish question. Despite facing difficulties, the Turkish economy stood stronger than those of the southern eurozone countries, with an improvement of economic indicators following the 2009 recession. Hence, in stark contrast to the southern eurozone, the lack of a severe economic crisis kept the incumbents in power, the positive perceptions of the AKP's (Adalet ve Kalkınma Partisi – Justice and Development Party) economic performance among the voters playing a major role in the electoral success of the party for the third consecutive time since 2002. The shift from the coalition governments of the 1990s to a one-party government in 2002 remained intact. Almost all of the opinion polls conducted prior to the election forecast the AKP to win the elections, though disagreement existed over the extent to which the party would be able to hold on to the sweeping 46.5 per cent of the vote which it obtained in its 2007 electoral victory. It was also largely predicted that the CHP (Cumhuriyet Halk Partisi – Republican People's Party) would turn out to be the main opposition party, with varying predictions regarding the expected increase in its share of the vote. Much controversy, however, concerned the electoral fate of the MHP (Milliyetçi Hareket Partisi – Nationalist Action Party) and whether the party would be able to attract enough votes to pass the ten per cent electoral threshold to enter the Turkish Grand National Assembly. The Kurdish political leadership followed its 2007 electoral strategy of bypassing the ten per cent electoral threshold by running its candidates as independents, while rising tension and violence in the southeast of Turkey prior to the elections provoked debate on the further consolidation of Kurdish votes in the BDP (Barış ve Demokrasi Partisi – Peace and Democracy Party).

The elections were nevertheless of high significance for Turkey's thorny path towards democratic consolidation. There is general agreement that the European Union (EU) has lost much of its credibility as an external anchor that promotes democratisation in Turkey. Left largely to its own internal dynamics, Turkey has recently been experiencing a bottleneck on the route towards further political reform, with increasing political and societal polarisation on the axis of the Islamist and secularist divide as well as that of Turkish and Kurdish nationalism (Çarkoğlu & Kalaycıoğlu 2009). Faced with the post-election prospect of creating a new constitution to replace the one resulting from the 1980 military coup, various different constellations of a post-election Turkish Grand National Assembly could have had diverse implications for the fate of Turkish democracy. This article first provides the longer-term background of the election and then introduces the main issues and developments during the election campaign. It then discusses the election results and presents an outlook on the post-electoral situation, particularly regarding its repercussions for the future of democratic consolidation in Turkey.

Hopes Turn Sour: The Background to the 2011 General Elections

In terms of political reform, the 2007–11 period can briefly be likened to the famous Ottoman janissary march: 'two steps forward and one step back'. This was particularly the case for developments in minority rights, judicial reform and the rule of law as well as civil–military relations. The Islamist–secularist tension and the ensuing polarisation were visible in all the major political incidents of the period. While recovery followed the economic downturn in 2009, this took place in a fragile economic environment with a high current account deficit.

The second AKP government in the aftermath of the July 2007 elections started off with high hopes, driven by Prime Minister Recep Tayyip Erdoğan's post-election speech that his policies in the second term would be geared towards minimising polarisation in society in order to consolidate Turkish democracy. The government started its preparations for the drafting of a new civilian constitution and emphasised its commitment to the EU accession process. The party's growing confidence after the elections received a further boost with its success in the October 2007 referendum in which the constitutional amendments introducing the popular election of the president were passed with 70 per cent of the vote.

It was not long before the tide turned. The constitutional project was put on hold in early 2008, followed by a proposal from the MHP to introduce a constitutional amendment to lift the ban on wearing the headscarf in universities. The AKP immediately picked up on this much-disputed MHP-led initiative, with the result that the amendment was later taken to the Constitutional Court by the CHP. At the same time, a comprehensive investigation into a neo-nationalist gang named Ergenekon was launched, on the grounds that it was engaging in plans to stage a violent uprising against the government. This led to some strong opponents of the AKP in the military, academia, press and the business community being taken into custody, and strengthened the belief among certain segments of society that the government was using this investigation as a tool to suppress oppositional forces.

This chain of events and the ensuing political instability reached a peak with the closure case against the AKP, filed at the Constitutional Court by the Chief Prosecutor of the Court of Appeals in March 2008. The Constitutional Court cancelled the constitutional amendment lifting the ban on headscarves in universities in June 2008 and in its decision on the closure case concluded that the AKP had become the focal point for activities against secularism. However, it ruled against banning the AKP, deciding instead to halve the party's state funding.

The political instability engendered by both cases, coupled with the waves of arrests in the Ergenekon trials, boosted polarisation between the AKP and the main opposition parties, as well as further exacerbating the tension between the AKP and the strictly secularist Turkish judiciary. This environment of growing polarisation and mistrust set the background for the March 2009 local elections in which the AKP remained the dominant party in the political system yet with a decline of approximately eight per cent in its vote share compared with its performance in the 2007 general elections, while the main opposition parties enjoyed only modest gains in their electoral support (Çarkoğlu 2009). The decline in the AKP vote was mainly attributed to two factors. One concerned the rising activity of the Kurdish nationalist terrorist organisation PKK (Partiye Karkaren Kurdistan – Kurdistan Workers Party) in the southeast, pushing the government into taking military action against the PKK bases in northern Iraq, and thus decreasing the AKP's popularity in the east and the southeast, where it is the only political party with a presence comparable to that of the BDP (Çarkoğlu 2009, p. 297). The second factor related to the impact of the global financial crisis on the Turkish economy, which led to an annual contraction of seven per cent in the gross national product and a four per cent rise in urban unemployment since July 2008. The crisis mostly effected the export-oriented sectors in the western part of Turkey and led to la loss of votes for the AKP in these regions (Çarkoğlu 2009, p. 298).

The local elections were followed by a new democratisation package announced by the AKP in the summer of 2009. The initiative was most notable for its resolve to solve the Kurdish issue, but also contained overtures to the Alevis and the Roma community in Turkey. While some progress has been achieved on the Roma front, little has been attained in resolving the Kurdish conflict and expanding the rights of the Alevis.

The resolution of the Kurdish issue in particular was the subject of high hopes initially. A group of 34 unarmed PKK rebels were questioned at the border with northern Iraq and then released to be greeted by gathered crowds in the southeast of Turkey. The expectation was that the PKK camps in Kandil would gradually be evacuated and a political settlement would be reached. The government, however, was pressured to take regressive steps by the massive public outcry and reactions from the main opposition parties to the celebrated reception of the PKK rebels. The Kurdish initiative was quickly renamed the 'democratic initiative', and later the 'unity and fraternity project', and the initially welcome rebels were soon to be prosecuted.

The summer of 2009 was also a time in which the possibility of another closure case being filed against the AKP began to be voiced, strengthening the AKP's drive to restructure the judiciary, with which its relations have been conflictual during both its terms in office. In August 2009, the government announced its Judicial Reform Strategy and put its main provisions to the vote in a constitutional referendum held on 12 September 2010. Despite the opposition of the CHP and the MHP, the constitutional amendments were approved by 58 per cent of the electorate and the outcome of the referendum was considered yet another victory for the governing party (see Kalaycıoğlu 2011a). Among the 26 amendments approved in the referendum, much of the controversy took place over those which related to the reform of the judicial system. While these amendments were welcomed by some as measures that would weaken the Kemalist guardianship role of the judiciary and thus make it more responsive to the demands of society, others pointed to the dangers that they posed for judicial independence in Turkey.[1]

Meanwhile, new prosecutions continued under the Ergenekon case, including those of two well-known oppositional journalists in March 2011 which raised great controversy both within Turkey and abroad. The EU and the Council of Europe raised open criticisms against the deteriorating levels of freedom of the press in Turkey, only to be rebuffed by the Prime Minister (see *Milliyet* 2011a). On the other hand, Balyoz (Sledgehammer) trials were initiated in December 2010 against around 200 officers in the Turkish military on the grounds of engaging in coup plots against the government. While the case was considered by some an important step towards the normalisation of civil–military relations in Turkey, other segments of society pointed to misconduct during the trials and perceived the manoeuvre as a pressure mechanism of the government in reorganising the military, generating yet another source of polarisation in society.

Growing political strain and polarisation was also evident on the Kurdish issue. While no substantial progress has been achieved towards the resolution of the conflict, tension grew first with the closure of the DTP (Demokratik Toplum Partisi – Democratic Society Party) in December 2009 (later to convene under the BDP), followed by the initiation of the KCK (Koma Ciwaken Kürdistan – Kurdistan Communities Union) trials in September 2010. These trials saw the prosecution of prominent political leaders of the Kurdish movement on the grounds that they constitute the political organisation of the PKK in the cities. The case has continued with compromises on the principle of the right to fair trial. Operations against the PKK continued up until the elections, causing spiralling reactions and violence among the Kurdish community in the southeast.

While the fate of democratic consolidation was being further clouded in the run-up to the general elections, there was a different story on the economic front. Unlike many of the crisis-ridden economies of Southern Europe, in Turkey the macroeconomic indicators picked up substantially from their recession-induced contracted levels in 2009, with an impressive growth rate and reduced unemployment levels. Gross national product increased in the last quarter of 2010 by 9.2 per cent from a year earlier.[2] Rapid growth has translated into reduced unemployment levels from 16.1 per cent in the first quarter of 2009 to 14.4 per cent in 2010 and 11.5 per cent in 2011.[3] Nevertheless, the increase in employment levels is still observed to be substantially higher in the agricultural sector than in the industrial and service sectors.[4] While the growing current account deficit seems to be a major problem for the Turkish economy, its effects still remain largely unfelt due to the continued infiltration of funds from international financial markets.

Personalised and Polarised: The Election Campaign

Much of the election campaign consisted of a bitter personalised feud between Erdoğan and the new CHP leader, Kemal Kılıçdaroğlu, which significantly contributed to polarising the pre-election political climate. Kılıçdaroğlu had replaced the outgoing Deniz Baykal only a year before the elections, when Baykal was forced to resign following the release of a video tape that revealed an illicit affair with his former assistant, later to become a member of parliament for the CHP. Especially in his earlier election rallies, Erdoğan made repeated references to the Alevi background of the new CHP leader, Kılıçdaroğlu, to discredit him in the eyes of pious Sunni voters. Instead of uttering explicit pejorative statements about his Alevi heritage, he exploited the existing prejudice among Sunni voters towards the Alevis by constantly reminding them of Kılıçdaroğlu's Alevi background. He repeatedly pointed out that the Alevi heritage stands against the 'immoral affair' that led him to power, thus reminding the voters of Kılıçdaroğlu's Alevi background without engaging in explicit discrimination, and at the same time portraying the CHP as a party devoid of ethical values and distanced from Islam proper. For example, between 29 April and 13 May, he brought this issue up in seven separate election speeches (Ergin 2011). He also often characterised Kılıçdaroğlu as an incompetent leader through references to the dire state of the public health system in the 1990s when Kılıçdaroğlu served as the general director of the Social Security Institution. In turn, Kılıçdaroğlu repeatedly accused Erdoğan of corruption and nepotism, and placed particular emphasis on his son's short term military service, which he defined as an expression of Erdoğan's hypocritical nationalism.

Since the AKP was no longer the underdog suppressed by the centrist bureaucracy, military and the judiciary in its second term in government, it mainly based its campaign on its relatively successful performance on the economy, on delivering public services such as in the health sector, and on the promise of further growth and development that would mobilise the new urban middle classes. Thus, there was considerable continuity with the party's 2007 election campaign, which also rested on the theme of 'economic stability and development', and the 2007 rhetoric on the struggle against the 'elitist oligarchy' of the secularist state apparatus was dropped (Bacık 2008; see also Çarkoğlu 2007). The economic appeal was combined with conservative rhetoric on the values front. The AKP repeatedly attacked the official opposition CHP on its historical heritage as the party of a centrist and secularist establishment that has little regard for conservative values.

In the case of the CHP, Kılıçdaroğlu ousted the former leadership cadres and steered the party away from the regime- and security-focused agenda that had demonstrated limited electoral appeal in the 2007 elections. Instead, his campaign rested on concrete societal problems such as unemployment, poverty and corruption on the discursive axes of social democracy, social justice and citizenship, while placing a pronounced emphasis on democratic rights and freedoms. Some of the tangible projects offered, such as the introduction of a Family Insurance Scheme in the fight against poverty and a substantial reduction in the duration of compulsory military service, attracted considerable attention in the media and society at large. The party repeatedly emphasised the need to reduce the ten per cent electoral threshold for parliamentary representation. While still timid due to the fear of losing its core nationalist voter base, it now displayed a relatively more open approach towards the Kurdish issue. Nevertheless, the CHP's parliamentary candidates displayed a rather eclectic profile, including a former Kurdish rights lawyer and activist alongside two prominent Ergenekon suspects. This facilitated AKP attacks on the CHP as a protector of coup plotters, as well as casting doubt on the commitment of the party to its revised social democratic agenda.

The campaign period also displayed major differences in the organisational strength of the two main contenders. It can be argued that, as in the 2007 elections, the AKP ran a successful campaign thanks largely to its strong and well-organised party organisation. It is well known that the AKP has very effective election coordination centres that are responsible for organising the campaign in each province and for sustaining close contact with the electorate outside the campaign periods. It enjoys the hard work of thousands of local volunteers and election observers in mobilising the electorate to vote. Furthermore, it can successfully combine this strong party apparatus with the advantages of being the sole party in government. For example, one of the main tasks of the party organisations in the provinces and the local branches is to help serve patron–client relations by pursuing the interests of its voters in the state bureaucracy (see Dinç 2008, pp. 6–9). The advantages of being the incumbent also relate to party finance. The AKP obtains more than twice the amount of election aid that CHP receives from the Treasury and has spent it on full-page advertisements in major daily newspapers, television channels and the billboards in major cities, on election rallies that drew large crowds and, towards the end of the campaign, on a professionally composed campaign theme song that was repeatedly aired on radio and TV. In provinces such as İzmir where the party has traditionally been weaker, current ministers were put forward as candidates so as to mobilise the local party organisation and also to convey the message to the electorate that their interests would be better served through being represented by reputable ministers in parliament.

In contrast to the professionalism of the AKP, the CHP campaign often exhibited a lack of effective organisation, enthusiasm and comparable finances. Whilst Kılıçdaroğlu held 300 election rallies in all 81 provinces, exceeding the 68 held by Erdoğan and almost tripling the number by his predecessor, the same vigour was not observed in the party apparatus. In fact, in the aftermath of the elections, it was reported that Kılıçdaroğlu himself attested to the lethargic nature of the party organisation in mobilising the electorate (see *Milliyet* 2011b). Although this was not a novel problem for the CHP, it was compounded in the 2011 elections by the exclusion of some of the prominent figures of the previous leadership from the party lists and the complete overhaul of some key provincial units such as that of Istanbul prior to the elections. This fuelled dissent and splits within the party which were exposed in the media and contributed to the declining motivation levels in the overall party organisation, which anticipated a purge of all the cadres that had served under the previous leadership.

The MHP campaign rested largely on the Kurdish question, attacking the AKP for the Kurdish initiative mainly on the grounds that it provided further encouragement to Kurdish separatism and terrorism. Having already lost some of its conservative-nationalist constituency in inner Anatolia to the AKP in the previous elections and the 2010 constitutional referendum, the party attempted to sustain the appeal to secularist-nationalist voters in the west and the coastal areas through this rhetoric. In fact, the campaign period witnessed a major debate as to whether the expected consolidation of the conservative central Anatolian vote in the AKP and a possibly improved performance of the CHP in the west and the coastal regions would leave the MHP under the ten per cent threshold required to enter the Turkish parliament. This was deemed crucial for the post-election scenarios on the distribution of seats in parliament, where the most prominent issue to be handled after the elections was expected to be the new constitution.

In the aftermath of the 2010 constitutional referendum, all of the main political parties promised a new constitution. The present Turkish constitution stipulates that the governing party needs to receive a minimum number of 367 seats in the 550-member Turkish Grand National Assembly to devise a new constitution without submitting it to a popular referendum. In the case that it obtains at least 330 seats, it can still draft a constitution without seeking a general consensus in the parliament, but the draft has to be approved in a nationwide referendum. It was clear that, among those political parties which stood a chance of being represented in parliament, the AKP and the CHP would not have a problem passing the electoral threshold, while the BDP would avoid the threshold requirement by running its candidates as independents who would only need to obtain enough votes in their respective provinces to enter parliament. Thus, the debate on representation in relation to the fate of the constitution centred on the MHP's chances of passing the electoral threshold, since the party's expected votes at around ten per cent would have serious ramifications for the distribution of parliamentary seats. Since the AKP was considered the main contender for MHP votes, primarily in inner Anatolia, its seats were expected to increase in disproportion to its votes if the MHP were to be excluded from parliament. This would increase its chances of drafting a constitution unilaterally, without seeking the broader societal consensus necessary for sufficient legitimacy. Given that both before and during the campaign period the Prime Minister also explicitly advocated the introduction of a presidential system under the new constitution, fears were aggravated among certain segments of the society that such a constitution would strengthen authoritarian tendencies on the part of the AKP and thus further hamper democratic consolidation.

During the campaign, the release of secret sex tapes of ten major politicians from the MHP resulted in their resignation from their candidacies and led to considerable speculation regarding the potential impact on the MHP's prospects of surpassing the threshold. There was widespread agreement that this was part of a plot to leave the MHP out of parliament by further alienating its conservative voter base. The lack of a thorough investigation and Prime Minister Erdoğan's public references to the tapes as evidence of moral corruption among the MHP cadres caused some speculation that the MHP could in fact acquire an underdog status that could help the party reach the threshold (Çağaptay 2011).

Positioned as diametrically opposed to the MHP, with its main agenda focused on the rights of the Kurdish minority, the BDP particularly drew attention to education in one's mother tongue, release of political prisoners, the KCK trials, cessation of military operations against the PKK and, under the banner of 'democratic autonomy', enhanced channels of self-governance in the southeast. The BDP in fact started an early campaign due to the decision by the YSK (Yüksek Seçim Kurulu – Supreme Election Board) to ban seven candidates of the party from running in the elections; this was later overturned (except in the case of one candidate) due to escalating tensions in the region and reactions from the media as well as from other major political players (with the exception of the MHP), including President Gül. The party presented the banning of its seven candidates as yet another plot devised by the state to keep the Kurdish movement out of democratic politics, given that the ten per cent electoral threshold is no longer effective in preventing its representation in the parliament.

Although the BDP attempted to expand its candidate base by including certain figures from the left, primarily in the western provinces under the coalition of a 'Labour, Democracy and Freedom Bloc', the party's election discourse remained strictly limited to the Kurdish issue, with little appeal to the wider electorate. It initiated a 'civil disobedience' campaign inspired by the Arab Spring movements, through which it attempted to further mobilise its constituency and, through extending it to organised prayers outside the state's mosques, unite the more religious Kurdish community with the ethnic nationalist wing (Çakır 2011, pp. 21–22). In a similar vein, the inclusion of certain candidates from an Islamist background was also considered to symbolise 'unity' among the Kurdish cadres (Çakır 2011, p. 24). These measures could be considered part and parcel of the strategy of uniting the Kurdish vote, which has been divided into religious and ethnic strands, as evidenced by the presence of the AKP and the BDP as the main respective contenders for Kurdish votes in the region.

The AKP's strategy in turn relied on adopting a rather conservative and nationalist approach to the Kurdish issue, reversing its earlier more liberal tone and placing the emphasis on religious ties and values rather than a rights-based discourse to attract the Kurdish voter. In choosing to appeal to the Turkish nationalist vote and the traditional Islamist streak of Kurdish identity, the Prime Minister went so far as to declare that there no longer exists a Kurdish issue. The AKP attacked the CHP for its increasingly lenient tone on the Kurdish problem, which it presented as part of the party's allegedly larger deal with the BDP. It thus tried to discredit the main opposition in the eyes of the Turkish nationalist electorate by discursively aligning the CHP with Kurdish ethnic nationalism and PKK terrorism.

It can be argued that, overall, domestic issues and highly polemical and personalised exchanges dominated the campaign period, with foreign policy matters receiving minimal attention. This is unsurprising given the fact that the main determinants of voting behaviour in Turkey are found to be party identification and the economic concerns of the electorate, with foreign policy issues playing a lesser role in shaping voters' opinion (Kalaycıoğlu 2009). Nonetheless, certain foreign policy issues made it to the agenda with possible implications for voters' perception of the parties (Kalaycıoğlu 2009, p. 82). For example, Erdoğan's harsh responses to the European criticisms of the state of press freedoms in Turkey in his address to the Council of Europe Parliamentary Assembly received wide coverage in the national media in the midst of the campaign period and ran counter to the party programme that reiterated the party's commitment to Turkey's EU membership and the reform process.[5] From a domestic perspective, this move may have appealed to the Eurosceptic voter by conveying the message that Europe can no longer meddle in the domestic affairs of a Turkey that is growing in confidence, whilst also sustaining the party's rhetorical commitment to accession, which is still valued by almost half of the electorate.[6] Kılıçdaroğlu, on the other hand, as part of the party's new agenda that places emphasis on democratic consolidation, displayed a more pro-European attitude than his predecessor, convening with the EU ambassadors in Turkey prior to the elections and underlining that, unlike the AKP, the CHP is committed to the EU accession process in substance through adherence to the reforms. Bahçeli, known for his party's and core constituency's explicit Euroscepticism, only invoked the issue in some of his election rallies to depict Erdoğan as a traitor who had made United States (US) and EU led concessions on Cyprus, the Armenian issue and the Kurdish question.

There seemed to be even less contestation between the parties regarding Turkey's foreign policy in North Africa and the Middle East. One exception concerned the reactions from the CHP and the MHP to the government's initially equivocal response to the Libyan crisis that erupted during the campaign period, whereby both parties accused the AKP of making ambivalent moves that jeopardised Turkey's potential role as an agenda setter in the region. Both parties later voted in favour of a parliamentary motion to allow the dispatch of Turkish soldiers in the North Atlantic Treaty Organisation (NATO) led operation against Libya. Another exception relates to the state of Turkish–Israeli relations and the conflict arising between the two countries over the *Blue Marmara* incident when Israel attacked a Gaza-bound aid flotilla in May 2010, killing nine people, most of them Turkish citizens. During the campaign period, Erdoğan raised the issue to portray the CHP as a pro-Israeli party in the eyes of the conservative voter by arguing that Kılıçdaroğlu had not sincerely condemned the incident. Kılıçdaroğlu retaliated by pointing to alleged attempts on the part of Erdoğan to reach a covert conciliation with Israel. While the issue was thus quickly personalised in the dominant spirit of the campaign period, it needs to be noted that the AKP's stance on relations with Israel, and the Gaza issue in particular, has a resonance particularly with the right-wing voters whom the party targets as its main constituency.

No Surprises at the Ballot Box

Like the 2007 general elections, when 84 per cent of the electorate went to the ballot box, the 2011 elections had a high turnout rate, with 83 per cent of the electorate choosing to vote. Table 1 shows the 2007 and 2011 general election results.

Unlike the 2007 general elections, there were no pre-election coalitions in the 2011 parliamentary elections. Political parties either faced the electorate on their own or, as in the case of the ANAP (Anavatan Partisi – Motherland Party), which had effectively vanished from the political scene after the 1999 parliamentary elections, chose not to run. In turn, these elections marked the last stage in the effective disappearance of the remaining splinter parties, particularly on the right of the political spectrum,

Table 1 Election results, 2007–11

	Vote share (%)			Seats	
	2007	2011	Gain, 2007–11 (%)	2007	2011
AKP	46.6	49.8	3.2	341	327
CHP	20.9	26.0	5.1	112	135
MHP	14.3	13.0	−1.3	71	53
DP	5.4	0.7	−4.7	0	0
Independents*	5.2	6.6	1.4	26	35
Sub-total	92.4	96.1		550	550
Other parties	7.6	3.9	−3.7		

Source: http://www.tuik.gov.tr/VeriBilgi.do?tb_id=42&ust_id = 12
* In 2007, Kurdish candidates from the DTP ran as independents and 20 were elected. In 2011, candidates from the BDP (formerly the DTP) ran as independents under the 'Labour, Democracy and Freedom Bloc' and 35 were elected to parliament.

such as the DP (Demokrat Parti – Democrat Party). The AKP, CHP and BDP all increased their vote share, while the MHP, having managed to pass the electoral threshold, faced a decline in its vote. The number of women elected was the highest in the history of the Republic, increasing from 48 in the 2007 elections to 78 in 2011.

The AKP, after two terms in government, raised its vote share from 47 per cent in 2007 to 50 per cent in 2011. It became the only party in the history of the Turkish Republic after the Democrat Party of the 1950s to win three consecutive elections. The party has clearly managed to overturn the trend of decline demonstrated in the 2009 municipal elections, when it secured only 38 per cent of the vote. Despite the increase in its votes, the number of seats that the AKP obtained in the General Assembly declined from 341 in 2007 to 327 in 2011. This was largely due to the success of the BDP's independent candidates in the southeast at the expense of the AKP and, following recent demographic changes, the reallocation of 33 seats from central and eastern Anatolia, where the AKP is the dominant party, to western provinces where there is a relatively more balanced distribution of power between the party and the main opposition.

The BDP scored a major success in these elections, having increased the number of its independent candidates in parliament from 20 in 2007 (3.6 per cent) to 35 (6.4 per cent) in 2011. Since the national percentage of the vote cast for the BDP by its mainly Kurdish nationalist constituency does not suffice for it to reach the ten per cent electoral threshold, the party (and its predecessor the DTP in 2007) chose to nominate its candidates as independents in those provinces where it has a substantial electoral base. The success of this strategy demonstrated once again the obsolescence of the ten per cent threshold.

The CHP also managed to increase its votes, from 21 per cent in 2007 to 26 per cent in 2011. Although the party has obtained its highest percentage of votes in the last three decades and experienced the largest increase in its votes since the 2002 general elections, the result was generally perceived as a disappointment for the new leadership, which had raised expectations to a share of around 30 per cent of the vote. One of the biggest questions of the campaign period was resolved when the MHP's vote share pushed the party above the electoral threshold. While the party experienced a decline in its votes from 14 per cent in 2007 to 13 per cent in 2011, the fact that it passed the threshold played a crucial role in determining the distribution of seats in parliament, with significant repercussions for the preparation of a new constitution in the aftermath of the elections.

Geography of the Vote

The AKP has on average the highest level of support in all of the seven regions, with vote shares of above 50 per cent in inner Anatolia, east and southeast Anatolia and the Black Sea region. The party increased its vote share in all regions except the Mediterranean region and east and southeast Anatolia, where it sustained modest declines. Its lowest vote share was recorded in the western and coastal regions, where it still managed to obtain on average more than 40 per cent of the vote.

Despite its changing rhetoric on the Kurdish issue, the CHP remained very weak in east and southeast Anatolia, at an average of less than ten per cent of the votes. Its highest vote share continued to come in the most developed and populous provinces of the western and coastal regions of Marmara, the Aegean and the Mediterranean, where it is traditionally strong. In fact, it increased its votes by six per cent in Marmara and the Mediterranean, and by nine per cent in the Aegean, but incurred losses in some key bases of support such as İzmir (by eight per cent). It also obtained more modest gains of around three to five per cent in inner Anatolia and the Black Sea region.

The expansion of the traditional MHP support base from inner Anatolia to the western and coastal provinces seems to have slightly declined with the 2011 elections. The party incurred losses of two to three per cent in Marmara, the Aegean and the Mediterranean, but retained its vote share of around 15 per cent in inner Anatolia. Unsurprisingly, it remained very weak in the southeast region, at around four per cent of the vote.

In terms of the geographic distribution of votes, little has changed on the BDP front. Most, but not all, of their independent candidates who entered parliament were elected from east and southeast Anatolia, where the Kurdish population is greatest. While 30 of the seats were won in these regions, three came from Istanbul and one each from Mersin and Adana. Hence, as in the 2007 elections, the party managed to mobilise the ethnic vote both in its traditional support area and in large cities like Istanbul where internal migration has created a significant demographic basis for the Kurdish vote.

Key Issues

Previous research has repeatedly highlighted the significance of the economy in shaping the outcome of elections in Turkey (see Esmer 2002; Çarkoğlu 2008; Kalaycıoğlu 2009). The 2011 general elections do not seem to pose an exception to this. The improvement in macroeconomic indicators and the reduction in unemployment after the 2009 crisis, which had cost the AKP a significant loss of votes in the 2009 local elections, have ameliorated the perception of the economic performance of the government among the voters. Economic satisfaction was also found to be among the main determinants of the 'yes' votes in the 2010 constitutional referendum (Kalaycıoğlu 2011a). It can be argued that in the case of the AKP, perceptions of economic satisfaction have also been closely bound to the perceived success of the government in delivering public services, particularly in the health and housing sectors. Taken together, these have also fed into sustaining among the electorate a relatively more credible impression of the government's future economic performance.

The CHP, on the other hand, seems to have suffered from a credibility problem in achieving a limited increase in its votes which continues to position it significantly behind the governing party. The new leadership's accelerated efforts for change six months prior to the elections do not yet seem to have found the expected resonance among a wider section of the electorate. It can also be argued that the mixed political signals from the main opposition party, such as liberalising its discourse on Kurdish rights while at the same time placing Ergenekon suspects on its electoral lists, added to the credibility problem. There was also some speculation that, especially following the sex-tape scandals, there was a modest transfer of votes from the CHP constituency to the MHP through tactical voting to prevent the exclusion of MHP from the parliament so as to prevent a possible disproportionate increase in AKP seats and/or as a reaction to the relative liberalisation of the CHP discourse on Kurdish rights. Nevertheless, in accounting for the CHP's vote share, one primarily has to consider the limited electoral appeal of what the electorate perceives as the 'left' on the Turkish political scene. Studies suggest that the Turkish electorate is growing increasingly more conservative and religious, which accounts also for the value related factors behind the AKP vote (Çarkoğlu & Kalaycıoğlu 2009).

The AKP's strategy of combining its rhetoric on conservative values with a more nationalist stance on the Kurdish issue also seems to have fared well for its electoral success in these elections. Not only did it increase its vote share in regions like inner Anatolia and the Black Sea, known for the strength of their Turkish nationalist constituency, but it also encountered only a modest loss of votes in east (by three per cent) and southeast (by two per cent) Anatolia. Nevertheless, the party incurred significant losses in certain highly Kurdish-populated provinces in the region (like Hakkari, Diyarbakır, Mardin and Van) which contributed to the success of the independent candidates in capturing seats from the AKP. Thus, it can be argued that, in addition to the enhanced organisational capabilities of the BDP in mobilising the ethnic vote, the AKP's shifting stance on the Kurdish issue also helped to reconsolidate the Kurdish vote (predominantly the ethnic strand) to a certain extent under the BDP umbrella. The continuing Kurdish conflict remains a key factor in the MHP's continued presence on the Turkish political scene. Although the party has no visible discourse on other principal issues of concern to the electorate, such as the economy and social matters, its reactionary stance on the Kurdish problem seems to grant it sufficient votes to continue being represented in the parliament. The fact that the party largely preserved its votes in inner Anatolia also suggests that the sex-tape scandals of the campaign period may not have had a major impact on the MHP's conservative voter base in the region.

Intra-party Struggles and Leadership

The results also imply a potential for intra-party struggles, most particularly in the case of the CHP and the MHP. Former CHP leader Deniz Baykal and his ousted cadres have already declared the election results a failure for the new leadership, but they remained short of gathering the 650 signatures required to hold an early party convention. It remains to be seen whether the impetus for change or the former party ideology of strict secularism and nationalism will prevail in the CHP. Another issue that the CHP may have to face in coming days concerns the eclectic mix of its new MPs. It may be difficult to impose party discipline on key issues such as the Kurdish conflict with the presence of the new MPs from the centre-right and the Ergenekon suspects, if and when the legal obstacles to their entry into parliament are lifted. As for the MHP, the 2011 elections once again displayed the limits of the party's discourse in reaching out to the wider electorate. Despite the presence of an intra-party opposition, the MHP's relatively strong party discipline means internal struggle may not be as pronounced as in the CHP. Nonetheless, the party convention to be held in 2012 may still lead to a challenge to the present leadership.

While such intra-party tensions are unsurprisingly not present in the AKP, the most pressing matter in the party regarding leadership concerns the presidential elections to be held in the next three years. It is not yet clear whether these elections will take place in 2012 or 2014. The constitutional changes undertaken in the immediate aftermath of the 2007 general elections to regulate the election of the president through a public referendum stipulate the election of the president for a five-year term. It is still unclear whether this or the former seven-year term will apply in the case of the current president, Abdullah Gül, who was elected by parliament before the relevant constitutional amendments entered into force. It is largely expected that Erdoğan will replace Gül as president when the latter's term ends. Erdoğan has previously declared this parliamentary term to be his last. It is, however, not clear whether he will take on the post of president with its current or extended constitutional powers under a possible presidential system. The outcome could have important ramifications for the future of Turkish democracy.

Turkish Democracy after the Elections: Quo Vadis?

It is true that the AKP took important steps in democratic reform primarily in its first term in government, moving the country towards starting accession negotiations with the EU. Yet, the process of democratic consolidation in Turkey remains far from complete. While some progress was attained in areas such as civil–military relations, the AKP's second term in government also bore witness to growing authoritarian tendencies on the part of the governing party, resulting in restrictions of fundamental freedoms such as the freedom of expression (European Parliament 2011). Questions continued on the issue of judicial independence, even among those who advocated for the 'yes' campaign during the constitutional referendum that aimed to restructure the judicial system (İnsel 2010). Attempts to resolve the Kurdish issue were halted and replaced by Turkish nationalism, resulting in the escalation of the conflict in the southeast.

Developments in the immediate aftermath of the elections also served to cloud positive expectations of the path towards the consolidation of Turkish democracy. Following the elections, the Supreme Election Board decided to strip a BDP candidate of his deputyship on the basis of his 2009 conviction of 'disseminating PKK propaganda'. On top of this, the courts declined requests to allow the entry into parliament of five more BDP deputies who are jailed suspects in KCK trials as well as two CHP deputies and one MHP deputy who are under arrest in connection with the

Ergenekon and Balyoz trials respectively. The BDP retaliated by deciding not to enter parliament with its remaining deputies, while the CHP deputies entered parliament, but did not participate in the oath-taking ceremony that is required for official participation in parliamentary activity. It took nearly two weeks for the CHP deputies to take their oaths, after agreeing on a joint declaration with the AKP stressing the significance of parliamentary activity in resolving the issue of imprisoned representatives and the importance of interpreting the laws in ways that expand individual freedoms. The statement was generally worded without any concrete indication of a legislative effort to bring the imprisoned deputies back to parliament. The BDP waited until the end of September before it agreed to enter parliament. Nonetheless, a legitimacy deficit will continue to loom over the Turkish parliament unless the problem of imprisoned deputies is resolved in the new parliamentary term.

The most significant and immediate test of the fate of democracy in the new parliament will be in the preparation of the new constitution. The AKP did not manage to acquire the 330 seats required for it to draft a new constitution unilaterally. This in turn means that the party will have to seek consensus with the opposition. In his post-election speech, Prime Minister Erdoğan described the election results as a mandate given by the electorate to the AKP to prepare the constitution through consensus with the opposition. The CHP responded positively by declaring that it was ready to cooperate without preconditions. Yet the actual implementation remains to be seen. While a constitutional consensus between the AKP and the CHP, and possibly including the BDP, could pave the way for a new text that upholds fundamental rights and freedoms along with the primacy of society over the state, with a broad basis of societal support, other political calculations could hinder such a possibility. If the AKP insists on introducing a presidential system with the new constitution as hinted by the Prime Minister prior to the elections, it would be very difficult for the CHP or the MHP to agree on a draft. The AKP could seek a compromise with the BDP group, yet the AKP's recent nationalist tone might put it into a difficult position in meeting some key BDP demands such as bilingual education and enhanced self-government. The worst-case scenario for the prospects of a text with high legitimacy would be a top-down constitution prepared by the AKP alone, possibly with the negotiated support of a few oppositional MPs in order to pass the 330 threshold, and including divisive issues, such as a presidential system, that could yet again polarise society at large and hinder the consolidation of democracy in Turkey.

Another pressing matter in relation to democratic reform concerns the Kurdish issue. Terrorist activity intensified significantly in the immediate aftermath of the elections and poses the risk of a return to the state of affairs in the 1990s, when the Kurdish issue was dealt with solely as a security matter that was used to restrict fundamental freedoms. The representation of the BDP in parliament with an increased share of seats provides yet another opportunity to approach the conflict through parliamentary means rather than via armed conflict. The CHP's changing discourse on the Kurdish issue and certain of its proposals, such as granting greater autonomy to local governments through full regard for the European Charter of Local Self-

Government, suggest that if the AKP were to return to a more liberal agenda on the issue, a more conducive environment for a feasible solution could be fostered with relatively less societal polarisation. Yet, the BDP's will to compromise on certain controversial demands, such as bilingual education, will also play a key role on the path towards a consensual solution.

Reform in civil–military relations will most likely continue, with the CHP also displaying a progressive attitude on the matter (Gürsoy, forthcoming). Nonetheless, perceptions of sustained misconduct in the Balyoz and Ergenekon trials may continue to fuel the existing polarisation and mistrust in Turkish society. The complete civilianisation of Turkish politics is a necessary but not a sufficient condition of democratic consolidation. Partial political reform in which the rule of law is compromised would continue to generate severe challenges for Turkish democracy (see Noutcheva & Aydın-Düzgit in press).

Although it was hardly an object of debate during the campaign period, democratic consolidation in Turkey cannot really be understood independently from the country's foreign policy orientations. In 2006, the EU suspended negotiations on eight chapters of the *acquis* and decided not to provisionally close any of the chapters in Turkey's accession negotiations until Turkey opens its seaports and airspace to Cyprus as required by the Turkish customs union with the EU. This, combined with persistent messages of rejection from Nicholas Sarkozy and Angela Merkel, has to a large extent served to block progress in accession negotiations and hampered the EU's democratic conditionality in Turkey.

The prospects for improved relations with the EU remain bleak, given both the EU's internal crisis over the economy and its continued reluctance to deal with the Turkish question. While the upcoming elections in France in 2012 and the German elections in 2013 may tilt the political balance in the EU in favour of Turkish accession, this may not be sufficient to revitalise relations between the EU and Turkey. The fact that the Prime Minister in his post-election speech made no reference to the EU, while devoting considerable attention to Turkey's greater neighbourhood, gave little hope in this respect. As this strengthens the conviction that Turkey's role as a regional power is now clearly a higher priority for the government than its EU accession, it also risks underestimating the importance of Turkey's democratic trajectory and its relations with the EU for its rising influence in its regional neighbourhood. Research suggests that Turkey's 'demonstrative effect' on its neighbourhood cannot be incurred without its standing as a 'democracy in progress' (Kirişçi 2011). The Arab Spring only serves to strengthen this imperative, especially given the resilience of Turkey's Kurdish issue and the necessity for Turkey to practise what it preaches in order to remain a credible actor and to prevent the escalation of its own ethnic conflict to the intensity of those in its immediate neighbourhood.

Much of this will undoubtedly also hinge on the state of the Turkish economy. While the Turkish economy currently seems to be in a much better shape than the rest of Southern Europe, it is still fragile with high levels of unemployment and a growing current account deficit. The post-election period thus needs to see significant structural reform to keep the economy on track and to sustain a more conducive environment for political reform. The shape of the economy to come will also prove crucial in determining whether Turkey will see yet another AKP victory in four years' time.

Acknowledgements

I would like to thank the editors of *South European Society and Politics*, Susannah Verney and Anna Bosco, as well as two anonymous referees for their valuable feedback on earlier drafts of this article.

Notes

[1] See the interviews with Sibel İnceoğlu and Serap Yazıcı, *Milliyet*, 20–21 June 2010.
[2] See the News Bulletin of the Turkish Statistical Institute No. 66 (31 March 2011), available online at: http://www.tuik.gov.tr/PreHaberBultenleri.do?id=8471
[3] See the News Bulletin of the Turkish Statistical Institute No. 85 (15 May 2009), available online at: http://www.tuik.gov.tr/PreHaberBultenleri.do?id=4054; News Bulletin of the Turkish Statistical Institute No. 84 (17 May 2010), available online at: http://www.tuik.gov.tr/PreHaberBultenleri.do?id=6247; News Bulletin of the Turkish Statistical Institute No. 123 (15 June 2011), available online at: http://www.tuik.gov.tr/PreHaberBultenleri.do?id=8531
[4] News Bulletin of the Turkish Statistical Institute No. 123 (15 June 2011), available online at: http://www.tuik.gov.tr/PreHaberBultenleri.do?id=8531
[5] See http://www.akparti.org.tr/site/akparti/parti-programi#bolum_
[6] For an assessment of recent Turkish public opinion on the EU, see Kalaycıoğlu (2011b).

References

Bacık, G. (2008) 'The parliamentary elections in Turkey, July 2007', *Electoral Studies*, vol. 27, no. 2, pp. 377–381.
Çağaptay, S. (2011) 'Turkey's June 12 elections', Policy Watch No. 1812, Washington Institute for Near East Policy, available online at: http://www.washingtoninstitute.org/templateC05.php?CID=3364
Çakır, R. (2011) 'The peace and democracy party', in *Political Parties in Turkey: From 2010 Referendum to 2011 June Elections*, SETA Policy Brief, no. 2, Ankara: SETA.
Çarkoğlu, A. (2007) 'A new electoral victory for the "pro-Islamists" or the "new centre-right"? The Justice and Development Party phenomenon in the July 2007 parliamentary elections in Turkey', *South European Society and Politics*, vol. 12, no. 4, pp. 501–519.
Çarkoğlu, A. (2008) 'Ideology or economic pragmatism: profiling Turkish voters in 2007', *Turkish Studies*, vol. 9, no. 2, pp. 317–344.
Çarkoğlu, A. (2009) 'The March 2009 local elections in Turkey: a signal for takers or the inevitable beginning of the end for AKP?', *South European Society and Politics*, vol. 14, no. 3, pp. 295–316.
Çarkoğlu, A. & Kalaycıoğlu, E. (2009) *The Rising Tide of Conservatism in Turkey*, Palgrave Macmillan, New York.
Dinç, G. (2008) 'Durmak yok, yola devam (No stopping, keep on going): a close look at AKP's election success', Friedrich Ebert Stiftung Fokus Türkei, No. 6, 8 April, available online at: http://library.fes.de/pdf-files/bueros/tuerkei/05726.pdf

Ergin, S. (2011) 'Erdoğan ve CHP liderinin Aleviliği' [Erdoğan and the Alevi background of the CHP leader], *Hürriyet*, 18 May, p. 24.
Esmer, Y. (2002) 'At the ballot box: determinants of voting behavior', in *Politics, Parties, and Elections in Turkey*, eds S. Sayarı & Y. Esmer, Lynne Rienner, London, pp. 91–114.
European Parliament. (2011) 'European Parliament resolution of 9 March 2011 on Turkey's 2010 progress report', available online at: http://www.europarl.europa.eu/sides/getDoc.do?pubRef=-//EP//TEXT+TA+20110309+ITEMS+DOC+XML+V0//EN&language=EN#sdocta3
Gürsoy, Y. (forthcoming) 'The final curtain for the Turkish Armed Forces?: civil–military relations in view of the 2011 general elections', *Turkish Studies*.
İnsel, A. (2010) 'HSYK seçimi şaibeli mi değil mi?' [Are the HSYK elections tainted or not?], *Radikal*, 19 October, available online at: http://www.radikal.com.tr/Default.aspx?aType=RadikalYazar&ArticleID=1024337&Yazar=AHMET%20%DDNSEL&Date=19.10.2010&CategoryID=98.
Kalaycıoğlu, E. (2009) 'Public choice and foreign affairs: democracy and international relations in Turkey', *New Perspectives on Turkey*, vol. 40, pp. 59–83.
Kalaycıoğlu, E. (2011a) '*Kulturkampf* in Turkey results in west versus the rest: 12 September 2010 referendum', *South European Society and Politics*. DOI: 10.1080/13608746.2011.600555
Kalaycıoğlu, E. (2011b) 'Turkey's views of the EU in 2011', GMF on Turkey Series, 21 September, available online at: http://www.gmfus.org/galleries/ct_publication_attachments/Kalaycioglu_TT2011Results_Sept11.pdf
Kirişçi, K. (2011) 'Turkey's "demonstrative effect" and the transformation of the Middle East', *Insight Turkey*, vol. 13, no. 2, pp. 33–55.
Milliyet (2011a) 'Bildiğimizi okuruz' [We will do as we see fit], 11 March, available online at: http://www.milliyet.com.tr/bildigimizi-okuruz/siyaset/haberdetay/11.03.2011/1362801/default.htm
Milliyet (2011b) 'Kılıçdaroğlu fena patladı' [Kılıçdaroğlu explodes], 13 June.
Noutcheva, G. & Aydın-Düzgit, S. (in press) 'Lost in Europeanization: the Western Balkans and Turkey', *West European Politics*.

Senem Aydın-Düzgit is an assistant professor in the Department of International Relations at Istanbul Bilgi University. Her book *Constructing Europe through Turkey: European Discourses on Turkey's Accession to the EU* (Palgrave) is forthcoming in 2012.

The 2011 General Election in Spain: The Collapse of the Socialist Party

Irene Martín and Ignacio Urquizu-Sancho

The 2011 general election in Spain had unprecedented results. The Spanish Socialist Workers' Party (PSOE) got its worst electoral results ever in general elections and the Popular Party (PP) won and obtained its second absolute majority since the establishment of democracy. We sustain that the defeat of PSOE can be considered a more defining feature of the elections than the victory of PP. Minority parties increased their electoral support and three new parties entered Congress. This article analyses the political and economic context that led to these changes with respect to the previous elections of 2008.

The eleventh parliamentary elections which took place on 20 November 2011 in Spain led to the victory of Partido Popular (Popular Party, PP) and put an end to more than seven years of socialist rule. The electoral support of PP (45 per cent of the votes) led to the fifth absolute majority obtained by any party in Spain since 1977 (186 seats out of 350) (Table 1).[1] The Partido Socialista Obrero Español (Spanish Socialist Workers' Party, PSOE), on its part, obtained its worst result since the inception of democracy in Spain (29 per cent of the votes; 110 seats). In spite of what this panorama conveys at first sight, these elections are better described as PSOE's collapse than PP's victory. One just needs to compare the number of votes and seats that PSOE lost between 2008 and 2011 (4,315,455 votes and 59 seats) and the number of votes and seats that PP won (552,683 votes and 32 seats).

A second feature was the increased support for small parties, both regional and not. The concentration of votes around the two main parties decreased from 84 per cent in 2008 to 73 per cent in 2011 and the concentration of seats from 92 per cent to 85 per cent. This meant a change in the trend followed during the previous 15 years. The number of parties represented in Congress increased from ten to 13. The most remarkable of the new parties entering Congress was Amaiur (the name refers to a place in the region of Navarra that offered great resistance to the conquest by the kingdoms of Castile and Aragon between the twelfth and the sixteenth centuries), a coalition of Basque left nationalists that obtained seven seats in Congress.

Table 1 Spanish General Elections 2011 and 2008

	2011			2008		
	Votes (N and %)		Seats	Votes (N and %)		Seats
PP	10,866,566	44.6	186	10,278,010	39.9	154
PSOE	7,003,511	28.8	110	11,289,335	43.9	169
IU-LV (Los Verdes)	1,685,991	6.9	11	969,946	3.8	2
UPyD	1,143,225	4.7	5	306,079	1.2	1
CiU	1,015,691	4.2	16	779,425	3.0	10
Amaiur	334,498	1.4	7			
EAJ (Euzko Alderdi Jeltzalea)-PNV	324,317	1.3	5	306,128	1.2	6
ERC (Esquerra Republicana de Catalunya)	256,985	1.1	3	298,139	1.2	3
BNG (Bloque Nacionalista Galego)	184,037	0.8	2	212,543	0.8	2
CC-NC-PNC (Coalición Canaria-Nueva Canarias-Partido Nacionalista Canario)	143,881	0.6	2	174,629	0.7	2
Compromís-Q	125,306	0.5	1			
FAC	99,473	0.4	1			
GBAI[1](Geroa Bai)	42,415	0.2	1	62,398	0.2	1
Turnout	24,666,392	68.9		25,900,439	73.9	
Abstention	11,113,099	31.1		9,172,740	26.2	
Invalid votes	317,555	1.3		165,576	0.6	
Blank votes	333,461	1.4		286,182	1.1	

Before 2011, Nafarroa Bai.
[1]*Source*: Ministry of Interior.

These phenomena have been accompanied by other factors such as a decrease in five points in the level of turnout (69 per cent, the third lowest since 1977) and a slight increase in the number of invalid and blank votes.

Below we analyse the background and context of these elections, paying special attention to the economic crisis that preceded them and analysing to what extent they had an impact on the result. We then go on to explore the circumstances under which the rise of the small parties took place and identify which of them benefited most from the Socialist defeat. It should come as no surprise that the economy has played a crucial role. But other phenomena such as the appearance of an unprecedented protest movement against the political and economic situation one week before the local elections of May 2011 (the 15-M movement), the legalisation of Basque independence formations in the context of historical steps towards the end of terrorism, the characteristics of the main party leaders and the peculiarities of the electoral campaign should not be ignored when trying to make sense of the electoral results.

The Delayed Impact of the Economic Crisis

In March 2008, PSOE had won a second consecutive election with José Luis Rodríguez Zapatero as its leader. The main issue during the electoral campaign that year had been the fight against terrorism. Economic issues, however, had been sufficiently present during the campaign. In the pre-electoral debate held on television on 21 February 2008 between the main PSOE and PP spokesmen on the economy—Pedro Solbes and Manuel Pizarro[2], respectively—Pizarro, stressed that the Spanish economy was characterised by high levels of inflation, unemployment, deficit and private debt. Solbes, on his part, insisted on the need for social expenses, as well as on the larger number of people in employment and the higher growth rate compared with 2003, when PP was in government. According to the different surveys carried out, Solbes won that debate. In any case, according to the electoral promises, one could say that none of the main Spanish parties foresaw correctly the development of the economy in the coming months: Zapatero had promised a rise in the minimum salary and pensions and Mariano Rajoy, the leader of PP, had promised to lower the taxes and raise minimum pensions. At that time the economy was still growing. During 2007 the Spanish economy had grown at a rate of 3.7 per cent (Figure 1, left axis). At the end of that year, even the International Monetary Fund shared the relative optimism of the Spanish government, predicting an economic growth rate of 2.7 per cent in gross domestic product (GDP) for 2008.

The truth is that, even if the Spanish economy was still growing, the rate of growth had started to decline in 2007 (Figure 1). The so-called 'real-estate bubble'—with the price of housing going up by more than ten per cent annually since 1997—exploded at the end of that year. Both external (subprime loans crisis in the United States [US]) and internal economic factors played a role in the rapid decrease in the demand for housing. This situation led to a dramatic and sudden decrease in prices in the sector,

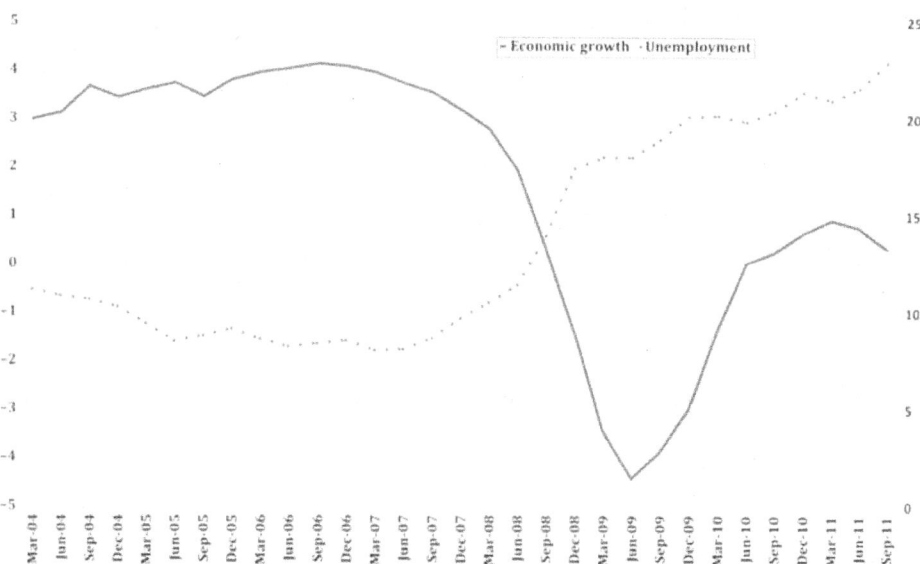

Figure 1 Economic Growth and Unemployment in Spain (2004–11).
Source: Bank of Spain and National Statistical Institute.

a huge increase in the number of empty houses available, a rise in unemployment (mainly in the building sector, on which the Spanish economy relies heavily)[3] (Figure 1, right axis) and a rise in personal debt.

In spite of this evidence, the government for months denied that Spain was going through an economic crisis. This may have proved a successful electoral strategy. The deterioration of the economy did not seem to have any impact on voting intention prior to the March 2008 elections (Figure 2) and PSOE won with 44 per cent of the votes. However, after the elections the trend of economic deterioration grew even faster. In July 2008 Zapatero finally admitted that Spain was going through an economic crisis following the same trend already observed inside and outside the Eurozone. A few months later the Spanish economy officially entered recession. Spanish citizens traditionally perceive PP as more competent than PSOE in handling economic issues (Urquizu-Sancho 2011b) and Zapatero's resistance to admitting there was an economic crisis reinforced this belief. During the crisis, 35 per cent of Spaniards believed that PP was the most qualified party to manage the economy, whereas only 20 per cent chose PSOE.[4]

The first attempt to fight the crisis was the Plan for the Encouragement of the Economy and Employment (called 'Plan E' because of the E in all three words), announced by Prime Minister Zapatero at the beginning of 2009. The plan followed the Keynesian idea of stimulating the economy through public investment. This resulted in a prospect of increasing public deficit and, in spite of the fact that public debt in Spain was lower than that of other countries,[5] the rating agency Standard & Poor downgraded the long-term debt of Spain to the AA+ category. In April 2009 the Minister of Economy, Pedro Solbes, who disagreed with the Plan E strategy, was replaced by Elena Salgado. Soon after assuming her new position, the new minister announced some signs

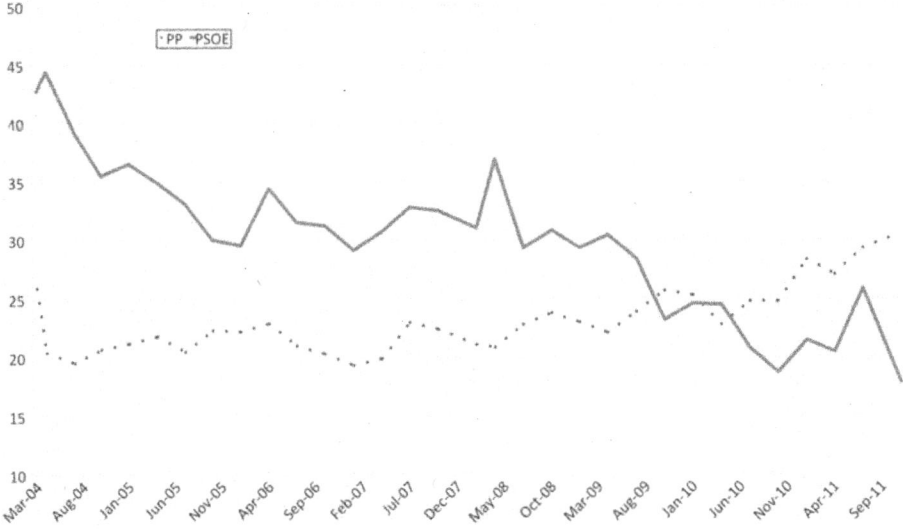

Figure 2 Vote Intention for PSOE and PP (2004–2011).
Source: CIS, several surveys, www.cis.es

of economic recovery (which she referred to as 'green sprouts', *brotes verdes*), which were met with general scepticism. In fact, by mid-2009 GDP growth had reached—4.5 per cent, unemployment was fast approaching the psychological barrier of 20 per cent and the first bailouts and reunification of banks were being discussed. Following the literature on economic voting (Ferejohn 1986; Lewis-Beck 1988), one could easily anticipate that this context significantly reduced the possibilities of electoral success for PSOE. And, in fact, it did.

The PSOE based its electoral campaign for the June 2009 European elections on blaming the previous PP government for developing an economic model too heavily based on housing and for having reduced workers' rights at a time when the economy was booming. They also emphasised the commitment of PSOE to social rights, education scholarships and support for the weaker social sectors and renewable energies. But both the optimism with regard to the economy and the emphasis on social rights did not seem credible any more. The PP won and PSOE lost more than four points with respect to the previous 2004 European elections (Table 2). In September the value-added tax (VAT) was increased and the government's popularity kept decreasing. Voting intention for PSOE went down to 23 per cent in October 2009 and, for the first time since March 2008, PP's electoral prospects looked better than those of PSOE (Figure 2).

At the beginning of 2010 the government announced an austerity plan that mainly affected public employment. Out of every ten public employees who retired, just one would be replaced. Soon after, the European sovereign debt crisis exploded when the new Greek prime minister George Papandreou declared that the public deficit in Greece in 2009 was considerably higher than had been estimated: more than 13 per cent—later announced to be, in fact, 15.4 per cent—instead of the estimated five per cent. With the bailout of Greece in the background, Spain's economy kept attracting international attention due to its increasing budget deficit (11 per cent in 2009). In fact, the rating agency Standard & Poor downgraded the long-term debt of Spain to the AA category on 28 April, just one day after that of Greece.

The second important blow to PSOE's popularity came in May 2010. Further adjustment measures were adopted, marking a final turn away from the previous emphasis on social policies. As a result of pressures by other European governments during the Eurogroup and the Ecofin meetings held in early May 2010 the Socialist government was forced to change its economic policy and to reduce the budget deficit. The government approved a cut of five per cent on average in the salaries of public

Table 2 Electoral Gains and Losses in the Spanish Elections 2008–2011 (%)

	European elections (2009 vs. 2004)	Catalonian elections (2010 vs. 2006)	Local and regional elections (2011 vs. 2007)	Parliamentary elections (2011 vs. 2008)
PSOE	−4.39	−8.45	−7.07	−15.2
PP	1.25	1.87	2.72	4.86

employees, a freeze on pensions (excluding the minimum ones), the end of the so called *cheque-bebé* (economic aid given to families for every new baby who was born) and cuts in public investment, in transfers to regions and local governments, pharmaceutical public expenses and in development cooperation. One month later, a reform of labour legislation which introduced greater flexibility in working conditions was approved by the government. This reform was contested in the streets with a general strike on 29 September called by the major trade unions. Even though there is disagreement as to the extent of the public response,[6] many citizens perceived that the incumbent party had betrayed their leftist values. Compared with March 2008, in October 2010 voting intention for PSOE fell by 37 points (from 57 to 20 per cent) amongst the more left-wing citizens, and by 23 points (from 65 to 42 per cent) amongst the moderate leftists.[7]

The impact of these measures was clearly felt in the Catalonian elections that took place in November 2010. After seven years of rule by a three-party leftist coalition (known as *tripartito*[8]), where PSOE was the main incumbent member, the centre-right nationalist party Convergència i Unió (Convergence and Union, CiU) won the elections and PSOE lost more than eight points compared with the previous contest (Table 2). The economic crisis and the performance of the central government played a more important role in these elections than in previous ones (Rico 2012).

In April 2011 Zapatero, realising that his deteriorating image was contributing to the constant decline in political support for PSOE, announced that he would not be a candidate in the next elections. Soon after, in a quite unexpected way, a huge protest movement that would become internationally known as the 'Indignados' (Outraged), was born in Madrid on 15 May after a demonstration organised by several citizen groups with the help of social networks to protest against the bleak future that awaited the most educated generation in the history of Spain. The demonstration was spontaneously prolonged by a gradually growing encampment in the Puerta Sol—a central square in Madrid—and their demands found such a wide echo in Spanish society that, in less than a week, similar encampments were created all over Spain. The initiative was probably facilitated by the pre-electoral climate but the resulting mobilisation, in turn, contributed to intensifying the final leg of the local and regional elections of 22 May.[9] The PSOE obtained its worst electoral results in elections of this kind since the establishment of democracy. It lost more than seven percentage points of support compared with the local elections in 2007 (Table 2). Moreover, the difference between the PSOE and the PP was close to ten points. The defeat was dramatic in the big cities and in most of the regions (Barreiro & Sánchez-Cuenca 2012). The economic crisis seemed to explain a big part of it (Urquizu-Sancho 2011c).

The Prime Minister took good note and opened the process that would lead to the election of his successor. The person elected by the party was the Minister of the Interior, Alfredo Pérez Rubalcaba. His nomination in July 2011 provoked the so-called 'Rubalcaba effect': the distance between PSOE and PP was reduced to less than four points (Figure 2). But the good news did not last long: as the economic situation in Greece and Italy deteriorated, Spain risked 'contagion'. Spain's bond spread—a measure of the risk of default of a country's public debt—reached a historical high exceeding 330 points. At the end of July, Zapatero called early elections for 20 November.[10]

The downward trend in popularity suffered by PSOE was so consolidated that not even the historical statement made by the terrorist organisation ETA (Basque Homeland and Liberty) in October 2011 announcing the permanent cessation of violence could stop it. One would have expected an important and positive impact of this event on intentions to vote for PSOE. Zapatero's efforts to put an end to ETA's violence had been by no means negligible[11] and the announcement was seen by many as the result of the successful antiterrorist policy of the Minister of the Interior since 2006 and new PSOE leader, Alfredo Pérez Rubalcaba. But, as vote intentions in October 2011 indicate (Figure 2), not even under these circumstances could the PSOE candidate recover ground. In all of the above, we can see a gradual decline in PSOE's popularity, related to the economic events, briefly interrupted in July 2011 by the nomination of Rubalcaba as the prime-ministerial candidate of PSOE.

The Rise of the Small

One of the most interesting issues to be analysed is where those more than four million votes that PSOE lost went. There are different possible scenarios. They could have gone to PP, in accordance with the widespread perception amongst citizens that this party is a competent economic manager. They could also have gone to smaller parties. Although the 15-M movement did not ask people to vote for any party in particular, the protests were clearly against the two biggest parties. The PSOE kept only half of its 2008 voters (Table 3). The rest moved to other parties or abstained from voting. The party that benefited most from the collapse of PSOE was PP, as 16 per cent of the 2008 PSOE voters decided in November 2011 to cross the ideological line that separates the two biggest parties. The second most important destination of 2008 Socialist voters was abstention (ten per cent). But smaller parties, such as Izquierda

Table 3 How Did the 2008 PSOE Electorate Vote in 2011?

Party	%
PSOE	49
PP	16
IU	7
UPyD	4
CiU	2
Others	4
Abstention	10

Note: The percentages indicate the proportion of citizens who said in the pre-electoral survey that they had voted in 2008 for PSOE and declared in the post-electoral survey that they had voted in 2011 for one of the parties in the first column.
Source: CIS survey no. 7711 (panel from October 2011 to January 2012).

Unida (United Left, IU) and Unión Progreso y Democracia (Union Progress and Democracy, UPyD), also received the support of seven and four per cent of prior PSOE voters, respectively. In the case of these two last parties, the additional number of voters compared with 2008 had a big impact on their electoral performance. The IU obtained 700,000 votes more than in the previous election and increased its representation from two to 11 seats in Congress. The UPyD lost an important number of votes to PP (18 per cent of those who had voted for it in previous elections, results not shown here) but, in total, it gained more than 800,000 votes and its representation rose from one to five seats.

The IU, a coalition of leftist and green organisations, built around the Spanish Communist Party, has been gradually losing electoral support in general elections since 1996. After its poor results in the 2008 general elections the internal disputes within the coalition became evident and the leader since 1999, Gaspar Llamazares, gave up his position as general coordinator. A new leader, Cayo Lara, was elected, but internal divisions did not disappear and some well-known members ended up leaving the party. In spite of the internal divisions, in the local elections of May 2011 the downward trend was reversed and the party obtained its best result since 1999. This was confirmed in the general elections. The IU focused its electoral campaign in the November parliamentary elections on the need for social policies to fight against unemployment, and the need to fight against fiscal fraud and corruption and to reform the electoral system to make it more proportional.

The UPyD, on its part, was born in September 2007 as a 'progressive' party, avoiding placing itself explicitly on the left or the right. Since the beginning, the leader of the party has been Rosa Díaz, previously a PSOE member and MP. The party programme demands a regeneration of democracy (including reform of the electoral system to make it more proportional), a more decisive fight against terrorism and a stand against decentralisation and regionalist parties. In 2008 the party's electoral support was very much concentrated in Madrid but in 2011 it managed to obtain support across Spain, with the exception of Catalonia and the Basque Country.

A third small non-regional party that is worth mentioning is Equo and the coalition in which it is integrated, Compromís-Q (Commitment-Q; the Q in the name of the coalition stands for 'Equo'). Compromís is a coalition formed by Valencian nationalists, leftists and ecologists which obtained one seat in Congress. Equo had joined the coalition in this region. This is a newly created party, led by the previous director of Greenpeace in Spain, Juan López de Uralde.[12] Its origin dates back to September 2010 when it was created as a sociopolitical movement to promote political ecology and social equity. However, it did not become a party until October 2011, as a result of a participatory process during which this decision was taken by the different assemblies that formed the movement. Some of the well-known members of IU who had abandoned the party joined Equo in 2011.

Regional and nationalist parties also increased their representation in Parliament (Table 1). This was clearly the case for CiU in Catalonia and Amaiur in the Basque Country. Even if regionalist parties are small when viewed from a country-wide perspective, some of them are the most popular parties in their electoral districts.[13] This has often been the case for CiU, and the 2011 general elections provided another example of this. The CiU had won the Catalonian regional elections in November 2010. A few months later, the Catalonian government adopted far-reaching adjustment measures that were met with discontent and protests from the citizens. In spite of this, CiU was the most voted-for party in the local elections of May 2011, and again in the general elections of November that same year. An important aspect of the electoral strategy of CiU has been mobilisation around the demand for more fiscal sovereignty (*pacto fiscal*) from the central government. This has proven successful enough to compensate for the cost of the cutbacks.

In the Basque Country it has also often been the case that a regionalist party is the one most voted for. In almost every general election this has been the Partido Nacionalista Vasco (Basque Nationalist Party, PNV); PSOE has usually come second. The 2011 general elections meant an important change in this share. The PNV was still the most voted-for party but it lost one seat. The real novelty, though, was that the second position was occupied by the new coalition of Amaiur, formed by various parties in favour of Basque self-determination.[14] The good results achieved by Amaiur were preceded by those of a similar coalition called Bildu in the local elections of May 2011. Bildu ('Meeting' in Basque) was formed in mid June 2010 and soon became the object of severe criticism and accusations of being the inheritors of Batasuna,[15] the independence party considered illegal since 2003 for supporting ETA. In April 2011, a police report concluded that Bildu had been promoted by Batasuna and by ETA itself. The party's lists were contested by the Attorney General and the State Attorney, and the Supreme Court considered that the party was, in fact, related to ETA. The government assumed this to be the right decision but many formations on the left, and even some members of PSOE, expressed their discontent with the Court's decision. Bildu appealed to the Constitutional Court and on 5 May, two weeks before the elections, the decision was announced that there was no proof of the party's relationship to ETA and, therefore, it could run in the local elections. The formation did astonishingly well, winning the second-highest vote (25 per cent) in the Basque Country. One month before the general elections, ETA for the first time declared a permanent, general and verifiable end to its terrorist attacks, after having killed about 1,000 people during the previous 40 years. Under these circumstances Amaiur, a new extended version of Bildu, got more than 300,000 votes and seven MPs in the November general elections.

Finally, two other small regional parties entered parliament. The first, Foro Asturias Ciudadano (FAC, Asturias Citizen Forum), is a splinter from PP led by a onetime minister, Francisco Álvarez Cascos (whose initials are the same as those of the party). He formed the party in reaction to the refusal of the PP to designate him as a candidate for the 2011 regional elections in Asturias. The other party, Geroa Bai ('Yes to the Future' in Basque), is a new version of Nafarroa Bai ('Navarra, Yes' in Basque), a coalition formed by Basque left nationalists of the Navarra region which had been represented in parliament with one seat since 2004. The change of name occurred after some of its members decided to join Amaiur.

Beyond the Economy

Besides the economy and the developments around the regionalist parties, other factors that played a lesser role are worth mentioning. These include the Indignados movement, the party leaders and the party campaigns.

The Indignados

As mentioned earlier, on 15 May 2011 the Indignados movement was born. Even if the pre-electoral context helped the mobilisation, the 15-M movement (as it is often referred to in Spain) continued being rather active. The encampment in Puerta del Sol was cleared in June but by that time hundreds of assemblies had been created in different neighbourhoods in Madrid and elsewhere in Spain. They were connected through a very sophisticated network based on the internet and assemblies that coordinated the work and decisions of the different groups in a region. Even if the reasons that led the young to mobilise were, to a large extent, economic (unemployment, high prices of housing, the disproportional influence of economic interests on political decisions), there has always been a strong political component in the demands of the Indignados. In fact, consensus amongst the different assemblies in Madrid was reached on four strictly political objectives: a change in the electoral system to make it more proportional and to facilitate citizens' participation; a determined fight against corruption;[16] a more effective separation of powers; and the creation of mechanisms for real accountability. The first of these objectives coincided with the demands of some of the small parties (not of the regional parties that are the most voted-for ones in their electoral districts; see note 13).

Three factors indicate that the 15-M movement could have had some impact on the electoral results. First, two of the parties that increased their electoral representation, Compromís-Q and IU, had the highest percentage of voters who had participated in activities related to the movement since May (Figure 3). Second, young people constituted an important proportion of participants in the movement, of the voters for IU and UPyD and of the voters who abandoned PSOE (Calvo, Gómez-Pastrana & Mena 2011; Likki 2012; Urquizu-Sancho 2011a; 2011c).[17] And, thirdly, invalid votes—an option widely discussed in assemblies as a possible way to express 'indignation'—almost doubled between 2008 and 2011 (Table 1 and Figure 3).[18]

The Leaders

When PSOE won the 2004 elections, Zapatero had a rather low profile. During his first term in office, though, he achieved international fame due to some of his most popular decisions: the withdrawal of troops from Iraq, his attempt to increase the role of women in politics (symbolised by the image of the pregnant Minister of Defence saluting the troops in Iraq), the change in the law allowing homosexuals to get married, and the attempt to recover the historical memory of the Republican side during the Civil War. Given the great personalisation of his government, these policies

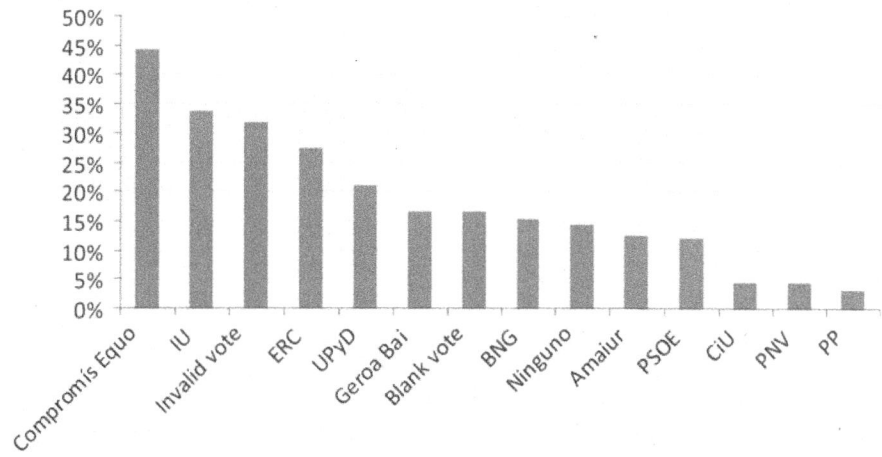

Figure 3 Participation in Indignados Activities and Vote in Spanish General Election (2011).
Note: Percentage of people saying that they had participated in an activity related to the 15-M/*Indignados* movement since May 2011 such as demonstrations, encampments, marches or protests.
Source: CIS survey no. 7711 (from October 2011 to January 2012).

were to a great extent associated with him. But this period of achievements in terms of civil and political rights came to an end as soon as the 'Great Recession' emerged, and the popularity that the Prime Minister had achieved quickly deteriorated.

The key economic decisions and results during the hard times were also identified with him personally, and so was the electoral fate of PSOE. As mentioned earlier, this was the reason why, after the defeat in the local and regional elections, Zapatero announced the holding of primary elections to find his successor. This declaration opened an internal debate in the party about the convenience of, alternatively, celebrating an extraordinary congress. This option in fact concealed a preference for one of the possible candidates—the Minister of the Interior, Alfredo Pérez Rubalcaba—against the other, the Minister of Defence, Carme Chacón. The former was a very experienced politician who had held the positions of minister of education and minister of the presidency during the 1990s in the governments headed by Felipe González. Under Zapatero, Rubalcaba became 'first vice-president', minister of the interior and government spokesperson. On the other hand, Carme Chacón belonged to the new generation that assumed the leadership of the party with Zapatero in 2000. She was vice-president of the Congress, minister of housing and minister of defence in his governments. Primary elections were not celebrated, as the pressure exerted by the proponents of holding a party congress undermined the will of Carme Chacón to present her candidacy. This freed the way for the Federal Committee to nominate Rubalcaba as candidate for the next general election. In spite of having been the minister with the highest popularity, his designation as the new leader was not enough to prevent the 'Socialist collapse'. In fact, the influence worked the other way around and the party's inevitable fate ended up damaging Rubalcaba's image.

Mariano Rajoy, the leader of PP, was nominated as candidate for the party leadership in 2003 by the then incumbent prime minister, José María Aznar. After Rajoy's loss of two elections (March 2004 and March 2008) his leadership started to be questioned by a section of his party, but, with the help of some regional leaders, he renewed his mandate at the National Congress in June 2008. The good results obtained by PP in the 2009 European elections and the 2011 regional and local elections strengthened his leadership of the party. But he has never been perceived as a strong leader. In fact, he won the elections in spite of having rather low personal popularity scores. Mariano Rajoy's levels of support were the lowest of any leader of the opposition since the 1980s. On a ten-point scale, he has never reached five. According to Centro de Investigaciones Sociológicas (CIS) surveys, in October 2011, right before the election, his evaluation (4.43) was lower than Rubalcaba's (4.54).

The Campaign

The 2011 election was preceded by a low-intensity campaign. Because of PSOE's large erosion in electoral popularity, PP's strategy consisted in taking as few risks as possible in order to arrive at the election without any mishaps. The main aim was to present the party and its leader as the alternative, to cast doubts on PSOE's capacity to manage the economy and to point at the contradiction between PSOE's ideology and policies. One of the criticisms most often heard about the PP campaign was the lack of specific proposals on offer. This can explain why PP did not get much additional electoral support compared with 2008.

The Socialist victory in 2008 had been due, to a considerable extent, to the mobilisation of left-wing voters who strongly rejected PP (Santamaría & Criado 2008; Urquizu-Sancho 2008). This was the reaction to the strategy of strong political confrontation followed by PP during the period 2004–08 (Fundación Alternativas 2008). In 2011, Mariano Rajoy abandoned the policy of confrontation and began a new phase of moderation. But this did not imply cooperation with the Socialist government. In fact, the main opposition party voted against the budgetary cuts and the labour market reforms that were adopted by the government in the context of the economic crisis. Only at the very end of the term did PP support the government in reforming the Constitution.[19] The content of the agreement was to introduce changes establishing that no government—central or regional—could incur a public deficit beyond the limits established by the European Union (EU), and that payment of the public debt had priority over other payments.[20]

The PP also had to face the problem of corruption by several of its party members and regional governments. In 2009, the media revealed that the PP was being financed via illegal methods through the so-called 'Gürtel network'.[21] After a long time, during which Rajoy's passivity was questioned even by some of his party members, most of those involved ended up resigning. Corruption, however, did not seem to affect PP's electoral results (Rivero Rodríguez & Fernández-Vázquez 2011).

The strategy of PSOE, on the other side, focused on emotional responses in order to counteract the demobilisation of their voters. The campaign aimed at keeping the support of its stronghold of voters, and focused on undecided leftist citizens. Thus, its principal slogan was 'Pelea por lo que quieres' (Fight for what you want). But the party in government also had to confront other problems. The denial of the crisis for several months had conveyed the idea that the party in government was not competent to manage the economy. Moreover, as mentioned before, many of its voters—especially those further to the left—felt ideologically betrayed. Since all polls predicted a clear victory for PP, it was difficult to mobilise these voters by appealing, like in previous elections, to the 'fear of the right'. The distance between PSOE and PP was too big as to make leftist voters think that they could make a difference with their vote for PSOE and, at least, avoid the victory of PP. This was the best scenario for PP: since the majority of Spanish voters are leftists (Cordero & Martín 2011), the best prospect for PP is when left-wing voters demobilise.

Given all of the above, did the electoral campaign have any consequences on voting decision? Electoral campaigns have four main effects: reinforcement, change, mobilisation and demobilisation (Martínez i Coma 2008). The first, reinforcement, means that people vote for the same party that they wanted to support before the electoral campaign. The second option, change, means that voters opt for a different party than they had thought of voting for before the campaign took place. Finally, there are two scenarios in which abstention plays a key role: when part of the electorate that previously thought they would abstain decides to vote and, vice versa, when citizens who thought of voting for a certain party end up not voting for anyone. Table 4 summarises the distribution of these effects in the 2011 electoral campaign.

As can be seen, the party that did best during the campaign was PP, as the high level of reinforcement (78 per cent did not change their vote choice during the campaign) and the low level of change to other parties (16 per cent of those who said they would vote for PP finally didn't) show. Compared to PP, PSOE was less successful in reinforcing its voters and in avoiding that they would end up voting for a different party. However, PSOE did better than other parties in mobilizing initial abstainers. On the other hand, the electoral campaign had strong and negative effects on UPyD and, especially, on IU voters. These parties present the lowest percentage of reinforcement and the highest percentage of change between October and the time of the elections.

Conclusions

The 2011 Spanish general election marked the end of Zapatero's two terms in government. After seven years in office, PSOE obtained the worst election results since the transition to democracy. The economic crisis for sure played a fundamental role. But the way it was managed by the government led many voters to confirm their impression that PSOE was a bad manager when it came to solving economic problems. The adjustment measures were also crucial in creating disaffection amongst the more leftist of its voters. The PP, on its side, did not need a strong strategy to win the

Table 4 Effects of the Electoral Campaign on Voting Behaviour (%)

	PSOE	PP	IU	UPyD
Reinforcement	71	78	57	69
Change	23	16	38	28
Mobilisation	11	8	4	2
Demobilisation	5	6	7	4

Note: The analysis measures 'reinforcement' as the percentage of voters who gave the same answer regarding their vote in the November elections in both the pre-electoral and post-electoral surveys. 'Change' identifies those who mentioned they would vote for the party mentioned in the columns (in the pre-electoral survey) but finally voted for a different one (as they declare in the post-electoral survey). 'Mobilisation' stands for those who, in the pre-electoral survey, said they would abstain but finally voted for the party mentioned in the columns and 'demobilisation' refers to those in the opposite situation.
Source: CIS survey no. 7711 (from October 2011 to January 2012). Authors' calculations.

elections: it basically waited for leftist citizens to abandon PSOE by themselves. One of the main problems that PP had to confront was corruption but, as mentioned, this proved to have limited electoral effects. In spite of the limited enthusiasm that Rajoy inspired, even amongst the party's own voters, the crisis and the way it was managed by the government brought victory to PP without much effort on its part. The 15-M movement may have played a small, even if important, role in the rise of some parties: mainly, of Compromís-Q and IU and, to a lesser extent, of UPyD. However, as we said above, the Indignados did not take sides with any of the parties. The future will show whether the success of these parties, and of Amaiur for different reasons, was the product of the exceptional context under which the elections took place, or whether the trend of decreasing concentration of the vote will continue.

As we have seen, Spaniards believe that PP manages the economy better than PSOE. However, this is the first time that PP has had to confront an economic crisis while in government. For that reason, their main challenge is to maintain this reputation. The PSOE, on the other hand, faces several and diverse challenges. Winning back the support of left-wing voters and choosing a leader who can inspire a sense of competence at the same time as a feeling of renewal are two of the most urgent ones.

Acknowledgements

We are grateful to the editors and one anonymous reviewer for their helpful comments and suggestions. The Spanish National Plan of Research and the Ministry of Science and Technology and the Ministry of Education have funded part of this research through the research project 'The Dilemmas of Democracy: Representation and Assigning Responsibilities' (CSO2009-10012) and the scholarship programme José Castillejo.

Notes

[1] Previous absolute majority governments were formed in 1982, 1986 and 1989 by PSOE and in 2000 by PP. In the case of the remaining six elections, single-party governments were formed with support from regional parties.

[2] Pedro Sobles was minister of economy in Felipe González's governments (1993–96) and in José Luis Rodríguez Zapatero's governments (2004–09). Manuel Pizarro is a businessman and he was 'signed' by PP in the 2008 elections.

[3] Since 2008 Spain has had the highest level of unemployment in the EU, starting with 11 per cent in 2008 and reaching 22 per cent in 2012. EU averages were seven per cent and almost ten per cent, respectively (Eurostat).

[4] CIS, survey no. 2847 (October 2010).

[5] In 2008, public debt in Spain was 40 per cent of GDP, whereas in Germany it was 67, in France 68 and in the United Kingdom (UK) 55 per cent (Eurostat).

[6] According to the Minister of Labour, 24 per cent took part in the strike in public enterprises and 7.5 per cent in the civil service. According to an estimate by the Think Tank 'Economistas frente a la crisis' the demand for electricity fell by 91 per cent compared with a normal day. http://www.economistasfrentealacrisis.com/

[7] CIS surveys measure ideology on a ten-point scale. We consider the most leftist citizens those who place themselves in points one and two, and moderate leftists, those who choose positions three and four.

[8] The coalition government was formed by the Partit dels Socialistes de Catalunya (Catalan Socialists' Party, PSC), the pro-independence nationalist Esquerra Republicana de Catalunya (Republican Left of Catalonia, ERC) and the eco-socialist Iniciativa per Catalunya Verds–Esquerra Unida i Alternativa (Initiative for Catalonia-Greens-United and Alternative Left, ICV).

[9] Local elections were held in all municipalities of Spain. The regional elections affected all autonomous communities except for Andalucia, the Basque Country, Catalonia and Galicia, which hold elections on different dates.

[10] It was suggested in the press that the date for the elections was not chosen by chance. It coincided with the anniversary of Franco's death and many saw it as an appeal to leftist voters who had previously voted for PSOE. Other interpretations focus on technical reasons. Basically, the date chosen allowed the government not to present the 2012 budget before the dissolution of parliament. However, this would also have been the case if the elections had been set for 13 November.

[11] During the term 2004–08, he opted to open discussions with the terrorist group, only to be betrayed by ETA during the truce when a bomb exploded in the Madrid airport in January 2007. This failed attempt had a political cost for PSOE in the 2008 elections.

[12] He became very well known after leading an initiative during the Copenhagen Summit of the UN on Climate Change to protest against the lack of will of the world leaders to reach an agreement. The peaceful protest consisted of sneaking into the Danish royal palace, to a reception offered by the Queen, with a poster. López de Uralde and other activists ended up in jail in the Danish capital, where they stayed for 19 days.

[13] The Spanish electoral system belongs to the proportional family, but it has a pluralist bias by which the two most voted parties in each electoral district are over-represented, while the smaller ones are under-represented. The small parties with electoral support distributed all over the country get less seats in parliament than their proportion of votes; however, the regional parties—which, by definition, concentrate their votes in a certain region and which are the most voted-for in their constituencies—are treated by the system like big parties.

[14] These are Eusko Alkartasuna, Alternatiba, Aralar and some independents.

[15] The other one being Sortu, another political formation created in February 2011. Sortu was declared legal by the Constitutional Court in June 2012, more than one year after Bildu.

[16] Since 2009 politicians and corruption have increasingly been perceived by citizens as significant problems in Spain. According to CIS, in the summer of 2008 around six per cent of citizens

thought that party officials were 'a serious problem' in Spain. In June 2011, a quarter of those interviewed shared the same opinion. The percentage of citizens who thought that corruption was one of the main problems in Spain went from 1.4 per cent in September 2009 to 12.3 per cent in January 2012.

[17] These results are confirmed by the post-electoral survey carried out by CIS but they are not shown for reasons of space.

[18] During the first days of the movement, the discussions about which kind of vote would best express the demands of the movement pointed to the small parties (without indicating any in particular) and to a blank vote. By October–November, though, there was an intense discussion in both social networks and the assemblies on whether a blank vote benefited the main parties or not. This cast doubts on the effects of a blank vote, influencing a preference of many in the movement in favour of an invalid vote.

[19] This was the second reform of a very rigid Constitution. The only other reform of the 1978 Spanish Constitution took place in 1992 and it was motivated by the signature of the Maastricht Treaty.

[20] See the new article no. 135 of the Spanish Constitution.

[21] Several senior PP politicians were involved: Luis Bárcenas, the PP treasurer, Francisco Camps, the President of Valencia, and regional deputies of Madrid were accused of receiving money and gifts from the Gürtel network.

References

Barreiro, B. & Sánchez-Cuenca, I. (2012) 'In the whirlwind of economic crisis: local and regional elections in Spain, May 2011', *South European Society and Politics*, 17, no. 2, pp. 281–294.

Calvo, K., Gómez-Pastrana, T. & Mena, L. (2011) 'Movimiento 15M: ¿quiénes son y qué reivindican', *Zoom Político*, no. 4, pp. 4–17.

Cordero, G. & Martín, I. (2011) *Quiénes son y cómo votan los españoles de izquierdas*, Catarata, Madrid.

Ferejohn, J. (1986) 'Incumbent performance and electoral control', *Public Choice*, vol. 50, nos 1–2, pp. 5–25.

Fundación Alternativas (2008) *Informe sobre la democracia 2007. La estrategia de la crispación*, Madrid.

Lewis-Beck, M. S. (1988) *Economics and Elections: The Major Western Democracies*, University of Michigan Press, Ann Arbor.

Likki, T. (2012) '15M revisited: a diverse movement united for change', *Zoom Político*, no. 11, pp. 1–15.

Martínez i Coma, F. (2008) *¿Por qué importan las campañas electorales?*, CIS, Madrid.

Rico, G. (2012) 'The 2010 regional election in Catalonia: a multilevel account in an age of economic crisis', *South European Society and Politics*, 17, no. 2, pp. 217–238.

Rivero Rodríguez, G. & Fernández-Vázquez, P. (2011) *Las consecuencias electorales de los escándalos de corrupción municipal, 2003–2007*, Fundación Alternativas, Madrid.

Santamaría, J. & Criado, H. (2008) '9-M: elecciones de ratificación', *Claves de la Razón Práctica*, no. 183, pp. 42–51.

Urquizu-Sancho, I. (2008) '9-M: elecciones tras la crispación', *Claves de la Razón Práctica*, no. 181, pp. 48–57.

Urquizu-Sancho, I. (2011a) 'Elecciones generales del 20-N', *Claves de la Razón Práctica*, no. 218, pp. 60–68.

Urquizu-Sancho, I. (2011b) '20-N: ¿ideología o economía?', *Revista fcr – Fundación Rafael Campalans*, no. 27, pp. 18–24.

Urquizu-Sancho, I. (2011c) 'El vuelco electoral del 22-M', *Claves de la Razón Práctica*, no. 214, pp. 32–41.

Irene Martín is a lecturer in political science at the Universidad Autónoma of Madrid and holds a PhD from the Juan March Institute. Her research interests cover political and electoral behaviour, political attitudes, and young people's relationship to politics, with special emphasis on Spain and Greece. Her last publications include *Quiénes son y cómo votan los españoles de izquierdas?* (with Guillermo Cordero, La Catarata and Fundación Alternativas 2011).

Ignacio Urquizu-Sancho received his PhD in sociology from the Complutense University. He is currently a lecturer in sociology at the Complutense University of Madrid and is a member of the progressive Spanish thinktank Fundación Alternativas. His works have been published in journals such as *Electoral Studies, South European Society and Politics* and *Revista Española de Ciencia Política*. His research interests include comparative politics, electoral behaviour and the theory of democracy.

Index

Page numbers in **bold** type refer to tables.
Page numbers in *italic* type refer to figures.
Page numbers followed by an 'n' refer to notes.

15 May movement (15-M) 155, 158, 224, 228, 232

abstention from voting *see* voter abstention
AKEL (Progressive Party of the Working People) 16, 167–8, 178; election campaign 171–2; results of election 174–6, **175**
AKP (Adalet ve Kalkınma Partisi) 14–15, 49–50, 201; decline in vote 2009 203; election 2011 results **210**, 211; election campaign 2011 205–6; Kurdish issue 209, 213; leadership issues 214; organisational strength 206–7; regional vote shares 212; second government 202–4
Akşit, Sait 5, 47–66
Alegre, Manuel 117, 118–19, 120, 121–3, **122**, **127**
Amaiur 19, 219, **220**, 226, 227
ANDARSYA (Anticapitalist Left Collaboration for the Overthrow) 18, 84
Asturias Citizen Forum *see* FAC
austerity policies: Greece 6, 69–70, 85; Portugal 182, 184–5; Spain 91, 155, 223–4
Aydın-Düzgit, S. 14, 201–17

bailouts 6–7, 14–6 68, 181, 185
Bakogianni, Dora 75, 80
Barreiro, Belén 17, 153–66
Basque country 158–60, **159**
Basque Homeland and Liberty *see* ETA
Basque Nationalist Party *see* PNV
Batasuna 18, 158–9, 227
BDP (Barış ve Demokrasi Partisi) 202, 208–9, **210**, 211, 212
BE (Bloco de Esquerda) 183, 187–8, 189, **189**, 190
Berlusconi, Silvio 2, 5; aftermath of Aquila earthquake 32; charismatic style 29; election success 42–3; electoral lists ruled ineligible 33, 34; fourth government, decline of 133–4, 135–40; legal problems and protection 31–2; local elections 2011, as an indicator of decline in popularity 16, 140–5, **141**, **142**; *Lodo Alfano* 31–2;
popular referendums, as an indicator of decline in popularity 145–7, **146**; popularity ratings *136*, 139, **146**, 147; relations with Gianfranco Fini 139–40; resignation 133, 135, 149; sexual scandals 31, 135–6, 137–8, 140; suspension of political talk shows 32–3
Bertolaso, Guido 32
Beşiktepeli, Zeki 53, **54**, 55, 56, 60, **61**
Bildu 18, 153–4, 158–9, **159**, 227
blank votes 99, 156–7; *see also* voter abstention
Bosco, Anna 1–26

C-PC (Ciutadans-Partido de la Ciudadanía) 96–7, **97**, 98–9, 102
Calvo, K. 156
candidate quality 113–14, 125–8, *126*, **127**, **129**
Carod-Rovira, Josep-Luís 95
Cascos, Francisco Álvarez 227
Catalan Socialist Party *see* PSC
Catalan Solidarity for Independence *see* SI
Catalonia *see* regional elections 2010, Catalonia
CDS-PP (CDS-Partido Popular) 183, 187, 189, **189**, 196
CDU (Coligação Democrática Unitária) 183, 187, 189, **189**
Centro de Investigaciones Sociológicas (CIS) 161, **162**, *163*, 164
Chacón, Carme 229
Chiaramonte, Alessandro 133–51
CHP (Cumhuriyet Halk Partisi) 201–2, 209; credibility issues 212–13; election 2011 results **210**, 211; election campaign 2011 206; intra-party struggle with MHP 213–14; organisational strength 207; regional vote shares 212
Christofias, Demetris 50, 62, 168, 169
Christophorou, Christophoros 5, 16, 167–79
CiU (Convergència i Unió) 18–19, 93–4, 98, 101–2, 107, 226–7

237

INDEX

Coelho, José Manuel 117, 120, 121, **122**, 123, **124**, 126, **127**
Coelho, Pedro Passos 184, 185, 186
Communist Party/Greens Coalition (Portugal) *see* CDU
Compromís-Q 226, 228
Corbetta, Piergiorgio 27–45
corruption 32, 86, 230, 233–4n16
Cox, G.W. 112, 113
CTP/BG (Cumhuriyetçi Türk Partisi-Birleşik Güçler) 48, 50, 52, 56, 62–3
Cyprus 3–4, 5, 6–7, 13, 168–9; AKEL party, reduction of influence 16; court decisions 169; economic crisis 9–10, **10**, 169–70; Greek Cypriot/Turkish Cypriot relations 48–50, 168–9; voter abstention 21; *see also* parliamentary elections Cyprus, 2011; Turkish-Cypriot presidential election 2010; Turkish Republic of Northern Cyprus (TRNC)

D'Addario, Patrizia 31
D'Alimonte, Roberto 133–51
Di Pietro, Antonio 41
DIKO (Democratic Party) 168, 172, **174**, **175**, 176, 178
DIMAR (Democratic Left) 73, 74, 79–80, 81
Dini, Lamberto 3
DISY (Democratic Rally) 168, 172, 175, **175**, 178
Draghi, Mario 7, 10

Eco-Greens **72**, 80, 82
Ecofin (EU Economic and Financial Affairs Council) 7
Ecologists Environmentalists Movement *see* Greens, The (Cyprus)
EDEK (Unified Democratic Union of the Centre) 168, 172, **174**, **175**, 176, 178
ELAM (National Popular Front) 20, 173, **174**, **175**, 176, 178
elections 2010–11: case studies 12–14, **13**; incumbent punishment 14–17, 164–5, **164**, 181–2; opposition parties, success of 17–20; voter abstention 21–2
Equo 226
ERC (Esquerra Republicana de Catalunya) 89–90, 93, 94–96, **97**, 98
Erdoğan, Recep Tayyip 56, 202, 205, 209, 210, 214
Ergenekon 203, 204, 206, 213, 216
Eroğlu, Derviş 47–8, 55; campaign 57, 59; election results 60–1, **61**, 63–4; party support 56–7; presidential candidate **54**, 55
Ertuğruloğlu, Tahsin 53, **54**, 55–6, 59, 60, **61**
ETA (Basque Homeland and Liberty) 18, 158–60, 225, 227

Eurobarometer data 22–3, **23**
European Court of Human Rights (ECHR) 169
European Court of Justice (ECJ) 169
European Union (EU): decision-making authority 4; Turkish Cypriot integration 50, 52, 61–2
EVROKO (European Party) 172–3, **175**, 176, 178

FAC (Astunas Citizen Forum) 227
far left parties 17–18
far right parties 20
Featherstone, Kevin 70
Fini, Gianfranco 134, 139–40
Fininvest 31
Finland 116
Five Stars Movement *see* M5s
Freedom and Ecology Left 41
FS (Federaziona della Sinistra) 28, **35**, 41

Garoyian, Marios 176
general election Spain, 2011: campaign 230–1; economic crisis, delayed impact of 220–4, *221*; effects of campaign on voting behaviour 231–2, **232**; electoral gains and losses 2008–2011 **223**; *Indignados* 228, *229*; party leaders 228–30; results compared with 2008 election **220**; smaller parties 219–20, 225–7; voting intention 222, *222*
Geroa Bai **220**, 227
Golden Dawn 20, 84, 173
Greece 13; austerity policies 6, 69–70, 85; corruption 86; economic and social problems 68–70; economic crisis 8, **8**; electoral victory of national incumbent 15; EU/IMF bailout 6–7, 68; far left parties 18; far right parties 20; government downfall 2–3; Kallikrates reform 73–4; local government system 73–5; Memorandum of Understanding vote 72–3; party support 71–2, **71**, **72**; three party coalition government 3; voter abstention 21, 70, **70**; *see also* local government elections, Greece 2010
Green, D. P. 125–6
Green Line Regulation 50
Greens, The (Cyprus) 173, **175**, 176
Grillo, Beppe 3, 20, 41–2, 142
Gül, Abdullah 56, 214

Iceland **115**, 116
ICV (Iniciativa per Catalunya Verds) 96
IDV (Italia dei Valori) 28, **35**, 41, **141**, 144
immigration 20
Immovable Property Commission 55, 59, 169

238

INDEX

Indignados 16, 19, 21, 154–5, 156, 161, 165, 224, 228, *229*
International Crisis Group 59
Ireland 7, **115**, 181
Israel 210
Italy 13–14; BTP-Bund spread 147–8, **148**; denial strategy 11; economic crisis 10, **10**, 135–7, **138**; economic reforms 148–9; electoral victory of national incumbent 15; government downfall 2–3, 5; national elections and winners 1994–2010 29, **30**; opposition parties, success of 17; scrutiny of public finance 138–9; technocratic government 3; unemployment 137, **138**; voter abstention 21; *see also* Berlusconi, Silvio; local elections and referendums 2011, Italy; regional elections 2010, Italy
IU (Izquierda Unida) 18, 157, **157**, **159**, **220**, 225–6, 228, 232, **232**

Jalali, Carlos 15, 111–32
Jones, M. P. 112
Justice and Development Party *see* AKP

Katz, J. N. 112, 113
Kaymak, Ayhan **54**, 56, 60, **61**
KCK (Kurdistan Communities Union) 204–5
Kiliçdaroğlu, Kemal 205, 206, 207, 209, 210
Kirdağ, Arif Salih **51**, **54**, 56, 60, **61**
KKE (Communist Party of Greece) 72, **72**, 77, 79, 80–1
Krasno, J. S. 125–6
Krastev, I. 23
Kurdistan Workers Party *see* PKK
Kurds 202, 203–5, 208–9, 213, 215–16

Laakso, M. 190, 198n16
Lago, I. 99
LAOS (Popular Orthodox Rally) 20, 72, **72**, 76, 78, 81, **83**
Laporta, Joan 95
Lario, Veronica 31, 138
Left Federation *see* FS
Leftist Bloc *see* BE
legislative elections Portugal, 2011: campaign 186–8; economic and social background 182–6; electoral change mechanics 190; government formation 195–6; policy preferences of electorate 192–5, *193*, *194*, 197; responsibility for the economy, voter opinion 191–2, **192**, *192*; results analysis 188–90; turnout 1975–2010 *188*; vote shares, turnout and seat shares 2002–11 **189**; voter abstention *188*, 189, 190
Lettieri, Giovanni 144–5
Levitt, S. D. 113
Libya 209–10

LN (Lega Nord) 28, 37, 38–9, *40*, 43, 135
local and regional elections Spain, 2011: background to elections 153–4; Basque country 158–60, **159**; campaign 155–6; context 154–5; evaluation of Government and opposition 161, 163, *163*, 165; five indicators of the capacity of parties **162**, 164; incumbent punishment 161, 164–5, **164**; *indignados* 155, 156, 161; local elections results 156–8, **157**; regional election results 160–1, **160**; voter behaviour and abstention 156–7; younger voters 161; Zapatero and Rajoy, mean approval 163, *163*
local elections and referendums 2011, Italy: Bologna 145; centre-left results 142, **142**, 143; centre-right electoral defeat 141, 142–5, **142**; comparison with 2010 regional elections 141–2, **141**, **142**; electoral systems, explanation 140–1; Milan 143–4; Naples 144–5; referendums 134–5, 145–7, **146**; Turin 145
local elections, Greece 2010 24n9; campaign 75–9; combined vote share of major parties 83–4, **83**; election dynamics 74–5; first-round result in Attica **84**; local government structure 73–4; outcome, assessment of 84–6; results analysis 79–82, 86; voter abstention 82–3, **82**
Lodo Alfano (Italian law) 31–2
Lopes, Francisco 119, 121, **122**

M5S 3, 20, 41–2, 142
Magalhães, Pedro C. 181–99
Magistris, Luigi, De 144–5
Mair, Peter 4
Martín, Irene 21, 219–35
Mas, Artur 106, 107
Mayhew, D. R. 112, 113
Memorandum of Understanding 20, 68, 69, 72–3, 75, 185
MHP (Milliyetçi Hareket Partisi) 202, 203, 207, 208, **210**, 211, 212, 213–14
Mills, David 32
Monti, Mario 3, 133
Montilla, José 90, 95, 103, 106
Moratti, Letizia 143–4
Moura, Defensor 120, **127**

Napolitano, Giorgio 140
National Popular Front *see* ELAM
Nationalist Action Party *see* MHP
New Democracy (Greece) 15, 69, 70; combined vote share 83, **83**; election results 80; local government election campaign 76–7; Memorandum vote 72–3; support for 71–2, **72**

INDEX

Nikolakopoulos, Ilias 75
Nobre, Fernando 119–20, 121, **122**, 123, **127**

Orams case 169
Organisation for Economic Cooperation and Development (OECD) 136, **138**, 154–5

Papandreou, Georgios 2, 68, 76, 77, 79–80, 84–5, 223
parliamentary elections Cyprus, 2011: background and context 168–70; campaign 170–3; economic crisis 169–70; Greek Cypriot/Turkish Cypriot relations 168–9; outcomes 177–8; results analysis 173–7, **174**, **175**; voter behaviour and abstention 173–4, **174**, 177–8
parliamentary elections Turkey, 2011: background 202–5; campaign 205–10; constitutional issues 207–8; democratic consolidation post-elections 214–17; foreign affairs, importance to voters 209; imprisoned parliamentary deputies, rights of 214–15; international incidents 210; intra-party struggles and leadership 213–14; results analysis 210–11, **210**; significance of economy to results 212; voting geography 211–12
PASOK (Panhellenic Socialist Movement) 68, 69, 71, **72**; combined vote share 83, **83**; election results 79–80; local government election campaign 76, 77
PD (Partito Democratico) 28, **35**, 37, *38*, 134
PDL (Popolo della Libertà) 28, 43, 135; relations between Berlusconi and Fini 139–40; support for 37–9, *38*, **40**
Peace and Democracy Party *see* BDP
Pisapia, Giuliano 143–4
Pizarro, Manuel 221
PKK (Partiye Karkaren Kurdistan) 203, 204–5
PNV (Partido Nacionalista Vasco) 159, **159**, **220**, 227
political parties: conflict between responsiveness and responsibility 4–5; distrust of 22–3, **23**; economic downturn, effect on 5; responsiveness 4; voter dissatisfaction 5–6
Portas, Paulo 187, 196
Portugal: austerity policies 182, 184–5; decline in socialist vote 2010–11 16; economic crisis 9, **9**, 182–3, 184–5; EU/IMF bailout 181, 185–6; far left parties 18; government downfall 2–3; party system 183–4; *see also* legislative elections Portugal 2011; presidential elections, Portugal
Portuguese Electoral Behaviour (CEP) project 190, 191, 192–5, **192**, *192*, *193*, **194**

PP (Partido Popular) 17, 96, 98, 100, *101*; Basque country local elections **159**; comparison of status with PSOE 164; corruption 230; effects of 2011 campaign on voting behaviour 231–2, **232**; electoral campaign 2011 230, 231; electoral gains and losses 2008–2011 **223**; general election 2011 219, **220**; indicators of capacity **162**, 164; local election results **157**, 158–60; regional election results **160**, 161; regions ruled by 164–5, **164**; vote intention 2004–2011 **222**, *222*
presidential elections, Portugal 15, 20; campaign budgets 123, **124**; candidates and campaign 117–21; direct effects of incumbency 123–5; incumbency, advantages of 112–14, 128, 130; incumbency re-election rates 111–12, 114–17, **115**; indirect effects of incumbency on challenger quality 125–8, *126*, **127**, **129**; presidential visibility 125; results analysis 121–3, **122**; voter abstention 121
protest voting 157–8
PS (Partido Socialista) 181–2; 2009 elections 183; 2011 election campaign 186, 187; defeat in 2011 elections 188–90, **189**; responsibility for the economy, voter opinion 191–2, **192**, *192*; voter abstention 190
PSC (Partit dels Socialistes de Catalunya) 89, 94–5, **97**, 100, *101*, 102, **102**
PSD (Partido Social Democrata) 117–18, 182, 183, 185; 2011 election campaign 186–7; 2011 election results 189–90, **189**; responsibility for the economy, voter opinion 191, **192**, *192*; voter abstention 190
PSOE (Partido Socialista Obrero Español) 16, 94, 154; Basque country local elections **159**; comparison of status with PP 164; decline in popularity 223–5; effects of 2011 campaign on voting behaviour 231–2, **232**; electoral campaign 2009 223; electoral campaign 2011 231; electoral gains and losses 2008–2011 **223**; general election 2011 219, **220**; indicators of capacity **162**, 164; local election results 156–8, **157**; regional election results 160–1, **160**; regions ruled by 164–5, **164**; vote intention **222**, *222*, 223, 224, 225, **225**
PxC (Platform for Catalonia) 20, 96

Radical Left Coalition *see* SYRIZA
Rajoy, Mariano 163, *163*, 221, 230
referendums, Italy 134–5, 145–7, **146**
regional elections 2010, Catalonia 18–19, 224; background and context 90–3; blank votes 99; campaign and parties 93–7;

INDEX

determinants of incumbent vote and defection 2006 and 2010 elections **106**; economic situation, voter perceptions 103–4, *104*; electoral competition 100; future implications 106–7; incumbent vote and defection determinants 104–5, **105**, 108n7; national level factors, effect on vote 103; regionalist parties and defence of regional interests 100–3, **102**; results analysis 97–9, **97**; three party government system 89–90; voter behaviour and abstention 97, 100, *101*; *see also* Spain

regional elections 2010, Italy: bipolar political system 28–9, 39–40; centre-right contest, northern regions 38–9; comparison with 2011 local elections 141–2, **141**, **142**; distribution between PDL and LN *40*; electoral campaign 29, 31–3; electoral system 27–8; left wing parties 41–2; party alliances 28; results analysis 35–8, **35**, *36*, *38*; UDC ambitions 39–40; voter abstention 33–5, *34*

Republican Left of Catalonia *see* ERC
Republican People's Party *see* CHP
Republican Turkish Party/United Forces *see* CTP/BG
Rico, Guillem 89–110
Rubalcaba, Alfredo Pérez 224, 225, 229–30

Salgado, Elena 222–3
Samaras, Andonis 72, 76–7, 80
Sánchez-Cuenca, Ignacio 16, 17, 153–66
semi-presidential regimes: candidate quality 113–14; incumbency re-election rates 114–17, **115**
SI (Catalan Solidarity for Independence) 19, 95, **97**, 98, 99
Silva, Carvaco 111; campaign budget 123, **124**; career and campaign 117–18; challenger quality **127**; election results 121, **122**
Soares, Mario 118, 123, **124**, **127**, **129**
Sócrates, José 2, 182, 183, 185, 187, 189, 195
Solbes, Pedro 221, 222
Southern Europe: austerity policies 6–7; financial bailouts 6–7; political and government changes 2–4; political cost of economic crisis 22; political parties, distrust of 22–3, **23**; recession, national variations 7–8
Spain: austerity policies 91, 155, 223–4; decline in socialist vote 2010–11 16, 17; denial strategy 11; economic crisis 11, **11**, 154–5, 221–3, *221*; financial autonomy of regions 93–4; financial bailouts 2; government downfall 2–3, 5; *Indignados* 19, 155, 156, 161, 224, 228, *229*; parliamentary seats, distribution 19, 24n10; Plan for the Encouragement of the Economy and Employment 222–3; regional nationalist parties 18–19; Statute of Autonomy and Catalonia 91–3; voter abstention 21–2; *see also* general election Spain, 2011; local and regional elections Spain, 2011; regional elections 2010, Catalonia

Spanish Socialist Workers Party *see* PSOE
SYRIZA (Coalition of the Radical Left) 18, 72–3, **72**, 78, 81

Taagepera, R. 190, 198n16
Talat, Mehmet Ali 17, 47–8, 50, 53, 169; campaign 57–9, 62; party support 56; presidential candidate **54**, 55
'Third Pole' 142, **142**
Tremonti, Giulio 136, 138, 147, 149
Trichet, Jean-Claude 7, 10
Tümkan, Mustafa Kemal **54**, 56, 60, **61**; election results 60, **61**
Turkey 14; AKP electoral victory 14–15; ban on wearing headscarves in universities 203; civil-military relations 204, 216; constitutional issues 207–8, 215; democratic consolidation 214–17; economic trends 11–12, **12**, 205, 216–17; Ergenekon 203, 204; foreign affairs 209, 217; imprisoned parliamentary deputies, rights of 214–15; Judicial Reform Strategy 204; KCK trials 204–5; Kurdish issue 202, 203–5, 208–9, 213, 215–16; polarisation 203; political instability 203; press freedom 204; *see also* parliamentary elections Turkey, 2011
Turkish-Cypriot presidential elections 2010 16–17; campaign 56–60; candidates 53–6, **54**; electoral rules 53; executive powers of president 52–3; historic background 48–50; legislative election results 2009 **52**; pre-election polls 58–9; results analysis 60–3, **61**; results for 2000, 2005, and 2010 elections **51**
Turkish Republic of Northern Cyprus (TRNC) 8, 14; economic indicators of crisis 12, **12**; integration with EU 49–50, 52, 61–2

UBP (Ulusal Birlik Partisi) 47, **51**, **52**, 55, 56–7, 60–1, 63
UDC (Unione de Centro) 39–40
Unified Democratic Union of the Centre *see* EDEK
United States of America 112
UPyD (Unión, Progreso y Democracia) 157, **157**, 220, **225**, 226, 232, **232**
Urquizu-Sancho, Ignacio 21, 219–35

INDEX

Verney, Susannah 1–26, 67–88
voter abstention 21–2; Catalonia, regional elections 2010 97, 100; Greece 70, **70**, 82–3, **82**; legislative elections Portugal, 2011 *188*, 189, 190; local and regional elections Spain, 2011 156, **157**; parliamentary elections Cyprus, 2011 173–4, **174**, 177–8; presidential elections, Portugal 121; regional elections 2010, Italy 33–5, *34*; *see also* blank votes

Wolfram, C.D. 113
Wu, Y.-S. 114

Zapatero, José Luis Rodríguez 2, 5, 91, 153, 156, 163–4, *163*, 220–1, 222, 224, 228–9